ADVENTURING THROUGH SPANISH COLONIES

DATE DUE

Brodart Co.   Cat. # 55 137 001   Printed in USA

Liverpool Latin American Studies

Series Editors: John Fisher, *University of Liverpool*
and Steve Rubenstein, *University of Liverpool*

1   Business History in Latin America: The Experience of Seven Countries
Carlos Dávila and Rory Miller eds

2   Habsburg Peru: Images, Imagination and Memory
Peter T. Bradley and David Cahill

3   Knowledge and Learning in the Andes: Ethnographic Perspectives
Henry Stobart and Rosaleen Howard eds

4   Bourbon Peru 1750–1824
John Fisher

5   Between Resistance and Adaptation: Indigenous Peoples and the
Colonisation of the Chocó
Caroline A. Williams

6   Shining Path: Guerilla War in Peru's Northern Highlands 1980–1997
Lewis Taylor

7   Latin American Independence: Gender, Politics, Text
Catherine Davies, Claire Brewster and Hilary Owen

8   Adventuring through Spanish Colonies: Simón Bolívar, Foreign
Mercenaries and the Birth of New Nations

Liverpool Latin American Studies, New Series 8

Adventuring through Spanish Colonies

Simón Bolívar, Foreign Mercenaries and the Birth of New Nations

Matthew Brown

LIVERPOOL UNIVERSITY PRESS

First published 2006 by
Liverpool University Press
4 Cambridge Street
Liverpool L69 7ZU

British Library Cataloguing-in-Publication data
A British Library CIP record is available

ISBN 1846310334 hardback
ISBN 184631044X paperback

Typeset by
Frances Hackeson Freelance Publishing Services, Brinscall, Lancs
Printed and bound in Great Britain by
Bell and Bain Ltd, Glasgow

For my parents

Contents

Figures, Maps and Tables   *page* viii
Preface   ix
Abbreviations   xiii

Introduction   1

1 The Context for Adventure   13

2 The Terrain of Adventure in Gran Colombia   39

3 The Practicalities of Adventure   61

4 Negotiating Honour   81

5 Nations and Armies   110

6 Race, Slavery and Abolitionism   133

7 Veteran Soldiers and the State   156

8 Settling In   173

9 After Adventure   202

Conclusion   214

Glossary   221
Bibliography   223
Index   259

List of Figures, Maps and Tables

Figures

1.1   Adventurers' Years of Birth   *page* 21
1.2   Private Soldiers' Experience in British Army   25
2.1   Summary of Adventurers' Fates   42
3.1   Alexander Alexander   62
3.2   At Prayer in Guayaquil   69
8.1   Daniel O'Leary   193

Maps

1   Gran Colombia   2
2   Regions of Ireland   28
3   Venezuela   43
4   New Granada   48
5   Ecuador   53

Tables

1.1   Adventurers Linked to Previous Service in British   22
        Armed Forces
1.2   Geographical Origins of Named Adventurers   27
2.1   Grouping the Expeditions   40
4.1   Duels involving Named Adventurers in the first years   87
        of the Wars of Independence
6.1   Distribution of Slaves across Gran Colombia, c.1820   134
8.1   Principal Occupations of Adventurers in Gran Colombia   174
        post-1822
8.2   Geographic Distribution of Adventurers across Gran   177
        Colombia post-1822
8.3   Adventurers' Marriages in Colombia   179

Preface

The Carnegie Trust for the Universities of Scotland and the Graduate School of University College London financed my research. Two European Union fellowships – a 'Marie Curie' at the Universidad Pablo de Olavide in Seville, and a 'Jean Monnet' at the European University Institute in Florence – gave me the time to think and write. I am extremely grateful for this support.

Many people have assisted me in the preparation, research and writing of this book, which began as a doctoral thesis at University College London under the challenging and encouraging supervision of Chris Abel and Nicola Miller. My examiners, John Lynch, Tony McFarlane, Josep Fontana and Raymond Buve were extremely helpful in guiding the work towards its present form. The following acknowledgements illustrate the wide diversity of countries and institutions in which I have had the fortune to work, and the great number of individuals who assisted my research.

In Europe I am grateful for the assistance of Amelia Almorza Hidalgo, Michael Angold, Christian Brannstrom, Keith Brewster, Philip Bucknor, Gloria Carnevali, María Eugenia Chavez, Stephen Conway, Michael Costeloe, Wendy Coxshall, Jo Crow, Jonathan Curry-Machado, Catherine Davies, Malcolm Deas, Paul Dinnen, James Dunkerley, Fae Dussart, Rebecca Earle, Charles Esdaile, John Fisher, Nicola Foote, Will Fowler, Catherine Hall, Manuel Herrero Sánchez, Karly Kehoe, Matthew Kelly, David Lambert, Asunción Lavrin, Jenny Lowe, Eleanor Malone, Habib Maroon, Jacob MacDonald, Iain McPhail, Maxine Molyneux, Keith Morris, Sven-Oliver Müeller, Luis Navarro, John North, Luke O'Sullivan, Kate Quinn, Kirsty Reid, Simon Renton, Julián Ruiz, Charles Sandeman-Allen, Najla Semple, Mimi Scheller, Amit Thakar, Clément Thibaud, Zsuzsa Torok, Mary Turner, Emily Walmsley, Caroline Williams, Edwin Williamson, Stuart Woolf and Bartolomé Yun Casalilla. Paddy and Maisie O'Toole were particularly warm and hospitable hosts in Dublin.

In the Americas, I would like to thank Ricardo Anteguera, Ramón Azpurúa, Guillermo Bustos, Germán Cardoso, María Milagro Carvajal, Adriana Castañeda, Carlos Dávila, Alejandro Gómez, Angela Gómez, Beatriz González, Margarita González, Adriana Hernández, Paul Jervis, Dion Jervis, Claudia Leal, Jason McGraw, Donny Meertens, Carmen Michelena, Francisco Modregón, Jorge Orlando Melo, Humberto Ovalle Mora, Luis Javier Ortiz

Meza, the late Jorge Palacios Preciado, Marco Palacios, Juan José Perdono, Karen Racine, Martín Alonso Roa, Carlos José Reyes, Gonzalo Sánchez, Susana Sará, Martha Jeanet Sierra, Hermes Tovar, Gilma Tovar, Mauricio Tovar, Ermila Troconis de Veracoechea, Gustavo Vaamonde, Grecia Vásquez, Yulieth Vásquez and Reuben Zahler. Margarita Garrido started me thinking seriously about honour. In Tunja, Javier Ocampo López found time to meet me for breakfast and fill me with ideas for further research. Amanda Caicedo at the Archivo Histórico de Cali and José Antonio Gómez at the Archivo Histórico de Guayas in Guayaquil both found me documents in whose existence I had ceased to believe. I met the Brito family on the bus to Ciudad Bolívar and their subsequent hospitality was outstanding. In Bogotá, Katia Urteaga and Vicente Vallies were hospitable, friendly, stimulating and generous. Other Peace Brigades International volunteers showed me friendship amid their bemusement at my research into nineteenth-century adventurers whilst they were daily risking their lives to protect those of others.

I am glad to be able to take this opportunity to thank the custodians and owners of the manuscripts and books I have consulted in the following institutions, and the staff who have fetched the materials: in Belfast, the Public Record Office of Northern Ireland; in Bogotá, the Archivo General de la Nación, Biblioteca Luis Angel Arango, Biblioteca Nacional, Academia Colombiana de Historia; in Cali, the Archivo Histórico de Cali; in Cambridge, the Cambridge University Library, Seeley Historical Library; in Caracas, the Archivo General de la Nación, Fundación John Boulton, Casa de Estudio de la Historia de Venezuela 'Lorenzo A. Mendoza Quintero', Biblioteca Nacional, Academia Nacional de la Historia; in Ciudad Bolívar, the Archivo Histórico de Guayana; in Dublin, the National Archive of Ireland, National Library of Ireland, University College Dublin Archive; in Edinburgh, the National Archives of Scotland, National Library of Scotland, Edinburgh University Library; in Florence, the library of the European University Institute; in Guayaquil, the Archivo Histórico de Guayas; in Ipswich, the Suffolk County Record Office; in London, the University College London Library, British Library, University of London Library, the British Library of Political and Economic Science, the Public Record Office at Kew (part of the National Archives), Colindale Newspaper Library, Casa Miranda, Institute of Historical Research; in Oxford, the Bodleian Library; in Popayán, the Archivo Central del Cauca; in Quito, the Biblioteca Ecuatoriana 'Aureliano Espinosa Polit', Biblioteca Nacional, Archivo Nacional del Ecuador; and in Tunja, the Academia Boyacense de Historia. Figure 2.1 is reproduced thanks to the Museo Nacional de Colombia. Figure 3.1 is reproduced thanks to the British Library. Figure 3.2 is reproduced thanks to the Fundación John Boulton. Map 1 is reproduced thanks to the Biblioteca Luis Angel Arango. In the process of researching and writing this book I have published some thoughts and interpretations on related topics based on similar sources in *Historia y Sociedad*, the *Bulletin of Latin American Research*, the *Journal of Latin American Studies*, and the *Feminist Review*. I am grateful to all reviewers who have assisted me in revising my thoughts and interpretations. I thank Hocol and the Museo Nacional de Colombia for their support of the publication of *Militares extranjeros en la independencia de Colombia. Nuevas perspectivas* (Bogotá, 2005), co-edited with Martín Alonso Roa Celis, a collection of documents related to this topic. Compiling *Militares extranjeros* encouraged me to think about the broader relevance of the present work; transcribing the documents helped me to focus on the detail. I began to research this book after having volunteered for several years in Hispanic America, first as an English teacher in Santiago de Chile, then working for the Peruvian Section of Amnesty International in Lima. I then led groups of young British students on adventure tours of Ecuador, Peru and Bolivia, an experience which left me perplexed and intrigued about the historical roots of present-day British travel in the continent. I am grateful to Anthony Cond and Andrew Kirk of Liverpool University Press, Frances Hackeson and Kate Possnett. My thanks go to Mandy Carver, Natasha Carver, Rebecca Earle, Charles Esdaile, Nicola Foote, Margarita González, Thom Rath, Jo Underwood, Caroline Williams and Reuben Zahler who read and commented on individual chapters. David Brown and Drew Ellis assisted with maps and images. I thank my parents for their encouragement and support. All errors in the text are my own responsibility.

Notes on Terminology, Spelling and Translation

In 1819 Simón Bolívar declared the independence of the Republic of Colombia, formed by the union of the territories encompassed by the Captaincy-General of Venezuela, the Presidency of Quito, and the Viceroyalty of New Granada. Historians have used the term 'Gran Colombia' (Greater Colombia) to refer to Bolívar's single republic, which existed from 1819 until 1830. When contemporaries referred to 'Colombia', they meant what is now understood as 'Gran Colombia'. When they referred to 'New Granada', they referred to the territory now called 'Colombia'. In this book I refer to the people of Gran Colombia as 'Gran Colombians' during the period 1819–1830. After 1830 I refer to them as New Granadans, Venezuelans and Ecuadorians, or collectively as 'the people of the Gran Colombian region'. When reproducing testimony from primary documents I have retained the original language as far as possible – it should be obvious, for example, when Bolívar talks of 'Colombia' that he means the larger nation comprising the three territories.

Bolívar's armies were Venezuelan until 1819 and Gran Colombian between 1819 and 1830. In 1830 the Gran Colombian state fragmented into the republics of Venezuela, Ecuador and New Granada, roughly based on the colonial administrative units that they succeeded. In 1863, the Republic of New Granada adopted the name Colombia, by which it is still known today.

Throughout the period studied here the capital of the Viceroyalty of New Granada, and later of the Republic of Colombia, changed its name several times. To avoid confusion, Bogotá is consistently used to refer to the city also known as

Santafé and Santafé de Bogotá. Similarly, the capital of Guayana is referred to as Angostura, even though it was also known as Santo Tomás de Guayana, Santo Tomás de Angostura, and was renamed Ciudad Bolívar in 1846.

The United Kingdom of Great Britain and Ireland was established in 1801. Great Britain is the largest island in the British Isles, and includes England, Scotland, and Wales. In 1922 the 26 county Irish Free State gained Independence from Britain, while the counties of Northern Ireland remained part of the renamed United Kingdom of Great Britain and Northern Ireland. In 1937 the Free State became the Republic of Ireland (Eire). During the period covered by this study, the British monarch (George III from 1760 to 1820; George IV as Prince Regent from 1810, and as King from 1820 to 1830; William IV from 1830 to 1837) also ruled territories across the globe, including North America (Canada), the British West Indies, much of India and Australia, and islands in the Atlantic and Pacific Oceans. The expeditions to Gran Colombia included men from the British empire and other parts of Europe, and these are noted where applicable.

Contemporaries and historians have used the terms 'adventurers', 'auxiliaries', 'foreign soldiers', 'mercenaries' and 'volunteers', to describe the members of these expeditions. All of these terms are in some way problematic, for reasons that are explored in Chapter 1. The Introduction and Chapter 1 provide a detailed explanation of my preference for 'adventurer', so that the cumbersome repetition of phrases such as 'the foreign volunteer–mercenary auxiliary soldier-adventurers' can be avoided.

To avoid confusion, ranks in the British army are given in English, whilst ranks in the Loyalist army (sometimes also known as 'the Spanish army' or 'the Royalist army') and the Independent armies (sometimes also known as 'the patriot army' or 'the Republican army') are given in Spanish. Further explanation for the choice of terms is provided in Chapter 1. The term 'Creole' is used to refer to predominantly white, American-born people. Creoles fought on both the Independent and Loyalist sides. The Spanish word *patria* is left untranslated from primary sources, as the usual English translations of 'fatherland', 'country' or 'homeland' do not catch the nuance of the period. *Patria* had a strong sentimental sense of 'home' and the land of one's fathers, to which one held a strong allegiance without being tied to strict administrative boundaries. The fact that British or Irish adventurers described their *patria* in Spanish language texts in the 1830s as 'Lincoln', 'Cork', 'England', 'Europe' or even 'Colombia' hints at the variable meanings given to the term. All translations from Spanish language sources are my own except where otherwise stated.

Particular adventurers have had the spelling of their names standardised. Hence John D'Evereux is always John Devereux unless in the reproduction of a primary document where it is spelt differently. Mary English is always Mary English, even after she had been widowed by James English, and married Colonel Lowe, and then Mr Greenup. Gregor MacGregor is preferred to McGregor or M'Gregor. Spanish names such as Simón Bolívar are written with their appropriate accents, unless quoting from a contemporary text that did not use accents, in which case the original spelling has been retained.

Abbreviations

AC	Asuntos Criminales
ACC	Archivo Central del Cauca, Popayán
ACHSC	*Anuario colombiano de historia social y de la cultura,* Bogotá
AGNC	Archivo General de la Nación de Colombia, Bogotá
AGNV	Archivo General de la Nación de Venezuela, Caracas
AHG	Archivo Histórico de Guayana, Ciudad Bolívar
AHR	*American Historical Review*
AL	Archivo del Libertador, Caracas, Sección Juan de Francisco Martín
ANE	Archivo Nacional del Ecuador, Quito
AOL	Archivo O'Leary
BANH	*Boletín de la academia nacional de historia,* Caracas
BCB	*Boletín cultural y bibliográfico,* Bogotá
BHA	*Boletín de historia e antigüedades,* Bogotá
BLAR	*Bulletin of Latin American Research*
BNC	Biblioteca Nacional de Colombia, Bogotá
CDM	Biblioteca Luis Angel Arango, Bogotá, Papers of Casa de Moneda
CHLA	*Cambridge History of Latin America*
CMP	*Carrick's Morning Post,* Dublin
CO	Colonial Office Papers
DEP	*Dublin Evening Post*
EP	James Towers English Papers, Suffolk County Record Office
FDJ	*Faulkner's Dublin Journal*
FJB	Fundación John Boulton, Caracas
FO	Foreign Office Papers
GDG	Gobernación de Guayana
GYM	Secretario de Guerra y Marina
HAHR	*Hispanic American Historical Review*
HDS	Hojas de Servicio
HYS	*Historia y Sociedad* Medellín
IP	Ilustres Próceres
JLAS	*Journal of Latin American Studies*
LARR	*Latin American Research Review*

MOL	*Memorias de O'Leary*
NLI	National Library of Ireland, Dublin
R	Sección La República
TCDOC	*The Correspondence of Daniel O'Connell*
TNA	The National Archives, London (formerly PRO, Public Record Office)
TRHS	*Transactions of the Royal Historical Society*, London
UCD	University College Dublin
WO	War Office Papers

Introduction

In 1826 the British Foreign Secretary George Canning declared that he had 'called the New World into existence, to re-dress the balance of the Old', thereby claiming British responsibility for Latin American independence.[1] His politic proclamation was more arrogant exaggeration, however, than accurate representation. The British government gave no formal military assistance to the Independent armies and, as John Lynch observed, its Latin American policy was 'diffident in its approach and vague in its intent'.[2] Nor did foreign traders dominate political élites and cajole them into accepting terms and conditions that were to the benefit of investors thousands of miles away. Rather, the 'Age of Revolution' in Europe and the Americas consisted of a number of interrelated events linked by ideology, trade, geopolitics, individuals and warfare. This book examines the Independence of Gran Colombia and the networks that brought 7,000 European adventurers to serve between 1816 and 1825 in the armies and navies commanded by Simón Bolívar. The presence of these foreigners in a war that produced nations had important repercussions for the identities of the new republics and also for the adventurers themselves. Many died, many returned home, and several hundred remained in the region, marrying local women and bringing up children who spoke Spanish and regarded themselves as Venezuelan, New Granadan or Ecuadorean.

Military historians have dedicated themselves to the narration of some aspects of this subject. They have mapped names and battles, listed the dead and injured, glorified heroes and denigrated villains. The cultural and social dimensions of these adventurers' experiences in Bolívar's armies have been neglected by these military historians.[3] The well-documented, wide-ranging and influential scholarship of Alfred Hasbrouck and Vicente Lecuna concluded that Independence as it came to pass would have been impossible without the professionalism and example of the foreign legionaries.[4] Eric Lambert expanded upon Hasbrouck's research, narrating the campaigns of the *gesta bolivariana* in great detail, and supplementing Hasbrouck's use of the Venezuelan and Colombian national archives with evidence drawn from contemporary newspapers.[5] But neither Hasbrouck nor Lambert accessed all the available archives. Neither used Spanish or Ecuadorean collections, nor those of provincial Venezuela or Colombia.[6] Both Hasbrouck and Lambert focused on the great battles and the brave officers who fought them. Campaigning was

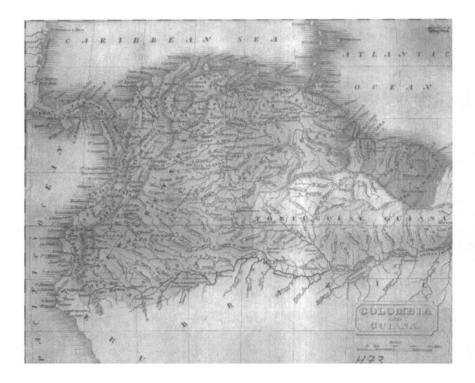

Map 1 *Gran Colombia*

what happened between military engagements, and the subsequent careers of
adventurers were reduced to a postscript. The unwillingness of these historians to engage with matters outside the narrowly defined military at once limited their use of the adventurers' own writings, and also meant that foreign
influence in the Independence period signified the statements and correspondence of diplomats, consuls and naval officers charged with monitoring and,
if possible, influencing developments in Spanish America. The pioneering
documentary collections of Charles Webster and R. A. Humphreys showed
how British concern for liberty and equality was often altruistic but always
suffused with British 'interest' in terms of geopolitics – stopping the USA or
France from acquiring the colonies that Spain could no longer control – and
commerce. The expeditions of adventurers merited barely an appearance in
this picture.[7] Studies of British commercial influence during the independence period depict British involvement as primarily commercial in design
and purpose. They inaccurately read the later period of 'informal empire' after 1870 back on to the Wars of Independence. The adventurers – if mentioned at all in these studies – are seen as a minor part of the process in which
British migratory capital and commercial supremacy, to which the navy was
'symbiotically linked',[8] led Latin American economic and political élites towards economic 'dependency' upon British capital.[9] This book attempts to

override these narrow specialisations and to unite diplomacy, commerce and fighting with socio-cultural, political and military processes. The scope of the subject is broadened, too, ranging from the recruitment of the volunteer expeditions, through the initial encounter with society, to the military campaigning and battles, which are the subject of Chapters 2 and 3. Chapters 4, 5 and 6 use the presence of foreigners as a lens through which to study wartime society in Gran Colombia, with particular attention paid to honour, national and racial identity, and slavery. Chapters 7 and 8 examine the post-war period and explore the ways in which retired adventurers became part of society in Ecuador, Venezuela and New Granada. Chapter 9 looks at how the foreign adventurers have been commemorated by peoples and states on both sides of the Atlantic.

Research into the period of Independence in Spanish America has only recently broken out of the 'historiographic prison' of battles, heroism and political drama in which investigators were trapped since historians defined the field in the nineteenth century, José Manuel Restrepo being a prime example.[10] From the perspective of a transatlantic 'Age of Revolution' spanning the century from 1750, Sarah Chambers, Victor Uribe Urán and Aline Helg have investigated the ways in which Spanish American subjects became republican citizens, stressing the continuing importance of colonial concepts relating to gender and honour.[11] The extended time-frame has also brought benefits for the study of Independence in Gran Colombia. Clément Thibaud has shown how the military units of the 1810s were rooted in colonial militias, which correspondingly affected their capacity. Thibaud argued that the very nature of military mobilisation, and the way Bolívar advanced through the 'national' territory between 1816 and 1821, fundamentally shaped the development of collective identities.[12] Moving away from the battlefield entirely, Karen Racine has shown how exile in Europe politicised the identities of Creoles, for example Bolívar and Andrés Bello, making London a key centre for turning prominent Spanish American Creoles into revolutionaries.[13] Eugenia Roldán Vera argues that the London book trade based around the publisher Rudolph Ackermann 'transmitted and promoted the creation of notions of national and continental identities in a crucial period of political reconfiguration of those countries', and played an important role in shaping the way Spanish Americans conceived of their relation to the rest of the world.[14] Racine and Roldán Vera both question the focus on military deeds and emphasise the cultural and social networks and changes that underpinned Independence. Both highlight the transnational networks that lay behind, enabled and affected the process of Independence itself.

In seeking to contribute to the developing historiography of Spanish American Independence, this study is also informed by recent trends in the history of British imperialism. Catherine Hall has argued forcefully that identities in Britain and the colonies were 'mutually constitutive'; indeed, that the imperial experience was integral to collective identities at home *and* abroad.[15] This interpretation argues that British imperial networks, and the colonial identities that evolved amongst them, were multidirectional and blurred the boundaries between metropolitan 'centres' and colonial 'peripheries'.[16] Valuable though such insights are, they do neglect the 'informal' empire, the importance of which was recognised by Gallagher and Robinson in 1953 and subsequently explored in some detail by economic historians of Latin America.[17] In their concentration on 'sites of empire' and on reconfiguring the relation between metropole and colony, areas outside of formal British imperial control – such as most of Latin America – 'remain marginal to most imperial historians'.[18] Even historians as prominent as David Cannadine, Niall Ferguson and Bernard Porter, who are more sceptical about recent fashions in imperial history, still omit Latin America from their discussions of the British empire.[19]

The time is right to re-examine this encounter between British adventurers and Spanish American societies in the transition from colonial to republican rule. An attempt is made in this book to reconcile the divergent interests and tendencies of military history, Latin American history and British imperial history by examining the cultural encounters between soldiers and civilians on the battlefield, round the campfire and at home, focusing on the formation and construction of collective identities during both warfare and peacetime. It is shown that Britons were active in commerce and in adventure outside of the formal empire during the early nineteenth century, and that processes of collective identity formation in Latin America took place against an ever-present background of transnational movements, migrations and networks.

The people called 'legionaries' by Hasbrouck, 'volunteers' by Lambert, 'errant heroes' by Giorgio Antei,[20] and 'mercenaries' and other derogatory names by the Spaniards they fought against are central to developing a new approach to the study of foreign involvement in the Wars of Independence.[21] The nomenclature applied to these people was politically charged even before the passing of the Foreign Enlistment Act in Britain 1819.[22] This is not to deny that a belief in liberty inspired some to volunteer their services and that others desired only pay and plunder. But their motivations, as Chapter 1 shows, were too diverse for either definition, and their experiences too varied for them simply to be approached from the viewpoint of the British Legion and Irish Legion, both of which dissolved very quickly upon arrival in Spanish America. I explain below why I prefer the term 'adventurer'.

This detailed study of the adventurers questions some of the arguments put forward by critics of travel writing as to the 'imperial eyes' of contemporaneous travellers. Mary Louise Pratt argued that European travel to Latin America created social spaces where cultures could meet, clash and grapple with each other, and where, in the period of independence, European ideologies and the 'vanguard of capitalism' generally emerged triumphant.[23] The exploration of the adventurers' diverse motivations, ideologies and attitudes towards progress and civilisation makes apparent the pressing need for a reconceptualisation of Britain's imperial activities in Latin America in the nineteenth century, and adds to the growing literature that sees the concept of 'informal empire' as an impediment to an understanding of the period 1800–70 in the region.[24]

Adventurers became some of the most influential chroniclers of the Wars of Independence. The most famous of their texts is the *Memorias de O'Leary*, the 32 volumes of documents and narrative compiled by Daniel O'Leary after Simón Bolívar's death, which were edited and published by O'Leary's son in the 1880s.[25] The *Memorias* are still one of the prime sources for historical writing on the Independence period.[26] O'Leary collected (and allegedly filtered and censored) a vast range of Bolívar's correspondence, proclamations and writings.[27] O'Leary's own account of the Wars of Independence took up just two of the published volumes, and it was part personal narrative, part biography of Bolívar and part political history. Because of the status he posthumously acquired as a result of the growing 'Bolívar cult', many historians took O'Leary's own narrative as definitive, especially on the occasions when he discussed the role of the foreign adventurers.[28] O'Leary concerned himself with only a few of the adventurers; specifically, those like himself who remained loyal to Bolívar until 1830 (such as Arthur Sandes, James Rooke, Thomas Wright and John Illingworth) and, in opposition to those heroes, those who were not worthy of the trust Bolívar had placed in them (principally Gustavus Hippisley and Henry Wilson).[29] Chroniclers like O'Leary became as valued for writing about things they had not witnessed as for their actions in military, political and social life, and this highlights the ambiguous nature of many of the sources available for this study.

Similar problems beset all of the published narratives of the Wars of Independence,[30] including the memoirs of the Venezuelan President, José Antonio Páez. Writing his autobiography some fifty years after the end of the Wars of Independence, Páez often relied upon memoirs written by British and Irish adventurers in order to trigger his memory and fill out his account. He did this even when describing events at which he had been present (and indeed instrumental) and from which the chroniclers he drew on were absent.[31] To make things even more difficult for the historian, fragmentary materials for the topic are distributed across the globe in national, regional, local and private archives. Those consulted in the course of my research are located in Colombia, Ecuador, England, Ireland, Northern Ireland, Scotland, Spain, and Venezuela. Sources include published memoirs, novels, poetry, histories and collections of correspondence, plus unpublished travel narratives, criminal court archives, government petitions, service records, military diaries and documents from both sides of the military conflict, private letters, hospital records, widows' petitions, censuses of foreigners, and interrogations of prisoners. The new sources consulted mean that the quantitative conclusions presented below are more authoritative than those of previous authors. The combination of a new approach with new sources strips away the veneer of objectivity of 'over-used authorities'[32] on the period, and allows new insights into the adventurers' role during this time. In addition, individuals whose very existence escaped previous historians appear in the new sources.[33]

The range of sources consulted has made possible the construction of a database of over 3,000 adventurers and also provides a window on to the ways in which foreigners and local people related to each other. By exploring what they talked about, squabbled over, traded in and considered important, we can get a better idea of what Independence really meant for contemporaries, than from re-treading the well-worn battlefield paths. To this end, this study uses the technique of group biography, or prosopography, which aims to steer 'a middle course between individual analysis and depersonalised social analysis'.[34] Much use, therefore, will be made of what in other contexts might be called circumstantial evidence: anecdotes, rumours, advertisements and jokes take their place alongside the official correspondence of high-ranking military officers.

The fragmentary nature of the sources means that very little is known about some individuals – predominantly those from the rank and file – and a lot is known about others, in particular those who wrote their own accounts. Only considered together can the sources allow generalisation. From an analysis of the 3,000+ minibiographies contained in the database, quantitative results can be laid against the wealth of qualitative detail. For example, there were over one hundred and fifty women who accompanied the expeditions. Very few of them were recorded in the sources by more than name but, treated as a group, it can be shown that they played an important role in shaping the ways in which the predominantly male adventurers interacted with Gran Colombian societies.[35]

This new focus on the prosopography of the foreign adventurers as a group questions straightforward assumptions about the 'power' or 'hegemony' of external actors in nineteenth-century Latin American history. It seeks to learn more about the myriad informal, relatively undocumented encounters that provided the background to the high-level political and diplomatic relationships which were long the staple of historical scholarship. In short, the soldiers serving in the Independent armies are examined as human individuals, with their attendant diversity of motivations, loyalties and abilities, rather than as one-dimensional military machines. As such, this is a theoretically informed study concerned with uncovering relationships of power and questioning assumptions of inherent or 'natural' identities. An emphasis on the categories of race, gender, and class pervades this work as it does much of the recent historiography on the period.[36]

Contemporaries made sense of the encounters between peoples and cultures during the Wars of Independence by using the concepts of status and honour. The conflation of colonial concepts of honour based on caste, lineage and blood[37] with the Romantic cult of the brave masculine military hero during the Wars of Independence produced a culture of adventure that led to the great honour and social prestige acquired during the 1810s and early 1820s by Creole aristocrats such as Bolívar, men of colour such as Manuel Piar and José Padilla and social outcasts such as Páez. Foreigners such as Gregor MacGregor also benefited from this cult of the adventurous hero. MacGregor was a peculiar creation of this time; subsequent generations have dismissed him as a crazy and self-important fraud, but during the early years of the Wars of Independence his charisma, endurance, military victories and unquestioned loyalty to his superiors established him as a patriotic hero at Bolívar's side.[38] This phenomenon was not unique to Gran Colombia of course: during warfare in the Romantic period in Europe, the brave and heroic soldier could also ascend to the pinnacle of society regardless of his origins. Napoleon Bonaparte is the obvious example, and he was a constant, although ambiguous, reference point for Bolívar and the foreign adventurers.[39]

The idea of a shared 'culture of adventure' between foreigners and Spanish Americans provides a useful way into the study of the encounter between peoples presented in this work. The concept first requires historicising and careful definition. During the Wars of Independence and early 1820s, men of all social and caste backgrounds, including foreigners, could quickly acquire honour by patriotic adventuring. Creoles and foreigners alike recognised the value of adventure as a public demonstration of love for the *patria* over and above concern for their own lives, achieved by virtue of successfully undertaking arduous campaigns across unforgiving terrain, protecting the men under their command and finally emerging victorious against the collective enemy, the Spanish army. This shared culture of adventure had transatlantic roots and was also common to other arenas of warfare in Europe and the Americas in this period and before, where honourable, manly and brave soldier heroes who were prepared to sacrifice everything in the name of the *patria* (rather than a monarch) were given great esteem by society.[40]

The key components of a culture of adventure were unprecedented military mobilisation alongside a search for a new collective identity that could justify taking up arms. This created both a set of social circumstances that was favourable to adventure, and a cult of the adventurer. This culture of adventure provides the background to the discussion in this book of the encounter between foreigners and Gran Colombians during and after the Wars of Independence. It is a necessarily broad concept. As is shown in Chapter 1, adventure was full of contradictions and tensions, and there were adventurers motivated solely by economic opportunity as well as those who hoped that they might form part of a civilising or imperial mission. Opportunity, prosperity, empire, liberty, enterprise and Romanticism were blurred together into the culture of adventure; the diverging directions that these forces took in Gran Colombia were manifested in conflicts over honour and status, and are explored in some detail in Chapter 4. Adventure, then, was much more than a simple response to boredom and uncertain economic situations.[41] Adventure was a word that contemporaries used and understood: travel memoirs and chronicles used the word to signal their intentions to the potential readership.[42] Broadly speaking, adventure was defined in this period for Europeans and Creoles alike as a confrontation with risk and danger, in which the obstacles posed by geography, circumstances or enemies were overcome, the adventurer finally emerging successfully to be crowned with laurels, medals or other symbols of honour.[43]

Geography and landscape were absolutely integral to the way in which ideas of adventure were imagined, described and acted out. The Spanish American interior was largely unknown and 'alien' to foreigners and Creoles alike.[44] In the words of one contemporary novelist, the Wars of Independence presented 'a service so replete with dangers and with difficulties' that adventure was both alluring and terrifying.[45] The landscape of mountains, plains and jungles described by Humboldt had to be overcome by physical exertion and incorporated into the territory of the new nation.[46] These ideas influenced how the Wars of Independence were reported and remembered, as Chapter 9 shows. In order to present themselves in the best possible light, the men who published narratives about their adventures (with few exceptions) exaggerated the dangers to which they had been exposed and the deceptions to which they had been subjected.[47] In 1820 the seasoned traveller Francis Hall recognised that hardship and danger were essential to any South American adventure narrative. If there were no difficulty involved, then there could be no adventure. As such, many writers were 'eager to exaggerate the general calamity' in order to highlight their success, and to declare their colleagues to have been 'annihilated, buried, scattered, famished, plague-smitten [and] murdered' so as to emphasise their own survival.[48]

As Chapter 3 shows, however, there was a kernel of truth in these accounts. Unlike the literary adventurers analysed by critics such as Northrop Frye, Graham Dawson and Martin Green, in all but the rarest scenario, real-life adventurers failed to ensure their recognition as the heroes of stories they imagined for themselves.[49] Whereas the stories of literary adventurers such as Robinson Crusoe ended with the 'exaltation of the hero',[50] most of the real-life adventurers studied here ended their careers in either anonymity or premature death, and more often than not, in both. Chapters 1 and 2 explore the context and realities of these adventures.

Notes

1   George Canning, 'Address on the King's Message Respecting Portugal', 12 December 1826, cited in Leslie Bethell, *George Canning and the Emancipation of Latin America* (London, 1970), p. 17.

2   John Lynch, 'British Policy and Spanish America 1783–1808', *JLAS*, 1 (1969), p. 1.

3   According to Hans Vogel, 'the military history of Latin America ought to be re-written, if not to be written, period'. Vogel, 'War, Society and the State in South America, 1800–70', in Patricio Silva, (ed.), *The Soldier and the State in South America: Essays in Civil-Military Relations* (London, 2001), p. 39.

4   Alfred Hasbrouck, *Foreign Legionaries in the Liberation of Spanish South America* (New York, 1928); Vicente Lecuna, *Crónica razonada de las guerras de Bolívar: Formada sobre documentos, sin utilizar consejas ni versiones impropias. Conclusiones de acuerdo con hechos probados, y la naturaleza de las cosas* (New York, 1950).

5   Eric T. D. Lambert, *Voluntarios británicos e irlandeses en la gesta bolivariana*, 3 vols. (Caracas, Vol. 1, 1983, Vols 2–3, 1990). The tradition is alive and well for other examples of British intervention in the Hispanic world, for example Edward M. Brett, *The British Auxiliary Legion in the Carlist War* (Dublin, 2005).

6   I explore these points in the Introduction to Matthew Brown and Martín Alonso Roa Celis, (eds), *Militares extranjeros en la independencia de Colombia. Nuevas perspectivas* (Bogotá, 2005), pp. 23–33.

7   C. K. Webster, (ed.), *Britain and the Independence of Latin America: Select Documents from the Foreign Office Archives*, 2 vols. (London, 1938); R. A Humphreys, (ed.), *British Consular Reports on the Trade and Politics of Latin America 1824–6* (London, 1940).

8   Geoffrey Best, *War and Society in Revolutionary Europe, 1770–1870* (London, 1982), p. 128.

9   On British trade see D. G. Goebbel, 'British Trade to the Spanish colonies, 1796–1823', *AHR*, 43 (1938), pp. 288–320; J. Fred Rippy, 'Latin America and the British Investment 'boom' of the 1820s', *Journal of Modern History* (1947), pp. 122–29; Humphreys, 'British Merchants and South American Independence', *Proceedings of the British Academy* (1969), pp. 153–74; T. W. Keeble, *Commercial Relations between British Overseas Territories and South America, 1806–1914: An Introductory Essay* (London, 1970); D. C. M. Platt, *Latin America and British trade 1806–1914* (London, 1972); W. M. Mathew, 'Britain and the Bolivarian Republics 1820–1850: Interimperium and the Tariff', in Reinhard Liehr, (ed.), *América Latina en la época de Simón Bolívar: la formación de las economías nacionales y los intereses económicos europeos 1800–1850* (Berlin, 1989), pp. 396–421; Frank Griffith Dawson, *The First Latin American Debt Crisis: The City of London and the 1822–25 Loan Bubble* (New Haven, CT, 1990). For Colombia in particular see Luis Eduardo Nieto Arteta, *Economía y cultura en la historia de Colombia* (Bogotá, 1941), pp. 77–107; for Venezuela see Nikita Harwich Valenilla, *Inversiones Extranjeras en Venezuela, siglo XIX*, 2 Vols. (Caracas, 1992, 1995). For general interpretations that see foreign influence in these terms, see Leslie Bethell, 'Britain and Latin America in Historical Perspective', in Victor Bulmer-Thomas, (ed.), *Britain and Latin America: A Changing Relationship* (Cambridge, 1989), p. 20; Anthony McFarlane, *The British in the Americas 1480–1815* (London, 1994), pp. 305–13; John R. Fisher, 'Britons and South America', in Fisher and James Higgins, (eds), *Understanding Latin America* (Liverpool, 1989), pp. 22–3; Rory Miller, *Britain and Latin America in the Nineteenth and Twentieth Centuries* (New York, 1993), pp. 33–46; Alan Knight, 'Britain and Latin America' in Andrew Porter, (ed.), *The Oxford History of the British Empire*, Vol. 3, *The Nineteenth Century* (Oxford, 1999), particularly p. 125.

10 Germán Colmenares, '*La Historia de la revolución*, por José Manuel Restrepo: Una prisión historiográfica', in Colmenares, *La Independencia: Ensayos de historia social* (Bogotá, 1986), pp.7–24. For a fine overview of the historiography see John Lynch, 'Spanish American Independence in Recent Historiography', in Anthony McFarlane and Eduardo Posada-Carbó, (eds), *Independence and Revolution in Spanish America: Perspectives and Problems* (London, 2001), p. 41.

11 For example Sarah Chambers, *From Subjects to Citizens: Honor, Gender and Politics in Arequipa, Peru, 1780–1854* (University Park, PA, 1999); Victor Manuel Uribe Urán, *Honorable Lives: Lawyers, Family and Politics in Colombia, 1780–1850* (Pittsburgh, Pa., 2000); Aline Helg, *Liberty and Equality in Caribbean Colombia 1770–1835* (Chapel Hill, NC, 2004).

12 Clément Thibaud, *Repúblicas en armas. Los ejércitos bolivarianos en la Guerra de Independencia (Colombia–Venezuela, 1810–1821)* (Bogotá, 2003), pp. 384–94.

13 Karen Racine, 'A Community of Purpose: British Cultural Influence during the Wars of Independence', in Oliver Marshall, (ed.), *English Speaking Communities in Latin*

America (London, 1998), pp. 3–32; Karen Racine, 'Imagining Independence: London's Spanish American Community 1790–1829', Unpub. Ph.D, Tulane University, 1996.

14   Eugenia Roldán Vera, *The British Book Trade and Spanish American Independence: Education and Knowledge Transmission in Transcontinental Perspective* (Aldershot, 2003), pp. 3–4.

15   Catherine Hall, *Civilising Subjects: Metropole and Colony in the English Imagination 1830–1867* (London, 2002).

16   This literature is summarised in the introduction to Alan Lester and David Lambert, (eds), *Colonial Lives: Imperial Careering in the Long Nineteenth Century* (Cambridge, 2006).

17   John Gallagher and Ronald Robinson, 'The Imperialism of Free Trade', *Economic History Review* 6:1 (1953), pp. 1–15.

18   Rory Miller, 'Informal Empire in Latin America', in W. Roger Louis, (ed.), *The Oxford History of the British Empire, Vol. 5, Historiography* (Oxford, 2001), p. 437.

19   David Cannadine, *Ornamentalism: How the British Saw Their Empire* (London, 2001); Niall Ferguson, *Empire: How Britain Made the Modern World* (London, 2003); Bernard Porter, *The Absent-Minded Imperialists: Empire, Society and Culture in Britain* (Oxford, 2004).

20   Giorgio Antei, *Los heroes errantes: historia de Agustin Codazzi, 1793–1822* (Bogotá, 1993). Antei discussed the heterogenous nature of the expeditions in order to set in relief the 'true heroism' of his subject, Codazzi. Nevertheless, his narrative is based on a fine survey of the published memoirs.

21   For ease of reading, this is the last time that I use apostrophes to mark off the constructed and contested nature of 'volunteer', 'mercenary' and 'adventurer'. For the use of 'mercenary' see 'Declaración de Pedro Alejandro Richon', undated, Puerto Cabello, AGI Cuba, Legajo 911A; *Correo del Orinoco*, 21 November 1818 and 15 December 1821; Francisco Burdett O'Connor, *Independencia Americana: Recuerdos de Francisco Burdett O'Connor, coronel del ejército libertador de Colombia y general de división de los del Perú y Bolivia. Los publica su nieto T. O'Connor d'Arlach* (Madrid, 1915), p. 197. For Francisco (Frank) O'Connor (b. 1781 Cork, d. 1871 Tarija) see James Dunkerley, *The Third Man: Francisco Burdett O'Connor and the Emancipation of the Americas* (London, 1999). On mercenaries' decline in prestige during the preceding period see Best, *War and Society*, pp. 27–8, and Janice Thomson, *Mercenaries, Pirates and Sovereigns: State-Building and Extraterritorial Violence in Early Modern Europe* (Princeton, NJ, 1994).

22   D. A. G. Waddell, 'British Neutrality and Spanish American Independence: The Problem of Foreign Enlistment', *JLAS*, 19 (1987), pp. 1–18.

23   Mary Louise Pratt, *Imperial Eyes: Travel Writing and Transculturation* (London, 1992), p. 4. I expand this critique in Matthew Brown, 'Richard Vowell's Not-So-Imperial Eyes: Travel and Adventure in Nineteenth-Century Latin America', *JLAS*, 38:1 (2006) pp. 95–122.

24   For example Roldán Vera, *The British Book Trade*, and Louise Guenther, *British Merchants in Nineteenth-Century Brazil: Business, Culture and Identity in Bahia, 1808–1850* (Oxford, 2004) pp. 1–2.

25   Daniel O'Leary (b. c. 1800 Cork, d. 1854 Bogotá) was appointed as an aide-de-camp by Bolívar within a year of arriving in Venezuela. In 1828 he married Soledad Soublette. Remaining loyal to Bolívar, in 1829 he was the general in charge of the suppression of José María Córdoba's rebellion in Antioquia. Before his death he returned to the region as a British diplomatic representative. The principal narrative of his life is Manuel Pérez Vila, *Vida de Daniel Florencio O'Leary: Primer Edecán del Libertador* (Caracas, 1957).

26   For an overview of the Bolivarian source material including that collected by O'Leary, see David Bushnell, (ed.), *El Libertador. Writings of Simón Bolívar* (Oxford, 2003), pp.

xviii–xxii. The original publication was Simón Bolívar O'Leary, (ed.), *Memorias del General Daniel Florencio O'Leary* (subsequently *MOL*), 32 vols (Caracas, 1879–87).

27 Several Colombian commentators have openly stated their belief that O'Leary doctored the evidence in order to 'divert the attention of history'. See, for example, Carmelo Fernández, *Memorias de Carmelo Fernández* (Caracas, 1973), p. 64, and Germán Arciniegas, in his prologue to *Cartas Santander – Bolívar 1813–1820*, Vol. 1 (Bogotá, 1988), p. xxv.

28 On the Bolívar cult, see Germán Carrera Damas, *El culto a Bolívar* (Bogotá, 1987) and Christopher Brian Conway, *The Cult of Bolivar in Latin American Literature* (Gainesville, FL, 2003).

29 For Arthur Sandes (b. 1793 Greenville, Co. Kerry, d. 1832 Cuenca) see Eric T. D. Lambert, 'Arthur Sandes of Kerry', *Irish Sword*, 12:47 (1975), pp. 139–47. For James Rooke (b. 1770 Dublin, d. 1819 Pantano de Vargas) see Matthew Brown, 'Soldier Heroes and the Wars of Independence in Colombia', *Hispanic Research Journal*, 7:1 (2006), pp. 41–56 and Lambert, *Voluntarios británicos e irlandeses*, Vol. 1, p. 32. For Thomas Charles Wright (b. 1799 Queensborough, Co. Louth, d. 1862 Guayaquil) see Alberto Eduardo Wright, *Destellos de Gloria: Biografía sintética de un prócer de la independencia*, (Buenos Aires, 1949). For John Illingworth (b. 1786 Stockport, Lancashire, d. 1853 Daule, Ecuador), often known as 'Juan Illingrot', see Camilo Destruge, *Biografía del Gral. Juan Illingworth* (Guayaquil, 1913). For Gustavus Mathias Hippisley (dates unknown), who wrote *Narrative of the Expedition* (London, 1820), see Lambert, *Voluntarios británicos e irlandeses*, Vol. 1, p. 47. For Henry Crosdile Wilson (dates unknown) see Matilde Moliner de Arévalo, 'Ingleses en los ejércitos de Bolívar: El coronel Enrique Wilson', *Revista de Indias*, 51 (1953), pp. 89–111, also D. A. G. Waddell, 'Los británicos y la política británica frente a Bolívar', in Alberto Filippi, (ed.), *Bolívar y Europa: En las crónicas, el pensamiento político y la historiografía* (Caracas, 1986, 1992), Vol. 2, p. 61.

30 In 'Richard Vowell's Not-So-Imperial Eyes', p. 16 I suggest an 'alternative canon' of narratives about Independence.

31 Páez reproduced nine pages from [Captain Cowley], *Recollections of a Service of Three Years during the War of Extermination in the Republics of Venezuela and Colombia, by An Officer of the Colombian Navy: 'Moving Accidents by Flood and Field'* (London, 1828) when dealing with the British Legion, and did not flinch from copying its lavish praise of Páez' own leadership, as in José Antonio Páez, *Autobiografía*, (New York, 1867), pp. 142–50. Páez (b. 1790 Curpa, d. 1873 New York) was President of Venezuela between 1830–34, 1839–43 and 1861–63.

32 Malcolm Deas, *Vida y opinión de Mr William Wills* (Bogotá, 1996), Vol.1, p. 302.

33 Most notably John Runnel, who is discussed in Chapter 5, and at length in Matthew Brown, 'Castas, esclavitud y extranjeros en las guerras de independencia de Colombia', *HYS*, 10 (2004) pp. 109–25.

34 William Taylor, *Drinking, Homicide and Rebellion in Colonial Mexican Villages* (Stanford, CA, 1979), p. 4. An edited version of the database can be consulted at www. bris.ac.uk/hispanic/department/resources.

35 See Matthew Brown, 'Adventurers, Foreign Women and Masculinity in the Colombian Wars of Independence', *Feminist Review*, 79 (2005), pp. 36–51.

36 For a discussion of the theories behind what was called 'a new cultural history' of foreign–local encounters in Latin America, which uses a similar approach, see Gilbert Joseph, 'Close Encounters: Toward a New Cultural History of US–Latin American Relations', in Joseph, Catherine LeGrand and Ricardo Salvatore, (eds), *Close Encounters of Empire: Writing the Cultural History of US–Latin American Relations* (Chapel Hill, NC and London, 1998), pp. 4–31. On gender, the principal reference point is Steve J. Stern, *The Secret History of Gender: Women, Men and Power in Late Colonial*

Mexico (Chapel Hill, NC, 1995), particularly pp. 157–77. Works that have followed this lead and cast new light on the period of Independence for Gran Colombia are Guiomar Dueñas Vargas, 'Gender, Race and Class: Illegitimacy and Family Life in Santafé, Nuevo Reino de Granada, 1770–1810', Unpub Ph.D, University of Texas, Austin, 1995; Rebecca Earle, 'Rape and the Anxious Republic: Revolutionary Colombia, 1810–1830', in Elizabeth Dore and Maxine Molyneux, (eds), *Hidden Histories of Gender and the State in Latin America* (Chapel Hill, NC, 2000), pp. 134–42; Arlene J. Díaz, *Female Citizens, Patriarchs, and the Law in Venezuela, 1786–1904* (Lincoln, NE, 2004).

37   Acquiring honour was a means to most ends in the colonial period. As Ann Twinam demonstrated, 'honour' was constantly subject to negotiation, and contemporaries 'used the single word to encompass a multitude of shifting meanings that were intrinsically linked'. Ann Twinam, *Public Lives, Private Secrets: Gender, Honour, Sexuality and Illegitimacy in Colonial Spanish America* (Stanford, CA, 1999), pp. 31–32.

38   On MacGregor (b.1786 Edinburgh, d.c.1845 Caracas) and the historiography surrounding his reputation see Matthew Brown, 'Inca, Sailor, Soldier, King: Gregor MacGregor and the early nineteenth-century Caribbean', *BLAR*, 24:1 (2005), pp. 44–71.

39   For the ambiguous sentiments of British admirers of Napoleon see Stuart Semmel *Napoleon and the British* (New Haven, CT, 2004). Naval heroes were closely-linked to British patriotism in the period, and were therefore seldom referred to by adventurers in Hispanic America; on Admirals Vernon and Nelson see Gerald Jordan and Nicholas Rogers, 'Admirals as Heroes: Patriotism and Liberty in Hanoverian England' *Journal of British Studies* 28:3 (1989) pp. 201–24.

40   For adventure in Germany in 1806–15 see Karen Hagemann, 'Of "Manly Valor" and "German Honor". Nation, War and Masculinity in the Age of the Prussian Uprising against Napoleon', *Central European History*, 30:2 (1997), pp. 187–220. For the general background to the culture of adventure and the 'cult of glory' in this period in Europe, see Best, *War and Society*, pp. 197–200.

41   As suggested in the comments of Magnus Mörner, *Adventurers and Proletarians: The Story of Migrants in Latin America* (Paris, 1985), pp. 21–22.

42   For the memoirs featuring 'adventure' in their title, see works in the bibliography by George Laval Chesterton, E. L. Joseph and Francis Maceroni.

43   See Angela Pérez Mejía, *A Geography of Hard Times: Narratives about Travel to South America, 1780–1849* (New York, 2004).

44   Oliver Marshall, *English, Irish and Irish–American Pioneer Settlers in Nineteenth-Century Brazil* (Oxford, 2005), p. 101.

45   Anon., *Soldiers of Venezuela: A Tale, in Two Volumes* (London, 1818), p. 193.

46   Pratt, *Imperial Eyes*, pp.147–53, examines the way that nature was described in writings of the period and concludes that, rather than being incorporated to the nation, the land was being discursively colonised by the agents of capitalism.

47   This was true even of narratives where the author did not even reach the Spanish American mainland, and the accounts were based on hearsay and rumour: James Hackett, *Narrative of the Expedition which sailed from England in 1817 to join the South American patriots* (London, 1818); and Anon., *Narrative of a Voyage to the Spanish Main in the ship 'Two Friends'* (London, 1819).

48   Francis Hall, *An Appeal to the Irish Nation on the Character and Conduct of General D' Evereux* (Dublin, 1820), p. 4.

49   Northrop Frye, *The Anatomy of Criticism: Four Essays* (Princeton, NJ, 1957); Graham Dawson, *Soldier Heroes: British Adventure, Empire, and the Imagining of Masculinities* (London, 1994); Martin Green, *The Adventurous Male, Chapters in the History of the White Male Mind* (University Park, PA, 1993).

50   Richard Philips, *Mapping Men and Empire: A Geography of Adventure* (London, 1997), p. 31.

CHAPTER ONE

The Context for Adventure

The Geopolitical Context

The 'Age of Revolution' encompassed both sides of the Atlantic, and repercussions from every event swept onwards to those areas as yet untouched.[1] While the Bourbon reforms were being implemented in Spain's American colonies in the second half of the eighteenth century, catalysing profound political, social, economic and cultural changes, elsewhere wars and revolutions were triggering a series of events that would eventually rebound upon Hispanic America.[2] The American Revolution of 1774 acted as a precedent for the French Revolution in 1789, which in turn precipitated the Haitian Revolution in 1790 and the subsequent attempts of British, French and Spanish imperial armies to subjugate the rebellious blacks of Haiti. The eventual declaration of Haitian Independence in 1804 and the huge losses of men and resources occasioned by their ill-fated involvement in the conflict persuaded the British government not to send another large armed force to the Caribbean a decade later, when Spain's American colonies began to fight for their Independence.[3] Nevertheless, the region 'remained a battleground where the northern Atlantic nations contested for military, political and commercial hegemony'.[4] Ideas – both radical and reactionary – and movements of commerce and people were catalysed by these events, and were fundamental in shaping the international context in which the Hispanic American Wars of Independence took place.

Creole élites in the Spanish colonies were influenced by Enlightenment ideas of liberty and equality but were also anxious to avoid the Haitian experience of *pardocracia* (rule by blacks). They desired freer trade and greater representation whilst maintaining a social and caste order in which Creoles would govern the rest of the population. The recourse to foreign mercenaries formed part of a recognition that local capacity would be insufficient to defeat the Spanish armies on their own, as well as an awareness of the fundamental importance of the international context of their conflict.

The Diplomatic Context

The European diplomatic context that shaped Hispanic American Independence was complex. The Spanish government hoped to avoid British meddling in their colonies, while at the same time welcoming the Duke of Wellington's armies in the Iberian Peninsula itself. The question of what constituted Spain's internal affairs, and to what extent Britain would intervene in them, was therefore a constant source of difficulties and tensions.[5] Politicians in London feared that other powers, principally France or the United States, could take advantage of any British inaction with regard to Spanish America. The British offer of 'mediation' between Spain and the rebellious colonies between 1810 and 1814 was not perceived by the Spanish government as 'disinterested', and for this reason it was repeatedly refused.[6] Spanish fear of Britain's covert intentions was also important in thwarting plans to introduce free trade as a means of mollifying the demands of Independent leaders.[7] Spain and Britain, then, while mutually suspicious of each other's intentions, were concerned to prolong their alliance in the uncertain geopolitical situation in Europe.[8] The precarious balance of power after the Congress of Vienna in 1815 persuaded such competitors to maintain a state of peace in order to assure the continued isolation of France. Thus British interests dictated an official policy of neutrality in Spain's colonial affairs.[9] Spain, in contrast, was in a particularly weak negotiating position, knowing that it could not afford completely to alienate Britain as the assistance or at least the neutrality of British naval power would be essential to Spanish attempts to recapture its rebellious colonies. Spanish officials in London and Madrid were intimidated by British power and assertion, and were reduced to regular complaints bewailing their lack of influence and the unfairness of the situation. Spanish policy was re-aligned in response to what was seen as consistent British obstruction of Spanish diplomatic attempts to negotiate or enforce an end to the conflict in the colonies.[10]

The Spanish representatives held 'well-justified doubts about the impartiality of the British', as Rebecca Earle has noted, attributing 'the persistence of the insurgency ... to the aid and support given to foreign mercenaries by their perfidious governments'.[11] The Spanish charge d'affaires in London recognised that Britain was going through the diplomatic motions, admitting that even if a law were passed to make 'foreign enlistment' of mercenaries illegal (which it eventually was, in 1819), then Britain would weasel out of any legal limits on its subjects' actions. This did happen; the recruitment of expeditions 'made a mockery' of their legal prohibition.[12] Waddell nevertheless concluded that it was by default rather than intent that between 1817 and 1819 Britain fell short of the perfect neutrality she professed.[13] This is over-generous. The claim to neutrality in the conflict was a smart and pragmatic position, waylaying Spanish claims at unprincipled intervention, while saving the British state the loss of resources, sailors and soldiers in what would be, judging by the Haitian experience, a draining and unpredictable conflict.

Private individuals took up the cause of intervention hoping that their investment would be repaid by grateful new governments after Independence. This
meant that the quality of the recruits, arms and ammunition was left in private hands, resulting in a lack of quality control in any sense. This official
British policy of wait and see, however, was only possible because of the strong
public support for the cause of Independence, which ensured that a steady
stream of individuals were attracted to expeditions which were organised by
entrepreneurs and to which the government turned a blind eye. In Carlos Pi
Sunyer's opinion, even when the British Home Office sent spies to monitor
the activities of those agents suspected of illegally recruiting mercenaries, 'they
did not see much or find out much, probably because they did not want to see
or find out much'.[14]

This public support was predicated on the repercussions of the French
Revolution and the Napoleonic Wars which 'tore great rents in the thick and
intimate web of relationships between Europe and the rest of the world'.[15] In
Ireland the radical rebellion of the United Irishmen against the British monarchy in 1798 ended in failure, exile and repression, and ultimately the political union between Britain and Ireland in 1801 and the dissolution of the Irish
Parliament. Britain was left isolated from its empire and markets by the economic crisis caused by the Napoleonic Wars and the Continental Blockade.
Socio-economic problems were augmented after victory at Waterloo in 1815
by the return of demobilised troops, who found that employment was increasingly scarce and poorly rewarded. In this situation many British and Irish
men turned to radical politics to improve their situation (leading, in the medium term, to the Great Reform Act of 1832), and others sought an outlet for
their efforts abroad. To this extent, the continuing conflict in Spanish America,
in which Britain was theoretically neutral, provided the ideal destination for
thousands of dissatisfied soldiers or farmers, whether radicals or moderates,
to try their hand as adventurers. The British government was content to see
the departure of discontented individuals, and official policy was improvised
according to events in Spain and Spanish America. After the failed attempts
at conquest in the River Plate in 1806–7, the prevailing mood was caution. A
force reluctantly assembled at Cork in 1808 was diverted to the Iberian Peninsula before it could cross the Atlantic.[16] Such diffidence and uncertainty in
British policy was the consequence of a relative lack of interest in the region
compared to the focus on Europe, North America and Asia, and of an awareness that any potential rewards were more likely to be assured by a stand-
offish, rather than interventionist policy. Even Canning's famous boast about
'calling the New World into existence' was made within the context of a parliamentary debate on the situation in Portugal in 1826, in which Latin America
was only invoked in passing.[17] By leaving intervention to private adventurers, the British government was dissolved from active concern with the region, and could concentrate on other regions until a decisive turn in events in
Spanish America, in either direction.

There was little connection between radical politics and the expeditions in terms of their organisation and leadership. In terms of personnel and ideology they were largely unrelated, even though Lord Castlereagh spoke in the same breath about the 'lamentable disorders' of the expeditions to Gran Colombia and the 'revolutionary meetings' being held across England in 1819.[18] Radical newspapers such as *Black Dwarf* and *The Republican* urged their readers to fight for justice at home, not abroad.[19] Adventure overseas ran against currents of patriotism in Britain and Ireland, even when it took place within the empire.[20] Moreover, events in Hispanic America touched a deeper chord than could be evoked by a small group of radicals. The call for liberty from a tyrannical and oppressive Spain was vague enough to touch on myths of El Dorado, the Black Legend of Spanish cruelty, and female Amazon warriors.[21] Romantics such as Byron and Keats saw events in Hispanic America as opening up a new world in a reprise of the adventurous and heroic deeds of the conquistadors.[22] As Luis de Onís, the Spanish Ambassador in London, noted, 'there was no prospect of changing public opinion, which saw in the Spanish American situation not only the prospect of an immense source of riches, but also the illusion of advancing the cause of liberty and civilisation'.[23] These sentiments were exploited by the Spanish American community exiled in London, who manipulated their high-level contacts in government and the press in order to advertise the recruitment of the expeditions.[24] The adventurers came out of a transatlantic ideological context in which 'liberty' stood for a weakly defined opposition to tyranny, and a bundle of beliefs encompassing opportunity, prosperity, empire, Romanticism and enterprise.[25] They travelled to Gran Colombia on networks laid by commerce and by private enterprise.

The Commercial Context of Enterprise

The individuals who decided to enlist and travel to Hispanic America did so within the wider context of the British imperial 'spirit of enterprise' and its desire to seek out new commercial opportunities, which provided the structure and finance to organise the expeditions.[26] 'Enterprise' was part of a set of outlooks and goals shared by entrepreneurs, intellectuals and patriots across the Atlantic world in the late eighteenth and early nineteenth centuries, and was by no means a peculiarly 'British' characteristic.[27] Commercial networks were precariously balanced upon geopolitical circumstance, and therefore subject to the vicissitudes of military success and metropolitan financial crisis. Several of the Caribbean islands had changed hands as a result of the Seven Years War, and the Continental Blockade had brought their full value into focus. The occupation of Trinidad in 1797 (it was formally ceded by Spain in 1802) gave Britain the ideal location for observing and influencing events on the Spanish mainland. For those who organised, financed and led them, the expeditions were about making profit through the enterprise of risking their capital and efforts, and maximising influence through contacts. The men who financed the expeditions hoped to establish positions of advantage, which they would be ready to exploit in the lucrative post-war years.[28] This was a speculative venture in every sense. They positioned themselves within pre-existing unofficial trade links between the British West Indian colonies and the mainland, and allied themselves with influential merchants from the colonial period.[29] Indeed, British enterprise in northern South America in this period was generally informal, short-termist, improvised and reliant upon pre-existing networks. From itinerant businessmen hauling their suitcases of goods in search of a market, to more stable merchant houses such as the House of Boulton and metropolitan companies such as the Anglo-Colombian Agricultural Society, British entrepreneurs tried every conceivable angle in order to extract profit from Hispanic America.[30] Some economic historians have echoed disillusioned Creoles of the 1820s, complaining that British merchants 'took control of the best positions in national commercial life'.[31] But in fact such an outcome was precluded by the overwhelmingly short-termist outlook, and the number of foreign businessmen in Gran Colombia was declining even before the 1826 London Stock Exchange crash which removed the most speculative financing for unlikely ventures. As Alan Knight has rightly concluded, 'for a time, Latin America promised a bonanza: Disraeli wrote prospectuses and Palmerston dabbled in Peruvian stocks. But the balloon soon burst. Latin American markets were shallow, cities small, and the huge, under-populated rural hinterland generated scant demand for imported manufactures.'[32] Creole merchants who looked to British mercenaries and their leaders to herald the restoration of a lost commercial dynamism were therefore disappointed. The Creole aspiration to incorporate themselves and their new republics into the North Atlantic and Caribbean networks of trade and investment remained, but they had to resign themselves to a peripheral role when the initial promise of investment was replaced with calls for debt repayment.[33]

In the 1810s the commercial imperative was the key catalyst for the recruitment of the expeditions, which were financed for the most part by City of London traders and investors. These were the 'gentlemanly capitalists' who, in the argument of Cain and Hopkins, were the bedrock of British imperialism, 'an extended network of personal contacts based on mutual trust and concepts of honour'.[34] There was a small group of gentlemanly capitalists in the City who remained directly interested in Gran Colombia before, during and after the Wars of Independence. This small community, joined by kinship and economic, political and social ties, invested in the expeditions, in loans, in agricultural and mining societies and in other trading enterprises. Not only did they invest their capital but they also had close personal relations with the figures who led expeditions.[35] For example, James Mackintosh was a leading parliamentarian who adopted the cause and later became chairman of the Colombian Association for Agricultural and other Purposes; his brother John was one of the expeditions' principal officers.[36] The same association's directors included the three men who arranged the first Gran Colombian loan in 1822: William Graham, Charles Herring, and J. D. Powles.

Another director was L. A. Goldschmidt, who in 1824 orchestrated the second major loan to Gran Colombia. The association's auditors included David Barclay, William Richardson and Richard Jaffray, all deeply involved in financing the expeditions. The same 'rich and powerful' people were behind the Colombian Mining Association.[37] Personal friendships were fundamental to underpinning the links between these financiers and the expeditions. Charles Herring described Coroneles John Blossett and Edward Stopford as 'persons of great importance to me', and General John Devereux thought of Herring and William Richardson as 'my great friends'.[38] As Mary English put it, these men were 'animated by the same spirit of speculation'.[39] There was also considerable overlap of personnel with the group of financiers investing in other Latin American countries.[40]

The enterprise was a private affair nevertheless, as noted above. The diplomatic and commercial priorities of Castlereagh and Canning lay elsewhere, even though they welcomed the commercial opportunities offered by independent states in Hispanic America.[41] In the short term, the British merchants' principal target was the arms trade created by the Wars of Independence, with which they hoped to supplement their earnings from the contraband hides, dyes and barks they had traded in the colonial period.[42] Caribbean islands such as St Thomas and St Bartholomew were used as depots for warehousing arms until the Independents could arrange to pay for and collect the goods. Adventurers in the service of Bolívar's armies were often involved in these transactions. In July 1818 Coronel Thomas Richards personally orchestrated Almirante Luis Brion's sale of a large batch of cotton to the merchant Aaron Monsanto.[43] The system was based on letters of credit and respect exchanged within a community of trustworthy gentleman. Promises had to be kept, and a gentleman's word had to be trusted implicitly, if the whole premise of the informal capitalist market was not to collapse. Merchants repeatedly emphasised the honour of the market when demanding payment for their cargos.[44] Creoles such as General Carlos Soublette agreed that it was 'loyalty and good faith that define the conduct of just and liberal governments in the fulfilment of their contracts'.[45] The adventurers were connected to these transatlantic capital networks by the many officers who relied on letters of credit to obtain cash from friends or relatives resident in the Caribbean.[46] The fact that the merchant James Hamilton took up an honorary colonelcy in the Independent army, and was often therefore referred to as 'Coronel' James Hamilton, demonstrates how military authority and commercial enterprise could be firmly linked in this period.

The Context of Emigration

The enterprise of raising expeditions for Gran Colombia was extended into colonisation schemes that were fully supported by the newly established government. The spirit of emigration suffused the expeditions. Many of the adventurers saw their military or naval service as a means towards land grants and prizes that would enable them to start new lives. At least one hundred and fifty women and children accompanied the expeditions. Their experiences were varied and, like the male adventurers, they petitioned the state for support and recognition during and after the wars.[47] The most prominent female adventurer, Mary English, was the widow of James English, the organiser of the British Legion who died in Margarita in 1819. Mary English remained in Gran Colombia, remarrying and setting herself up in society and business. Her biographer concluded that a 'mysterious evil' of scandal prevented Mary English from returning to Britain, and she died in New Granada in 1845.[48] Lambert insisted that the colonisation schemes were an improvised 'smokescreen' to escape the Foreign Enlistment Act of May 1819, but there is a wealth of evidence to substantiate the claim that emigration, for all manner of personal, social or economic reasons, was an integral part of the expeditions from the beginning.[49]

Writing in London in July 1817, the Venezuelan agent Luis López Méndez told Simón Bolívar, 'I have not only managed to encourage people to arm ships for privateering and the arms trade, but I have also stimulated labourers and artisans to go to establish themselves in the Republic's territory under a very generous protection, where they will be free from all religious persecution and able to obtain their own land to work.'[50] López Méndez was assisted in this aim by the pre-existing trade in emigrants from Ireland to North America which was beginning to boom after 1815, and which was diverted south without too much difficulty. By 1816 merchants were regularly advertising in newspapers to put emigrants on ships that would otherwise have returned empty from trading voyages, although the numbers involved were still extremely small in comparison with the major emigrations three decades later. One ship involved in transporting emigrants from Belfast to Baltimore, the *Nikolai Palowitch*, in 1820 took a group of adventurers from Belfast to Barbados, and it is likely that other ships were converted for this purpose.[51] Assisted emigration to the Cape colonies and Australia was beginning in this period too, and there was competition between potential destinations. One adventurer claimed to have been offered a land grant 'twice the size of what I would have got if I had gone to the USA'.[52]

The rise of the emigrant trade coincided with the decline of the slave trade, prohibited by British law in 1807. Many of the ships used in transporting emigrants to North America and adventurers to the cirum-Caribbean may previously have been used in early nineteenth-century slave trading. Ships named *Plutus*, *Peggy*, *Britannia*, *Jupiter*, *Henrietta*, *Prince of Wales*, *Sarah*, *Hannah*, and *Tartar* all journeyed between Africa and the Caribbean in the early years of the century, and identically-named ships all transported adventurers between 1816 and 1822.[53] In the absence of firm documentary evidence, such suggestive links indicate the extent to which the transportation of the expeditions extended previous trading patterns, using existing ships and the skills and experience of their captains and crews.

Some adventurers believed the commercial nature of the expeditions to be similar to the businesses of transportation and piracy.[54] But while there may have been links to previous businesses which profited from carrying people across the Atlantic, once in Hispanic America it was hoped that the establishment of colonisation schemes would make this trade more permanent and act as a beacon for further enterprise. In early 1819 two of the financiers of the expeditions sent a colonisation project to Bolívar. They proposed to exploit the 'spirit of emigration existing in these kingdoms' by providing Venezuela with 'a bold and free peasantry'.[55] Pamphlets were printed and potential colonists were painted a picture of paradise on earth that 'may almost be said to possess perpetual spring', where only half the normal labour was required to cultivate the land.[56] Potential migrants were offered 'a most favourable opportunity to improve their Fortunes'.[57] One adventurer claimed that he had been told that any fighting would be cursory, and that he was 'as much a settler as a soldier'.[58] The details of a scheme for colonising the land of the Orinoco and the Caroní missions with the Irish and British poor were set out in the *Correo del Orinoco* in May 1819, and later reported in Dublin and London.[59] The proposals were signed by Charles Herring, Richard Jaffray and James Towers English, the first two being major financiers of the expeditions from London and the latter being the highest-ranking military officer at the head of those expeditions.[60] The capital of New Erin, the proposed new federal province of Venezuela, would be New Dublin.

The schemes for emigration and colonisation received a powerful impetus from Creoles hoping to populate the extensive 'empty' lands of the territory with productive free foreigners rather than slaves or Indians.[61] The plans were much discussed and debated. An editorial in the *Correo del Orinoco* claimed that the project would be economically advantageous because many empty boats were already making the journey up the Orinoco to collect cattle and other products for export to the British West Indian colonies.[62] Some of the promoters of these schemes, such as John Princep and James Hamilton, subsequently made profits out of exporting cattle to the British West Indies, but they were initially most interested in profiting from colonisation projects.[63] They adopted a pre-existing idea originally proposed by a New Granadan entrepreneur,[64] and promoted the region as the ideal terrain for Scottish colonists.[65] Francisco Antonio Zea confirmed these plans in a letter to Bolívar which stressed the power of the City of London financiers supporting Hamilton and Princep. It was of vital importance, Zea argued '[to] persuade them to buy the best estate in Caroní, so that they can start a colony for poor Scots. This project can give them the profits that they want, and give us a large rural establishment in the Missions'.[66] The interest in bringing foreign colonists to Venezuela continued beyond the Wars of Independence and throughout the 1820s.[67]

Emigrants and adventurers were of all ages when they arrived in Gran Colombia. Some came at the start of their lives, others towards the end, spanning almost forty years in age. Peter Dinnon from Cork was the eldest, born in

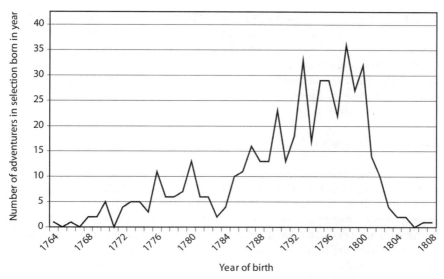

Figure 1.1   *Adventurers' Years of Birth*

1764 and aged fifty-five when he first arrived in Venezuela. George Finlay was the youngest, born in 1808 and aged just fourteen when he joined the Gran Colombian navy in 1822.[68] Most individuals listed themselves as 'Single' when they were asked. In 1819 the adventurers' mean age was 28 years; they were on average three years older than the Venezuelan soldiers they served alongside.[69] As is illustrated by Figure 1.1, the expeditions consisted of a large number of inexperienced youths accompanied by a small number of older men.

An analysis of the adventurers' literacy levels again suggests that the expeditions were recruited from a cross-section of society. Most of the officers were literate; most of the rank and file were not. Literacy was essential for officers, who needed to write down the names of their men and send notes, orders and memoranda to each other. No records have been found indicating any illiterate foreign officers. Based on the number of individuals who left their mark 'X' on requests for pensions, discharges and other documents, it can be estimated that around 60 per cent of the private soldiers were illiterate.[70] Those who could read and write had a marked difficulty in spelling hispanified versions of their names, such as Francisco or Juan.[71] One adventurer, John Hill, learnt to write in Gran Colombia.[72]

The level of Spanish spoken by adventurers was very low, at least initially. Those few who could speak Spanish on arrival were singled out for special mention, and were often given positions of influence. Thomas Jackson, George Woodberry and Thomas Richards served as aides-de-camp to Luis Brion, José Antonio Páez, and Manuel Manrique and Mariano Montilla, one of their principal responsibilities being to translate orders from Spanish to English.[73] Daniel O'Leary dedicated himself to learning Spanish so that he could take

up a similar position close to Bolívar.[74] Those who remained in Gran Colombia after 1823 had learned enough Spanish to petition the government
and write to friends, but before this the widespread ignorance of the Spanish
language (let alone the languages of the many indigenous groups they encountered in Gran Colombia) was one of the principal initial obstacles to relations with Hispanic Americans.

Military Experience

The orthodox historiography assumes that the adventurers were predominantly professional soldiers, seeking a mercenary outlet for their military vocation after demobilisation in 1815.[75] But, as has already been shown, the
expeditions recruited settlers as much as soldiers, and were marketed to potential adventurers rather than military veterans. Figure 1.2 below records all
those who were explicitly linked, in memoirs or personal correspondence, to
previous service in the British armed forces (even where neither dates nor
regiments nor ranks were given):

Table 1.1   *Adventurers Linked to Previous Service in the British Armed Forces*[76]

Name, and rank held in independent service	Dates served	With whom served/ where served
General		
English, James Towers	Unknown	18th Light Dragoons
Von Reimboldt, Julius	Unknown	Unknown
Almirante		
John Illingworth	1801–16	Royal Navy
Leonard Stagg	Unknown	Royal Navy
Coronel		
Chamberlain, Charles	Unknown	West Indies
Crofton, Richard	Unknown	Unknown
Derinzy, William	1814–16	12th Foot
Ferrier, Thomas[77]	Unknown	43rd Foot
Foster, William	Unknown	Waterloo
Gordon, I. D. R.	Unknown	Iberian Peninsula
Hall, Francis	1810–18	12th Light Dragoons/North America, Waterloo
Hippisley, Gustavus	c. 1810–15	West Somerset Militia
Lyster, William	c. 1812	Iberian Peninsula
MacDonald, Donald	c. 1812	Aide-de-camp to General Ballesteros in Iberian Peninsula
Manby, Thomas	1812–c. 1816	East Suffolk Militia to 1812, 12th Foot/Tuam

Name, and rank held in independent service	Dates served	With whom served/ where served
Needham, John	To c. 1816	In 7th Light Dragoons to 1812, then West Indies
Piggott, Richard	To 1816	54th Foot
Power, William Middleton	To 1814	28th Foot
Rafter, William	1806–18	Holland, Iberian Peninsula, West Indies
Rooke, James	c. 1800–16	Aide-de-camp to Prince of Orange at Waterloo
Sandes, Arthur	To 1815	Not known
Skeene	1807–16	Maidstone Cavalry Depot
Stopford, Edward	c. 1810–17	Not known
Uslar, Johannes	1809–16	Iberian Peninsula (Talavera, Badajoz), Waterloo
Wilson, Henry	To 1810	3rd Light Dragoons
Young, Brooke	1813–17	8th Foot
Teniente-Coronel		
Burke, Luke	c. 1805–16	98th Foot, then West Indies
Gillmore, Joseph	c. 1800–15	Portugal, West Indies
Grant, Peter	Unknown	79th Foot
Robertson	Unknown	Unknown
Woodley	Unknown	18th Hussars
Teniente		
Alexander, Alexander	1801–16	6th Artillery/Ceylon, Ireland
Mahary	Unknown	Royal Navy
McCarthy	Unknown	East India Company
Schwitzgibel, François	Unknown	Unknown
Mayor		
Graham	To 1815	Iberian Peninsula
Minchin, John	To 1815	Unknown
Sargento-Mayor		
Boyd, Charles	c. 1806–16	Unknown
Egan, Denis	Unknown	Unknown
Minuth, John	1805–15	Royal Navy
Rudd, Charles	c. 1815	40th Foot/ Waterloo
Capitán		
Chesterton, George	c. 1812–1818	Iberian Peninsula, North America, West Indies
Clubley, Thomas	c. 1805–16	84th Foot
Dillon, John	Unknown	Royal Navy
Edgar, Raymond	c. 1808–16	8th Foot/ Iberian Peninsula
Goodfellow, Samuel	1813–17	Cumberland Volunteers
Langson, James	1804–16	Royal Navy

Name, and rank held in independent service	Dates served	With whom served/ where served
Palmer, Thomas	Unknown	Nottingham Militia
Phelan, James	c.1805–1815	St Helena
Ryan, Cornelius	Unknown	Royal Navy
Saddler, Nathaniel	Unknown	69th Foot
Simpson Hughes, John	Unknown	Royal Navy
Thomas, George	1799–1816	Royal Navy
Sargento		
Fortune, James	Unknown	Horse Artillery
Leard	Unknown	Iberian Peninsula
Shaw, Robert	Unknown	France
Musician		
Powling, James	Unknown	3rd Foot
Seamen		
Adams, John	Unknown	Royal Navy
Brown, George	Unknown	Royal Navy

The available evidence suggests that just one in twenty-five officers had any verifiable experience in the British Army, Royal Navy or defence militias.[78] Some sympathetic sources put the figure a little higher, although in rather a disparaging manner. One wrote that 'two thirds of these … officers … had never fired a gun in their lives'.[79] Another estimated that half of the officers in Gregor MacGregor's expeditions had some military experience.[80] It should be noted that the British Army was by no means the only place in which to gain military experience during the Napoleonic Wars. A handful had served in the French Army.[81] Other officers had served in the Spanish army in the Peninsular War and, like the famous Navarrese leader Martín Javier Mina, continued their military adventures in the Spanish colonies.[82] Given the tendency of memoirs and archival documentation to focus on officers, it is no surprise that few of the men recorded as having British Army experience came from the ranks. However, it is generally also assumed in the historiography that the bulk of those private soldiers who travelled to Hispanic America had also been demobilised from the British Army after the Napoleonic Wars, and thus took their military experience with them across the Atlantic. Reinforcing this interpretation, Loyalist correspondence regularly described the mercenaries as 'well-disciplined, battle-hardened veterans', a verdict which made any success against such foes all the more impressive.[83]

But nowhere has this been demonstrated with hard evidence. There were many contemporaries who expressed frank disdain for the soldiers' lack of

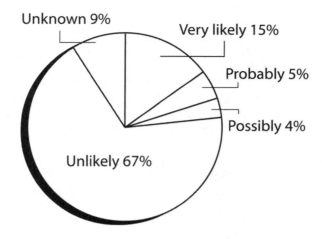

Figure 1.2   *Private Soldiers' Experience in the British Army*

experience. Weatherhead estimated that, of the private soldiers in MacGregor's expeditions, just one third 'had ever handled a musket before'.[84] Of the Irish Legion, Francis Hall wrote that the majority 'had either a very feeble or very mistaken notion of the duties of a soldier'.[85] In particular the Irish Legion was singled out as having 'not even one hundred veteran soldiers in all its ranks'.[86] In his memoirs, José Antonio Páez indicated that the British soldiers at Carabobo had proved themselves to be 'worthy compatriots of those who fought a few years previously at Waterloo'.[87] In an attempt to verify whether the expeditions were composed of the same men who had been at Waterloo, as is implicit in the historiography, or whether (as Páez hinted) they were merely inspired by them, a sample of adventurers was checked against a collection of British Army discharge papers for the period corresponding to the end of the Napoleonic Wars. Wherever possible the benefit of the doubt was given towards a positive identification.[88] Testing 226 adventurers against the British Army discharge papers gave the results shown in Figure 1.2.[89]

Even when all the uncertain results were incorporated into the total just 33 per cent of private soldiers had any verifiable experience in the British Army. Given the aforementioned fragmentary and inconclusive nature of the sources, a figure of around one in three is the most generous possible, and is in all likelihood a significant exaggeration. This is a very long way from the picture of thousands of demobilised veterans painted by Lambert and Hasbrouck, even whilst it is a considerable minority, and a much higher proportion than a random selection of Britons in the period.[90]

Those private soldiers with experience in the British Army shared some general characteristics. They had served in the West or East Indies, and had been discharged because of the damage the climate was held to have inflicted on their ability to serve. Francis Fuge was a typical veteran. He was discharged from the British Army in Mauritius in June 1816, when he was 39 years old and with 24 years' service behind him. He had suffered from 'strictures and chronic rheumatism' and was therefore 'considered unfit for further service abroad'.[91] Despite their experience in imperial locations, veterans such as Fuge were by no means a 'crack force' of élite British soldiers. Rather than being demobilised because of post-war reductions, many had been discharged before the end of the wars on health grounds. William Ryan was suffering from 'chronic hepatitis and gut debilitation'. Thomas Francis had been seriously wounded 'by a market bull' in Hindustan in 1805.[92] Only very few had served at Waterloo and one of those, Robert Brinkworth from Bath, received a gunshot wound in his left thigh during the battle, so rendering him 'unfit for service'.[93]

Even this arresting group of half-blind, gunshot-wounded and amputee soldiers did not form a majority in the expeditions.[94] Most of the adventurers had no verifiable military experience at all. They signed up not out of a frustrated military vocation, but rather as emigrants and adventurers using military service as a means of achieving their goal of a fresh start in the New World, just as the British and Spanish armies were often understood as a form of subsidised emigration.[95] 319 adventurers recorded their previous profession, trade or occupation in a unique document preserved in Guayaquil.[96] 148 described themselves as labourers. The next most popular occupation was 'Weaver' (twenty-six). In descending order, eleven volunteers said that they were shoemakers, and another eleven were tailors. Seven were bakers, seven were mariners and six were musicians. There were five carpenters, and four each of book-binders, breeches-makers and painters. There were three respondents each for bricklayer, butcher, hatter, miner, servant and watchmaker. There were two respondents each for accountant, chandler, clerk, cloth-cutter, cordwainer, craftsman, farrier, gardener, glass blower/stainer, glazier, hairdresser, potter, printer, silk-maker and water-man. There was one respondent each for apothecary, basket-maker, blacksmith, boat-maker, cabinet-maker, cooper, cotton spinner, courier, draper, founder, gunsmith, ham-beater, horseman, lawyer, lightman, machinist, mason, merchant, miller, papermaker, poulterer, roller, rope-maker, saddler, sawyer, shearer, slater, soapmaker, stocking-maker, stone-cutter, tanner, tin-man, varnish-maker, wood-cutter, wood merchant and woollen draper. Only one, Private Felix McKean from the Curragh, described himself as a soldier.[97] There were also a few 'sprigs of nobility' amongst the officers, such as Charles Semple, son of Lord Semple.[98]

The analysis of the adventurers' previous occupations again reveals what a cross-section of society sailed to Gran Colombia. There are 73 different trades listed above. 47 per cent were labourers. Even more, 49 per cent were artisans. Weavers, shoemakers and tailors were the most popular of these trades, which is consistent with research into backgrounds of British Army soldiers in the Napoleonic period.[99] But the very high numbers of men claiming to be artisans supports the thesis that these were not just demobilised military men who, upon the end of the Napoleonic Wars, could do nothing else but enlist in yet another army. These were men with other skills, who found that demand for their trades collapsed with the post-war recession, as in the case of Thomas Livingstone, a printer from Edinburgh, or following major structural changes in the economy, as in the case of John Howard, a labourer from Lancashire.[100] There were more hairdressers, painters and silk-makers in this sample than there were soldiers or sailors. By adventuring in Hispanic America, they may have been hoping to tide themselves over in a time of crisis, or seek a new life where their skills might have been in higher demand. In the expeditions that sailed to Gran Colombia, military veterans were outnumbered by inexperienced labourers and artisans. They came from across Britain, Ireland, Europe and beyond.

Geographical Origins of the Adventurers

Table 1.2   *Geographical Origins of Named Adventurers*[101]

Origin	Number of named adventurers	Overall % of named adventurers
Ireland	644	48.71
England	269	20.35
France	86	6.51
Germany	81	6.13
Scotland	54	4.08
Spain	41	3.10
North America	36	2.72
Italy	22	1.66
British colonies	18	1.36
Netherlands	13	0.98
Wales	9	0.68
Others	49	3.71
Total in sample	*1322*	*100*

The principal conclusion to be drawn from these statistics shown in Table 1.2 is that the majority of the individuals in the expeditions were Irish. Ireland's overrepresentation is consistent with the high percentage of Irishmen serving in the British army in this period, but this is still a finding worth emphasis: the majority of adventurers were Irish, not English, out of a pool of mercenaries from across the globe.[102] By extrapolating from the evidence available for the origins of a quarter of the adventurers, I estimate that there were 3,650 Irish (54 per cent of the total), 1,525 English (22 per cent), 459 Germans (7 per

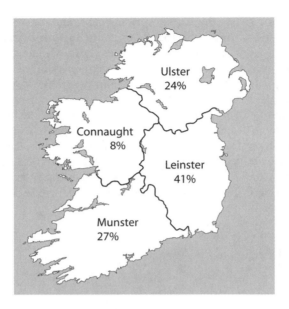

Map 2   *Regions of Ireland*

cent) and 300 Scots (5 per cent). The other 12 per cent were made up of Spaniards, North Americans, subjects of the British colonies, Italians, Welsh, Dutch, Poles, Haitians, Africans, Swiss, Maltese, Cubans, Brazilians, Puerto Ricans, Swedes, Portuguese, Russians, Danes and Norwegians.

There are several provisos to these figures. First, the sources available tend to lean towards the British and Irish Legions at the expense of the legions raised by Gregor MacGregor. Taken in conjunction with the contemporary unwillingness of the Scottish or Welsh to define themselves as such (preferring to be *inglés*, or North or West British), the involvement of such groups in the legions is probably underestimated.[103] Secondly, the subsequent division of the unnamed adventurers has been slightly weighted towards Britain and Ireland. This reflects the likelihood that the men who remained anonymous were lower-ranked soldiers in the expeditions, the type of person most likely to have escaped documentation. Finally, the figure for the British colonies includes men who listed their place of birth as either in Asia ('Calcutta', 'Bengal' and 'Asia') or in the West Indies ('Bermuda', 'Jamaica' and 'West Indies').[104] Despite these caveats, the figures enable some useful generalisations to be made. The expeditions were principally made up from the poorer regions outside of the British empire's metropolitan centre, and comprised a diverse collection of identities and loyalties under their British and Irish banners (which are discussed in detail in Chapter 5).

The adventurers were also regionally diverse.[105] 37 per cent of the English adventurers came from the South-East (mainly Kent and Middlesex), 14 per cent from across the South-West, 10 per cent from the East (principally

Norfolk), 25 per cent from the Midlands (with most from Staffordshire) and 14 per cent from the North (predominantly Lancashire). These figures show that there was a wide cross-section of English society, and almost every county was represented. The bias to the south can be explained by the area's greater population, and by the fact that most of the ships sailed from that area.

As in the case of England, the background of the Irish adventurers was weighted towards the principal port from which the expeditions sailed. This aside, the four regions generally shared the composition. Ulster, Munster, Leinster and Connaught were represented, supporting the claim of one of the Legion's promoters, Charles Phillips, that this was a project which would unite Irishmen, 'where neither sect nor party are opposed; where every man in the country may clasp his brother by the hand'.[106] Leinster provided 41 per cent (principally from Dublin and Wexford), Munster 27 per cent (predominantly from Cork), Ulster 24 per cent (mainly from Down and Antrim) and Connaught 8 per cent.

Most of the documents revealing county origin were forms completed in Achaguas in 1820, but very few of those enlisted in Gregor MacGregor's legions reached this town, so the sample of Scots is probably again unrepresentative. The twelve in the selection came from Aberdeenshire, Forfar, Lanark, Midlothian, Perthshire, Renfrewshire and Stirlingshire – from all over Scotland. Similarly, adventurers came from across Wales, although always from counties with a coastline – Carmarthenshire, Denbighshire, Monmouth and Pembrokeshire.

The adventurers were, geographically, a cross-section of British and Irish societies. Both in England and Ireland there was a tendency towards the recruitment of men living in or near the principal ports – London and Dublin. There was a broad spread of men from across the regions. Within these regions they came from predominantly rural areas as well as urban centres. In Kent, adventurers came from Bonnington, Canterbury, Deal, Gravesend, Sevenoaks, Tunbridge, Wingham and Woolwich. In Co. Cork, adventurers came from Cork itself, Ballygarvan, Bandon, Clonakilty, Gouganbarra, Kanturk, Macroom and Mallow. As the British Legion assembled at Gravesend in 1819, John Blanton, a weaver who had travelled down from Bradford in Yorkshire, mingled amongst others with John Middleton, a watchmaker from Dublin, John Williams, a labourer from Wrexham in Denbighshire, John Cane, a labourer from Co. Derry and John Hill, a labourer from Kent.[107] The expeditions were already a melting-pot for new identities even before they had crossed the Atlantic.

Religion

The expeditions incorporated Catholics and Protestants and laid little emphasis on religious persuasion. As can be seen above, adventurers came from areas of Ireland associated with both Catholics and Protestants, from which it can be inferred that Protestant men associated with the Ascendancy in both North and South were involved, as well as poor Catholic labourers more commonly involved in military service. However, adventurers' religious denominations were only rarely recorded in the archival documents consulted.[108] In the early stages of the Wars of Independence several officers did stress their Catholic background when they arrived in Spanish America. John Devereux claimed to be 'a member of one of the British empire's oldest and most noble Catholic families' who had left Ireland because of 'religious persecution'.[109] Certainly the prevalence of Irish adventurers noted above suggests that Catholics were much better represented in the expeditions than previous historians have supposed.[110] The substantial gaps in the archival record mean that it is impossible to state with any accuracy the proportion of Catholics and Protestants in the expeditions as a whole.[111] Religion was never far from the surface in political conflicts during the Wars of Independence, however, and the way that this affected the adventurers is discussed in Chapter 3.

The statistical analysis above shows how the expeditions were much more about emigration and adventure than they were about experienced military professionals seeking remunerative employment. Socio-economic explanations for migration merged with cultural expectations about the rewards of adventure in South America. The expeditions consisted of young and old, labourers and artisans, and they represented cross-sections of British and Irish society in geographical and class terms. Amongst their number they included some mercenaries with military experience, and other volunteers inspired by the idealism of the cause of liberty. Others had 'no great desire to fight against Spain', but rather came seeking adventure in lands about which they knew next to nothing.[112] They did so carried by commercial and geopolitical networks with their roots in the eighteenth century. In Gran Colombia they encountered new lands and peoples, and practical difficulties that confounded their dreams and changed their aspirations.

Notes

1 Eric Hobsbawm, *The Age of Revolution, 1789–1848* (New York, 1962); Kenneth J. Andrien and Lyman L. Johnson, (eds), *The Political Economy of Spanish America in the Age of Revolution 1750–1850* (Albuquerque, NM, 1994); Victor M. Uribe Urán, (ed.), *State and Society in Spanish America During the Age of Revolution* (Wilmington, DE, 2001).

2 The best summary of the changes occurring in eighteenth-century Spanish America is Lynch, 'The Origins of Spanish American Independence', *CHLA*, Vol. 3, pp. 3–48.

3 David Geggus, *Slavery, War and Revolution: The British Occupation of Saint Domingue 1793–1798* (Oxford, 1982).

4 Luis Fernández-Martínez, *Torn between Empires: Economy, Society and Patterns of Political Thought in the Hispanic Caribbean, 1840–1878* (Athens, GA, 1994), p. 1.

5 Charles Esdaile, *The Duke of Wellington and the Command of the Spanish Army, 1812–1814* (London, 1990).

6 John Rydjord, 'British Mediation between Spain and her Colonies', *HAHR*, 21 (1941),

pp. 29–50.

7 Michael P. Costeloe, 'Spain and the Latin American Wars of Independence: The Free Trade Controversy, 1810–1821, *HAHR*, 61:2 (1981), particularly p. 233.

8 D. A. G. Waddell, *Gran Bretaña y la independencia de Venezuela y Colombia* (Caracas, 1983). Waddell traced this policy in 'International Politics and Independence' in Leslie Bethell, (ed.), *CHLA*, Vol. 3 (Cambridge, 1987), and 'Anglo-Spanish Relations and the "Pacification of America" During the Constitutional Triennium 1820–1823', *Anuario de estudios americanos*, 46 (1989), pp. 455–86.

9 As argued in Waddell, 'British Neutrality and Spanish American Independence', pp. 1–18.

10 My thanks for Josep Fontana for his insightful comments on an earlier draft of this section.

11 Rebecca Earle, *Spain and the Independence of Colombia* (Exeter, 2000), p. 34.

12 Waddell, 'Anglo-Spanish Relations', p. 455.

13 Waddell, 'British Neutrality and Spanish American Independence', pp. 1–18.

14 Carlos Pi Sunyer, *Las expediciones de los legionarios británicos vista desde Inglaterra* (Caracas, 1970), p. 60.

15 Stuart Woolf, 'The Construction of a European World-View in the Revolutionary–Napoleonic Years', *Past and Present*, 137 (1992), p. 89.

16 I rely here on John Lynch's interpretation, which best explores the complexities and ambiguities of British policy in this period. Lynch, 'British Policy and Spanish America 1783–1808', pp. 1–30. For an insightful summary of the consequences of the River Plate conquests, see Klaus Gallo, *Great Britain and Argentina: From Invasion to Recognition 1808–1826* (New York, 2001), pp. 66–70.

17 See note 1, and also Juan Diego Jaramillo, *Bolívar y Canning 1822–1827: Desde el congreso de Verona hasta el congreso de Panama* (Bogotá, 1983), p. 182.

18 Duque de San Carlos to Manuel González Salmón, 30 September 1819, London, AGI Estado, Legajo 89, N.24, fo.1v.

19 A sample of these periodicals for the period in question revealed very little coverage of the expeditions being sent to Spanish America.

20 See the comments of Feargus O'Connor cited in James Dunkerley, *Americana: The Americas in the World around 1850 (or 'Seeing the Elephant' as the Theme of an Imaginary Western)* (London, 2000), p. 432.

21 Peter Marshall, *'A Free Though Conquering People': Britain and Asia in the Eighteenth Century, An inaugural lecture in the Rhodes Chair of Imperial History delivered at Kings College London on Tuesday 5 March 1981* (London, 1981), pp. 8–9.

22 For example Lord Byron, 'Childe Harold's Pilgrimage' (1818) Canto the First, Stanza 89; John Keats, 'On First Reading Chapman's Homer' (1815).

23 Luis de Onís to Secretary of State, London, 1822, cited in Waddell, 'Anglo-Spanish Relations', p. 468.

24 Carlos Pi Sunyer, *Patriotas Americanos en Londres* (Caracas, 1978).

25 On liberty in Gran Colombia, see for example Elías Pino Iturrieta, *Las ideas de los primeros venezolanos* (Caracas, 1993), pp. 127–45, and Javier Ocampo López, *El proceso ideológico de la emancipación en Colombia* (Bogotá, 1999), pp. 19–28.

26 Ferguson, *Empire: How Britain Made the Modern World* lays particular emphasis on this supposedly British virtue.

27 Penny Liss, *Atlantic Empires: A Network of Trade and Revolution 1713–1826* (Baltimore, MD, 1983), pp. 223–24.

28 Alvaro Tirado Mejia, *Introducción a la historia económica de Colombia* (Bogotá, 1976), p. 11; Marco Palacios, 'Las consecuencias económicas de la independencia en Colombia: sobre los orígenes del subdesarrollo', *BCB*, 29:31 (1992), pp. 12–13.

29 R. J. Shafer, *The Economic Societies and the Spanish World 1763–1821* (Syracuse, NY, 1958); Liehr, (ed.), *América Latina en la época de Simón Bolívar*; Adrian Pearce, 'British Trade with the Spanish Colonies, 1788–1795', *BLAR*, 20:2 (2001), pp. 233–50.

30 For the English hawker (*mercachifle*) Mr Christie, see Thomas Manby to Tomás Cipriano de Mosquera, 21 October 1833, Bogotá, ACC, Sala Mosquera 1832, d. 6833.

31 Luis Ospina Vasquez, *Industria y protección en Colombia 1810–1930* (Medellín: ESF, 1955), p. 132. See also Lola Vetencourt Guerra, *El imperio británico en la economía de Venezuela 1830–1870* (Caracas, 1981).

32 Knight, 'Britain and Latin America', p. 127.

33 This process was traced on a regional level in Roger Brew, *El desarrollo económico de Antioquia desde la Independencia hasta 1920* (Bogotá, 1977), and for the continent as a whole in Carlos Marichal, *A Century of Debt Crises in Latin America, from Independence to the Great Depression, 1820–1930* (Princeton, NJ, 1989).

34 P. Cain and A. G. Hopkins, 'Gentlemanly Capitalism and British Expansion Overseas, I: the Old Colonial System, 1688–1850', *Economic History Review*, 39 (1986), p. 507.

35 Listed in J. M. Castillo, *Cuentas del emprestito de 1824, y de los resagos del de 1822, hasta fin de diciembre de 1825* (Bogotá, 1826), BNC, Fondo Quijano.

36 For the long repercussions of Mackintosh's investment, see Gobierno de la Nueva Granada, *Cuestión Mackintosh: Historia de ella y documentos. Publicación oficial del gobierno de la Nueva Granada* (Bogotá, 1852).

37 Anon., 16 January 1819, Angostura, in AL, Legajo 14, fo. 17. For the prospectuses of these companies see the collection preserved in *Prospectuses of Public Companies*, British Library 8223.e.10.

38 Herring to Fernando Peñalver, 10 April 1820, London, copy in EP, HA157/6/93; John Devereux to Daniel O'Connell, 16 July 1822, Bogotá, O'Connell Papers, UCD, P12/3/142. For a mini-biography of John Devereux (b. 1778 Wexford, d. 1860 London) see Brown and Roa, (eds), *Militares extranjeros*, p. 39.

39 Mary English, 'Account of the relations of Mary Coulthorpe Greenup with Herring and Co., Written for W. M. Greenup', n.d., EP, HA157/2/1.

40 Cross-referencing my database against a database of British holders of Mexican bonds reveals the recurrence of several of the individuals named above. I am extremely grateful to Michael Costeloe for the loan of his database, upon which is based Costeloe, *Bonds and Bondholders: British Investors and Mexico's Foreign Debt 1824–1888* (Westport, CT, 2003).

41 R. A. Humphreys' analysis in 'British Merchants and South American Independence', p. 174, suggests that 'their sympathy and their interests went hand in hand'.

42 Aside from arms, most of the materials imported to Colombia by British merchants were aimed at the adventurers, rather than any local markets. Upon its arrival at Angostura in 1819, the *George Canning* unloaded: 'Saddlery, horsewhips, dressing cases and ladies work-boxes, ladies dresses; Scented Soap of various kinds; Hair, tooth, Shaving and Coat Brushes; ready made duck trousers of the best quality; Razors, Penknives and scissors; Shoe-brushes and blacking; and also Pistols and Swords, and good Porter'. *Correo del Orinoco*, 20 February 1819

43 Tomás Richards, 9 May 1823, Caracas, CDM, Db5766, fo. 3. Luis Brion (b. 1782 Curacao, d. 1821 Curacao) was a wealthy merchant whose substantial investment in the Independents' cause earned him the command of the naval forces.

44 For example James Hamilton to the Government of Venezuela, 7 March 1819, Angostura. FJB Archivo Histórico C825, ff. 273–76; Herring to William Adam, 11 September 1822, London, EP, HA157/5/6; Edward Hall Campbell to Bolívar, 11 November 1818, Newcastle-upon-Tyne, AL, Vol. 14, Roll 45, fo. 12.

45 Soublette to Matthew Macnamara, 5 December 1820, Angostura, in *MOL*, Vol. 8, p.

114. Carlos Soublette (b. 1789 La Guaira, d. 1870 Caracas) was a loyal Bolivarian general throughout the 1820s, and served as President of Venezuela between 1837–39 and 1843–47.

46 Thomas Manby to Mary English, 26 October 1835, Bogotá, EP, HA157/3/210. For Manby's life and career, see de Mier, 'Tomás Manby: Soldado en Europa y en América', p. 11.

47 Sixty-seven named women appear on the database. For the specific experiences of female adventurers, see Brown, 'Adventurers, Foreign Women and Masculinity'. For women who accompanied the British army in this period, see Richard Holmes, *Redcoat: The British Soldier in the Age of Horse and Musket* (London, 2001), pp. 293–95.

48 Drusilla Scott, *Mary English: Friend of Bolívar* (Lewes, 1991), p. 240. This biography provides much excellent insight into the expeditions and the world that adventurers moved in.

49 Lambert, *Voluntarios británicos e irlandeses*, Vol. 2, p. 188.

50 López Méndez to Bolívar, 22 July 1822, copy in FJB, Archivo Histórico, C825, ff. 25–37. Luis López Méndez (b. 1758 Caracas, d. 1841 Curacaví, Chile) was the Venezuelan representative in London who organised the recruitment of the volunteer expeditions at the same time as pressing for official recognition of Venezuelan Independence. He was several times imprisoned in London for unpaid debts, and in 1821 was stripped of his powers by the Colombian Congress.

51 *Belfast News Letter*, 23 October 1818, referenced in William Forbes Adams, *Ireland and Irish Emigration to the New World from 1815 to the Famine* (New Haven, CT, 1932), p. 73.

52 'Declaración de Cristóbal Ricaus', 11 April 1819, Puerto Cabello, AGI Cuba, Legajo 911A. This competition continued throughout the century; see Marshall, *English, Irish and Irish-American Pioneer Settlers*, pp. 107–15.

53 I cross-referenced David Eltis, Stephen D. Behrendt, David Richardson and Herbert S. Klein, *The Trans-Atlantic Slave Trade: A Database on CD-Rom* (Cambridge, 1999) with my own database of the 53 ships known to have been involved in transporting adventurers to Gran Colombia. For a description of these vessels, see Hadelis Jiménez López, *La armada de Venezuela en la Guerra de la Independencia* (Caracas, 2001).

54 James H. Robinson, *Journal of an Expedition 1,400 Miles up the Orinoco and 300 Miles up the Arauca; With an Account of the Country, the Manners of the People, Military Operations, etc* (London, 1822), p. 4, p. 26.

55 Herring and Richard Jaffray to Bolívar, 29 January 1819, London, copy in FJB, Archivo Histórico, C–825, ff. 269–70, an interest continued in Herring to Zea, 13 May 1821, Paris, copy in EP, HA157/6/95.

56 Printed Sheet, 'South America', copy in FJB, Archivo Histórico, C–825, fo. 281; also the Irish Legion recruiting sheet (in Spanish, although signed in Dublin by John Devereux and Matthew Sutton), NLI, MS 8076; and *The Times*, 12 April 1819.

57 Repr. in *CMP*, 8 January 1820.

58 'Declaración de Jayme Powling', 12 April 1819, Puerto Cabello, AGI, Cuba, Legajo 911A.

59 *Correo del Orinoco*, 8 May 1819; *FDJ*, 22 November 1819; *CMP*, 13 February 1820. These plans to found a New Ireland in Latin America recurred in the 1860s in Brazil. See Marshall, *English, Irish and Irish-American Pioneer Settlers*, Ch. 3.

60 For James Towers English (b. 1782 Taney, Co. Dublin, d. 1819 Juan Griego) see Eric T. D. Lambert, 'La muerte y entierro del General English', *Boletín histórico*, 24 (1970) pp. 317–27.

61 Ermila Troconis de Veracoechea, *El proceso de la inmigración en Venezuela* (Caracas, 1986), pp. 61–64; John H. Hambleton, *Diario del Viaje por el Orinoco hacia Angostura (julio 11–agosto 24, 1819) Con las instrucciones para el viaje dadas por el Secretario de*

Estado, John Quincey Adams, ed. Juan Friede (Bogotá, 1969), p. 57; Frédéric Martínez, 'Apogeo y decadencia del ideal de la inmigración europea en Colombia, siglo XIX', *BCB*, 34:44 (1997), pp. 3–45.

62 *Correo del Orinoco*, 7 August 1819.

63 Wilfredo José Hernández Brito, 'Notas sobre el arriendo de nueve misiones del circuito Caroní a los ciudadanos británicos James Hamilton y John Princep', *Boletín histórico del Instituto para el rescate, conservación del patrimonio histórico y desarollo cultural del Estado Bolívar*, 1 (1985), pp.12–21.

64 Elias de Santa Croix to the Supreme Government of Venezuela, 24 January 1819, in English, AGNV GDG, Vol. 10, fo. 312.

65 John Princep, *Diario de un viaje de Santo Tomé de Angostura en la Guayana Española a las Misiones Capuchinas del Caroní*, translated from the English and edited by Jaime Tello (Caracas, 1975), pp. 21–24. See also Hamilton to Zea, 11 May 1819, Angostura, copy in FJB, Archivo Histórico, C–825, ff. 282–83.

66 Zea to Bolívar, 3 June 1818, Nueva Guayana, AGNC R GYM, Vol. 24, ff. 1–15, also repr. in Princep, *Diario de un viaje*, pp. 65–74.

67 Interest in colonisation schemes continued throughout the 1820s. See Herring to William Champion Jones, 15 January 1823, London, EP, HA157/5/7; Troconis de Veracoechea, *El proceso de la inmigración en Venezuela*, pp. 65–67; Hans P. Rheinheimer, *Topo: The Story of a Scottish Colony near Caracas 1825–1827* (Edinburgh, 1988).

68 The date of birth of 465 adventurers is known. For Dinnon see AGNC R GYM, Vol. 16, fo. 728. For Finlay see Hasbrouck, *Foreign Legionaries*, p. 405.

69 The comparison comes from Thibaud, *Repúblicas en armas*, p. 498. There was no discernible difference in age between officers and the ranks.

70 This figure may be too low. Of the remaining 40 per cent, some adventurers were able to sign their names in fluent hispanised renditions of their names, suggesting that Colombian clerks signed forms on their behalf. The signatures of John Butcher, 17 March 1824, Bogotá, CDM, Db0762, fo. 4; John Davis, no date, 1823, Bogotá, CDM, Db1010, fo. 6, Samuel Dolloway, 7 October 1822, Bogotá, CDM, Db0299, fo. 4; Julian Lobley, 7 October 1822, Bogotá, CDM, Db0176, fo. 4; and John Ledger, 3 October 1822, Bogotá, CDM, Db0311, fo. 3 all appear to have been signed with the same hand.

71 Francis Mulligan, 7 October 1822, Bogotá, CDM, Db0127, fo. 4. Francis Kean, 29 November 1826, Maracaibo, CDM, Db0734, fo. 7.

72 Upon his discharge from the Colombian Army in 1825 Hill signed himself with an X, but 17 years later, long-married and settled in Coro, he signed reasonably fluently. John Hill, 6 September 1825, Maracaibo, AGNV IP, Legajo 42, fo. 209; John Hill, 23 July 1842, Coro, AGNV IP, Legajo 42, fo. 214.

73 For Jackson, see Lambert, *Voluntarios británicos e irlandeses*, Vol. 1, p. 22; for Woodberry see Carlos Pérez Jurado, 'Tras las huellas del Coronel George Woodberry', *BANH*, 84:335 (2001), pp. 116–18; for Richards, see AGNV IP, Legajo 74, ff. 17–70. Manuel Manrique (b. 1793 San Carlos, d. 1823 Maracaibo) commanded the Independents' forces on the Venezuelan coast in the early 1820s. Mariano Montilla (b. 1782 Caracas, d. 1851 Caracas) commanded the Independents' attacks on Barcelona, Cumaná and Riohacha in 1819 and 1820.

74 Daniel Florencio O'Leary, *Narración: Memorias de O'Leary* (Caracas, 1952), Vol. 1, p. 491.

75 Representative examples are Roberto Ocampo López, 'El proceso político, militar y social de la Independencia', p. 39; in Darío Jaramillo Agudelo (ed.), *Nueva Historia de Colombia*, Vol. 2 (Bogotá, 1989), pp. 9–64; Javier Ibáñez Sánchez, 'La independencia', in Alvaro Valencia Tovar (ed.), *Historia de las fuerzas militares de Colombia*, Vol. 1 (Bogotà, 1993), p. 300; Racine, 'Imagining Independence', p. 212; Christon Archer (ed.), *The*

Wars of Independence in Spanish America, p. 29, p. 187; Frank Safford and Marco Palacios, *Colombia: Fragmented Land, Divided Society*, (Oxford, 2002), p. 98.

76 Most of those listed here were referenced by either Lambert in *Voluntarios británicos e irlandeses* or Hasbrouck in *Foreign Legionaries* as having served in the British Army, both of whom consulted the *British Army Officer Lists* in the TNA. Information for the others comes from: Major Graham and James Fortune in Hippisley, *Narrative of the Expedition*, p. 123, p. 483; Denis Egan, *DEP*, 29 July 1820; James Powling, AGI Cuba, Legajo 911A; Charles Boyd in a letter to Bolívar, undated, AL, Vol. 14, fo. 292; John Simpson Hughes, López Méndez to Bolívar, 20 April 1817, London, repr. in FJB, Archivo Histórico, C-825, fo.49; John Dillon, AL, Vol. 14, fo. 306; Chesterton in *Peace, War and Adventure*, p. 18, p. 246; Alexander Alexander in *The Life of Alexander Alexander*, Vol. 1; I. D. R. Gordon (p. 4) and Sgt. Leard (p. 104) in Weatherhead, *An Account of the Late Expedition Against the Isthmus of Darien*; George Thomas, George Brown and John Adams in *Morning Chronicle*, 4 December 1818; Mahary (pp. 247–48) and McCarthy (p. 266) in Michael Rafter, *Memoirs of Gregor M'Gregor; Together with the Events Subsequent to the Recapture of Porto Bello, till the Release of the Prisoners from Panama; Remarks on the Present State of the Patriot Cause and on the Climate and Diseases of South America* (London, 1821); James Langson, in *DEP*, 3 February 1820; Robertson, *Freeman's Journal*, 8 February 1820; Woodley, in *DEP*, 29 July 1820; Robert Shaw and Samuel Goodfellow, in letters of introduction to Bolívar, June 1817, repr. in FJB, Archivo Histórico, C825, ff. 7–10. The claim about James English's service, made in William Jackson Adam, *Journal of Voyages to Marguaritta, Trinidad and Maturin; with the Author's Travels Across the Plains of the llaneros to Angustura, and Subsequent Descent of the Orinoco in the Years 1819–1820; Comprising his Several Interviews with Bolivar, the Supreme Chief; Sketches of the Various Native and European Generals: And a Variety of Characteristic Anecdotes, Hitherto Unpublicised* (Dublin, 1824), p. 18, was disputed by Lambert.

77 For Thomas Ilderton Ferriar (b. 1785 Manchester, d. 1821 Carabobo), sometimes referred to as 'Ferrier', see Hasbrouck, *Foreign Legionaries*, p. 79.

78 59 officers from 1,445 on the database.

79 Anon., *Colombia: Being a Geographical, Statistical, Agricultural, Commercial and Political Account of that Country, Adapted for the General Reader, the Merchant and the Colonist*, (London, 1822), Vol. 2, p. 433.

80 Weatherhead, *An Account of the Late Expedition Against the Isthmus of Darien*, p. 4.

81 For examples see Hasbrouck, *Foreign Legionaries*, p. 309; Eric T. D. Lambert, 'Irish Soldiers in South America 1818–1830 (Illustrated)', *Irish Sword*, 16:62 (Summer 1984), p. 23; Francis Maceroni, *Memoirs of the Life and Adventures of Colonel Maceroni* (London, 1822), p. 448.

82 General Horé and Teniente Coronel Jaime Albernoz/Arbuthnot continued service on the Loyalist side during the Wars of Independence. For Horé's ancestry, see Rafter, *Memoirs of Gregor M'Gregor*, pp. 236–37. For Arbuthnot (a Protestant Scot with an Irish Catholic grandmother, known to his colleagues as Albernoz), see Chesterton, *Peace, War and Adventure*, p. 208, and Pablo Morillo, *Mémoires du Général Morillo, Comte de Carthagène, Marquis de la Puerta, relatifs aux principaux événements de ses campagnes en Amérique de 1815 a 1821* (Paris, 1826), p. 288. Mina was killed in Mexico in 1815; see M. Ortuño, *Xavier Mina: Guerrillero, Liberal, Insurgente* (Pamplona, 2000).

83 José Solis to Juan Sámano, 19 October 1819, Riohacha, copying his letter of the same day to Coronel de las Milicias del Valle Dupar D. Juan Salvador Anslemo Deoza, AGI Cuba, Legajo 745.

84 Weatherhead, *An Account of the Late Expedition against the Isthmus of Darien*, p. 4.

85 Hall, An *Appeal to the Irish Nation on the Character and Conduct of General D'Evereux*, p. 23.

86 Mariano Montilla to Minister of War, 4 January 1820, Juan Griego, *MOL*, Vol. 17, fo. 23.
87 Páez, *Autobiografía*, p. 206.
88 The WO 97 series of War Office papers held at TNA contains the discharge papers of all soldiers discharged from the British Army in the period c. 1780 to c. 1850. It records the birthplace, birth date, occupation, height, physical description, army career and reasons for discharge of each soldier who left the armed forces in this manner. The only soldiers to slip through this bureaucratic net were those who died in the forces (irrelevant to this study) or those who deserted. From the 848 named adventurer private soldiers' records collected, a sample of 226 soldiers was selected (27 per cent). Soldiers were selected for inclusion in the sample on the essentially random criteria that sufficient information (first and surnames, place and year of birth) should be known about them from other sources, in order to establish a positive identification. Principal among the selection criteria was that the individual had a reasonably uncommon surname and that both first names and surnames were known – for example, Private Francis Fuge. Fuge was known to have arrived in Angostura as part of the British Legion in January 1819. Finding the British Army discharge papers for Private Francis Fuge, dated June 1816, was presumed as sufficient proof of his British Army experience, even though neither Fuge's place of birth nor his age were known. Fuge's discharge papers are at TNA WO 97/420/123. When there was some confusion regarding a match between an adventurer and a British Army soldier, the benefit of the doubt was given on the side of a positive match. This was to balance the inherent negative tendency created by the difficulties of inconsistent spelling of surnames, or the occasional change in first names between Spanish language sources (Julián for William, Juan for James, for example). This method could not be relied upon always to provide 100 per cent certainty that the individual soldier in question did serve in the British Army. However, when used over a sample of 226 soldiers, it was deemed to provide a plausible indication of what proportion of soldiers did have such experience.
89 Very likely – positive match found with British Army Discharge Papers: 34. Probably – positive match found, but serious reservations held: 11. Possibly – no match found, but some reservations held: 8. Unlikely – no matches found with British Army Discharge Papers: 153. Unknown – no match found due to the name bringing up an unfeasibly large number of potential marches, i.e. Private Patrick Kelly brought up 89 matches: 20.
90 From Best, *War and Society*, p. 125, pp. 144–48, a rough estimate can be made that no more than 15 per cent of British men had military experience by 1815. According to Best, 315,000 Britons with military experience were killed in the Napoleonic Wars.
91 Fuge joined the Independents in 1819. He campaigned from Angostura to Quito, and in June 1823 in Bogotá he petitioned the government for his *haberes militares*. See TNA WO 97/420/123; CDM, Db0272.
92 William Ryan, TNA WO 97/796/35; Thomas Francis, TNA WO 97/420/117.
93 For Robert Brinkworth, see TNA WO 97/504/126. Unlike all those soldiers noted previously, Brinkworth was not recorded in Lambert, *Carabobo*, as present in 1821 – instead, he was with the Albion Battalion in Cali. While Lambert did not mention Brinkworth at all, he was named in three other documents, AGNC R GYM, Vol. 778, fo. 766, fo. 794, fo. 840. Amongst those who were at the Battle of Waterloo were Private James Oldham from Manchester, TNA WO 97/102/95; Private Thomas Whitesides from Killaire in Co. Armagh, TNA WO 97/897 fo. 151; Private John James from Roscommon, TNA WO 97/72/16; and Private Robert Brinkworth from Bath, TNA WO 97/504 fo. 126.

94 George Moore had a leg amputated upon discharge from the British Army in 1816: see TNA WO 97/365/77. He joined Bolívar's army in 1819 or 1820. Eric T. D. Lambert, *Carabobo 24 Junio 1821 Algunas relaciones escritas en inglés* (Caracas, 1974), p. 34; 'Descriptive Roll', AHG G, Acta 2; AGNC R GYM, Vol. 326, ff. 13–25.

95 For Scottish Highlanders, see Stephen Conway, *The British Isles and the War of American Independence* (Oxford, 2000), pp. 99–101. Manuel Moreno Fraginals and José J. Moreno Mosó, *Guerra, migración y muerte: El ejército español en Cuba como vía migratoria* (Colombres, Asturias, 1993), Chapter 1, 'El ejército como via migratoria', makes a similar argument for the nineteenth-century Spanish army, which is at variance with the many accounts from the 1810s and 1820s in which 'nothing could be more loathsome and fearful to a Spaniard than the prospect of death on the other side of the world', Margaret L. Woodward, 'The Spanish Army and the Loss of America 1810–1824', *HAHR*, 48 (1968) p. 587.

96 The majority of this information comes from the 'Descriptive Roll' compiled by the officers of the British Legion at Achaguas in late December 1820, held in the AHG G. By this time, the British Legion was formed by men who had come out as part of either the British or Irish Legions, and so can be taken as being a largely representative sample. Additional information was taken from invalid records in AGNC R GYM, Vol.16.

97 Felix McKean was 31 in 1820. No record could be found of him in TNA WO 97. His description of himself as a soldier appeared in 'Descriptive Roll', AHG G, Acta 2.

98 The nephews of Lord Byron and Lord Rosse were also adventurers. See Besant, *Narrative of the Expedition, p. 52*; Hasbrouck, *Foreign Legionaries*, p. 79; Lambert, *Voluntarios británicos e irlandeses en la gesta bolivariana*, Vol. 2, p. 38.

99 Sylvia R. Frey, *The British Soldier in America: A Social History of Military Life in the Revolutionary Period* (Austin, TX, 1981), pp. 9–16.

100 For Livingstone, see Lambert, *Carabobo*, p. 37; AGNC R GYM Vol. 16, fo. 591; and AHG G, Acta 2. For Howard see AHG G, Acta 6. On the post-war recession, see Boyd Hilton, *Corn, Cash and Commerce: The Economic Policies of the Tory Governments* (Oxford, 1977).

101 The surviving documentation gives a clear national origin to 1,322 of the 3,013 named individuals, either through their own testimony or that of an officer or colleague. Of the rest, an almost equal number, 1,319, could only be tentatively labelled as 'British or Irish' (for example, when a Spanish language source called them *inglés*), which probably contributed to under-representing Irish, Scots and Welsh in the final totals. 372 defied any labelling at all. For similar reservations see Marshall, *English, Irish and Irish-American Pioneer Settlers*, p. 73.

102 P. Karsten, 'Irish Soldiers in the British Army 1792–1922: Suborned or Subordinate?', *Journal of Social History*, 17 (1983–84), pp. 36–54; David Fitzpatrick, "A Peculiar Tramping People': The Irish in Britain 1801–1870', in W.E. Vaughn, (ed.), *A New History of Ireland*, Vol. 1, *Ireland Under the Union 1801–1870* (Oxford, 1989), p. 614.

103 See the essays collected in Laurence Brockliss and David Eastwood, (eds), *A Union of Multiple Identities: The British Isles c. 1750–c. 1850* (Manchester, 1997).

104 Soldiers giving their places of birth in Asia appear in the 'Descriptive Roll, Achaguas, 22 December 1820', AHG G, Actas 1–6.

105 386 named adventurers provided details as to their county of origin, in addition to being 'British', 'English', 'Irish', 'Scottish', or 'Welsh'. In the following section, these individuals – 143 from England, 225 from Ireland, 12 from Scotland and 6 from Wales – are used as a random sample with which to analyse collective identities within the expeditions.

106 Charles Phillips, quoted in *Fairburn's edition of the speech of Chas. Phillips, Esq., the*

Celebrated Orator, to General D'Evereux and the Regiments under his Command Previous to their Embarkation at Dublin to Join the Spanish Patriots in South America (London, 1819), p. 4.

107 For Blanton see AL Vol. 14, fo. 272; AGNC R GYM Vol. 1447, fo. 465; CDM Db2720; AHG G, Acta 3. For Middleton see AHG G Acta 2. For Williams see AHG G Acta 4. On Cane see AHG G, Acta 5. On Hill see AGNV IP, Vol. 42; AHG G Acta 2.

108 Of 3,013 records on the database, 195 named individuals were recorded as Catholics, 45 as Protestants. This information largely came from Loyalist interrogations of Independent prisoners in the AGI, and some doubt must be cast upon the reliability of this information, in that Protestants may have claimed to be Catholic in order to avoid the wrath of the feared Spanish Inquisition.

109 Devereux to Crisanto Valenzuela, Secretary of State of the United Provinces of New Granada, 16 June 1815, Bogotá, in *MOL*, Vol. 14, pp. 257–59.

110 Some historians assumed that British adventurers had to be Protestant. For example, Friede and Ortiz both followed a Loyalist officer's account which stated that Catholic officers serving under Gregor MacGregor by definition had to be French. See José Solis, 'N.1°. Lista de los que se han podido alberiguar murieron quemados y de balas en el Castillo de San Jorge en día once del pasado de octubre', Riohacha, 21 October 1819, AGI Cuba, Legajo 745. The document is published, with some transcription errors, in Juan Friede, 'La expedición de Mac-Gregor a Riohacha, Año 1819', *BCB*, 10:9 (1967), pp. 71–74, and Elías Ortiz, *Colección de documentos para la historia de Colombia*, pp. 272–73. Cross-referencing with the database of adventurers, and especially Rafter, *Memoirs of Gregor M'Gregor*, pp. 421–22 shows that 'Er' was 'Eyre', 'Grande' was 'Grant', 'Bruin' was 'Brown', and soforth, all either Scottish or Irish Catholics.

111 Neither is there any record of the variety of Protestant denominations and evangelicalism that prospered in Britain at this time, and which scholarship has shown to have caused tensions in other British armed forces. H. J. Hanham, 'Religion and Nationality in the Mid-Victorian Army', in M. R. D. Foot, (ed.), *War and Society: Historical Essays in Honour and Memory of J. R Western 1928–71* (London, 1973), pp. 159–81.

112 'Petición de oficiales presos', AGI Cuba, Legajo 745, repr. in Friede, 'La expedición de Mac-Gregor', p. 74.

CHAPTER TWO

The Terrain of Adventure in Gran Colombia

Welcome at this favourable hour, illustrious defenders of liberty; welcome to the arms of your brothers, and to the bosom of your adopted country. ... This cause is worthy of you: it is the cause of wisdom and industry, of the arts and commerce – the sacred cause of social intercourse, and consequently that of every people and all men. ... Such is the sublime undertaking in which you have embarked with us, and to which we are conducted by a chief, covered with glory and full of virtue, generous, magnanimous, ever a patriot, always a citizen, and always the best friend of the defenders of liberty. Fly to his arms, follow him on his victorious march: – be careless of your fortune, and that of your children, for whom he himself has provided; and intent alone on the grand idea of freeing the land of Columbus, rush forth with us upon the Spaniards, and hurl them from our territory to the Sea of the Antilles! – Let us at once shew what any army of friends can do, composed of Britons and Venezuelans!

(Francisco Antonio Zea, 1818)[1]

This chapter examines the often harsh realities that met the adventurers in Gran Colombia. Each group of adventurers is traced from Britain and Ireland to Hispanic America, and the regional variations across the lands in which they travelled are described. Despite the fragmentary and unreliable nature of many of the sources, which were often founded upon mistaken assumptions and untrustworthy accounts, providing figures for the number of adventurers is still an essential starting point. Previous narrative histories have not attempted to provide any quantitative analysis of the expeditions, instead relying on the estimates and guesstimates of contemporaries. The results presented in Figure 2.1 largely agree with Lambert's estimate of a total number of 5,500 to 6,000 soldiers, plus around 1,000 sailors.[2] The groups were recruited over several years by different individuals.

Tracing the Adventurers

This section provides a quantitative breakdown of where the adventurers went and in what numbers. Most of these numbers are approximate unless otherwise stated. The subsequent section details the regional characteristics of the places they went, and describes the campaigning activity that they were involved in.

Table 2.1 *Grouping the Expeditions*

Group	Description	Number of individuals
A	First units, recruited by Luis López Méndez, Gustavo Hippisley, et al., 1817	720
B	British Legion, recruited by James Towers English, 1818–19	c. 1200
B	British Legion, recruited by George Elsom, 1819	572
B	Hanoverian Legion, recruited by Johannes Uslar, 1819[3]	300
C	Irish Legion, recruited by John Devereux, 1819–20	1729
D	MacGregor Legions, recruited by Gregor MacGregor, 1819	c. 600
D	MacGregor Legions, recruited by Francis Maceroni, 1819[4]	300
E	Others enlisting individually	387
E	Naval adventurers c. 1,000	
Total		*c. 6808*

Group A: 720 individuals enlisted in the first contingents in 1817. Of these, 200 drowned when the ship they sailed on, the *Indian*, was shipwrecked off the coast of France. There were no survivors. 390 adventurers left the service in the Caribbean without reaching Gran Colombia (either returning to Europe or dying in the Caribbean), and just 200 of these first contingents arrived in Angostura.[5] Of this group, 100 survived to cross the Páramo de Pisba in 1819 and then served at the Battle of Boyacá. Of the other 100, probably 20 died or left Angostura without taking part in any active campaigning, and around 80 served in the Apure and eventually fought at Carabobo in 1821.

Group B: Of the 2,072 members of the British Legion (including the Hanoverian Legion) around 1,000 served in the 1819 campaign on the Venezuelan coast, culminating in the attack on Barcelona. Of these 1,000, perhaps 100 died on campaign, with 900 returning to Margarita. Here, 100 died or departed, leaving only 800 to reach the Independents' headquarters inland at Angostura. Of these survivors, around 500 were present in the llanos at Achaguas in December 1820, and then went on to serve at Carabobo. Of these 500, about 100 died, 100 joined the Albion battalion, and 200 went on to serve in the navy on the Venezuelan coast and were later based around Coro and Maracaibo. This leaves a figure of around 100 who died in, or deserted from, Angostura. Taking the figure of 1,000 for the campaign on Barcelona means that 1,072 died *en route* to or in Margarita, or departed the service there and returned home.[6] Given the often catastrophic descriptions of conditions in Margarita in this period (see below) these high figures are not unreasonable.

Group C: Of the 1,728 members of the Irish Legion who travelled in 1819–20, just 678 formed part of the campaign on Riohacha in 1820. 544 of these rebelled and were transported to Jamaica. Some were dispersed throughout the Caribbean and others travelled on to North America. 134 remained in the Independent service, fighting at La Ciénaga, the siege of Cartagena, and later were incorporated into the Albion Battalion. 12 of these were killed in combat. Of the other 1,050 who did not leave Margarita for Riohacha, probably 300 travelled on to Angostura, of whom 100 were incorporated into the British Legion and 200 either died or departed from the service.[7] This leaves 750 who either died at Margarita or departed and returned home. Of these, given the evidence provided by memoirs of the period, approximately 600 died and 150 were able to depart.[8]

Group D: Of the 900 individuals recruited by MacGregor and Maceroni, about 300 deserted in the Caribbean before taking part in any military action and either died, remained in the Caribbean, or returned home. 300 joined the attack on Riohacha and another 300 on Portobello. Of these 600 adventurers who did join the attacks very little is known beyond the executions of 150 and the imprisonment of 100 (almost all of whom died in captivity, with the exception of around a dozen who escaped) and 150 said to have escaped from Riohacha before the Loyalist occupation (some of whom re-joined the Independent army at a later stage). This leaves 200 who did serve at Riohacha or Portobello but then either died or deserted.

Group E: The careers of a minority of the individuals who enlisted independently are known in some detail but they are so disparate that it is impossible to generalise about them. The early career of Gregor MacGregor and the arrival of John Runnel exemplify the ways in which Caribbean and Pacific networks linked into the Gran Colombian region, bringing adventurers in their wake.[9] Very little is known about the naval volunteers, beyond their mobility within the Caribbean region (but not the mainland interior).

The discussion of the adventurers in the groups above enables the summary shown in Figure 2.2 of what happened to them after they arrived in the Caribbean.

Campaigning in Gran Colombia

Between 1817 and 1825 the adventurers travelled across almost all of the Gran Colombian territory. They encountered areas that differed greatly in topography, population, labour relations, religion and economy. This section describes these variations and the ways in which they affected the adventurers. The Captaincy-General of Venezuela was the first point of arrival for most volunteers. The region had been beset by debilitating warfare since the declaration of Independence in 1810. A total population of around 700,000 consisted of around 26 per cent whites, 13 per cent Indians, 39 per cent pardos, 8 per cent (free) blacks, and 14 per cent slaves.[10] Within this region there were marked local variations.

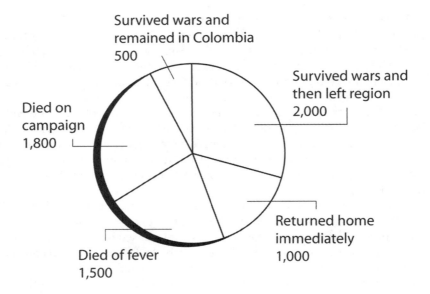

Figure 2.2   *Summary of Adventurers' Fates*

Angostura and Guayana

From 1817 the Independents' capital was Angostura, a small town perched on a hill by the Orinoco river several hundred miles inland, a journey that provided the adventurers with an uncertain, 'swampy, rainy and hot' welcome to mainland Venezuela.[11] Angostura's population was around 6,000 in 1810.[12] Most of Venezuelan Guayana's settlements hugged the edges of rivers, leaving expanses of unexplored hinterland to the indigenous peoples, and to the adventurers' imaginations.[13] Guayana was a relatively neglected outpost of Spanish power, scattered with Capuchin missions and providing a temporary stop-off for colonial officials, the last of whom was an Irishman in the service of Spain, Laurence Fitzgerald.[14] In 1817 the Independents' advance triggered a mass exodus, and the 41 remaining Capuchin friars either fled or were killed or captured by the Independent army led by Manuel Piar.[15] In the years 1817 to 1821, the population of Angostura was swollen by the arrival of the Independents' leaders, their armies and the associated traders, women and followers who accompanied them. A *hacendado* from the llanos, Don Feliciano Pérez, reported in February 1819 that Angostura was 'virtually a foreign colony, as it is mainly populated by foreigners'.[16] The town became a meeting-place for people from across the Gran Colombian region, and around 1,500 foreign adventurers spent some time there, an extraordinary number given the size of the town. In addition, refugees came in from the missions, where the combined impact of disease and the requisitioning of men and supplies by

Map 3   *Venezuela*

competing armies had led to the collapse of the local population.[17] Angostura was a melting-pot for the new Venezuelan republic where, in a small urban centre, Independent officers rubbed shoulders with Indians and free blacks in the military service, where whites, pardos and blacks came together in a common enterprise. During 1817 and 1818, Angostura was the only fixed point in the Venezuelan Republic. Bolívar declared the independence of the Republic of Colombia there on 17 December 1819. The presence of foreign soldiers and officers was one more element in this rapidly changing, tense and pressurised environment.[18]

British traders had been linked to Angostura since Spain ceded the island of Trinidad in 1797. These commercial contacts had continued through the periods of free trade, neutral trade and prohibition of trade that accompanied the varying Spanish fortunes in the Napoleonic wars, and foreigners were therefore in a good position to press for better terms upon the establishment of republican government in Angostura.[19] Foreigners such as James Hamilton and Samuel Forsyth occupied prestigious positions in Angostura society as a result of the debts owed to them by the government, and they often hosted important receptions in the houses they took over from Spanish governors and high-level officials. The trade in hides, beef, mules and tobacco continued to interest the British colonies, and the income that this commerce earned the nascent republic largely financed these pivotal years of the war against Spain.[20]

The forts along the Orinoco had been held by small units of the Loyalist army, which were quickly dislodged when the Independents took control of the region. The Loyalists were replaced by regiments of the Independent army, often manned by the foreign adventurers, who were sent away from Angostura to smaller postings where they could be drilled and prepared for campaigning and fighting. One hundred adventurers left Angostura to cross the Andes and marched over the Páramo de Pisba in 1819, into the Eastern Cordillera of New Granada and up to Bogotá. A total of around 700 joined the army campaigning on the llanos, eventually moving to Achaguas in late 1820, and then on to the Battle of Carabobo in 1821.

Margarita

The other principal holding area for newly arrived foreign adventurers was the island of Margarita, 15 km. north of the Venezuelan Caribbean coast. Margarita was very important in receiving, barracking and dispersing large numbers of the British Legion, and almost all of the Irish Legion. Probably 4,000 adventurers passed through Margarita between 1816 and 1822, many of whom died without reaching the mainland. Most of the island's local population of 15,000 resided in the valleys on the eastern side of the island where fresh water was most plentiful, and in the four principal towns, La Asunción, Juan Griego, El Norte and Porlamar.[21] As an island which had received many travellers and immigrants during the colonial period, the population was a mixture of whites and pardos who had long travelled to fish and trade. They were apparently 'eager to perform any office of kindness for strangers'.[22] Their traditional tolerance towards foreigners was one reason why Bolívar chose it as the meeting-point for the adventurers, rather than the more distant and quickly overcrowded Angostura.[23]

In colonial times slave labour was used to harvest pearls from the seabed around Margarita. This trade was in decline by the beginning of the nineteenth century. Several sugar plantations relying on slave labour were dotted around the island, although by 1819 many of the slaves had been recruited into the Independent army.[24] The movements led by two future heroes of Venezuelan Independence, Santiago Mariño and Juan Bautista Arismendi, converted the island into a standard bearer of the Independents' cause, earning it the title of 'New Sparta'.[25] In addition, Margaritan women were famed for their conduct in resisting Spanish attempts to capture the island, and were often portrayed as 'gallant Amazons'.[26]

The island's agriculture and cattle-raising was sufficient for its own needs, but was limited by the short rainy season which only lasted from December to January. Those adventurers who arrived outside this period, and were temporarily barracked on beaches away from the population centres, struggled to find enough drinking water. These conditions allowed fevers and illnesses to flourish. Robert Young described the scene in his diary in late 1819:

I passed several Huts by the wayside, converted into Hospitals, but in the [most] miserable plight from want of everything; the unfortunate sufferers lying without blankets, or any kind of covering, on the cold earthen floor, most of them raving mad; several of them lying dead or dying, under prickly pears, or anything which could secure them from the burning rays of the sun. I stopped some minutes to contemplate this scene of human misery, and then proceeded on my way.[27]

The Venezuelan Coast, including Cumaná, Barcelona, Coro, and Maracaibo

Many of the adventurers who gathered at Margarita were used to attack Loyalist strongholds on the Venezuelan Caribbean coast.[28] Between 1816 and 1823 all of the principal ports – Puerto Cabello, Coro and La Guaira – and towns where rivers from the llanos meet the Caribbean – Cumaná and Barcelona – were attacked and occupied by expeditions of Independents that largely consisted of foreign adventurers. The maritime adventurers also spent most of their time in operations on this section of the coast, especially around Coro, Puerto Cabello and Maracaibo. This coastal region was home to a heterogeneous mix of people throughout the late colonial period, its 200,000 population made up of 15.2 per cent whites, 8.1 per cent Indians, 38.8 per cent pardos, 11.6 per cent free blacks and 26.3 per cent slaves according to a late colonial census.[29] This population was largely urban, with the many and largely undocumented indigenous groups occupying the interior, where the Society of Jesus was active in founding settlements.[30] Slavery – on plantations and pearl fisheries – was an important constituent of the coast's plantation economy, both before and after Independence, and the region was the scene of Venezuela's principal colonial slave rebellions.[31]

At the end of the colonial period, the populations of Cumaná and Barcelona were growing rapidly and their markets were full of indigo, cotton and tobacco, products which were fundamental to Venezuela's late-colonial economic prosperity.[32] Security was a minor consideration. Maracaibo had a reformed militia but other coastal towns were left relatively undefended. Consequently they regularly passed between the competing armies in the first stages of the war. Coro, Maracaibo and Puerto Cabello remained loyal to Spain well into the 1820s, with much of their antipathy to the Independents' cause being explained by their relative prosperity under the colonial trading systems and by their reluctance to be ruled from Caracas.[33]

On 14 July 1819 Barcelona was taken by an Independent expedition, led by Rafael Urdaneta, made up of 300 Margaritans and approximately 1,000 adventurers from the British Legion, including 300 Germans from the Hanoverian Legion. While the Loyalist forces slipped away, the adventurers devoted themselves to plunder and drinking.[34] Between 1821 and 1823 Puerto Cabello was besieged by forces largely composed of foreign adventurers, who also took part in the Campaigns of Coro and Zulia, designed to force Loyalist forces out. The port was finally taken only after the naval battle of Maracaibo on 24 July 1823, under the command of Admiral Padilla, which 'destroyed for the remainder of the war the naval power of Spain on the north coast of South America'.[35]

Venezuelan Coastal Range, including Caracas

The Venezuelan coastal range, or *cordillera*, sits just behind the coast in the central and eastern portion of Venezuela. Although representing only a small fraction of Venezuela's surface area, the 'stabilized network of hamlets, villages, towns and cities' in the rich intermontane valleys made this the most densely populated part of the region, and it held the principal economic and political centres of the area from the mid-eighteenth century onwards.[36] The region had a unique 'three-way external orientation – Colombian, Caribbean, and Atlantic'.[37] Its demography was similar to that of the Coast, except in that the white population was rather larger (29.4 per cent of the total), reflecting the attraction of its more temperate climate to European settlers. The rest of the 164,000 population was made up of 8.8 per cent Indians, 34.3 per cent pardos, 6.0 per cent free blacks, and 21.5 per cent slaves.[38]

This high percentage of slaves reflected the development of a 'dynamic cacao economy' in the seventeenth and eighteenth centuries.[39] In response to the resultant demographic imbalance, white hacienda owners developed closely-linked kinship networks, and protested energetically when they felt that their interests were threatened by colonial initiatives.[40] This group had benefited from Caracas' 'golden age of economic expansion and political maturity' at the end of the eighteenth century and they formed the *consulado* (local body or tribunal, formed to protect commercial interests) of Caracas in 1793.[41] By relative standards the Church was much less powerful in Venezuela than in New Granada.[42] In the wake of the influx of slaves, the pardo-dominated population boomed, consequently blurring ethnic differences and 'creating an integrated middle-class' of white and pardo plantation and ranch owners who were largely content with the colonial order.[43] This prosperous region suffered from the disruptions of the Napoleonic Wars, however, which affected its capacity to find markets for its products. The previously moderate, consensual political equilibrium was replaced by something akin to desperation to recoup lost halcyon days of wealth.[44] Mercantile and commercial élites represented in the Caracas *cabildo* therefore argued for increased economic and political independence from colonial rule.[45]

The colonial militia in Caracas, officered by the white and pardo landowners and traders, formed the basis of the armies of the First Venezuelan Republic. It proved an inflexible weapon for waging war in the region between 1810 and 1816, and the recruitment of foreign adventurers was in part designed to remedy perceived deficiencies.[46] The principal military set-piece battle of the second phase of the Wars of Independence on Venezuelan soil was at Carabobo, near Valencia, on 24 June 1821. Around 900 adventurers fought at the battle. Victory was won by skilful tactics from the commander, Bolívar, and, according to Hasbrouck, assured by stout defence from a British battalion stranded on a hillock and under constant fire from the enemy. Eventually the British Legion charged out of their defences and up 'two hundred yards of sun-baked hillside'. In this astonishing counter-attack, again according to Hasbrouck, the British demonstrated 'heroic courage', 'Herculean endurance' and 'bulldog determination'. Over one hundred foreign adventurers died at Carabobo, mostly on that small hillside.[47] After the battle, around 200 adventurers settled in Caracas amidst a general attitude of tolerance. The first official Protestant cemetery was consecrated in Caracas in 1834, and the British Consul regularly performed Anglican services including marriages.[48]

The llanos

The area known as the llanos forms the interior heartland of Venezuela, and rolls westwards into New Granada, covered with grass, clumps of trees, and marshes. The llanos were the major arena for Independent military campaigning in 1818 and 1819. Rivers and streams dissect the region, regularly flooding vast areas and regulating the lives of its cattle-herding inhabitants.[49] Given the immense territory encompassed, the population of 134,174 – 41.7 per cent of whom were pardos – was spread extremely widely.[50] It included many escaped slaves or *cimarrones,* who had fled the plantations to find a life of relative freedom on the llanos. According to Miguel Izard, this led to the formation of a 'dangerously egalitarian' informal society.[51] The llanos were far from formal Venezuelan colonial politics, and life was only very weakly institutionalised. The Church manned the only outposts of colonial rule in the larger towns, but even its presence was in decline by 1810.

Until the Wars of Independence, the llanos had witnessed no military mobilisation at all, although some commentators believe that 'violence was already a way of life'.[52] However, the Comunero rebellion of the 1780s had demonstrated how the very isolation of the region could act as a haven for subversive groups, and the Independents took full advantage of this after 1817 under Páez and Francisco de Paula Santander.[53] The llanos formed a sparsely populated frontier between Venezuela and New Granada, and between the export economy of the coast and the subsistence agriculture of the highlands, although the informal llanos economy was increasingly being incorporated into the prosperous Venezuelan economy.[54] Contact with non-Spaniards from across the Atlantic was minimal during the colonial period, but the llaneros were highly mobile people, and meeting strangers was an integral part of any travel in the region. In this frontier, identities were flexible and cultures merged rather than clashed.[55] Foreigners were tolerated and welcomed – providing they were on the right side of the partisan struggle.[56] It was in this region that the Independent armies prepared for the major campaigns of the wars, and across which they marched to enter New Granada, a terrible journey in harsh wet and cold conditions that left many soldiers dead. Around 1,000 adventurers were barracked in the Barinas, Apure and Maturín Llanos in 1819 and 1820. They travelled constantly throughout the region on horseback or on foot.

The New Granadan Caribbean Coast: Santa Marta and Riohacha

The New Granadan Caribbean coast west of Maracaibo was in many ways similar to its Venezuelan counterpart. The area was integrated into the maritime trading economy of the circum-Caribbean, particularly through contraband with British traders operating out of Jamaica and Dutch traders from Curacao. Because of the relative prosperity derived from this trade, ports such as Santa Marta and Riohacha remained loyal to the colonial status quo into the 1820s.[57] Their hinterlands were occupied by unconquered Indians who had established complex relations of resistance and co-operation with their Hispanic neighbours.[58] There were slave plantations along the coast, and mountains and marshland left the coastal towns isolated from the rest of New Granada and at threat from the depredations of pirates and buccaneers.[59] Ecclesiastical establishments were reduced to a bare minimum by the 1810s.

The sheer number of free, non-white men who formed the vast majority of society on the coast made élites acutely conscious of how precarious their rule

Map 4   *New Granada*

could become in the event of racial upheaval.[60] Their response to the incursions of foreign adventurers was therefore ambiguous. They wanted to maintain their present prosperity and hierarchy, but also wanted more freedom to trade. Gregor MacGregor occupied Riohacha with 300 men in 1819 and almost 700 members of the Irish Legion attacked the town in 1820. Both expeditions attempted to negotiate with Santa Marta, having already occupied Riohacha but in the short term neither was successful. Poor communication and a lack of resources plagued both expeditions, which were largely derided as failures by many commentators. The nature of the region, however, and the relative strength of neighbouring Cartagena, meant that any attacks on Riohacha or Santa Marta were necessarily improvised and short term in their success. Only in 1821, after the fall of Cartagena, could Mariano Montilla's campaign eventually secure the region for the Independents.

Cartagena and Panama

Cartagena de Indias was the best defended of Spain's South American possessions, as virtually all the efforts of Bourbon military reform in New Granada were focused on this vital port. Sea defences were reinforced, the militia system was overhauled, and at the end of the colonial period the town had a functioning defence force which proved vital to provisioning and resistance during the long sieges that it suffered in 1815 and in 1821.[61] Its reinforced walls were virtually impregnable to contemporary weapons and lengthy siege warfare was the only alternative. Attackers massed outside Cartagena were often plagued by yellow fever, and the combination of strong defences and disease defeated several British forces during the eighteenth century.[62]

As the principal Spanish American entrepôt for the transatlantic slave trade, Cartagena itself had developed a substantial enslaved and free black population by 1800.[63] These black communities were linked to Caribbean networks of communication and were thus aware of the processes and consequences of the Haitian Revolution.[64] Freed slaves and pardo artisans also formed important sections of the Independents' terrestrial and maritime mobilisation after Cartagena was wrested from Spanish control in 1821.[65] Labour structures varied across the region, as did relations between people from a large diversity of ethnic backgrounds. The 'extreme fragmentation of the territory and social fabric of the vast Caribbean region precluded mass rebellion'.[66] The Church was important in Cartagena, providing a focal point for society and providing some assistance to those left in poverty and need by slavery or warfare.

A distinctive regional identity developed around Cartagena, which can largely be explained by the difficulty of communication with the viceregal capital Bogotá, from which it was separated by a boat journey up the Magdalena river and then a mule ride over the *cordillera*. The vicissitudes of the Wars of Independence served to reinforce this sense of difference from the rest of New Granada.[67] The residue of the Irish Legion took part in the 1821 campaign and thenceforth Cartagena welcomed the many maritime adventurers who adopted the city as a place of residence and rest between campaigns.

In contrast to Cartagena, Panama was a commercial outpost, perched on the mainland but existing only to facilitate transoceanic trade, acting as a link between the Atlantic and the Pacific and between Spain and the Viceroyalty of Peru. After the abandonment of the old galleon fleet system in 1739 Spain's possession of Panama was largely symbolic.[68] Gregor MacGregor attacked Portobello in 1819 with 300 men, many of whom were quickly captured by Loyalists and held prisoner in Panama. Several dozen died during months in captivity before the remainder were executed.

New Granada Eastern Cordillera, including Bogotá

In the late-colonial period, highland New Granada consisted of several distinctive sub-regions and an axis of interconnected local economies.[69] Warmer areas in the far north produced sugar, cacao, cotton, gold and tobacco. In the south, around the fast-growing town of Socorro, cotton production thrived and the enterprise culture led the Spanish General Pablo Morillo to describe it as the 'Manchester' of New Granada.[70] This burgeoning prosperity and increased agricultural production had led to frustration with imperial attempts to control revenue, triggering the 1780–81 rebellion of the Comuneros.[71] Further south again, and at a much higher and colder altitude, was the *tierra fría* of the colonial capital Bogotá, and Tunja, both cities with populations of around 30,000.[72] *Mestizos* (persons of mixed heritage) provided the labour for the agriculture that was the basis of economic life across the region, and subsequently supplied many men for the armies.[73] In 1820–21 alone, Socorro sent around 10 per cent of its men to the Independent army.[74] Black slavery was virtually non-existent in the highlands and much of the population were *mestizos* from generations of mixed-race relationships. The remaining indigenous peoples of the region lived in *resguardos,* Spanish-initiated institutions that regulated the dispersed settlement pattern of their pre-conquest ancestors.[75] Until the eruption of warfare these communities existed without much contact with the white communities huddled in the urban centres. The British and Irish officers who crossed the *cordillera* with Bolívar in 1819 were charged with recruiting in this region and spent lengthy periods there, operating especially in Tunja and Pamplona.[76] The Church was well-established at the centre of viceregal power and owned land and controlled mortgages much more extensively than it did in outlying areas. The institutions of the State and Church provided the central focus for employment, status, and honour in colonial Bogotá.[77] The Viceroy and *audiencia* (high court) often conflicted, but their presence in the city persuaded residents of their loyalty to the institutions of the state.[78]

The battle of Pantano de Vargas took place in the Andean highlands on 25 July 1819. Bolívar forced the issue by riskily marching his men over the inhospitable mountain pass at Pisba from the Venezuelan llanos, perhaps surprising but certainly inconveniencing the Loyalists in New Granada.[79] A quarter of the foreign adventurers on the expedition lost their lives at Pisba. Regrouping quickly, Bolívar engaged the enemy by the *pantano* (swamp) at Vargas. Coronel James Rooke, who led the 100-strong British battalion in the battle, was wounded in the arm and subsequently died after an unsuccessful amputation.[80] The result of the battle was indecisive, and the armies met again at the bridge of Boyacá two weeks later. This bridge controlled access to the capital, crossing a river that was swollen because of heavy rain. Bolívar marched his men from Tunja towards the bridge on the morning of 7 August, and the Loyalist army was routed and forced to flee or surrender. Bogotá's lack of military defences was roundly demonstrated when Bolívar subsequently marched straight into the city without further resistance from the Loyalist authorities, who fled in the opposite direction when their fate became apparent.[81] In Bogotá the foreign survivors of Boyacá were joined by another 100 who had been campaigning on the Venezuelan coast. These men formed the basis of the Albion Battalion, which continued southwards in late 1820. Despite its isolated location, Bogotá had a diverse population and was receptive to newcomers, open to change and tolerant towards differences of opinion.[82] Many of the Albion Battalion returned to settle in Bogotá after completing their service in Ecuador.

The Chocó and Antioquia

Unlike other parts of New Granada, the Chocó and Antioquia regions were relatively untouched by the Wars of Independence and hence received only rare and sporadic visits from adventurers. With its perceived lack of accessibility and reliance on fluvial transport, plus its high indigenous and black populations, the Chocó was visited only by the most adventurous adventurers.[83] Antioquia, whose population contained 20–40 per cent slaves, was prospering in the late colonial period as its mining industry took off, fostering an entrepreneurial culture that produced some of New Granada's principal commercial figures.[84] Antioqueño businessmen negotiated the first Gran Colombian loans with British financiers, and foreign adventurers were instrumental in suppressing an anti-Bolívar rebellion there in 1829.[85]

The Cauca Valley, including Cali and Popayán

The Cauca Valley, on the other hand, saw a great deal of conflict during the Wars of Independence. Before it reaches Antioquia and the Chocó the River Cauca flows through the Cauca Valley, a varied region based around the towns of Cali and Popayán. In the late colonial period the population was 15.2 per cent whites, 17.6 per cent Indians, 46.4 per cent free *mestizos*, pardos and blacks, and 20.8 per cent slaves.[86] Cali was a tropical, lower-lying settlement, with a large black (free and enslaved) proportion of its 11,000 population in 1797.[87]

Popayán had a very different identity, enjoying a more temperate climate and surrounded by the Indians living in the many autonomous *pueblos de indios*.[88] The cabildos in Cali and Popayán represented the land-owning and slave-owning élites, who, along with the region's main power-broker, the Church, dedicated themselves to maintaining precarious social and racial hierarchies.[89] Alongside this traditionalist, white-dominated and conservative society, new social groups made up largely of free blacks emerged in the second half of the eighteenth century. They began to take advantage of their increased numbers and the upheaval of the Wars of Independence to negotiate better conditions. Free-born blacks and manumitted (recently freed) slaves, poor whites, and pardos were able to live off small parcels of land on the margins of the large haciendas.[90] Further from the urban centres, areas of subsistence farming remained, which provided a similar refuge for those fleeing conflict, poverty, or enslavement.[91]

Because of its economic wealth and key location on the road from Bogotá to Quito, the Cauca Valley was repeatedly fought over throughout the Wars of Independence. Its slave-based economy was devastated by the loss of much of its labour, and its mining industry (which had been in decline throughout the eighteenth century) was destroyed by flooding.[92] Many labourers, both free and enslaved, therefore joined the campaigning armies. Some adventurers such as John Runnel were involved with guerrillas and banditry, which flourished in the region's difficult topography. The Albion Battalion was barracked in Popayán in 1821–22, and campaigned regularly in its environs.

Pasto and Patía

South of the Cauca Valley, the indigenous people in Pasto and Patía (60 per cent of the total population) were much more closely tied to *haciendas* than others in New Granada.[93] The substantial distance from colonial capitals in Bogotá and Quito meant that élites in Pasto developed a marked autonomy from colonial legislation and the Pasto Indians learned to 'organise themselves independently of the élite' in order to resist unwelcome developments.[94] Correspondingly, the region remained loyal to the Spanish Crown during the Wars of Independence, as much due to a sense of local identity than to the power of the clergy.

In Patía, warfare detached many men from the land they had worked, and the land leant itself to the operations of bandit bands, often led by pardos and freed slaves, who were eventually suppressed by or incorporated into regular armies.[95] The recurrent banditry, and the image of black savagery and anarchy that this fostered with Creoles and foreigners, meant that overall contact with outsiders remained limited. Pasto was seen to be 'far from everywhere'.[96] When adventurers did venture into the region, the result was often violent confrontation. The foreign officers in the Rifles Battalion were prominent in Bolívar's controversial suppression of Loyalist resistance in Pasto in 1822.[97]

Map 5   *Ecuador*

Quito and highlands

Set high up in the Andes and surrounded by a scattered and largely indigenous population, the *audiencia* and Presidency of Quito were even further away from the currents of Atlantic thought that took so long to reach Bogotá.[98] This did not stop white land-owning élites in Quito declaring their Independence from Spain in 1809, but the subsequent Loyalist reconquest was swift and complete. Quito was only forcibly taken for the Independent cause by an army commanded by Antonio José de Sucre after the battle of Pichincha in 1822, in which the Albion Battalion fought.[99] Given the topographical diversity of the region, local and regional identities remained strong into the nineteenth century.[100] The urban artisans and servants of Quito had a markedly different outlook from their rural counterparts, whose involvement in colonial rebellions was limited.[101]

Defended primarily by its surrounding mountains and distance from the sea, the region did not develop any military tradition until the arrival of the Venezuelan officer who became its first President, Juan José Flores.[102] Flores had served alongside the foreign adventurers of the Rifles and Albion Battalions, and many of them later rose to positions of authority in the region under his patronage. Quito and the Ecuadorean northern highlands therefore occupied a paradoxical place with regard to the adventurers. Historically distant from the transatlantic networks of trade and ideas that had so affected Venezuela, Quito and its surroundings by the mid-1820s found itself governed by Venezuelans, and largely occupied by an army officered almost entirely by non-locals. These included the few hundred adventurers who had made it that far, many of whom continued on to Guayaquil.

Guayaquil

South America's second-largest Pacific port, Guayaquil was booming in the late eighteenth century as a result of its export of textiles and cacao.[103] In contrast to the conservatism of Quito, the world of the Guayaquil traders was one of 'fearful and wonderful fluidity, of questioning old norms, widespread disagreement, and political bickering'.[104] This increasingly wealthy town turned its face towards the Pacific trade routes that provided its life-blood and its back to the indigenous people and slaves who laboured to produce its products. In Ecuador slavery was particularly prevalent on the coastal plantations leading north from Guayaquil up the coast to Esmeraldas, and less prevalent in the interior, creating a situation where indigenous peoples and blacks mixed only in a few small areas in the north, and in urban centres such as Guayaquil.[105]

The Guayaquil traders dominated the political manoeuvring that led to the proclamation of the Independence of a city-republic in 1820.[106] Guayaquil had a paradoxical relationship with foreigners, especially after Bolívar annexed it to Gran Colombia. As a cosmopolitan port city it was open to and tolerant of incomers, especially sailors and foreign merchants, many of whom had been resident for several decades, and there had long been a tradition of the daughters of merchant élites marrying into the families of newly arrived Spaniards. At the same time the city had built a strong local identity in opposition to Quito and Cuenca in the highlands and Lima further south. Guayaquil marked the end of the road for the Albion Battalion, whose five-year contracts were terminated here in 1823. Rather than settle, many foreign soldiers travelled by land back to Bogotá, where they could petition the authorities for recognition, unpaid wages, prizes and pensions. Those adventurers who settled or remained in Guayaquil tended to pertain to the naval forces based there.

In conclusion to this brief summary of the Gran Colombian region as it was encountered by the adventurers, it can be seen that Gran Colombia was a topographically, economically, demographically diverse place which the disintegration of Spanish colonial rule had brought to varying degrees of social decomposition. In some areas, institutions were in disarray, while in others, loyalties to the colonial system remained strong. The experiences of the foreign adventurers were correspondingly diverse, and these are explored in Chapter 3.

Notes

1 [Francisco Antonio Zea], 'Proclamation to the British Troops', 1818, repr. in Anon., *Colombia: Being a Geographical, Statistical, Agricultural, Commercial and Political Account of that Country*, Vol. 2, pp. 373–75. Zea (b. 1766 Medellín, d. 1822 Bath) was President of the Congress of Angostura, and the most important civilian in the Independents' administration. In 1820 he travelled to Europe to negotiate loans for the new republic of Colombia.

2 Lambert's figures were based on an unpublished card index which he occasionally mentioned in his published work. This was primarily the three volumes of *Voluntarios británicos e irlandeses*, but his findings were best synthesised in 'Irish Soldiers in South America' in *Irish Sword*, and 'Los legionarios británicos' in Fundación de Bello, *Bello y Londres*, Vol. 1 (Caracas, 1980), pp. 355–76. In 'Irish Soldiers in South America', Lambert estimated that there were 5,500 soldiers in total, and that 5,000 actually arrived on the shores of South America. In addition, he proposed a figure of 500 sailors. Such inconsistency between different sections of his work was typical of Lambert. Here I have taken his (higher) figures from 'Los legionarios británicos', which are more in line with my own findings. On several occasions in what follows the term 'named adventurers' is used. This is understood to mean an adventurer whose name has been preserved in the documentary record – there are 3,013 such individuals on the database used for this study.

3 The Hanoverian Legion raised by Uslar harked back to the King's German Legion that was part of the British Army between 1803 and 1815. However, by 1808 only a minority of its members were Hanoverians, and, as such, Uslar's forces are referred to as 'German' in this work.

4 Francis Maceroni (dates unknown) was a veteran of the Napoleonic armies who became associated and then disillusioned with Gregor MacGregor. The principal source for Maceroni's life is his own autobiography, *Memoirs of the Life and Adventures of Colonel Maceroni*.

5 All of this basic information has been extracted from Hasbrouck, *Foreign legionaries*, and Lambert, *Voluntarios británicos e irlandeses*, unless otherwise stated.

6 Anon. [Cowley], *Recollections of a Service of Three Years*, p. 8 stated that 2,000 took part in the Barcelona campaign. [G. A Lowe], 'A brief sketch of operations', estimated 1,500. Both appear to be excessive numbers proposed by men interested in promoting the size of the expedition for their own benefit.

7 Anon., [Cowley], *Recollections of a Service of Three Years*, p. 175 estimated that 500 died on the outward voyage.

8 Benjamin M'Mahon, *Jamaica Plantership: A Description of Jamaica Planters viz Attorneys, Overseers and Book-Keepers, with Several Interesting Anecdotes, Compiled by the Author during a Residence of Eighteen Years on Twenty-Four Properties, in the above Capacity, Situated in Different Parts of the Island* (London, 1839), p. 13; O'Connor, *Independencia Americana*, p. 32.

9 For MacGregor, see Brown, 'Inca, Sailor, Soldier, King', pp. 44–70; for Runnel, see Brown, 'Castas, extranjeros y esclavitud', pp. 109–25.

10 John V. Lombardi, *People and Places in Colonial Venezuela* (Bloomington, IN, 1976), p. 110.

11 Lombardi, *People and Places*, p. 9.

12 'Ciudad Bolívar', *Diccionario de la Historia de Venezuela*.

13 Lombardi, *People and Places*, p. 23.

14 R. B. Cunninghame Graham, *José Antonio Páez* (London, 1929), p. 106.

15 John Lynch, 'Revolution as a Sin: The Church and Spanish American Independence', in

Lynch, *Latin America Between Colony and Nation: Selected Essays* (London, 2001), p. 133.

16 'Copia de la declaración tomada a Don Feliciano Pérez benido de Guayana', 19 February 1819, La Bannosa, AGI Cuba, Legajo 898A, 'Asuntos pertenecientes a la comandancia de los llanos'.

17 Neil Whitehead, *Lords of the Tiger Spirit: A History of the Caribs in Colonial Venezuela and Guayana 1498–1820* (Dordecht, 1988), pp. 149–50. In 1825, the population of all Guayana was estimated at 16,310, Miguel Izard, *Series estadísticas para la historia de Venezuela* (Mérida, 1970), p. 14.

18 See Matthew Brown, 'La renovación de una élite, Angostura 1810–1830', in Luis Navarro (ed.), *Las élites urbanas en hispanoamérica* (Seville, 2005), pp. 341–53.

19 Elias A. Pino Iturrieta, 'Antecedentes generales y esbozo del comercio inglés en Angostura' (1968), pp. 131–43.

20 J. P. Harrison, 'The Colombian Tobacco Industry from Government Monopoly to Free Trade 1778–1876', University of California, Unpub. Ph.D., 1951.

21 Izard, *Series estadísticas*, p. 14.

22 Anon. [Cowley], *Recollections of a Service of Three Years*, Vol. 1, p. 31.

23 Francisco Javier Yanes, *Historia de Margarita* (Caracas, 1948), p. 155, p. 162, p. 167.

24 M'Mahon, *Jamaica Plantership*, p. 14.

25 Santiago Mariño (b. 1788 Valle del Espíritu Santo, d. 1854 La Victoria) was the principal caudillo of the Venezuelan East. He was involved in many of the political rebellions of the post-Independence years. Juan Bautista Arismendi (b. 1770 La Asunción, d. 1841 Caracas) commanded Margarita's resistance to Loyalist reconquest, and for a period in late 1819 he was Vice-President of Colombia. He was prominent in Venezuelan politics throughout the 1820s and 1830s.

26 Anon. [Cowley], *Recollections of a Service of Three Years*, Vol. 1, pp. 27–32.

27 Robert Young, 'Diary of the Voyage of Robert James Young, and of General Devereux's Expedition to Margherita with the Irish Legion, Bolivar', 1819, PRO NI D/3045/6/3/2, fo. 17.

28 Lombardi, *People and Places*, p. 7.

29 Lombardi, *People and Places*, p. 133; Rosa María Guillén Serrano, 'Vida cotidiana en Cumaná en vísperas de la independencia', in Maria Carmen Mena Garcia, (ed.), *Venezuela en el siglo de las luces* (Seville and Bogotá, 1995), p. 203.

30 'Provincia de Nueva Andalucía', *Diccionario de Historia de Venezuela*.

31 Federico Brito Figueroa, *Las insurrecciones de los esclavos negros en Venezuela 1777–1830* (Caracas, 1961), pp. 42–98; Miguel Acosta Saignes, *Vida de los esclavos negros en Venezuela* (Caracas, 1967), p. 291.

32 Guillén Serrano, 'Vida cotidiana en Cumaná en vísperas de la independencia', pp. 206–9.

33 Enrique Nobrega, 'Notas sobre la élite militar en la provincia de Maracaibo, 1750–1814', in Mena Garcia, (ed.), *Venezuela en el siglo de las luces*, pp. 255–80; María Antonieta Martínez Guarda, *La region histórica de Coro y su articulación en tres momentos de la historia de Venezuela: 1528–1824* (Caracas, 2000), pp. 63–70; Yanes, *Historia de la provincia de Cumaná en la transformación política de Venezuela desde el día 27 de abril de 1810 hasta el presente año de 1821* (Caracas, 1949), pp. 229–44.

34 Hasbrouck, *Foreign legionaries*, pp. 120–1.

35 Hasbrouck, *Foreign legionaries*, p. 291.

36 With on average eight people per km². Lombardi, *People and Places*, p. 26.

37 Lombardi, *People and Places*, p. 26.

38 Lombardi, *People and Places*, p. 133.

39 Robert J. Ferry, 'Encomienda, African Slavery and Agriculture in Seventeenth Century Caracas', *HAHR*, 61:4 (1981), pp. 609–35.

40 Robert Ferry, *The Colonial Elite of Early Caracas: Formation and Crisis, 1567–1767* (Berkeley, Calif., 1989), pp. 177–216.

41 P. Michael McKinley, *Pre-Revolutionary Caracas: Politics, Economy and Society 1777–1811* (Cambridge, 1985), p. 3.

42 McKinley, *Pre-Revolutionary Caracas*, p. 29; Lloyd Mecham, *Church and State in Latin America: A History of Politico-Ecclesiastical Relations* (Chapel Hill, NC, 1934), p. 124.

43 McKinley, *Pre-Revolutionary Caracas*, pp. 9–17.

44 McKinley, *Pre-Revolutionary Caracas*, p. 169.

45 Pedro M. Arcaya, *El Cabildo de Caracas* (Caracas, 1968).

46 Thibaud, *Repúblicas en armas*, pp. 73–85.

47 Hasbrouck, *Foreign Legionaries*, p. 237.

48 Mecham, *Church and State in Latin America, p. 124*; Hans Dieter Elsching, *Cementerios en Venezuela. Los camposantos de los extranjeros del siglo XIX y los antiguos cementerios en Caracas y el Litoral* (Caracas, 2000), pp. 40–47; Manuel Alberto Donio Ríos, 'Sir Robert Ker Porter y los inicios del Protestantismo en Venezuela', *BANH*, 72:327 (1999), pp. 157–81; Robert Ker Porter, *Diario de un diplomático británico en Venezuela* (Caracas, 2000), *p. 642*. All subsequent references to Ker Porter's diary are taken from the Spanish edition; the English edition is Walter Dupouy, (ed.), *Sir Robert Ker Porter's Caracas Diary 1825–1842: A British Diplomat in a Newborn Nation* (Caracas, 1966).

49 Lombardi, *People and Places*, p. 9.

50 Lombardi, *People and Places*, p. 133.

51 Miguel Izard and Richard Slatta, 'Banditry and Social Conflict on the Venezuelan Llanos', in Slatta, (ed.), *Bandidos: The Varieties of Latin American Banditry* (Westport, CT, 1987), p. 42.

52 Robert Paul Matthews, *Violencia rural en Venezuela 1840/1858: antecedentes socioeconómicos de la guerra federal* (Caracas, 1977), pp. 61–63.

53 Jane Loy, 'Forgotten Comuneros: The 1781 Revolt in the Llanos of Casanare', *HAHR*, 61 (1981), pp. 235–57. Francisco de Paula Santander (b. 1792 Rosario de Cúcuta, d. 1840 Bogotá) was the principal New Granadan military leader during the Wars of Independence. He was Vice-President of Colombia from 1821, and served as President of New Granada from 1833–37.

54 Miguel Izard, 'El comercio venezolano en una época de transición 1777–1830', *Miscelánea Barcinoseia: Revista de investigación y alta cultura*, 10:30 (1971) pp. 7–44..

55 See especially David J. Weber and Jane M. Rausch, (eds), *Where Cultures Meet: Frontiers in Latin American History* (Wilmington, DE, 1994), p. xiv, and Jane M. Rausch, *Territorial Rule and the Llanos Frontier* (Gainesville, FL, 1999), pp. x–xi.

56 See for example [Richard Vowell], *Campaigns and Cruises in Venezuela and New Granada and in the Pacific Ocean; From 1817–1830: With the Narrative of a March from the River Orinoco to San Buenaventura on the Coast of Chocó and Sketches of the West Coast of South America from the Gulf of California to the Archipelago of Chiloe. Also, Tales of Venezuela: Illustrative of Revolutionary Men, Manners, and Incidents in Three Volumes* (London, 1831), Vol. 1, pp. 100–29.

57 Jorge Conde Calderón, 'Poder local y sentimiento realista en la independencia de Santa Marta', *Historia caribe* 2:4 (1999), pp. 77–86.

58 Eduardo Barrera Monroy, *Mestizaje, comercio y resistencia. La Guajira durante la segunda mitad del siglo XVIII* (Bogotá, 2000), p. 221.

59 Arturo E. Bermúdez Bermúdez, *Piratas en Santa Marta: Piratas que atacaron la Provincia de Santa Marta* (Bogotá, 1978).

60 Steiner Andreas Saether, 'Identities and Independence in the Provinces of Santa Marta and Riohacha (Colombia) ca. 1750–ca. 1850' (University of Warwick, Ph.D, 2001), p. 325.

61 John R. Fisher, 'Soldiers, Society and Politics in Spanish America 1750–1821', *LARR*,

7:1 (1982), pp. 217–22; Alan J. Kuethe, *Military Reform and Society in New Granada 1773–1808*, (Gainsville, FL, 1978), pp. 18–47.

62 For an analysis of how these actions were interpreted for the burgeoning British identity, see Kathleen Wilson, 'Empire, Trade and Popular Politics in Mid-Hanoverian Britain: The Case of Admiral Vernon', *Past and Present*, 121 (1988), pp. 74–109.

63 Aline Helg, 'Raices de la invisibilidad del afrocaribe en la imagen de la nación colombiana: independencia y sociedad, 1800–1821', in Gonzalo Sánchez and María Emma Wills Obregón (eds), *Museo, memoria, nación* (Bogotá, 1999), pp. 219–51; Arturo Rodriguez-Bobb, *Exclusión e integración del sujeto negro en Cartagena de Indias en perspectiva histórica* (Madrid, 2002).

64 María Laxxo, 'Haiti as an Image of Popular Republicanism in Caribbean Colombia: Cartagena Province (1811–1828)', in David Patrick Geggus, (ed.), *The Impact of the Haitian Revolution in the Atlantic World* (Columba, SC, 2001), pp. 176–90.

65 Aline Helg, 'Simón Bolívar and the Spectre of Pardocracia: José Padilla in Post-Independence Cartagena', *JLAS*, 35:3 (2003), pp. 447–71.

66 Aline Helg, 'A Fragmented Majority: Free "Of All Colours", Indians and Slaves in Caribbean Colombia During the Haitian Revolution', in Geggus, (ed.), *The Impact of the Haitian Revolution in the Atlantic World*, pp. 157–75; Jorge Conde Calderón, 'Provincias, ciudadanía y 'clase' social en el caribe colombiano, 1821–1855', Unpub. Ph.D thesis, Universidad Pablo de Olavide, 2001.

67 Alfonso Múnera, 'El caribe colombiano en la república andina: Identidad y autonomía política en el siglo XIX', *BCB*, 33:41 (1996), p. 36; Anthony McFarlane, 'Comerciantes y monopolio en la Nueva Granada: El Consulado de Cartagena de Indias', *ACHSC*, 11 (1983), pp. 43–69; Alfonso Múnera, *El fracaso de la nación. región, clase y raza en el caribe colombiano (1717–1821)* (Bogotá, 1998).

68 McFarlane, *Colombia before Independence: Economy, Society and Politics Under Bourbon Rule* (Cambridge, 1993), p. 203.

69 McFarlane, *Colombia Before Independence*, p. 51.

70 Pablo Morillo, quoted by Gabriel Puyana García, 'La Primera República y la Reconquista', in Valencia Tovar, (ed.), *Historia de las fuerzas militares de Colombia*, Vol. 1, p. 79. General Pablo Morillo (b. 1778 Fuentesecas, Spain, d. 1837 Baréges, France) fought alongside British officers in the Peninsula War against Napoleon, before being named in change of the expedition to re-conquer New Granada and Venezuela. He became disillusioned with the lack of resources and support coming from Spain, and left the continent in 1820. For more detail on Socorro, see John Leddy Phelan, *The People and the King: The Comunero Revolution in Colombia 1781* (Madison, WI, 1978), pp. 39–45.

71 McFarlane, *Colombia Before Independence*, pp. 264–71. See also Maurice Brungardt, 'Tithe Production and Patterns of Economic Change in Central Colombia, 1764–1833', Unpub. Ph.D, University of Texas, Austin, 1974, p. 324.

72 McFarlane, *Colombia Before Independence*, p. 361. *Tierra fría*, literally cold land.

73 Jaime Jaramillo Uribe, ''Algunos aspectos de la personalidad histórica de Colombia', in Jaramillo Uribe, *La personalidad histórica en Colombia y otros ensayos* (Bogotá, 1977), p. 141; McFarlane, *Colombia Before Independence*, pp. 50–2.

74 Safford and Palacios, *Colombia: Fragmented Land, Divided Society*, p. 102.

75 Glenn T. Curry, 'The Disappearance of the Resguardos Indígenas of Cundinamarca, Colombia, 1800–1863', Unpub. Ph.D, Vanderbilt University, 1981; Aydee García Mejia, 'The transformation of the Indian Communities of the Bogotá Sabana During the Nineteenth Century Colombian Republic', Unpub. Ph.D, New School for Social Research, 1989.

76 For example, AGNC R GYM, Vol. 56, ff. 235–6, Vol. 480, fo. 9, and Vol. 1441, fo. 544.

77 Uribe Urán, *Honorable Lives*, pp. 5–7.

78 José María Opts Capdequi, 'The Impact of the Wars of Independence on the Institutional Life of the New Kingdom of Granada', *The Americas*, 17:2 (1960) pp. 111–98.
79 Earle, *Spain and the Independence of Colombia*, p. 135, doubts whether this much vaunted attack was much of a surprise to the Loyalists at all.
80 For Rooke's career and subsequent elevation to patriotic hero, see Matthew Brown, 'Soldier Heroes', pp. 45–49.
81 Kuethe, *Military Reform and Society in New Granada 1773–1808*, p. 187.
82 Guiomar Dueñas Vargas, 'Adulterio, amancebamientos, divorcios y abandono: La fluidez de la vida familiar santafereña 1750–1810', *ACHSC*, 23 (1996), pp. 33–49.
83 For Capitán Henry Macmanus's travels to the Chocó, see AGNC R GYM, Vol. 1447, fo. 399.
84 McFarlane, *Colombia Before Independence*, p. 356.
85 Twinam, *Miners, Merchants and Farmers in Colonial Colombia* (Austin, TX, 1982), p. 149; Fernando Botero Herrera, *Estado, nación y provincia de Antioquia. Guerras civiles e invención de la región, 1829–1863* (Medellín, 2003), p. 48.
86 McFarlane, *Colombia Before Independence*, p. 353.
87 McFarlane, *Colombia Before Independence*, p. 362.
88 Martha Herrera Angel, 'Configuración territorial, dominación y resistencia. Provincia de Popayán, siglo XVIII', Unpub. Paper presented to XII Congreso de Historia, Popayán, Colombia, August 2003.
89 Demetrio García Vásquez, *Los hacendados de la otra banda y el Cabildo de Cali* (Cali, 1928), especially pp. 143–84; Mecham, *Church and State in Latin America*, p. 141.
90 Germán Colmenares, 'Castas, patrones de poblamiento y conflictos sociales en las provincias del Cauca 1810–1830', in Colmenares, (ed.), *La Independencia*, p. 152; Zamira Díaz de Zuluaga, 'La fuerza de trabajo en el Cauca grande 1810–1830', in Colmenares, (ed.), *La Independencia*, p. 67.
91 José Escorcia, 'Haciendas y estructura agraria en el valle del Cauca, 1810–1850', *ACHSC*, 10 (1982), p. 138.
92 Colmenares, 'Castas, patrones de poblamiento y conflictos sociales', pp. 143–46.
93 Colmenares, 'Castas, patrones de poblamiento y conflictos sociales', p. 140; McFarlane, *Colombia Before Independence*, p. 353.
94 Rebecca Earle, 'Indian Rebellion and Bourbon Reform in New Granada: Riots in Pasto, 1780–1800', *HAHR*, 73:1 (1993), pp. 100–17, particularly p. 110.
95 Eduardo Pérez Ortiz, *Guerra irregular en la independencia de la Nueva Granada y Venezuela* (Tunja, 1982), pp. 201–4; Francisco Zuluaga Ramírez, *Guerrilla y sociedad en el Patía: Una relación entre clientelismo político y la insurgencia social* (Cali, 1993), p. 72, pp. 115–16; Gerardo León Guerrero Vinuenza, *Pasto en la guerra de independencia, 1809–1824*, Vol. 2 (Bogotá, 1994), p. 10, p. 162; Earle, 'Popular Participation in the Wars of Independence in New Granada', in McFarlane and Posada-Carbó, (eds), *Independence and Revolution in Spanish America*, pp. 97–101.
96 Sergio Elías Ortiz, *Agustin Agualongo y su tiempo* (Bogotá, 1979), p. 393.
97 Guerrero Vinuenza, *Pasto en la guerra de independencia*, Vol. 2, p. 144.
98 María Susana Vela Witt, *El Departamento del Sur en la Gran Colombia 1822–1830* (Quito, 1999); Brooke Larson, 'Andean Highland Peasants and the Trials of Nation-Making during the nineteenth century', in Frank Salomon and Stuart B. Schwartz, (eds), *The Cambridge History of the Native Peoples of the Americas*, Vol. 3, *South America, Part 2* (Cambridge, 1999), pp. 594–95.
99 Manuel Chiriboga, 'Las fuerzas del poder durante el proceso de la independencia y la Gran Colombia', in Enrique Ayala, (ed.), *Nueva historia de Ecuador, Vol. 6, Independencia y el período colombiano* (Quito, 1989), p. 280. Antonio José de Sucre (b. 1795 Cumaná, d. 1830 Berruecos) was a young Bolivarian loyalist who was assassinated when travelling

between Bogotá and Quito, presumably by political rivals. See Thomas McGann, 'The Assassination of Sucre and its Significance in Colombian History, 1828–48', *HAHR*, 30:3 (August 1950), pp. 269–89.

100 Roger Davis, 'Ecuador Under Gran Colombia, 1820–1830: Regionalism, Localism and Legitimacy in the Emergence of an Andean Republic', Unpub. Ph.D, University of Arizona, 1983.

101 Anthony McFarlane, 'The Rebellion of the 'Barrios'. Urban Insurrection in Bourbon Quito', in John R. Fisher, Allan J. Kuethe, and McFarlane, (eds), *Reform and Insurrection in Bourbon New Granada and Peru* (Louisiana, 1990), p. 253; Kenneth J. Andrien, 'The State and Dependency in Late Colonial and Early Republican Ecuador', in Andrien and Lyman L. Johnson, (eds), *The Political Economy of Spanish America in the Age of Revolution*, p. 184.

102 General Juan José Flores (b. 1800 Puerto Cabello, d. 1864 Santa Rosa, Ecuador) was a Bolivarian loyalist who was President of Ecuador between 1830–34, 1839–43, and 1843–51.

103 Chiriboga, 'Las fuerzas del poder durante el proceso de la independencia', pp. 280–81. For an analysis of these changes over the longer term, see Michael T. Hamerley, *Historia social y económica de la antigua provincia de Guayaquil, 1763–1842* (Guayaquil, 1975).

104 Camilla Townsend, *Tales of Two Cities: Race and Economic Culture in Early Republican North and South America* (Austin, TX, 2000), p. 77.

105 Nicola Foote, 'Race, Nation and Society in Ecuador, c. 1900–40', Unpub. Ph.D., University of London, 2004.

106 Chiriboga, 'Las fuerzas del poder durante el proceso de la independencia', p. 282.

CHAPTER THREE

The Practicalities of Adventure

Chapter 2 established the terrain across which the Wars of Independence took place. Now it is necessary to trace the practicalities which shaped the ways in which foreign adventurers experienced this environment. This chapter examines the mobility inherent in military campaigning during the Wars of Independence, and the obstacles to the professionalisation of armed forces which were undermined by the recurrent death or desertion of the soldiers enlisted into their ranks. The practicalities of adventure, particularly health, food, drink and pay, underscored and often overshadowed weightier matters of identity and ideology.

Mobility and Personnel Turnover in the Military

The adventurers' previous military experience is taken in the existing historiography to have been essential to their contribution to the Wars of Independence. Chapter 1 showed that the adventurers were in fact not a crack force of military veterans, but in fact a much more improvised body. They were therefore unlikely to effect any immediate or wholesale 'modernisation' or 'professionalisation' of the army. Thibaud emphasised the highly improvised nature of all military campaigning and training in this period, along with the high turnover of troops through illness and desertion. The regularisation of units therefore depended on the skills of individual officers charged with transforming their men into disciplined units in short time-scales.[1] In this sense, some adventurers may have contributed effectively. Lambert observed that a kernel of brave foreign officers could inspire discipline and courage in local troops, dissuading nervous and unenthusiastic troops from retreat or desertion.[2] Thibaud posited that the small band of experienced mercenaries was a crucial component of a 'third generation' of military officers reaching positions of authority in 1818–21 and 'professionalising' the Independent forces.[3] Some foreign officers clearly did think that the Independent army could be improved by their know-how. Coronel Joseph Gillmore produced a prospectus for the design of a new rifle, and Capitán James Fraser translated British Army drilling instructions.[4] More tangibly perhaps, the value of the minority of British Army veterans in the expeditions lay in the vital experience they

Figure 3.1   *Alexander Alexander*

had acquired of being victorious in military conflict, something most Hispanic Americans still lacked in this period. According to Brian Vale, veterans of the Royal Navy brought with them 'a high level of technical experience, aggression and a confidence in victory derived from years of unquestioned British supremacy at sea'.[5]

Long-term plans to improve the efficiency of the army and navy were constantly undermined by loss of personnel through desertion or death. As Chapter 2 showed, over half of the adventurers (c. 3,633 of c. 6,808) died in the Caribbean after serving only briefly with the Independents, or else deserted and returned home after rapidly becoming disenchanted with the service. Those who departed quickly still left a mark on the Independents' morale, with widespread bad feeling the result of the promises and threats employed by Bolívar to try to retain desperately needed manpower.[6] As such, the initial military consequences of Bolívar's recruitment of foreign mercenaries were almost entirely negative. Many others died before they could leave the region.

Disease decimated the foreign expeditions when they first reached Gran Colombia. Yellow fever dispatched far more than the 60 named individuals for whom documentary evidence survives.[7] The figure was probably 20 times that, as anonymous private soldiers were accommodated in far worse conditions than officers, and the names of those who died were seldom felt worth reporting. Many died of fever on their ships even before they could reach the mainland. The corpses of these men were thrown overboard before they could infect the rest of the crew – often a forlorn hope.[8] During the years 1818 to 1820, fevers swept through Angostura and Margarita.[9] New arrivals brought 'the seed of yellow fever with them … [it] spread like a pestilence, and the unfortunate newcomers were swept away daily'.[10] High numbers of deaths from fever were not out of keeping with the experience of soldiers in the British West India garrisons, however. In the same period 80 per cent of white British soldiers in the Caribbean died from either yellow fever or malaria.[11] 90 per cent of the Spanish soldiers serving in the Wars of Independence also died from tropical fevers, and soldiers often deserted in large numbers when an epidemic threatened.[12] The lower figures presented here for Britons can perhaps be explained by the fact that they were relatively mobile after 1819, rather than being permanently barracked in unhealthy areas.

The piecemeal recruitment of adventurers by private individuals as described in Chapter 1 meant that units arrived throughout the period 1816 to 1822, rather than in one fleet *en masse*. What could therefore have been a short-lived epidemic, dying out once survivors had developed immunity, was continually renewed by the regular arrival of new groups who had not previously been exposed to the mosquitoes.[13] One observer saw 'piles upon piles of human bones, of both sexes and all ages'.[14] Early improvised experiments with the use of quinine provided little empirical data and so saved few lives.[15] Fever rates only declined once marching and campaigning began, as adventurers were able to flee from their confinement in the low-lying barracks in Margarita and Angostura that had fostered epidemics.[16] The Caroní missions in Guayana were in turn ravaged by the diseases brought by the mercenaries and lost a substantial proportion of their population to yellow fever and warfare.[17] Those who recovered from yellow fever were immune in the future, yet other tropical fevers such as malaria continued to claim victims even when mercenaries reached the highlands of Ecuador.[18]

The initial condition of the soldiers probably contributed to the high levels of wastage due to illness. Since the expeditions were unofficial and illegal, there were no medical examinations before a soldier or officer could enlist. Those soldiers who did have experience in the British Army had been physically weakened and could have been more susceptible to illness. Nutrition was a contributory factor, as local economies in Margarita and Angostura struggled to provide enough food for the adventurers, let alone a balanced diet of fruit or vegetables. Officers stressed the efforts they made at least to bury their colleagues 'in as becoming a manner as possible, considering the circumstances of [their] situation', erecting small wooden crosses in the sand to mark their place of rest.[19]

Despite ravaging them, yellow fever did not destroy the expeditions. Adventurers drowned, died in battle, or were killed by firing squads and duellists. Around two hundred men survived to be killed in formal set-piece battles. Eleven officers and ninety-five men were killed in combat at Carabobo, and others died at Villa del Ortiz, El Semen, Boyacá, Pantano de Vargas and La

Ciénaga de Santa Marta.[20] At least 120 more were executed by Loyalist troops after being taken prisoner, mainly after Gregor MacGregor's attacks on Portobello and Riohacha.[21] Several adventurers died of wounds they received in battle.[22] The names of those killed in battle were much more likely to be recorded than the many others who perished as a result of the harsh campaigning lifestyle. Their neglect by historians can be traced back to a comment by James Rooke, who said that the men who died crossing the mountain pass at Pisba had 'deserved their fate – those men were the worst behaved in my unit, which can only prosper from their deaths'.[23] Dying on the march was more the consequence of sharp variations in climate and incomplete provisioning, clothing and shoeing of the men, rather than some divine retribution for bad character as Rooke implied. Even disciplined, experienced men died marching in all regions and all climates.[24] Others drowned while being transported by sea or river. Over two hundred officers, soldiers and crew perished when the *Indian* sank off the French coast in late 1817.[25] In Venezuela, men continued to die when they fell into rivers, at least a dozen perishing in this way while fishing or travelling.[26] Six soldiers died when their boat overturned whilst they were rowing the fevered corpse of an officer to his burial ground.[27] Matters of honour and discipline accounted for the lives of several adventurers. At least a dozen officers were killed in duels or physical confrontations with other adventurers. Twenty-five were executed after failed attempts at desertion or thwarted insubordination.[28] Ten were killed in violent encounters with indigenous people, giving rise to many stories of adventurers 'found with [their] heads cut off' on beaches shortly after arrival at Margarita.[29]

The rapid rate of personnel turnover through death and desertion meant that effective training had to focus on the short term, especially during the peak years 1816–22, when both turnover and adventurer numbers were at their highest.[30] Because of the high rates of desertion, a good soldier was often simply one who did not run away in the night.[31] Thibaud saw popular desertion as partly related to subaltern resistance to élite projects, illustrating widespread 'popular dislike of the republic and its wars'.[32] The topography and underpopulation of much of the region provided substantial opportunities for escape and then subsistence and modest insertion into legal and contraband trading networks, just as it had for slave maroons in colonial times.[33] Hasbrouck dismissed adventurers' desertion as 'inconsequential' but in fact it was a widespread tactic of resistance and survival for them as much as it was for other recruits.[34]

Most of the adventurers whose desertion was recorded were those who were unlucky enough to be recaptured. One officer who did desert the service, Dennis O'Reilly, was expelled from Gran Colombia as punishment in 1821, but just two years later he returned and rejoined the army.[35] Soldiers did not receive such lenient treatment and regulations were introduced in 1819 to hunt down deserters and to punish those who harboured them.[36] Occasional references to mass desertion in the Caribbean and the ease of mobility between the naval and terrestrial services do show that, at least for those adventurers operating on the coast, it was not impossible to depart the service in small groups. Indeed, British adventurers deserted even before they arrived in Hispanic America. Coronel Hippisley reported that 40 of his men deserted on the island of Grenada, 'many of whom died in their new employments of clerks, overseers, bailiffs and bailiffs' followers'.[37] One of the few recorded examples of British desertion was that which occurred in response to a proclamation by General Morillo inciting them to join the Spanish army in 1819.[38] That night, Rafael Urdaneta reported, some forty British soldiers escaped, and five were captured the next morning. Urdaneta submitted the first recaptured group to a court martial and they were all executed.[39] Some were more fortunate and, like Private John Evans, reached the Loyalist camp, gave themselves up, and eventually made their way home to England.[40] George Laval Chesterton wrote that 'it was evident that the whole force was prepared to follow their example', and in subsequent days the British troops 'continuously deserted, and seemed to prefer death to re-joining our columns'.[41] Soldiers captured by Loyalists claimed that desertion was so great, and the fear of rebellion so prevalent, that the British troops in the llanos in mid-1819 were surrounded while they marched, with cavalry at their flanks, and Creole infantry in front and behind them.[42]

Like their Gran Colombian counterparts, British and Irish private soldiers tried to desert when they felt that they could escape the bands sent in their pursuit. This happened near the coast and also in the llanos, where groups of five or six soldiers struck out for the Loyalist camps.[43] Over one hundred adventurers successfully deserted from the llanos in 1819 and 1820, totalling about 7–8 per cent of the foreign contingent operating in the region. This evidence reveals that although British and Irish adventurers were perhaps more reluctant to desert than other groups, they certainly did desert, and when they did go, they went in larger groups. Perhaps this was because of their fear of a threatening environment. After conversing with several retired adventurers, the traveller C.S. Cochrane observed that 'some at first turned their thoughts to desertion, but a moment's reflection convinced them of the impossibility: how could this be affected without guides? How could they traverse those immense plains? And how explain themselves? How exist?'[44] Nevertheless, despite these denials the correspondence of the Independent authorities in Guayana reveals that by 1820 they were accustomed to the regular desertion of groups of *ingleses*, and they had drawn up procedures for redistributing the rifles and bayonets of those who left the service.[45]

Examination of naval documentation shows how the Independent navy mopped up many of these foreign deserters from the terrestrial forces. Between periods of service these men resided temporarily in ports in Jamaica and Haiti, 'literally starving, and pitiable to look upon, ragged and lame, pale and thin from hunger'.[46] Members of Gregor MacGregor's expeditions, which made very few incursions inland, can also be traced within this mobile Caribbean community of 'sailors from every nation', privateers, soldiers and corsairs.[47] For example, Private William Johnson served in MacGregor's 1819 attack on Portobello, where he was among those captured by the Loyalists. In

1823 he was at Maracaibo serving as a sailor on the Independent corsair *Marte*, and in April 1824 he was on the frigate *La Venezuela*.[48]

The crew listings of Independent ships demonstrate that foreigners tended to be grouped together and that they left and returned to the service when it suited them. Smaller launches were filled with local men. Personnel turnover was such that between March and December 1824 only 22.8 per cent of the crew of *La Venezuela* served without interruption under the command of Walter Chitty.[49] Mobility and desertion was common amongst both foreigners and Hispanic Americans. A handful of sailors disappeared in May but had returned by December. There were several men on the ship who had fought three years earlier at Carabobo, among them Bandsman Joseph Olive and Cabo James Gilbert, a cotton-spinner from Portaferry in Co. Down.[50] Those sailors who left their duties on a Gran Colombian vessel often rejoined another soon after.[51] There was also some movement of personnel between the British Royal Navy and the Independent navies, as men sought better prospects according to the military climate.[52]

Naval service offered far greater opportunity for desertion or, less dramatically, a change of ship, than the soldier who was dependent upon his company for rations in an unfamiliar environment. Documentation reveals that only very rarely was a ship able to maintain any continuity of personnel. In 1823 the Independent naval forces at Maracaibo produced a full roll-call of their officers and crewmen. Several of the foreigners listed (who made up 20 per cent of the crews) had joined up via other branches of the Independent service, such as William Gow of Perthshire who had fought at Carabobo.[53] Those adventurers who became Caribbean privateers are even more difficult to track down, as very few records survive relating to privateering activities. Soldier/sailors such as William Gow probably found work as privateers in the gaps in the records of their 'official' military and naval career. The vicissitudes of privateering during the Wars of Independence meant that sailors often had to be ready to change masters at a moment's notice.[54] Capture and reaffiliation of loyalties were frequent.[55]

The Enemy

The adventurers' experiences of the Wars of Independence were also shaped by the enemy they faced. Like the Independents, the Loyalist forces were also plagued by desertion and the often short-term enlistment of many of their Hispanic American soldiers. In contrast to the forces serving under Simón Bolívar, however, Pablo Morillo's Expeditionary Army did originally consist predominantly of veterans of the Peninsular War when it arrived in Venezuela in 1815. Morillo's forces were intended to supplement the regular army battalions and colonial militias who had succeeded for so long in protecting Spanish America from foreign aggression, but which, as Juan Marchena Fernández demonstrated, had been deteriorating in efficiency in the late eighteenth century. The regular army included a small percentage of foreigners and 'soldiers of fortune' in its ranks, but mostly it was composed of conscripts from Spain, with many prisoners forced to serve unwillingly.[56] As Rebecca Earle has observed, Morillo's regular army was not assured of discipline or success in the face of climatic and geographical obstacles and the opposition of better-motivated individuals. The 'reconquest' of Venezuela and New Granada in 1815–16 took advantage of pre-existing weaknesses and divisions in the Independent forces, but disease, illness and desertion gradually depleted Morillo's forces to such an extent that by 1819 the stock of veterans was almost exhausted.[57] Morale amongst the Spanish troops was terrible as 'nothing could be more loathsome and fearful to a Spaniard than the prospect of death on the other side of the world'.[58] Morillo's army was therefore 'rapidly Americanised', but remaining Spaniards showed little respect for their new American colleagues. Morillo's soldiers and officers 'emerged from an environment where American inferiority was taken for granted' and they were unwilling or unable to adapt their beliefs to new circumstances. Officers such as Morillo distrusted black, pardo and *mestizo* troops, who correspondingly often defected to the Independent army.[59] Soldiers, disgusted by their 'miserable quality of life'[60] were rude to Hispanic Americans, brawled, drank to excess and sometimes attacked civilians without provocation.[61]

Conflicts and tensions between Loyalist commanding officers and their subordinates – which of course existed on the Independent side too – were 'serious and important' factors explaining Loyalist defeat in the battles at Pantano de Vargas, Boyacá and Carabobo.[62] By the early 1820s, Loyalist morale was so diminished, desertion so endemic and sympathy for the cause of Independence so entrenched amongst the Loyalist officer corps, that Independent victory seemed to many to be only a matter of time.[63] The armistice signed by Morillo and Bolívar at Santa Ana in 1820 was an expression of shared concerns and recognition, Bolívar believed, of the resonance of the Independent cause amongst Morillo and other senior officers. After the victory at Carabobo in 1821, Loyalist resistance in Venezuela and New Granada was quickly reduced to a few enclaves and to irregular bands of guerrillas who ambushed the campaigning Independent armies.

Religion

Desertion remained extremely dishonourable for officers on both sides of the conflict, at least while the cause itself was still felt to be honourable. British officers declared that inducements to desert were a stain on their honour.[64] Service in the Loyalist army was equally unattractive to many of those adventurers who fled the Independent forces, and many deserters tried to make their way home. The honourable man should not 'desert the cause of liberty',[65] and therefore all of the memoirs written before 1824 presented the author's departure from the Independent army as something forced upon him by circumstance or bad health, rather than having been actively sought. One of the favourite ways of deflecting attention from their desertion was by evoking the idea of a clash of cultures and, in particular, a clash between religious denominations. One complained that 'the priesthood in Barcelona ... had taught that we English were ... savages, cannibals ... that nature had been so bountiful as to furnish us with tails like monkeys'.[66] These themes were most often brought out with regard to death: commentators raged that the corpses of Protestant adventurers were thrown into the sea or river rather than be buried on a Catholic continent.[67] Religion was often invoked by adventurers as a cause of their problems, but close examination of the available sources suggests that this was more rhetoric that a real cause of division. Protestant officers were in fact often buried with great ceremony, such as General English, whose funeral party was followed by a considerable cortège at Juan Griego in 1820.[68] Indeed, stories of religious animosity owed much to conventional travel narratives and to the so-called Black Legend of Spanish cruelty. Archival sources from Hispanic America suggest that religion was not a divisive issue. Protestants attended Catholic masses which celebrated victory, and even included sermons praising the British monarch.[69]

One of the most popular myths from the early period of the Wars of Independence, amongst Creoles and adventurers alike, centred on a Protestant adventurer Charles Chamberlain, who was in command of the fort at Barcelona in 1816 when it came under siege from Loyalists. When the situation was lost and the fort was about to be taken, Chamberlain killed his Venezuelan wife Eulalia Ramos and then committed suicide. This story – which stressed Chamberlain as a patriotic foreigner, and such a fervent defender of his wife's honour that he preferred to end her life rather than let her live dishonoured by Spaniards – appealed to the imaginations of Catholics, Protestants, Creoles, Britons and Irishmen.[70] The persistence of the story of Chamberlain's actions can be explained by the weight that Benedict Anderson lays on the importance of gestures of sacrifice at the centre of national sentiments. Sacrifice had roots in diverse religious traditions.[71] Retired adventurers often claimed to have 'sacrificed their youth' for the sake of Gran Colombia. The chivalric language of 'sacrifice' had religious origins too, and overrode any potential 'clash' between religious denominations in Bolívar's armies. When brought before a court, Gran Colombians of all origins swore to tell the truth in court by placing their hand on the bible or their sword.[72]

Religious difference was not a major source of conflict, but there are examples in private correspondence suggesting that it could occasionally cause tension, generally when the participants had been drinking. In the officers' drinking club attended by Robert Young, the only taboos were 'religious and political questions'.[73] Later, Coronel George Augustus Lowe wrote that Rafael Urdaneta had a 'Quakerish tongue', and Mariano Montilla accused John Devereux of being a 'vain Methodist'.[74] In a drunken dispute over a card game in a Bogotá bar in 1826, Capitán Henry Macmanus accused Cabo Jacob Teeson of being 'a cheating Jew'.[75] A more persuasive interpretation suggested by these insults and corroborated by other sources is that, for most soldiers and officers, religious observance was more a matter of duty than belief. The *Correo del Orinoco* published a satirical version of the Lord's Prayer in 1821.[76] The possibility that religious ceremonies were often more for show than prayer was illustrated in a caricature (Figure 3. 2), probably sketched by a British officer.[77] In this rare visual depiction of life with the Independents, Simón Bolívar was drawn on his knees at a pew in a church, reading a newspaper, while Daniel O'Leary sipped a cup of coffee. As O'Leary himself recorded in his *Detached Recollections*

> General Bolivar was a complete atheist. Notwithstanding, he thought religion necessary for government. His indiscretion, which was very great at all times, knew no bounds when he spoke of religion, which he used to ridicule in a disgusting manner. At mass he was sure to have some book or other in his hand and sometimes a gazette.[78]

For most adventurers, as for Bolívar, religious differences were neither insurmountable nor of great concern. Tolerance was based more on a lack of enthusiasm to enforce distinctions than any genuine commitment to a doctrine of tolerance. Conceptions of honour, service, sacrifice, belonging and loyalty were all suffused with a non-denominational Christian sentiment.[79] Curry-Machado's study of Britons in Cuba in the mid-nineteenth century suggests

Figure 3. 2   *At Prayer in Guayaquil*

that religious difference was only evoked when political differences were exhausted.[80] As Malcolm Deas noted in his biography of William Wills (who settled in Bogotá in 1826), despite British Protestants' abiding prejudices against Catholics, many Britons did not have an explicitly 'religious temperament' and religion was not an important issue in their relations with Gran Colombians.[81]

Rationing and Payment

The principal cause of conflict for the adventurers was sustenance, not religion. Those who left the Independent army often justified their return home by lamenting the insufficiency of rations. Warfare had triggered economic dislocation, poverty and crisis.[82] The movement of armies around the region further disrupted traditional food supply networks, and meant that the mercenaries passed above and between the short-range and loosely connected economies that made up local markets.[83] Military commanders struggled to form new relationships with suppliers in each town or village they passed through, which proved a major drain on the small reserves of coinage that they carried with them. In this sense any markets to which the adventurers had access were small and informal and often set up on an improvised basis to meet their needs as they passed through. Where food was scarce, soldiers went hungry.

The foodstuffs available in each area differed from town to town and between the seasons, and soldiers had to take what they could get. On occasion, Independent officers withheld available food from the adventurers, claiming that they did not wish to create unequal conditions between the foreigners and other troops.[84] The weekly allowance in the British Army at the time consisted of 'seven rations': seven pounds of bread or flour, seven pounds of beef or four pounds of pork, six ounces of butter, three pints of peas, and a half pound of rice or oatmeal.[85] In Angostura in 1819, a local official noted that 'the English never stop complaining about the rations they have not received, but there is nothing here apart from bread and beef. There is no rum, paper, salt, tobacco or soap, all of which they request every day.'[86] This was in stark contrast to the mouth-watering prospects described in recruitment advertisements, which promised beef, pork, bread, potatoes and whisky every day.[87] These offers were fanciful if not intentionally fictional, and initially many adventurers had to survive on their remaining 'sea-rations', known as 'bad biscuit'.

Drink was also a problem. There was little awareness among soldiers or officers that high daily alcohol intake was unhealthy and could worsen existing maladies in hot tropical climates. Drinking alcohol was one of the adventurers' principal recreational activities: the daily regime of one was apparently 'at five in the morning a glass of sling, a smoke at 7, breakfast at 8, a glass of grog after, some toddy at 11 o'clock, Solomon Grundy at one, dinner at 3 o'clock, two tumblers of grog after, a smoke at 5 o'clock, tea at 7, a nip at 8, and

THE PRACTICALITIES OF ADVENTURE   71

a smoke at 9, and then turn in, except upon the meetings of the Club, which enabled him to take four additional tumblers'.[88] Unsurprisingly, doctors accompanying the expeditions perceived excessive alcohol consumption as one of the main causes of illness.[89] Judging by the protests made whenever it was withheld or unavailable, however, soldiers regarded their daily rum ration as a necessity, a pleasure and a right. Rum was often believed to be healthier than the local water, and new distilleries were set up on appropriated haciendas to cope with the soldiers' 'extraordinary rum consumption'.[90] Officers and soldiers alike recognised that both too much and too little alcohol could trigger rebellion.[91]

Food and drink were principal causes of disillusion and discontent. One of the main reasons why Coronel Hippisley returned home was that he 'could not eat the [unsalted] beef, nor drink the ration rum', describing the beef as 'mangled' and 'fit only for dogs'.[92] Some officers felt they were dishonoured by 'miserable' rations. One 'begged' the Minister of War 'to consider that [his] companion and [he] were Britons, and unused to such treatment'.[93] Locals in Angostura heard these complaints and felt that the foreigners were unrealistic in their demands in a time of inescapable hardship and pronounced shortages.[94] One adventurer detected 'great jealousy amongst the native troops' at their perceived preferential treatment.[95] Creole officers recognised that dissatisfaction with food supplies was a major barrier to the efficient performance of foreign troops.[96]

The reality, however, was that even the essentials such as beef, cereal, salt and alcohol were not uniformly available across the region and supplies were often irregular. In Coro, adventurers received bread, meat, salt and bananas but no beef.[97] Vicente Lecuna reported that he had not been able to feed the patients in the Angostura Hospital on 18 October 1819, as his flour supplies had run out so he could not produce any bread.[98] Because of the importance of keeping the adventurers fed (and drunk), British and Irish officials were often given the sensitive position of Chiefs of Staff and were charged with keeping the officers and troops rationed and armed and their movements co-ordinated, and the prisoners guarded, and their complaints controlled. This was especially so when campaigning on the Caribbean coast, so that British officers could maximise their perceived links to regional traders. Coronel George Woodberry and Coronel Thomas Richards served in this position under General Páez and Almirante Brion respectively.[99] In early 1820 Richards negotiated the purchase of cod and flour to feed the troops stationed at Pampatar, but the diet of the troops changed according to geographical location, transport and market availability, from beef in the llanos to bananas in the tropical valleys.[100] On occasions foreigners received special treatment. In March 1820 in Neiva, a local official received delivery of salted meat and biscuits, and recorded having to ration those destined for 'the English soldiers who don't eat bananas', and who had requested extra flour to bake bread.[101]

Soldiers got a particularly raw deal. As Michael Howard commented with reference to the Napoleonic Wars, 'soldiers are not always the best of ambassadors or missionaries, especially soldiers who, for lack of pay and supply, have to take what they need from the peoples they are supposed to be liberating'.[102] The distribution of rations was often chaotic, especially when, as in Neiva in 1820, 'more than a hundred men compete for what there is, grabbing whatever they can get their hands on'.[103] The subsequent rioting often led to more fights and desertions.[104] Lacking sustenance, enterprising and ruthless private soldiers took food from those who had it. In September 1820, at Soledad across the Orinoco from Angostura, Private George Wall was accused of stealing 'food, some liquor, some clothing, a shaving blade and other articles' from Capitán Herrenyn, whom he had served as a domestic servant.[105]

Travelling armies taking local resources caused irritation and discontent amongst the affected communities. The fear of marauding troops undermined confidence in the market economy, already weakened by the lack of currency and mules caused by military requisitioning. As the Duke of Wellington noted in 1810, 'war is a terrible evil, particularly to those who reside in those parts of the country which are the seat of the operations of hostile armies'.[106] All this contributed to peasants keeping food back from market, so making worse the very food shortages that caused hunger and increasing looting tendencies amongst the mercenaries.[107] Such well-founded complaints often resulted in pillaging, even by those battalions reputed to be the best-behaved.[108] For this reason, officials tried to manoeuvre unpaid campaigning units into 'enemy' territory, so that they could loot with more impunity.[109] As at Ciudad Rodrigo in the Iberian Peninsula, 'a town taken by storm was by tradition regarded as the legitimate prize of the men concerned'.[110] Stories of drunken abandon always accompanied the news of the plunder of captured towns, such as Barcelona and Portobello in 1819, and Riohacha in 1820.[111] This meant that, as in Europe, 'a civilian family in an assaulted city was unlikely to come out of it without some experience of house-breaking, vandalism, robbery, rape, maiming or murder'.[112]

The lack of wages was as big a concern as the scarcity of rations. Much correspondence of the period related to problems of coinage, its availability and its reliability. Adventurers hoped to take some riches home, but they also wanted money to alleviate their wants, their boredom or their curiosity. But quite simply, the Independent leaders did not have enough in the treasury to pay their troops.[113] As one official wrote in Angostura in 1819, 'there is no money to buy anything'.[114] To combat this, some officers reported that they were forced to sell their spare shirts, and other inessential items, but these resources were quickly exhausted, and some attempted to use metal buttons as coins.[115] Such exchanges were sought by the local population as well – upon the imminent arrival in Angostura of a regiment of the British Legion in April 1820, local officials felt it necessary to 'prohibit any person from buying clothes, accessories, etc, from the arriving troops'. Anyone caught engaging in this illicit trade was to be fined.[116] Private soldiers did not carry trunks full of such goods and therefore had even less capacity to exchange. Such a situation probably encouraged looting and desertion. One Irish soldier, Sargento Thomas Cannon, was apprehended late one night outside Popayán in 1822 by his own unit's patrol, as he and his accomplice Encarnación Ximenes led two cows by ropes around their necks, which they intended to sell to the neighbouring village of Yanacones. Evidence suggests clear links between lower-class mercenaries, local Independent soldiers and indigenous leaders in this cow-rustling operation.[117]

On long-distance journeys, adventurers had to rely on the charity of locals for food and shelter. In Socorro in 1822 a group of stragglers from the Albion Battalion were given 'three shirts, as they were naked, and rations for four days'.[118] Another group caused discontent in Cali by stealing mules and saddles from the local community as they passed through.[119] This was but one example of the resort to small-scale criminality on the part of the adventurers. After the mayor of the village of Amaine purchased a bull with which to feed a group of adventurers, he complained that 'the troops overpowered me and took *all* of the meat: there was nothing I could do'.[120] 'With the same disorder' they also took all the salt they could find.[121]

The problems faced by these travelling armies highlight the extent to which much military activity in this period was essentially local – when armies could not feed their troops, the rank and file tended to return to their villages where they could gain sustenance.[122] Without such links to local communities, foreigners such as the Albion Battalion seized what they needed. Their conceptions of honour did not prevent them from engaging in such actions, because these rural communities were not perceived by the British and Irish as a potential source of honour. Civilians therefore increasingly saw the military, and especially the 'foreign' military, as a burden to be tolerated during times of danger, to be limited in peacetime. 'Foreign' in this sense was understood in very local terms as someone from outside the local economy and community, who would not contribute to production but would instead demand to be supplied.

These local arrangements across Gran Colombia differed greatly from the conditions for merchants or diplomats in the major urban centres. In 1824, Commissioner John Potter Hamilton informed the British Foreign Secretary of some standard prices in post-war Bogotá, converting them into British currency for ease of understanding. A dozen silk pocket handkerchiefs cost £10, a pound of beef 4d., a dozen bottles of claret £5, a dozen bottles of champagne £12 and a well-furnished house about £400 a year.[123] Possibly only a commissioner appointed by the British Foreign Office could have made a pound of beef appear inexpensive in post-war Gran Colombia. In contrast, the adventurers were forced to accept what they were given, and to take what they could. The large distances they travelled meant that only rarely could they develop formal relations with the regions they passed through. Whilst Thomas Cannon's rustling and the Albion Battalion's cow-snatching could be seen as 'enterprising', they operated on an even more improvised basis than the medium-scale arms traders and food suppliers who followed them, or the investors back in London proposing colonisation schemes and arms deals. Forced into these transactions by hunger, discontent, lack of currency and supply difficulties, non-commissioned officers and soldiers were left to their own devices. When this was not enough, and opportunities to leave arose, they contemplated and attempted desertion. The reality of adventure was founded on these short-term concerns and on everyday battles for survival.

Notes

1 Carlos Soublette described the services of Mayor Daniel Maclaughlin as 'embarrass-ing and useless, because he does not understand Spanish. This is an essential skill for instructing troops, and by lacking it his contribution is effectively negative. Please, give him something else to do, as even if we gave him the best of all our troops, he couldn't do a thing with them'. Soublette to Páez, 28 January 1823, Caracas, AGNC R GYM, Vol. 44, fo. 201.
2 Lambert, *Voluntarios británicos e irlandeses*, Vol. 3, p. 455.
3 Thibaud, *Repúblicas en armas*, pp. 379–83, pp. 411–25.
4 Santiago Fraser, *Manuel de táctica de infantería* (Mérida, 1824), copy in AGNC R GYM, Vol. 56, ff. 34–51; Joseph Albert Gillmore, 'Observaciones sobre el fusil y avisos sobre su adelantamiento', undated, copy in FJB, Archivo Histórico, C-825, ff. 235–9. For Gillmore (b. Bogshead, Co. Antrim, dates unknown) who was a barrack master in Glasgow in the 1840s see TNA FO 80/36, fo. 123.
5 Brian Vale, *A War Betwixt Englishmen: Brazil Against Argentina on the River Plate, 1825–1830* (London, 2000), p. 15.
6 For an example see 'Declaración de Don José Antonio Velasco, practicante de cirugía', 19 March 1819, Gamarra, AGI Cuba, Legajo 911A.
7 Documentary sources reveal the names of just 60 individuals who died from fever, 25 who died from other diseases, 307 who died violently (in combat, or executed after being taken prisoner) and ten who drowned (from a total of only 402 named adventurers whose cause of death was recorded).
8 For examples see Charles Brown, *Narrative of the Expedition to South America which sailed from England in 1817, for the service of the Spanish patriots: Including the Military and Naval Transactions, and ultimate fate of that expedition: Also the Arrival of Colonels Blosset and English, with British troops for that service, their reception and subsequent proceedings, with Other Interesting Occurrences* (London, 1819), p. 50; Hippisley, *Narrative of the Expedition*, Appendix R; [Cowley], *Recollections of a Service of Three Years*, pp. 17–22.
9 Capitán William Hill was said to have died from a raging fever at the very moment that he stepped off his ship at Porlemar in early 1820. *Freeman's Journal*, 6 March 1820.
10 [Vowell], *Campaigns and Cruises*, p. 152.
11 Phillip Curtin, *Death by Migration: Europe's Encounter with the Tropical World in the Nineteenth Century* (Cambridge, 1989), p. 30. Figures for Jamaica in 1817 to 1836 come from Roger Norman Buckley, *The British Army in the West Indies: Society and the Military in the Revolutionary Age* (Gainesville, FL, 1998), p. 215.
12 Rebecca Earle, 'A Grave for Europeans? Disease, Death and the Spanish American Revolutions', *War and History*, 3 (1996) pp. 371–83.
13 For the way this happened, see Curtin, *Death by Migration*, p. 69 and Michael Duffy, *Soldiers, Sugar and Seapower. The British Expeditions to the West Indies and the War against Revolutionary France* (Oxford, 1987), pp. 356–59.

14 Robinson, *Journal of an Expedition*, p. 94.
15 For the development and use of quinine, extracted from South American bark in this very period, see Curtin, *Death by Migration*, p. 62; Weatherhead, *An account of the late expedition against the Isthmus of Darien*, p. 130; Dr Joseph Clark to Vicente Lecuna, 19 September 1819, Angostura, AGNV GDG, Vol. 10, fo. 126.
16 For the effects of these conditions see papers relating to James Constant, AGNV IP, Vol. 21, ff. 73–85.
17 Jonathan D. Hill, 'Indigenous Peoples and the Rise of Independent Nation-States in Lowland South America', in Salomon and Schwartz (eds), *Cambridge History of the Native Peoples of the Americas*, p. 728.
18 Deaths from malarial fevers were recorded in Arthur Sandes to Daniel O'Connell, 10 September 1822, Quito, UCD, P12/3/110; papers relating to the death of Edward Fitzpatrick, 5 November 1824, Bogotá, CDM, Db0676, fo. 10; 'Inventario de bienes del finado Guillermo Maquinec [William McGuinness]', 3 February 1828, Antigua Guayana, AHG CB, 2. 1. 1. 111. 15; Weatherhead, *An Account of the Late expedition against the Isthmus of Darien*, pp. 130–32.
19 William Sullivan to Mr Fenton, 8 November 1819, on board the San Rafael, anchored off Long Island, Bahamas, UCD, P12/3/247.
20 Lambert, *Carabobo*, pp. 28–31. [Cowley], *Recollections of a Service of Three Years*, Vol. 2, p. 99, p. 196, estimated 12 deaths at La Ciénaga and 150 at Carabobo.
21 Another 21 died after being taken prisoner at the same engagements. For listings of those executed see Governor Juan Solís to Viceroy Juan Sámano, 10 November and 20 November 1819, Riohacha, in Friede, 'La expedición de Mac-Gregor', pp. 81–85; for those initially imprisoned see Solís to Sámano, 13 October 1819, Riohacha, rpd. in Elías Ortiz, *Colección de documentos para la historia de Colombia (Epoca de la Independencia)*, III Serie, pp. 270–73. Rafter, *Memoirs of Gregor M'Gregor*, p. 421 listed those he believed killed in the actions, several of whose names coincide with those listed by Solís as having been executed after the event.
22 For example the death of Teniente Hepote in the Cauca Valley in mid-1820, as related in Manuel Valdés to José Concha, 4 July 1820, Quilchao, ACC, Sala Independencia, M1-4-C, Sig. 6532, fo. 3.
23 O'Leary, *Narración*, Vol. 1, p. 572.
24 For example John Wilton between Maracaibo and Bogotá, CDM, Db1496, Db4825, Db0696.
25 A list of some of those who died is repr. in FJB, Archivo Histórico, C-715, fo. 89. Other men drowned during the Atlantic crossing on other ships, such as Robert Lewis; anonymous letter to *DEP*, 29 June 1820.
26 Drownings recorded in Brown, *Narrative of the Expedition to South America*, p. 52; Hippisley, *Narrative of the Expedition*, p. 364; Rafter, *Memoirs of Gregor M'Gregor*, p. 425; 'Review of Rifles under John Mackintosh', 1 March 1819, AL, Vol. 14, fo. 37; Declaration of John Devereux, 25 December 1823, Baltimore, EP, HA157/6/32; *DEP*, 30 November 1820; *DEP*, 23 November 1820.
27 Lambert, *Voluntarios británicos e irlandeses*, Vol. 2, p. 104.
28 These deaths, which occurred in Soledad in 1820, are all examined in more detail in Chapter 4.
29 James Towers English to Luis Brion, 10 September 1819, Juan Griego, AL, Vol. 14, fo. 46. This manner of death is discussed at length in Chapter 3.
30 Thibaud estimated that desertion reached 5–15 per cent per month in campaigning units of the Bolivarian armies during 1819–21, *Repúblicas en armas*, pp. 334–46. For the similar situation in the Loyalist armies, see Juan Marchena Fernández, *Oficiales y soldados en el ejército de América* (Sevilla, 1983), p. 325.

31 Alvaro Tirado Mejia, *Aspectos sociales de las guerras civiles en Colombia* (Bogotá, 1976), p. 42.
32 Thibaud, *Repúblicas en armas*, p. 517.
33 Anthony McFarlane, 'Cimarrones and Palenques: Runaways and Resistance in colonial Colombia', in Gad Heuman, (ed.), *Out of the House of Bondage: Runaways, Resistance and Marronage in Africa and the New World* (London, 1986), pp. 131–49.
34 Hasbrouck, *Foreign Legionaries, p. 122*, followed by Racine, 'A Community of Purpose', p. 12.
35 Pedro Briceño Méndez to Dionisio O'Reilly, 5 March 1821, Trujillo, in *MOL*, Vol. 18, p. 107. O'Reilly's return to the service was recorded in CDM, Db0569. Pedro Briceño Méndez (b. 1792 Barinas, d. 1835 Curacao) served as Bolívar's personal secretary for many years, moving naturally on to be Secretary of War and Marine from 1820.
36 Santander, 'Reglamento para la conservación de los exércitos de la república', 26 November 1819, Bogotá, AGNC R GYM, Vol. 323, fo. 900; also Vowell, *Campaigns and Cruises*, p. 211.
37 Hippisley, *Narrative of the Expedition to the rivers Orinoco and Apure*, p. 175. For desertion from MacGregor's forces at Amelia in 1817, see Rafter, *Memoirs of Gregor M'Gregor*, p. 103.
38 Morillo's proclamation was printed in English on a handbill; see EP, HA157/5/34, and rpd. in Spanish and English in Brown and Roa, (eds), *Militares extranjeros*, pp. 68–9, pp. 271–72.
39 Urdaneta, *Memorias del general Rafael Urdaneta*, p. 233. General Rafael Urdaneta (b. 1788 Maracaibo, d. 1845 Paris), was later Secretary of War. Urdaneta estimated (pp. 237–39) that eighteen adventurers were later killed in the skirmish attempting to recapture them, and a further nineteen gave themselves up and were permitted to rejoin the Independent ranks.
40 John Evans, letter to *CMP,* 23 November 1820.
41 Chesterton, *Peace, War and Adventure*, pp. 68–69.
42 'Declaración de Cristóbal Ricaus', 11 April 1819, Puerto Cabello, AGI Cuba, Legajo 911A.
43 Report from captured Loyalist correspondence, repr. in 'Relación histórica del Exto. de Occidente al mando del Sr. General José Antonio Páez desde la Villa de Achaguas en 1 de noviembre de 1819', AGNC R GYM, Vol. 323, ff. 325–42.
44 C. S. Cochrane, *Journal of a Residence and Travels in Colombia during the Years 1823 and 1824* (London, 1825), Vol. 1, p. 470.
45 José Montes to Provincial Governor, 25 May 1820, Nueva Guayana, AGNV GDG, Vol. 13, fo. 289.
46 Howell (ed.), *The Life of Alexander Alexander,* Vol. 2, p. 241.
47 'Declaración de Pedro Alejandro Richon', undated, Puerto Cabello, AGI Cuba, Legajo 911A.
48 For William Johnson, see Elías Ortiz, (ed.), *Colección de documentos para la historia de Colombia*, pp. 244–45; AGNC R GYM, Vol. 326, ff. 13–25; and Vol. 363, ff. 850–936.
49 Of the 202 sailors to appear on the three roll lists (from March, May and December), 122 (60. 4 per cent) were Hispanic Americans, listing a wide range of towns and villages across Venezuela and New Granada as their place of birth. The 80 foreigners (39. 6 per cent) were from Norway, Germany, Brazil, Wales, Italy, Peru, Africa, St. Bartholomew, Jamaica, and Holland. There were five each from Ireland and Scotland, 10 from the United States of America and 29 from England.
50 For Olive, see Lambert, *Carabobo*, p. 39; Hasbrouck, *Foreign Legionaries*, Appendix H; AGNC R GYM, Vol. 363, ff. 850–936. For Gilbert see 'Descriptive Roll', Acta 3; Lambert, *Carabobo*, p. 34; Hasbrouck, *Foreign Legionaries,* Appendix H; AGNC R GYM,

Vol. 363, ff. 850–936.
51 See for example the remarkably mobile career of Guillermo Jeffery in Jeffrey, 20 November 1828, Puerto Cabello, AGNC HDS, Legajo 24, f. 123, repr. in Brown and Roa, (eds), *Militares extranjeros*, pp. 77–78.
52 Charles Chabaud-Arnault, *La Marine pendant les Guerres d'Independence de l'Amerique du Sud* (Paris, 1894); L. Florez Álvarez, *Acción de la marina colombiana en la guerra de independencia 1806–1830* (Bogotá, 1919) and Jiménez López, *La armada de Venezuela en la Guerra de la Independencia*.
53 For Gow see TNA WO 97/1122/160; Lambert, *Carabobo*, p. 35; AGNC R GYM, Vol. 363, ff. 850–936.
54 On privateering in the period, see Jane Lucas de Grummond, *Renato Beluche: Smuggler, Privateer, and Patriot, 1780–1860* (Baton Rouge, LA, 1982); Anne Perotin-Dumon, 'Les corsairs de la liberté', *Histoire*, 43 (1982), pp. 24–29.
55 See Sullivan to Fenton, 8 November 1819, Long Island, Bahamas, UCD, P12/3/247; Rafter, *Memoirs of Gregor M'Gregor*, p. 425.
56 Marchena Fernández, *Oficiales y soldados*, p. 96, p. 325.
57 Earle, *Spain and the Independence of Colombia*, pp. 69–74.
58 Woodward, 'The Spanish Army and the Loss of America', p. 587.
59 Earle, *Spain and the Independence of Colombia*, p. 72.
60 Marchena Fernández, *Oficiales y soldados*, p. 351.
61 Earle, *Spain and the Independence of Colombia*, pp. 109–11.
62 Earle, *Spain and the Independence of Colombia*, p. 74.
63 Earle, *Spain and the Independence of Colombia*, p. 159.
64 *Correo del Orinoco*, 27 November 1819.
65 Adam, *Journal of Voyages to Marguaritta, Trinidad and Maturín*, p. v.
66 [Cowley], *Recollections of a Service of Three Years*, p. 80. See also Vowell, *Campaigns and Cruises*, p. 20. Guenther quotes Henry Koster who claimed in the same period that the Brazilians saw the British as 'pagans, animals and horses'. Guenther, *British Merchants in Nineteenth-Century Brazil*, p. 65.
67 Hippisley, *Narrative of the Expedition*, p. 261; Brown, *Narrative of the Expedition to South America*, pp. 148–55.
68 Lambert, 'La Muerte y Entierro del General English', pp. 355–76.
69 *Correo del Orinoco*, 20 February 1819, 24 April 1819; Morgan O'Connell to Daniel O'Connell, 25 August 1820, Barranquilla, repr. in *DEP,* 28 November 1820.
70 See for example Gustavus Butler Hippisley, *The Siege of Barcelona* (London, 1842); James Mudie Spence, *The Land of Bolivar; or War, Peace and Adventure in the Republic of Venezuela* (London, 1878), pp. 85–87; José Dolores Monsalve, *Las mujeres de la revolución de la independencia* (Bogotá, 1926), p. 78.
71 Benedict Anderson, *Imagined Communities: Reflections on the Origin and Spread of Nationalism* (London and New York, 1991), pp. 144–48. For a discussion of *The Siege of Barcelona*, see Matthew Brown, 'Inca, Sailor, Soldier, King', pp. 65–66.
72 As in AGNV GDG, Vol. 12, ff. 167–84.
73 PRO N1, 'Diary of the Voyage of Robert James Young and of General Devereux's Expedition to Margherita with the Irish Legion, Bolivar', D/3045/6/3/2, p. 8.
74 [Lowe], 'A brief sketch of operations', EP, HA157/6/28; Montilla to Bolívar, 20 August 1820, Soledad, repr. in Montilla, *General de División Mariano de Montilla: Homenaje en le Bicentenario de Sunacimiento 1782–1982* (Caracas, 1982), Vol. 1, p. 572. See also the sardonic references to prospective immigrants who might be *'quakercitos, irlandesitos'* in a letter signed by 'El Anti-Mago', 24 September 1821, Bogotá, published in *Gazeta de Santafé de Bogotá*, 7 October 1820.
75 Macmanus, 7 March 1826, Bogotá, AGNC R AC, Legajo 60, fo. 902.

76 *Correo del Orinoco*, 14 April 1821.
77 Anonymous sketch of Bolívar, O'Leary, Ibarra and servant, undated, FJB. A comment hand-written above the scene, in English and in the same hand as the name-captions, reads: 'This was the attitude in which they were seen at mass one day in Guayaquil. The Liberator reading a newspaper, O'Leary taking a cup of coffee which his servant had brought him, and Ibarra striking the *mea culpa* on his heart from behind.' The presence of all three in Guayaquil makes 1822 the likely date of composition, around the time of Bolívar's celebrated interview with José de San Martín.
78 Daniel O'Leary, *The 'Detached Recollections' of General D. F. O'Leary*, ed. R. A. Humphreys (London, 1969), p. 29.
79 According to Boyd Hilton, religious feeling 'permeated all aspects of thought' in Britain in this period. Hilton, *The Age of Atonement: The Influence of Evangelicalism on Social and Economic Thought 1785–1865* (Oxford, 1988), p. ix.
80 Jonathan Curry-Machado, 'Contradiction, Exclusion and Disruptive Identities: The Interaction of Engineering Migrants with Mid-nineteenth century Cuban Society', in A. Asgharzadeh, E. Lawson, K. Oca and A. Wahab (eds), *Diasporic Ruptures: Globality, Migrancy and Expressions of Identity*, Vol. 1 (New York, forthcoming, 2006).
81 Deas, *Vida y opinión de Mr William Wills*, Vol. 1, p. 213.
82 Halperin Donghi, 'Economy and Society in post-Independence Spanish America', *CHLA*, Vol. 3, pp. 299–345.
83 McFarlane, *Colombia before Independence*, p. 351.
84 José María Ossa to Director of Finance, 26 May 1819, Angostura, AGNV GDG, Vol. 10, fo. 64.
85 Frey, *The British Soldier in America*, pp. 30–33.
86 Joaquín Moreno to Director of Finance, 3 March 1819, Angostura, AGNV GDG, Vol. 10, fo. 235.
87 *CMP,* 8 January 1820.
88 Young, 'Diary of the Voyage of Robert James Young', fo. 10.
89 Dr Edward Kirby to Governor of Angostura, 11 May 1819, Angostura, AGNV GDG, Vol. 7, fo. 154.
90 [Vowell], *Campaigns and Cruises*, p. 237; also Anon., 20 April 1818, AGNV GDG, Vol. 6, fo. 179.
91 'Declaraciones de Juan de la Concepción Rueda, Licinio Franco, and Manuel Quiñónez', undated, Puerto Cabello, AGI Cuba, Legajo 911A.
92 Hippisley, *Narrative of the Expedition to the Rivers Orinoco and Apure*, p. 275, p. 315, p. 422.
93 Adam, *Journal of Voyages to Marguaritta, Trinidad and Maturín*, p. 112.
94 Robinson, *Journal of an Expedition*, pp. 67–71.
95 Anon., [An Officer Late in the Colombian Service], *The Present State of Colombia; Containing an Account of The Principal Events of its Revolutionary War; The Expeditions Fitted out in England to Assist in its Emancipation, Its Constitution, Financial and Commercial Laws; Revenue Expenditure and Public Debt; Agriculture; Mines; Mining and Other Associations; With a MAP Exhibiting its Mountains, Rivers, Departments and Provinces* (London, 1827), p. 99.
96 D. Y. C to Don Juan Elías López, 25 April 1819, Jamaica, repr. in *Gazeta de Santa Fe de Bogotá*, 19 August 1819.
97 Woodberry, 'Diario de operación', in Arturo Santana, (ed.), *La campaña de Carabobo (1821) Relación histórica-militar* (Caracas, 1921), pp. 177–315.
98 Vicente Lecuna, 18 October 1819, Angostura, AGNV GDG, Vol. 10, fo. 134. Note that this Vicente Lecuna (b. 1790 Valencia, Venezuela, d. 1862 Caracas), one of Colombia's principal civilian administrators, should not be confused with his great-grandson,

the historian Vicente Lecuna (b. 1870 Caracas, d. 1954 Caracas), author of *Crónica razonada*.

99 For many more documents relating to Woodberry's organization of Páez' army in 1823, see AGNC R GYM, Vol. 44. Woodberry was of such standing that he had his own personalised printed headed paper; for an example see AGNV IP, Vol. 84, fo. 310. See also Pérez Jurado, 'Tras las huellas del Coronel George Woodberry', pp. 116–18. For Thomas Richards, see AGNV GDG, Vol. 6, ff. 33–40; for his links to the financier Charles Herring, see Mary English, 'Diary of Mary English', [1822], EP, HA157/11/10.

100 Richards to Minister of Marine, 22 January 1820, Juan Griego, *MOL*, Vol. 17, pp. 45–8.

101 José Fructuoso Durán to Domingo Caycedo, 21 March 1820, Neiva, repr. in Guillermo Hernández de Alba, Enrique Ortega Ricaurte and Ignacio Rivas Putnam, (eds), *Archivo Epistolar del General Domingo Caycedo*, Vol. 1 (Bogotá, 1943), pp. 100–1.

102 Michael Howard, *The Invention of Peace and the Reinvention of War* (London, 2000), p. 36.

103 Durán to Caycedo, 23 March 1820, Neiva, in Hernández de Alba et al. (eds), *Archivo Epistolar*, Vol. 1, pp. 101–3.

104 For examples of these disturbances see Libro de Ordenes, 2 July 1819, Angostura, AGNV GDG, Vol. 9, fo. 295; Unsigned and undated (probably Angostura, late 1819), AGNV GDG, Vol. 8, fo. 415.

105 J. Herrenyn to Juan José Conde, 24 September 1820, Angostura, AGNV GDG, Vol. 11, ff. 43–44.

106 Cited in Best, *War and Society*, p. 104.

107 On the widespread lack of confidence in the New Granadan economy in this period see McFarlane, *Colombia Before Independence*, p. 162. On requisitioning see Thibaud, *Repúblicas en armas*, p. 447.

108 On the 'scandalous behaviour' of the Rifles Battalion see Briceño Méndez to José María Carreño, Rosario, 21 May 1820, *MOL*, Vol. 17, p. 192. For the similar depredations of the Loyalist soldiers, see Earle, *Spain and the Independence of Colombia*, pp. 111–12.

109 Briceño Méndez to Páez, 25 May 1820, San Cristóbal, *MOL*, Vol. 17, p. 203.

110 Charles J. Esdaile, *The Peninsular War: A New History* (London, 2003), p. 380.

111 Three examples from many are Urdaneta, *Memorias del general Rafael Urdaneta*, p. 230; [Cowley], *Recollections of a Service of Three Years*, p. 77; and Young, 'Diary of Robert James Young', p. 53.

112 Best, *War and Society*, p. 102.

113 For the examples of Ibagué and Cali, see ACC, Sala Independencia, M1-11-ad, C1-5f.

114 José María Olivares, Military Governor of Angostura, to Director of Finance, 19 November 1819, Angostura, AGNV GDG, Vol. 10, fo. 144; see also Hippisley, *Narrative of the Expedition*, p. 430.

115 Chesterton, *A Narrative of Proceedings in Venezuela and South America in the years 1819 and 1820; with general observations on the country and people; the character of the republican government; and its leading members, etc. And also a description of the country of Caraccas; of the force of General Morillo; the state of the royalists; and the spirit of the people under their jurisdiction* (London, 1820), pp. 19–20.

116 José María Olivares, 'Proclamación', 15 April 1820, Angostura, AGNV GDG, Vol. 12, f. 233.

117 Comandante Luis Castillo, 'Investigation into the arrest of Sargento Tomás Cañon', 14 September 1822, Popayán, ACC, Sala Independencia, J1-15-cr, Sig. 6109.

118 Note in the margin of a passport for Albion Battalion soldiers, initially signed by Mariano Montilla in Cartagena 2 June 1822, completed in Socorro on 11 July 1822,

AGNC R GYM, Vol. 1447, fo. 606.
119 Alcalde Ordinario Francisco Molina to José Concha, 3 September 1822, Cali, ACC, Sala Independencia, M1-8-ad, Sig. 1244, fo. 1.
120 José Antonio Barrelas to Francisco Molinas, 2 September 1822, Cali, ACC, Sala Independencia, M1-8-ad, Sig. 1244, fo. 4 [original emphasis].
121 ACC, Sala Independencia, M1-8-ad, Sig. 1244, ff. 9–14.
122 See the comments to this effect from the Loyalist General Basilio Palacios to Comandante General, 17 April 1826, Popayán, ACC, Sala Independencia, M1-1-c, Sig. 2400, ff. 3–4.
123 Hamilton to Planta, 9 April 1824, Bogotá, TNA FO 18/3 ff. 32–37.

CHAPTER FOUR

Negotiating Honour

What gives value to travel is fear. It breaks down a kind of internal structure ... stripped of all our crutches, deprived of our masks ... we are completely on the surface of ourselves ... This is the most obvious benefit of travel.

(Albert Camus, 1937) [1]

This chapter explores how adventurers negotiated their honour with each other and with Gran Colombians. An examination of disputes that ended in duels or court cases can illustrate the ways that honour was negotiated and conceptualised. An adventurer's honour was a compound of prestige and romantic conceptions of 'glory', race and national pride. The adventurers' desire for honour meshed well with the concerns of Creoles, for whom it was also a central preoccupation throughout the colonial period.[2] Indeed, as Chapter 5 argues, a culture of adventure was one of the principal consequences of foundational fighting in Gran Colombia.[3] Adventurous heroes such as Bolívar were converted into national heroes as the nineteenth century wore on.

In late-colonial Spanish America, honour was both 'a motivating sentiment and code of conduct observed by individuals and families looking for ways to accumulate prestige, esteem, influence, and other opportunities to increase their social standing',[4] which was then 'convertible' into material advantage. As Elías Pino Iturrieta has argued for the Venezuelan republic, and Victor Manuel Uribe Urán for New Granada, the upheavals of wartime and the accompanying social and economic changes meant that ideas of honour began to ascribe more value to conduct and, correspondingly, less to birth.[5] The *honra* (virtue) of the good citizen was incorporated into élite Venezuelans' understandings of what it meant to be honourable after the break from Spain. But both Pino Iturrieta and Uribe Urán consciously focused on civilian aspects of society, seeing these as the true bases for nationhood. In both cases unprecedented levels of military mobilisation conditioned and transformed civilian codes of honour, even though New Granada experienced a lower degree of military conflict than did Venezuela. The vast majority of the military in this period were not professional soldiers, but were rather lawyers (like Santander), *hacendados* (like Bolívar), peasants or slaves who had taken up arms either for opportunistic reasons or from necessity. During over a decade of warfare, therefore, aspects of the 'warrior's honour'[6] were superimposed upon pre-existing conceptions of honour, ascribing increased importance to those individuals who had performed with bravery and success in the military sphere.[7]

The contemporary resurgence of interest in chivalric codes in Britain and Ireland underscored the way adventurers thought about honour when they arrived in Gran Colombia. Paradoxically, because only a third of them had any prior military experience before reaching Gran Colombia, they were even more anxious to recognise the importance of heroism, bravery in battle and other aspects of the warrior's honour. This was a period in which Walter Scott's Romantic hero was popular: 'brave, dashing, honourable, proud of his birth, pure-minded, gentle to women and loyal to his masters'.[8] Honour, however, was not equally accessible to all. As Cannadine has observed, 'Britons generally conceived of themselves as belonging to an unequal society characterised by a seamless web of layered gradations, which were hallowed by time and precedent, which were sanctioned by tradition and religion, and which extended in a great chain of being from the monarch at the top to the humblest subject at the bottom.'[9] Some people were conceived of as more honourable than others, and the high status of one was at least in part dependent upon the recognition and deference shown by lower-status individuals. Some adventurers achieved very high status in Gran Colombia, often through dying in the service of the state. These included Coronel James Rooke, who died after the battle of Pantano de Vargas in 1819, and whose last words were '*Viva la patria*',[10] and William Ferguson, who was killed protecting Bolívar from an assassination attempt.[11] They epitomised the figure of the self-sacrificing, chivalric hero which emerged from the Wars of Independence as an integral part of the new republican patriotism.[12]

Adventurers in the rank-and-file found that military rank was often as good a guide to status as class or race. Even though they gained advantages and status because of their whiteness, their rank as soldiers meant that they served in the subordinate positions alongside freed slaves and indigenous peoples. In the Independent army, race or poverty were increasingly unlikely to impede the ascent of a capable officer, as was demonstrated by the rise of pardo officers like Manuel Piar and José Padilla to positions where they could challenge the authority of Simón Bolívar.[13] The issues surrounding race and slavery are explored in Chapter 6.

Social tensions were both crystallised and exposed by the formal and explicit hierarchies of military rank.[14] This was true of the British Army in the Napoleonic period, and was equally the case during the Wars of Independence in Gran Colombia. Problems were exacerbated by the differences in translation between the British and Spanish military models. The Independent armies, in their most regular incarnations, were the heirs to the codes and regulations of the Spanish army. Each rank had an English translation, but they corresponded to different grades of authority, especially for mid-ranking officers. Especially relevant were the smaller units of men that operated in the Independents' army, which meant that middle-ranked officers such as *mayores*, *tenientes* and *capitanes* often found themselves with little real authority with which to distinguish themselves from each other. Such a simple issue provided the background for tension, conflict and resentment between officers, both foreigners and locals. Effectively, a teniente was a much lower rank than a Lieutenant felt himself to be and a capitán a higher rank than a Captain. British and Irish officers competed to gain the respect which they felt they were owed, based on their own translations of these ranks into English.[15] This problem was aggravated by the fact that officers had been recruited in London with the promise that they would be raised by one rank upon arrival in Hispanic America, and that many of them had no military experience upon which to base their claims. Officers therefore quarrelled publicly amongst themselves as to who was allowed what respect and prestige, and soldiers were made even more aware of the advantages and luxuries they were correspondingly denied. Yet despite the blurred boundaries between the officer ranks, the divisions between officers, non-commissioned officers, and private soldiers were well-defined and strictly observed. These distinctions provided the principal basis for assessing status and respect owed by colleagues. Assuming that all officers were named in archival sources at some point, it can be extrapolated that 22 per cent of the adventurers occupied an officer rank, 28 per cent were non-commissioned officers, and 50 per cent private soldiers.

Chivalry

Chivalry was an important reference point for the officers in the expeditions. Several authors and chroniclers linked the expeditions to Don Quijote, the principal Hispanic chivalric figure of their imaginations, a new translation of whose adventures was advertised in London as the expeditions were being recruited.[16] The Irish Legion was 'a gallant and well-appointed band' who went to defend the 'brave, but much enduring people of Spanish America' against their 'imbecile though remorseless oppressors'.[17] The chivalric theme continued throughout the Wars of Independence. In 1821 the celebrations of the second anniversary of the Battle of Boyacá were marked in Bogotá by 'a ceremonial march in which all the gentlemen of ancient times paraded' followed by 'more music and patriotic singing'.[18] The following year there was 'a magnificent display in imitation of the ancient tournaments. Horsemen [were] attired after the manner of the knights-errant of old, belonging to the four quarters of the world. ... The most adroit of the knights were then selected by the judges, and received various prizes from the Queen of the Tournament, who was generally the most beautiful young lady of the place.'[19] The language of chivalry infused much of the adventurers' correspondence. Some officers were 'noble knights'.[20] Others sought 'to encounter as many perils and dangers as most knights-errant of yore'.[21] One officer defended breaking into a Bogotá merchant's house on the grounds that he had heard 'the screams of a maiden'.[22]

Women were at the centre of much of the men's chivalric discourse but they also claimed their own place in it by serving as soldiers, spies and cooks, or by performing tasks in propaganda and communications throughout the wars.[23] Élite women such as Manuela Sáenz played vital roles in military and political affairs.[24] The presence of women in the armies of the Wars of Independence was crucial to fashioning understandings of honour and identity. O'Leary described with admiration the British wife of a soldier giving birth to a child in the snow half-way up the Páramo de Pisba mountain pass.[25] Women shared the deprivations and victories of the campaigning armies and petitioned the authorities when in need of resources.[26] The claims of foreign women to the same levels of respect and recognition as their male counterparts were particularly uncomfortable for the male political and military élites who sought to cement a social order based upon new forms of masculinity and fraternal bonds between men. The recourse to the language of chivalry declined considerably once peace was established.[27]

Fear of the Unknown

The recruitment of adventurers in Britain and Ireland contrasted the riches and glory to be gained with the perils that could await them in the unknown South American hinterland. By definition, adventure had to entail dangerous risk in unknown areas, and for the metropolitan British subject, South America was the very epitome of the unknown, more mysterious even than the lands of empire. A novelist in 1817 imagined a dialogue between a mother and her son about to set off for Venezuela:

> Oh! my son, when you are exiled beyond the western ocean, when the sun that gilds your morn leaves his evening beams on yonder hill – when months must revolve 'ere a line from you can cheer my lonely life – these, Eugene, these are harrowing anticipations, and I sink beneath their weight. Imagination will be gloomily exercised in beholding you sick, wounded, shipwrecked or a captive! Deprived of every tender care, exposed to all the dangers and difficulties of hostile operations in another quarter of the globe. Perhaps, without a friend to cheer, or a voice to whisper consolation. Oh! my son, reflect yet again 'ere you embark in a service so replete with dangers and with difficulties.[28]

One of the dangers that caused most anxiety was the fear of being captured by pirates or Indians, which, as Linda Colley has shown, was a constant in the imaginations of British adventurers across the globe in this period.[29] In South America, these anxieties crystallised quickly around the death of the leader of one of the first expeditions, Coronel Donald MacDonald. MacDonald was a high-profile figure already, having been an adventurer in the Peninsular War in Spain where he served as aide-de-camp to General Ballesteros. Stories of the manner of MacDonald's death circulated among the adventurers for several years and they illustrate the variety of fears of the unknown held by members of subsequent expeditions. There is no definitive account of what happened, but the combination of a hostile and impenetrable environment and of ambush by the 'savage barbarity' of local Indians was common to all accounts.[30] The role of indigenous women in luring MacDonald to his death was also much discussed, despite there being little evidence to support the claim. But these three factors, Indians, environment and women, provided an essential backdrop to casting Gran Colombia as a landscape for adventure. All three needed to be dominated for honour to be secured. Similar stories became commonplace, leading to troops 'complaining that they could not stir from their immediate neighbourhood, without the danger of having their throats cut by the natives'.[31] Anxious adventurers feared being 'overwhelmed by a horde of Indians'.[32]

Taking these stories at face value, Eric Lambert concluded that what happened to MacDonald and his colleagues was 'the inevitable' result of entering Indian territory.[33] More accurately, repeated descriptions of MacDonald's death were important tools in creating and conditioning adventurers' fears of the Venezuelan environment. Even if the rumours and anecdotes were all based on fact, no more than a dozen adventurers were ever captured or killed by hostile Indians – many more died fishing or duelling. The constant repetition of these stories, however, which spread through word-of-mouth reports coming out of camp-fire discussions, and which were embroidered during the inaction between military duties and passed on though colonial news networks before crossing the Atlantic, enabled other adventurers to present their own adventures as dangerous and therefore as confirmation of their manliness.[34]

Duelling

Adventurers were encouraged to assert their honour in front of other groups by these largely unsubstantiated reports. One of the ways in which they did this was through duelling. Duelling was an established part of British and Irish aristocratic society in the early nineteenth century, and a manifestation of the value ascribed to notions of courage and bravery. Also crucial to the duelling culture, however, was the idea of the sense of duty to which it corresponded, and the social cohesion to which it contributed – the duellist was left 'to confront his destiny supported by nothing but his pride in membership of a chosen section of mankind'.[35] As Kiernan explained, the very illegality of duelling was extremely important for the cohesion of the aristocracy, in that by putting himself above the law the duellist also put himself 'outside any social contract' and 'demonstrated that his self-respect or, what came to the same thing, his respect for his class, mattered more to him' than 'any social contract'.[36] In the early nineteenth century, duelling was increasingly emulated by the rising middle classes as a means of asserting and gaining individual honour. Duellists included literati such as Sheridan, Byron and Marx and politicians such as Canning, Castlereagh and Daniel O'Connell.[37] In Ireland both Protestants and Catholics came to 'defend their bravery under fire'.[38] By 1850 the increased access to duelling for wider sectors of society had undermined its exclusivity and hence its use and purpose in society, but in the 1810s and 1820s the duel was still a key arena for addressing issues of honour and equality in societies where religious and social identities were rapidly changing. The adventurers carried this culture with them across the Atlantic and with it the understanding that duelling could affirm group identity and assert differences between one group and another.

Outside of Northern Europe, duelling was much less prevalent in this period. The principal history of the duel, Kiernan's authoritative *The Duel in European History* (1988), hardly dealt with the Hispanic world and was inconsistent and contradictory when it did.[39] Duelling was ridiculed in Cervantes' *Don Quijote* and colonial constructions of honour were too strongly grounded in blood and family for duelling to 'prove' anything, which was the whole point of it in Northern Europe. Steve Stern has argued that the equality assumed between duellists was substituted in Mexican culture by concentration on the assertion of honour by 'using [one's] power to punish a subordinate' instead.[40] The persistence of the duel in early nineteenth century Europe, and its growth in the Americas and its resurgence in France and Germany throughout the nineteenth century, has confused historians.[41] In theory, the spread of republican and liberal ideologies – of which the Wars of Independence in Hispanic America are held to form part – should have meant that honour was less defined by public reputation, and henceforth was defined much less publicly. Yet the duel survived and flourished in periods of 'practically endless warfare' in Europe and the Americas in which 'permanent mobilisation and the high prestige of military élites' nourished the spread of military virtues and chivalric honour throughout civil society.[42] The duel especially flourished in imperial armies. When British and Irish men left home for the outside world and empire, when they formed new relationships of power and authority with previously unknown men, they felt the need to mark out their honour in public. Duelling was part of this conscious attempt to assert honour in a new environment.

Even though duelling was illegal in Gran Colombia, it was accepted by Creole élites as unavoidable baggage brought by the adventurers, and best ignored.[43] One British businessmen resident in Angostura in 1820 described how large crowds gathered on the outskirts of town 'in full knowledge of everyone' to watch these events, while the authorities looked the other way.[44] Everything known about the duelling of mercenaries in Hispanic America comes from their own accounts in memoirs, rather than official documents. Alexander Alexander recorded a period in Angostura in 1819 when 'foolish duels became frequent, two and three of a morning'.[45] Table 4.1 lists what is probably only a small fraction of the duels that took place. There are a total of 22 named adventurers involved in duelling. With a minimum of two seconds per duel, this means that over forty men were directly involved, without mentioning the surgeons who usually attended, and these are just the duels where documentary record has remained. Circumstantial evidence suggests that the

Table 4.1   *Duels involving Named Adventurers in the first years of the Wars of Independence*[47]

Duellist 1	National identity	Outcome	Duellist 2	National identity	Location and date of duel
Teniente John Sutton	Scottish or Irish	Killed by	Mayor Lockyer	British or Irish	Isle of Wight, December 1817
Cornet John Dewey	British	Outcome unknown	Cornet Humphries	British or Irish	St Bartholemew, c. 1818
Capitán Zenetitch	Not known	Wounded by	Capitán Bombatch	Not known	On board the *Monarch* off Margarita, January 1819
Capitán Smith	Irish	Outcome unknown	Capitán Boyd	Irish	Margarita, August 1819
Capitán Daniel O'Leary	Irish	Outcome unknown	Not known	Not known	Hatoviejo, New Granada, August 1819
Lieutenant C——	Irish	Outcome unknown	Capitán De B——	Irish	Ballyhackmore, near Belfast, January 1820
Assistant Surgeon Gray	British or Irish	Killed by	Mayor William Davy	British	Maturín, November 1819
Capitán Rupert Hand	Irish	Wounded by	Teniente William Lynch	English	Maturín, November 1819
Capitán Block	English	Outcome unknown	Capitán ——	Scottish	Cumaná, January 1820
Surgeon Compton	Irish	Killed by	Mayor	British or Irish	Barbados, June 1820
Coronel John Blosset	Irish	Killed by	Coronel William B. Middleton Power	Irish	Achaguas, August 1820

actual number of duels was much higher. Those duels which did not result in fatalities were much less likely to leave a trace. Nevertheless, Table 4.1 is useful in that it reveals some basic trends. Duels tended to be fought between men of equal military rank, or where the difference in rank was minimal (between *teniente*, *capitán*, and *mayor*, for example). No private soldiers were involved and there were no women. The duel was a way of rectifying small differences in perceptions of status and honour – not a challenge to existing social hierarchies. Duels took place everywhere: before leaving Europe, on board ship, on the Caribbean islands and in Venezuela. At this stage (all the duels recorded occurred before the end of 1820) there were explicitly no duellists from outside the expeditions, nor any non-whites or Hispanic Americans. As Kenneth Greenberg has observed, 'since the whole point of the duel was to heal a breach within the community of gentlemen ... it made no sense to duel with a stranger'.[46] The stranger in this sense could be alien in terms of race, gender, or class: the duelling community was extremely exclusive.

Peter Linebaugh and Marcus Rediker have stressed how the Atlantic Ocean was the setting for the negotiation and challenging of social hierarchies in this period. The crew and passengers of a ship were a microcosm of society in a confined space, and this often caused rebellions and disorder in a way that would not have happened back on land.[48] Benjamin M'Mahon despaired at the 'frequency of petty quarrels amongst the officers, which invariably led to a duel', claiming to have witnessed 15 duels in the two months' duration of his passage.[49] M'Mahon ridiculed this duelling culture, and explicitly contrasted it with the harmony he perceived amongst the rank and file. But duelling continued on shore as well and was characteristic of the adventurers as a group rather than their land- or sea-based activities.

Because they took place in an otherwise non-duelling environment, the adventurers' duels on arrival in Venezuela were extremely noticeable and public affairs, 'almost as well attended as any other entertainment'. [50] Following Greenberg's writings on the American South, it could be argued that the duelling adventurers were trying to reaffirm their superiority to the new, supposedly subservient, social groups which they found surrounding them, by making it clear that they did not fear death. It is hard to tell if this had the desired effect. Those commentators who did record the events denounced the duels as 'trivial', and soldiers tended to mock the elaborate rituals.[51] Many observers, including Creoles, mocked the proceedings.[52] According to Alexander, after witnessing these demonstrations of honour, lower-ranked soldiers would pretend to duel with blanks and would then fall about laughing at their 'mock heroics'.[53] Creoles began to 'play at duelling, which caused them great entertainment'.[54]

Most authors sought to emphasise the 'triviality' of the affairs when recalling these duels for the benefit of their readership, stressing that although such behaviour may have been widespread, it was by no means acceptable for civilised and rational people. Radical and evangelical sections of society had no sympathy with duelling, seeing it as outdated a custom as cruel sports and slavery and arguing that it was a practice that could 'only help out of the world those who are too silly to do it any good by remaining'.[55] But in the context of the Wars of Independence, duelling was a crucial way for anxious adventurers to assert and retain honour in an arena of 'heightened sensitivity over character and reputation'.[56] At issue were usually accusations of dishonour and duplicity – many related to how those involved in the recruitment of the expeditions had somehow 'duped' others into signing up.[57] Kiernan argued that the Irish, and particularly the Protestant Anglo-Irish, deserved their stage reputation as trigger-happy duellists, and this conclusion is lent some support by Kelly's study of the duel in Ireland, and by the number of Irishmen featured in Table 4.1.[58] But it is also possible that their duels were recorded with more detail than others precisely because of the stereotype of the 'naturally brave' Irishman, with his 'impulsive courage and self-sacrifice' as portrayed on the contemporary stage.[59]

Rumours circulated throughout the Caribbean about duels involving Creoles and adventurers. In late 1818 news spread that Luis Brion had been killed in a duel with an English officer.[60] Two years later it was reported that 'Mariano Montilla has been killed in a pistol-duel with an Englishman' triggered by Montilla's supposed cowardice in battle.[61] But these rumours did not reflect reality. British and Irish officers did not consider 'the natives' as worthy duellists, as such an action would imply a certain amount of equality between the participants, and this disdain was matched by Creoles' disinterest in duelling as an activity. Despite the many complaints they had with leaders such as Brion and Montilla, apparently no adventurers ever challenged either of them to a duel, and both eventually died of natural causes. When the possibility arose of a challenge being laid down to a Hispanic American officer, every effort was made to avoid it resulting in a duel.[62] Duelling was primarily a way of asserting honour within the closed community of foreign officers, and thereby demonstrating that honour to those who stood outside.

By 1821, the amount of duelling had markedly declined, although 'back-biting and enmity were as great as ever'.[63] This was not only because many of the duellists were now dead or had returned to Europe, but because those who remained recognised that there were other more effective ways of asserting one's honour in the Hispanic American context. When General John Devereux issued a challenge to the Gran Colombian Vice-President, General Antonio Nariño, he was imprisoned and hastily backtracked, claiming that he had been mistranslated.[64] Bolívar described Devereux's challenge as 'madness ... a real disgrace, a stupidity that compromises the Government and its functionaries, and the Congress which is supporting him. The case should have remained personal.'[65] It is clear from his private correspondence that Antonio Nariño thought duelling dishonourable, and did not deem either Mary English – the woman he was alleged to have insulted – or Devereux, as worthy of his respect. He described English as 'a woman who says she is General English's widow', and complained that the 'foreigners here are driving me mad'.[66] Devereux was 'an absentee officer, with no army, no current command' whose demands were 'a formal insult to our government'.[67] Nariño felt that his personal honour was bound up with the dignity of his office, and that he must 'continue with this case until the government's honour is completely satisfied, so that these adventurers will stop coming here and treating us like they treat their subjects in the East Indies'.[68] Nariño wanted Gran Colombians and Britons to be equals, highlighting the treatment he himself would receive if positions were substituted:

Let us just suppose that I *did* insult the English woman, that I kicked her even, or beat her to death. What right does an official like D'Evereux have to judge our government? If one of us had presumed the same, not even to the English Government itself but just to the Governor of Jamaica – just how long do you think they would have let us live?[69]

The Minister of Justice and the Interior, Diego Bautista Urbaneja, agreed with Nariño, writing that Gran Colombia's honour must not be undermined by the lack of respect shown to the government by foreigners. Devereux was investigated for 'insolence, insulting language, and showing disrespect to the Government'.[70] By this stage, 1821, and in this manner, the prospect of duelling became most dishonourable for Creoles and foreigners alike. The republican court system was now functional and responding to the established and institutionalised Gran Colombian state.

Honour Disputes

Disputes over honour were often taken into the new republican courts. Surviving records of court cases from Angostura in 1818–20 involving foreigners provide an opportunity to explore the extent to which adventurers were able to protect their perceived superiority and individual honour in these cases. The British officers at Waterloo, according to John Keegan, had a stark, individual sense of honour, concerned with proving themselves to the men around them, demonstrating that they were not cowards and that they were fit to lead.[71] The reputation of the brave British was underlined by stories told about their involvement in the Battles of Pantano de Vargas and Carabobo. Despite suffering 'horrific mortality'[72] under fire without ammunition to defend themselves, the British were said to have entered the fray 'in formation, marching in good order, launching a brilliant bayonet charge and gaining the heights' that allowed the Independents to win the battle.[73] In battle, the ideal was to stand firm, never to yield, and to fight on when wounded. This attitude was epitomised in a celebrated anecdote about John Mackintosh's actions during the battle of Pantano de Vargas: 'When bullets were raining down on us like hailstones, one of his officers commented that "it was impossible to take those heights". To that, Mayor Mackintosh replied, "Be quiet officer, and get forward – nothing is impossible for British bayonets"'.[74]

This element of a soldier's honour, while founded upon the collective honour and perceived superiority of whites, Britons and officers, was of prime importance. The individual had to demonstrate his honour by being strong, brave, loyal, and unwilling to give in to even the most unfavourable odds and greatest obstacles. Hasbrouck and Lambert provide much evidence for the argument that British officers did behave in this way on several occasions. Away from the battlefield, however, which was where adventurers spent the vast majority of their time, asserting this type of honour was more problematic. The law in Gran Colombia was administered by Gran Colombians, and so –

duelling apart – the final decision on the adventurers' disagreements and conflicts was made by Gran Colombian officers.

The emphasis on the 'individual' aspect of honour, as opposed to that of the 'group', was in part based upon the fear of shame, the internal counterpoint to external honour.[75] The adventurers' individual honour was peculiar to their particular circumstances, as discussed in Chapter 1, and conflated a liberal concept of citizens' individual rights with honour, and merged honour with contract agreements that necessitated fair payment and recognition of rank and status. Their ideas about honour stood at the crossroads between the corporate subjects of the early modern period, and the liberal republican ethos of the modern world. In this sense the next section brings to the fore the honour disputes recorded by contemporaries.[76] Military historians such as Hasbrouck and Lambert ignored the documentation of honour trials from Angostura in 1818–20, presumably because they regarded them as irrelevant to campaigning and military activity. Yet the trials cast a light on the encounters between adventurers and Gran Colombians in Angostura, a town that witnessed the most concentrated and intense involvement of foreigners in any particular Hispanic American society in the whole period under study. Like the diverse immigrants to Buenos Aires in the late eighteenth century described by Johnson, men in Angostura were 'divided by ethnicity, language and culture, but shared a desire to protect themselves from insult and intimidation'.[77] The city's fluid social make-up constantly challenged ideals of masculine social hierarchy and individual honour. White male officers did well in the cases studied, although, as in the colonial period, justice was not routinely awarded to those already possessing established 'purity of blood', honour and rank.[78] Creole ideas of race, gender and class took the foreground in what were often flexible and pragmatic interpretations of justice, crime and punishment. Codes of honour defined the acceptable dealings between officers and their soldiers, between gentlemen and their subalterns, and between Creoles and foreigners. These court sessions were a means of 'fixing' honour in public in this time of social and political change.

Understandings of honour were changing in Spanish America at the beginning of the nineteenth century. In the colonial period, honour based on what Steve Stern called 'cultural displays of forcefulness' was at once a code to mark out divisions between groups, and a means of restoring any imbalance created when social boundaries had been transgressed.[79] Social boundaries were under attack during the Wars of Independence, and republican courts acted as a means to shore up distinctions under threat from previously subordinate groups. Creole officers judged all but one of the cases involving foreigners, and the trials were paid for by the local political authorities. The court was thus a 'contact zone' in which adventurers' understandings of honour were publicly negotiated with Creoles.[80] These Creoles were at the same time defining the limits of their own decision to fight against Spanish authority in the name of a new 'national' honour which had necessarily redefined colonial conceptions of honour. Subjection to an absolute monarch was now held by some to be demeaning and dishonourable in that it was felt to impinge upon the independence of individuals and their right to govern themselves and their communities. The conduct of foreign adventurers within these communities – and the ability of the republican leaders to assert themselves as the judges of honourable behaviour – was therefore integral to the new legitimacy of the republican government based in Angostura, and a touchstone of nascent national self-definition.

In contrast to much of what we know about honour in Hispanic America, in very few cases was adventurers' honour explicitly linked to the behaviour of 'their' women.[81] This was because of the frequently isolated nature of their service, transient and often thousands of miles from their families. In one exceptional instance, the merchant James Hamilton encouraged Ana Rooke (wife of Coronel James Rooke) to leave Venezuela for Barbados when it was discovered that she had been conducting an affair with another officer while Rooke was away recruiting indigenous troops from the Caroní missions. She asked Hamilton 'as you know the motives … you will I trust, never allow any comments to be made, in your presence, detrimental either to my dearest Rooke's character, or my own'.[82] Coronel Rooke's honour was to be preserved by maintaining a discreet silence about his wife's infidelities. But the debates over honour in the other surviving documents made little or no reference to relations with wives, girlfriends, mistresses, lovers or prostitutes. In one case involving an alleged attempted rape of a Venezuelan woman by a Scottish officer, the crime was seen as less important than the alleged blow that he landed on the man trying to defend her, for which the officer was reprimanded. Indeed, most honour disputes recorded in the archives revolved around property, or physical 'insults' to the male body.[83]

Campaigning and drilling away from urban centres necessarily meant that the separation between officers and soldiers could no longer be as rigidly enforced as during time spent barracked in towns. Private soldiers therefore had occasional opportunity to dispute the respect owed to them, or the rights they felt they had earned. In October 1820 Capitán Rupert Hand was tried by a military court for the offence of having drawn his sword and struck one of his own men with it. Hand's physical assault was in response to the verbal and physical abuse he had received from the British soldier Private Lons while out marching in Guayana.[84] Hand's reaction led the entire battalion to rebel and take up arms against him, chasing Hand with rifles and bayonets and shouting 'Kill him! Kill him!'[85] Hand's life was saved when General Santiago Mariño came into the street to discover the cause of the commotion. Mariño restored order with the help of 100 local troops and allowed Hand to hide in his house while the soldiers were dispersed.[86]

Private Lons could not be tried for his insubordination because he died as a result of his injuries. The soldiers who rose up in outrage at the actions of their officer were also punished severely. Various witnesses, including several of the soldiers themselves, testified that 'the men had risen up as one, there was no leader'.[87] In a collective petition to the court, the men admitted that 'their actions were mistaken, but were triggered by the sight of their *compañero* being injured'.[88] The court (which was composed of four Creole and three British officers) ordered a collective exemplary punishment, and one in ten of the soldiers implicated in the rebellion was executed.[89]

Once the men had been dealt with, the authorities turned their attention to Capitán Hand's actions. Given the harsh punishment of the rebels, witnesses were perhaps understandably cautious in criticising Hand. However, the sources reveal that ongoing tensions between officer and soldier both underscored and catalysed the incident. Private James Haworth reported that 'Lons said to Hand that "he had been born just the same as him", upon which Hand ordered the troops to arrest Lons'.[90] After Hand had struck him three times, Lons threw his blood-soaked cap at his officer, a symbolic gesture which encouraged his colleagues in the ranks to abuse and ridicule Hand. John Taylor, a British merchant resident in the town, confirmed that Lons claimed to be 'just as much of a man' as Hand. According to Taylor, Lons called Hand a 'rogue, a wanker and a thief'.[91] Capitán Hand stressed his 'duty' to maintain discipline, 'to protect [his] person, and to vindicate the insults made on [his] character'.[92]

The final verdict on the case was given by Sargento Mayor Santiago de España, temporary commander of Angostura. He recognised the 'serious accusation', but affirmed that Hand had 'fulfilled the most sacred duty of an official', using his sword only 'as he saw necessary' which was 'fully within his rights if the soldier was obstinately refusing to go'.[93] The Creole officials absolved Hand of any wrongdoing, commended him for fulfilling his duty, and even stated that in the long run, the firm example (that of striking a soldier with his sword) was to the benefit of the army and its discipline; all this despite the fact that Hand had killed a private soldier and triggered rebellion amongst his men.[94] The insubordination of a subaltern (Lons) was seen as having been justly punished, and Capitán Hand's honour upheld. In this way the Creole officials sided with the officer in order to maintain military hierarchies structured around rank, and the social order that this represented in an increasingly militarised environment, regardless of the justice of the private soldiers' cause. Nevertheless, the same case provides clear evidence that lower-status groups did openly challenge these hierarchies by taking on the language of equality and disrupting the order imposed upon them from above. Status was not fixed but was rather disputed and challenged by all groups during this period.[95] Whereas the officer was given the benefit of the doubt, private soldiers received vastly different treatment from the republican dispensers of justice. The Creole military officers confirmed their own position as the arbiters of disputes in Venezuela, by arbitrarily and randomly punishing the soldiers for rebellion, and by publicly affirming Hand's honour and approving his conduct.

Hand killed Lons with a sword, symbolically the officers' weapon. In another case, a very public honour dispute between officers of different rank, the symbolism of the sword was integral to the articulation of the degrees of 'respect' due to an individual. In July 1820, Teniente FitzThomas of the British Legion was accused by Coronel William Lyster of the Irish Legion of 'unofficerlike conduct, and [of] using threatening and disrespectful language to a Superior Officer'.[96] The dispute, triggered by FitzThomas's refusal to carry out an order because of the late hour, was just a squabble between officers sensitive to incursions on their authority until Lyster formally arrested FitzThomas. The latter refused to surrender his sword. FitzThomas used the symbolism of his weapon to register his status as a 'a decent man'.[97] He recognised that Coronel Lyster was his 'superior officer', but objected to Lyster addressing him 'in a sharp, loud voice inappropriate for discussing issues of service with a gentleman'.[98] Considering all the evidence, the presiding officer at the trial, Teniente Coronel José Martínez, concluded succinctly that the charges did not merit any more punishment than the time FitzThomas had already spent under arrest. The case was dismissed and FitzThomas was released and allowed to return to the service.[99] The hierarchies amongst the officer ranks were not of such concern to Creoles as the absolute division required between officer and soldier, enforced with such rigour in the Hand–Lons case studied above.

On occasions honour was disputed across the boundary between the military and civilian spheres. In December 1818 a Venezuelan fisherman-turned-soldier who was temporarily resident in Angostura, Sargento José Herrera, was charged with having used a knife to attack the North American merchant Samuel Forsyth at his home. Herrera was accused of a premeditated assassination attempt triggered by a disagreement over money. According to one witness, Herrera had told Forsyth that 'all the English are thieving rogues who steal from the Republic: they all have bread to eat while we starve', and that when Forsyth told him to leave, Herrera responded that 'he was an official of the Republic' and that he could not be thrown out of a house by a civilian. In response Forsyth pushed him, which was the reason Herrera went to get the knife. His attack never came to fruition, however, as the merchant's friends attacked Herrera with sticks and then threw him out of a window.[100]

When the matter came to trial, the sentence was again flexible and adapted to unique circumstances. Herrera was found guilty of attacking Forsyth, but was held to have 'already been sufficiently punished by the very hand of those offended who wounded him and left him useless for armed service ... [it was decided to] absolve him of the imputation and return him to his employment'.[101] This secured the honour of the powerful merchant, as Forsyth was not charged with the physical attack. Herrera was free to rejoin the armed forces, despite public recognition of his guilt. Teniente Asunción Ferrera, representing Herrera, contested the Court's verdict. He asserted that it was 'indecorous to those who wear the military uniform that a private individual can have broken the sacred respect for those, like Herrera, who have been adorned with military honours'.[102] In the view of Ferrera, a mid-ranking Creole officer, Herrera's military profession provided him with more residual honour than any civilian, despite his low social status when compared to the wealthy businessman Forsyth. However, in the view of the high-ranking Creole officers sitting in judgement, Herrera was acting dishonourably by striking a man they judged his social superior, whether his resentment was valid or not. The vigilante beating Herrera received was therefore legitimated, and Herrera was even made to kneel to be informed of the Court's decision.[103] Authority and hierarchy were enforced by the Court's apparent pragmatism, made necessary by the power and influence of merchants such as Forsyth, who were closely linked to the authorities because of the money owed to them by the new republic.

These public honour disputes were ostensibly conflicts between men over the respect they were due, but tensions about race and gender suffused them too. This was made clear in the case of Teniente Coronel Peter Grant, who was tried for wounding the Venezuelan sailor Seferino Sarmiento in his own Angostura house on the night of 12 August 1820. As in the Hand–Lons dispute, a superior officer was accused of striking a lower-ranked man, but here neither was on duty, and the victim was Venezuelan, not foreign.[104] It was alleged that Grant had broken into the house, attempted to rape Sarmiento's lover's sister, and then violently struck out at the sailor. Several witnesses claimed that, during the attack, Grant had publicly spoken of his antipathy towards blacks and local women. Sarmiento took the case to court in the hope that his own loss of honour – by the attack on one of his dependants – could be publicly redressed.[105] All the witnesses testified to Grant's unprovoked aggression. Domingo Mancino, a bemused sail-maker, was resting outside the arsenal after the events in question (around midnight), when he was hit by Grant passing by in a raging fury. 'When I asked him why he had hit me', Mancino told the enquiry, 'he replied that he thought that I was a woman and it was nothing; he sheathed his sword and marched away.'[106] The woman whom Grant was accused of trying to rape, 20-year-old María Andrea de la Gardera, affirmed that Grant had demanded to be allowed into her hammock, and had struck her when she refused.[107] Grant was also accused of antagonism towards people of colour. Another witness, a 36-year old black sailor, claimed that he had heard Grant saying that 'he was going to kill all the blacks that he could find in the house'.[108] Chapter 6 below discusses the importance of race to adventurers' honour. When Peter Grant was invited to give his own statement, he accused the other witnesses of lying. He denied everything. He claimed

[I had been walking along] with a girl of my acquaintance, when a *sambo* came up and … said to me 'What are you doing here, you fucking Englishman?' ['*inglés de carajo*'], to which I replied, 'I do not wish to molest you my friend', to which he responded 'Go away Sir and I will refrain from killing you'. When he said this, two other coloured men appeared with sticks and other weapons, and joining the first they tried to offend me. One of them said, 'Let's kill this fucking Englishman' and another said 'Leave him to me and I will beat him to death'. Despite these threats, I replied 'Please go away, as I am not scared of you'. When I said this, one of them charged at me with his dagger, and I responded by striking him with my sword.[109]

This account, completely at odds with those of all the other witnesses, conjured up demons of aggressive coloured people who held, Grant claimed, deep-seated resentment of him and foreigners like him. His version evoked the stories told about the death of Coronel MacDonald two years previously, with a quarrel about a woman and jealousy on the part of the local population all ending with unjustified aggression against an innocent Scottish officer. Grant claimed that he had acted in self-defence and that he was not a coward. Because there were no impartial witnesses, and the accused denied everything, the Chairman of the Court concluded that 'although there is a strong suspicion of Grant's guilt, and that his denial is simply malicious, he cannot be punished by more than eight days arrest'. Grant was therefore given the benefit of the doubt and was moved to another unit and away from Angostura.[110] There was no attempt either to find other potential witnesses or to formally assert the honour of Sarmiento or the female victim.

In the testimonies of the victim and her friends, we have a rare insight into the way foreigners were viewed outside of élite circles in Angostura. Grant was portrayed as an aggressive and ignorant foreigner, seeking physical gratification with local women with or without their consent, entering private homes without permission, expressing anger and resentment at coloured men, using his sword to strike an unarmed inferior, and lashing out in anger at strangers. Yet the allegations, acknowledged by the Court as probably an accurate reflection of events, were punished by just a short stay in prison. This was because Grant's actions dishonoured common sailors and their women, people of colour and other subalterns (in contrast to Herrera, who in the case studied above picked a fight with one of the most influential foreign merchants in Angostura). So while Grant's perceived 'malicious' lying in court did dishonour him in Creole eyes, his physical actions did not dishonour any of the Creole officers themselves or threaten existing social hierarchies, and he was therefore allowed to pass without further punishment.

Honour disputes could not and did not exist in a social vacuum. The adventurers were in the service of the Republican government, and their individual honour was necessarily affected by the bonds linking them to the state and the army. According to an English officer, Thomas Simpson, the adventurers believed that honourable behaviour was contingent upon certain conditions being met. If service had not been formally purchased by the state (through pay or provision of sustenance) or formalised by the individual through an oath of allegiance (which adventurers were loath to do),[111] then honour remained individual and consequently unblemished by any flouting of local military law. In August 1818, a junior officer John Brown was arrested and charged with breaking orders for having allowed Coronel Henry Wilson to receive visitors while under house arrest, when Brown was acting as Officer of the Guard. (Wilson himself had been charged with insubordination and conspiring to overthrow Bolívar, and shortly afterwards was expelled from the Republic).[112] Brown's defence was that he had not acted dishonourably, even though he admitted breaking the rules.[113]

Brown's case is an example of when Creole officers did accept the adventurers' arguments about honour. Brown named Simpson to defend him in court, and he argued that the 'literal interpretation of the law had already been neglected by the Government for more than a month', that Brown was 'still awaiting the promotion to teniente he had recently been promised' and that his daily rations were arriving late. This meant that nothing joined him to 'a literal execution of the Government's instructions' and that he had not broken any 'bonds of honour'.[114] In passing judgement, the members of the War Council recognised that although Brown was guilty of 'not fulfilling orders', 'as the crime committed has not produced any great evil ... Brown should be .... given an arbitrary punishment of the amount of time he has already been imprisoned ... and therefore released'.[115] They accepted Simpson's argument, based on the recognition that 'Brown ha[d] not sworn either loyalty or obedience to the Government' and that 'he [said] that what he was offered in London ha[d] not been fulfilled.'[116] This formulation demonstrates that, although Creoles usually imposed their own customs and rulings upon the disputing parties, on occasions during the early periods of the Wars of Independence they were prepared to accept the different understandings of honour brought with them by adventurers, on the condition that the potential repercussions were not serious.

Only one case survives in the archives where adventurers set up a court of enquiry to judge the actions of one of their own, and it revolved around an alleged incident of 'ungentlemanly conduct'. The case demonstrates the extent to which the foreign officers shared Creoles' concerns about maintaining a sharp dividing line between officers and their subalterns. In Angostura in June 1819, Capitán Gustavus Butler Hippisley was accused of 'conduct highly unbecoming an officer and a gentleman in striking and otherwise obstructing Sergeant William Delaney', and 'unofficerlike conduct in associating and drinking at the same table with two non-commissioned officers and two Creole shopkeepers being inconsistent in every respect with the character of an officer or gentleman'.[117] The clash occurred after the wake of a colleague who had died of fever. Hippisley was drunk at the time of the events in question, and was alleged to have struck Sargento Delany. One witness, when asked if Delany had fallen from the effect of the blow or from intoxication, replied 'Both.'[118] Because Hippisley had associated with non-commissioned officers and Creole civilians, the presiding officers judged him to have been 'laying himself open to the insults of those inferior to him in life'.[119] No formal verdict survives, but Hippisley soon returned to Britain, and this verdict may have hastened his departure from the Independent service. By 'laying himself open' to the insults of the lower classes, Hippisley's behaviour brought shame on the officers and gentlemen of the British Legion. The charge of 'ungentlemanly conduct' was felt to be so serious that it could only be assessed by a closed group of peers of the accused, rather than representatives of Venezuelan society.

The records of the military courts reveal the richly nuanced world of honour within which the adventurers met the microcosm of Venezuelan society living in Angostura. The cultural encounters across national, regional and local boundaries in this circumscribed location meant that 'cultural displays of force-fulness' were complicated.[120] Race, gender and class all competed with (and often took second place to) individual conceptions of inherent and exercised honour. The inventory of the possessions of an English Capitán Poole, who died at Upata in Guayana in November 1819, reveal that he was buried wear-ing his sword, recalling the visual nature of these demonstrations of honour.[121] The cases discussed above provide an insight into the adventurers' world of honour, indicating how drunkenness, encounters with strangers outside the 'community of honour', the death of comrades and monetary relations all oc-casionally caused adventurers to overstep the codes of honour which they felt entitled them to privilege and respect in Angostura. Women and people of colour were sometimes the victims of these displays of honour, but in those cases recorded in the archives, adventurers most often disputed amongst them-selves. The Creole authorities in Angostura generally gave the benefit of the doubt to officers and, as the case of Private Lons showed, they were extremely unsympathetic to subaltern troops' claims to equality, which were punished severely with few qualms.

1821 was a watershed with regard to the ways in which adventurers negoti-ated their honour in Gran Colombia. Before that date they duelled, fought and complained directly to Bolívar as the personification of justice in Gran Colombia.[122] The Creole authorities responded by judging extreme behaviour in their own courts, and by 1821 they were successful in asserting the primacy of republican officials and courts in the mediation of conflict. Duelling de-clined markedly. Public honour disputes were much less useful in the post-Independence world with its 'new, more egalitarian and republican sense of honour'.[123] Instead of duelling and complaining, adventurers began to nego-tiate their honour with the state after 1821, using the courts and petitions to government and, above all, making public their recognition of the authority of the Gran Colombian state. These changes are examined in Chapter 7.

Leisure and Gambling

When they were not explicitly disputing their respect and honour, officers could enjoy themselves alongside colleagues of different origins at social func-tions and activities on the fringes of warfare. These occasions took the forms of balls and parties, hunting trips, gambling and drinking sessions, and even picnics. Balls were organised by governmental authorities in honour of im-portant anniversaries, or sometimes by foreign merchants resident in Venezu-ela and seeking influence.[124] One *pardo* plantation owner near Maturín organised a picnic for 12 local women and some British and Irish officers under Coronel Blosset in 1819. He hoped to gain prestige and perhaps influ-ence through organising the event.[125] Rafael Urdaneta wrote in the same year of his intention to 'cultivate the honour of the officer class of the division' that he commanded, which contained foreigners, Venezuelans and New Granadans alike. He saw the officer-class as an extended family.[126] Drinking and eating in separate areas from the soldiers was one way of cementing this group loyalty, which was then enforced by the honour codes discussed earlier in this chapter. Masonic groups were another way of creating exclusivity and establishing difference.[127]

Social occasions were used to establish group identities, and on occasions they could bridge political divides. The meeting between Bolívar and Morillo at the Santa Ana armistice was one celebrated example, involving 'hugs, greetings, conversations, dinners, toasts, promises of friendship'.[128] The regular hunting trips described in memoirs were different, as hunting was an activity that the British and Irish officers enjoyed on their own as an expression of their masculine honour and competence. They hunted without their Creole colleagues and were accompanied only by local guides and assistants.[129] Gambling was an important component of the foreign officers' honour-asserting lifestyle in the first years of their involvement in the Wars of Independence. Gambling was 'another kind of adventure', a recreation more compatible with their transitory lifestyles than any formal business investment.[130] The late 1810s and early 1820s were a time of 'gambling propensity' in London.[131] In this sense, the 'adventure' of travel to Gran Colombia was just another gamble taken by those hoping to capitalise on their own daring risk-taking: wagering their own lives against the inhospitable climate, savage Indians, the Loyalist army, and the often treacherous sea voyage, all in the hope of returning with honour and improved status. A novel featuring mercenaries as its main characters had a penniless gambler leave his native land for Venezuela after a failed suicide attempt – casting the expeditions as one final throw of the dice.[132]

Gambling reflected the extent to which the adventurers were in constant close proximity to death and were living for short-term pleasures. Yet it was a type of adventure that the Independents were indulging in even before the foreigners arrived. Some of the adventurers found this disconcerting, as it suggested worrying intimations of equality. Adam described high-stake Angostura gambling meetings with 'upwards of fifty native officers' concentrated together.[133] The adventurers criticised the Creoles for their gambling, suggesting that it was a symptom of idleness.[134] In 1824 Robert Sutherland, a British consular official sending his first impressions to Foreign Secretary Canning, passed on a story he had heard from a retired adventurer. Rafael Urdaneta was alleged to have received a large amount of money from Bolívar 'to provide shoes for a British corps that had long marched barefooted, and he lost the sum at a gambling table; this corps continued for weeks afterwards unprovided'.[135] This story, inserted into a generally favourable portrait of one of Bolívar's most loyal officers, contrasted the uncomplaining virtue and hardy endurance of the British troops with the frivolous Creoles frittering away their money.

The British criticism of Creole gambling was that it threatened to undermine social hierarchies. One critic noted, 'there appears to be no distinction of rank: a general is often seen gambling at the same table with one of his common soldiers, on terms of perfect equality. Many negroes hold commissions in the army.'[136] According to this writer, the equality of the gaming table was dangerous, and directly related to the spectre of black men holding positions of responsibility in the armed forces. As such it was not gambling itself that the British or Irish commentators were criticising when they saw Creoles playing – it was the equality that it embodied between different social groups who ought to be at opposite ends of the social and racial orders.[137]

With time, reservations about equality and gambling were eroded. By 1820 many foreigners were gambling alongside Creoles. One example of this was a horse race organised in Angostura in April 1820.[138] On one level, national and regimental honour was being disputed between one horse representing Britain and the Albion battalion, and another representing Ireland and the Irish Legion. On another level, around five hundred dollars were bet on the outcome, 'all the Native Officers and Respectable Inhabitants were there', and other races took place after the main event, in which Creoles were well represented.[139] In contrast to the experience in Brazil, where according to Louise Guenther horse-riding was an opportunity for British merchants to escape 'Brazilian space, out towards the more neutral – and perhaps less familiar – realm of "nature"'[140], in Gran Colombia horse-racing was a rare opportunity for foreign adventurers to show off some horsemanship in front of their llanero colleagues who, on other occasions, laughed at their inability to ford rivers or overcome other obstacles posed by the environment.[141] After around 1820 there were no hard and fast rules about non-association with Creoles and other supposedly subordinate social groups, despite the fact that officers like Capitán Hippisley were reprimanded by their peers for sitting and drinking with Creole shopkeepers. Indeed, in some circumstances, officers would gamble regardless of national and racial distinctions. Louis Perú de la Croix (a French adventurer) described the nightly gaming and card-playing between Bolívar, Daniel O'Leary, himself and the other assistants in Bucaramanga in 1828.[142] Perhaps the most revealing story in which foreigner and Gran Colombian gambled together was recalled by Francisco Burdett O'Connor: in Huamachuco in Peru in March 1824:

> my countryman Coronel Arthur Sandes came to visit me. While we were chatting, General Sucre entered my room, and told Coronel Sandes that an officer was about to march for Quito, and that he was finishing a letter to a friend of his there. 'Sandes', he said, 'I know that in Quito you were engaged to be married to the Marques of Solano's daughter. But I always wished to marry that girl, and so I propose to you now, if you will allow me, that we trust our destinies to Lady Luck. Let us throw a coin in the air, to see who will win the hand of the little Marchioness. If you lose, I will include the order in my current letter, so as to marry her myself'.
>
> 'Agreed', replied Sandes. 'Because, who knows if we will ever return to Quito, or if we are soon to die in battle'. So they named me as witness to their bet, and I threw the coin in the air. General Sucre was the winner. And so it came to pass, that four years later he did return to Quito, where he married Solano's daughter.[143]

Chapter 8 examines in some detail the marriage strategies of adventurers and Creole élites in the post-war period. O'Connor's anecdote illustrates how, at least during war-time, such strategies were often rendered meaningless by the realities of campaigning. The story demonstrates the cheery fashion in which Sandes gave way to a superior Creole officer's point of view and the toss of a coin, indifferent to any personal preference that he or indeed the woman at stake might have had.[144] Creoles and foreigners would gamble with whatever prize they felt they could afford to lose. Initially at least, for some of the adventurers, this included their lives, as shown in their duelling. But by the early 1820s, duelling had largely given way to other forms of honour disputes. Gambling was a form of adventure which persisted and which foreigners shared with Hispanic Americans on an equal footing. There are parallels here with British activity in India, where although race was fundamental to all colonial encounters, important bonds were formed by common perceptions of shared status among the upper classes of both local and incoming actors.[145]

The transition from colonial to republican systems, however, and the consequences that military mobilisation had for identity formation, complicated these matters still further than in India. Chivalric individual honour clashed with new republican ideas of virtue, and post-war processes of institutionalisation, despite the way that it neatly dovetailed with the 'warrior's honour'. Creole attempts at nation-building were set against the adventurers' (and some Creoles') concerns with personal individual honour. Duelling and chivalric parades therefore suffered the same fate as other supposedly outdated practices. The courts and Congress became established as the new field of honour in the post-war period. For example, the 1821 honour dispute between Antonio Nariño and John Devereux surpassed their individual differences and became the tool for working out differences of authority between military and civilian leaders, and between the Executive and Legislative powers.[146] Devereux felt (at least initially) that he had acted in a chivalrous fashion to protect the honour of a defenceless woman. Nariño wanted to defend the dignity of his office and the state from the scurrilous insults of a newly arrived foreigner who had not earned his respect in campaign or battle. There was no duel because Nariño was able to secure his own honour by the physical imprisonment of his challenger, and eventually by sending him for judicial trial in Caracas. Nariño thus confirmed that, by 1821, the state had become the ultimate arbiter on matters of honour and consequently Devereux backtracked considerably. Devereux repeatedly stressed that he had never proposed a duel, nor intended to offend the honour of the Vice-President or the Republic. He blamed his translator's 'essential misunderstanding of the concepts'.[147]

For the first adventurers, therefore, honour remained an individual affair until around 1821, to be publicly affirmed against a hostile environment through displays of bravery, duelling and the physical defence of the integrity of social and military hierarchies. During the Wars of Independence the nature of their honour underwent a transformation as a result of the encounter with Creoles and other sections of Gran Colombian society. Republican courts were confirmed as the ultimate arbiters of honour. The state was increasingly recognised as the fountain of justice, and honour was increasingly defined by relationships with Creoles and upon a glorious and heroic new national history shared by Gran Colombians of all backgrounds. As a means towards understanding how and why this happened, Chapter 5 considers the changes in collective identities that spread across the relationships formed by adventurers and Gran Colombians during the Wars of Independence.

Notes

1   Albert Camus, 'Carnets 1935–7', NRF/Gallimard 26 (1962) p. 26, quoted in Peter Phipps, 'Tourism, Terrorists, Death and Value', in Raminder Kaur and John Hutnyk, (eds), *Travel Worlds: Journeys in Contemporary Cultural Politics* (London, 1999), p. 80.
2   For a synthesis, see Lyman L. Johnson and Sonya Lipsett-Rivera (eds), *The Faces of Honor: Sex, Shame and Violence in Colonial Latin America* (Albuquerque, NM, 1998), pp. 8–14. For Venezuela, see Luis Pellicer, *La vivencia del honor en la provincia de Venezuela 1774–1809* (Caracas, 1996); for New Granada, see Margarita Garrido, *Reclamos y representaciones: variaciones sobre la política en el Nuevo Reino de Granada, 1770–1815* (Bogotá, 1993), pp. 18–28. Twinam, *Public Lives, Private Secrets*, pp. 31–33 contains a sophisticated criticism of much of the historiography on honour.
3   It should be clear that this analysis is only appropriate to the Gran Colombian case, where military mobilisation was so widespread and long-lasting. Elsewhere in Latin America the transition from colonial to republican rule differed considerably, and this had diverse consequences in the post-Independence era.
4   Uribe Urán, *Honorable Lives*, p. 11.
5   Elías Pino Iturrieta, *País Archipiélago*, pp. 68–69.
6   Michael Ignatieff, *The Warrior's Honour: Ethnic War and the Modern Conscience* (London, 1998), pp. 109–63.
7   Ignatieff, *The Warrior's Honour, p.* 17.
8   Mark Girouard, *The Return to Camelot: Chivalry and the English Gentleman* (London, 1981), p. 36, p. 93.
9   Cannadine, *Ornamentalism*, p. 5.
10 Manuel Antonio López, *Recuerdos históricos del coronel Manuel Antonio López, Colombia, Perú 1819–1826* (Bogotá, 1955), p. 12.
11 *El Colombiano de Guayas*, Edición Estraordinaria, 4 November 1828.
12 Bernardo Tovar Zambrano, 'Porque los muertos mandan. El imaginario patriótico de la historia colombiana', in Carlos Miguel Ortiz Sarmiento and Bernardo Tovar Zambrano, (eds), *Predecir el pasado* (Bogotá, 1997), pp. 125–69; Rebecca Earle, '*Padres de la Patria* and the Ancestral Past: Commemorations of Independence in Nineteenth Century Spanish America', *JLAS*, 34:4 (2002), pp. 775–805.
13 Aline Helg, 'Simón Bolívar and the Spectre of *Pardocracia*: José Padilla in Post-Independence Cartagena', *JLAS*, 35:3 (2003) pp. 447–71.
14 Clive Emsley, 'The Impact of War and Military Participation on Britain and France 1792–1815', in Emsley and James Walvin, (eds), *Artisans, Peasants and Proletarians 1760–1860* (London, 1985), pp. 57–80; also Carolyn Kay Steedman, *The Radical Soldier's Tale* (London, 1988), pp. 27–48.
15 This tension is generally hidden by the common tendency of military and naval historians to translate all ranks into English, as in Vale, *A War Betwixt Englishmen*, or

into Spanish, as in Lambert, *Voluntarios británicos e irlandeses*. In order to retain some of the uncertainty of the time, in this book all ranks in the Spanish and Independent (Colombian) armies are given in Spanish, whereas ranks in the British army are given in English. The spelling of General is the same in both languages but it is always apparent by context to which force the General in question belonged.

16 Anon., *The Soldiers of Venezuela: A Tale in Two Volumes*, Vol. 1., p. 114; E. L. Joseph, *Warner Arundell*, pp. 250–53; Robinson, *Journal of an Expedition*, p. 5; [Vowell] *The Earthquake of Caraccas, p. 197*; [Vowell], *The Savannas of Varinas*, p. 36. Francisco de Miranda and Sir Robert Ker Porter had *Don Quijote* in their travelling libraries, Dupouy, (ed.), *Sir Robert Ker Porter's Caracas Diary*, p. lxxix; Pedro Grases and Arturo Uslar Pietri, *Los libros de Miranda* (Caracas, 1967), p. 13; *Morning Chronicle*, 2 November 1818. Daniel O'Leary read *Don Quijote* while on campaign in 1829. Pérez Vila, *Vida de Daniel Florencio O'Leary*, p. 446.

17 Jean-François Dauxion-Lavaysee, *A Statistical, Commercial, and Political Description of Venezuela, Trinidad, Margarita and Tobago: containing various anecdotes and observations Illustrative of the Past and Present State of these Interesting Countries, with a Beautiful Map of the United and Independent Provinces of Venezuela and New Granada* (London, 1820), p. vi. The volume was authored by a landowner in Trinidad, and edited by supporters of John Devereux to encourage Irish enlistment; it was dedicated to 'Major-General John Devereux'.

18 José Manuel Groot, *Historia de la Gran Colombia 1819–1830, Tercer volumen de la historia eclesiástica y civil de Nueva Granada* (Caracas, 1941), p. 126.

19 C. S. Cochrane, *Journal of a Residence and Travels in Colombia*, Vol. 2, p. 285.

20 For example C. S. Cochrane to Mary English, 9 October 1825, London, EP, HA157/3/168.

21 John Potter Hamilton, *Travels Through The Interior Provinces of Colombia*, Vol. 2 (London, 1827), p. 25.

22 Francisco Sierra, 6 April 1824, Bogotá, AGNC R, AC, Legajo 29, fo. 940.

23 Summarising the historiography on this subject, see Claire Brewster, 'Women and the Spanish-American Wars of Independence', *Feminist Review*, 79 (2005), pp. 20–35.

24 Manuela Sáenz (b. 1797 Quito, d. 1856 Paita, Peru) was married to an English merchant, James Thorne. See Pamela S. Murray, 'Loca or Libertadora? Manuela Sáenz in the eyes of History and Historians, 1900–c. 1990', *JLAS*, 33:2 (2001), pp. 291–310.

25 O'Leary, *Narración de O'Leary*, Vol. 1, p. 568.

26 For example Manuel Manrique, 23 January 1819, Angostura. AGNV GDG, Vol. 9, fo. 11.

27 This topic is explored in much greater depth in Brown, 'Adventurers, Foreign Women and Masculinity in the Wars of Independence in Colombia'.

28 Anon., *The Soldiers of Venezuela*, Vol. 1, p. 193.

29 Linda Colley, *Captives: Britain, Empire and the World 1600–1850* (London, 2002), p. 147.

30 Robinson, *Journal of an Expedition*, p. 147.

31 Chesterton, *A Narrative of Proceedings in Venezuela and South America*, pp. 46–47.

32 Wright, *Destellos de Gloria*, pp. 35–36.

33 Lambert, *Voluntarios británicos e irlandeses*, Vol. 1, pp. 158–60.

34 Various interpretations of Donald MacDonald's death are discussed in Matthew Brown, 'Scots in South America', in Iain McPhail and Karly Kehoe, (eds), *A Panorama of Scottish History: Contemporary Perspectives* (Glasgow, 2004), pp. 124–44.

35 V. G. Kiernan, *The Duel in European History: Honour and the Reign of Aristocracy* (Oxford, 1988), p. 152.

36 Kiernan, *The Duel in European History*, p. 152.

37 Robert Shoemaker, 'Male Honour and the Decline of Public Violence in Eighteenth-century London', *Social History*, 26:2 (2001), pp. 195–96; Green, *The Adventurous Male*, p. 193; O'Connell Papers, UCD, P12/3/223; James Kelly, *'That Damn'd Thing Called Honour'*, Duelling in Ireland 1570–1860 (Cork, 1995), pp. 242–47.

38 Kelly, *'That Damn'd Thing Called Honour'*, pp. 239–40.

39 Kiernan, *The Duel in European History*, pp. 71–72, p. 258. The Catholic Church formally prohibited duelling at the Council of Trent in 1563. An excellent study of issues of duelling and honour in this period, Pieter Spierenburg, (ed.), *Men and Violence: Gender, Honor and Rituals in Modern Europe and America* (Chicago, Ohio, 1998), ignores both Spain and Hispanic America. See also Pablo Piccato, 'Politics and the Technology of Honor: Dueling in Turn of the Century Mexico', *Journal of Social History*, 33 (1999), pp. 331–54. Mark A. Burkholder, 'Honor and Honors in Colonial Spanish America', in Johnson and Lipsett-Rivera, (eds), *The Faces of Honor*, contains a short section on sixteenth- and seventeenth-century duels and sword fights, p. 34.

40 Stern, *Secret History of Gender*, p. 161; also Julian Pitt-Rivers, 'Honour and Social Status', in J. G. Peristiany, (ed.), *Honour and Shame: The Values of Mediterranean Society* (Chicago, 1966), p. 30.

41 In his sole reference to the continent, Kiernan in *The Duel in European History* (p. 300) claimed that South Americans duelled with blow-pipes loaded with poison. This was a wilfully erroneous reading of an article in the *Edinburgh Review*, 86 (1826) pp. 299–314, which itself was speculating mischievously that these hunting weapons 'will become the weapons of gentlemen in the new republics of South America'. The travel book that both were commenting upon, Charles Waterton, *Wanderings in South America* (London, 1826) did not mention duelling at all.

42 Shoemaker, 'Male Honour and the Decline of Public Violence', p. 197, pp. 204–5; Robert A. Nye, *Masculinity and Male Codes of Honor in Modern France* (New York, 1993), p. 23, p. 132; John Keegan, *The Face of Battle*, p. 316.

43 Alexander Alexander wrote that out of regard for Britain, Simón Bolívar allowed the adventurers to duel, while threatening Creoles with the firing squad should they join in. Howell (ed.), *The Life of Alexander Alexander*, Vol. 2, pp. 26–28.

44 W. C. Jones to President of Colombia, 4 November 1820, Angostura, AGNC, Sección República, Fondo Negocios Administrativos, 11, ff. 42–43.

45 Howell (ed.), *The Life of Alexander Alexander*, Vol. 2, p. 39.

46 Kenneth S. Greenberg, *Honor and Slavery: Lies, Duels, Noses, Masks, Dressing as a Woman, Gifts, Strangers, Humanitarianism, Death, Slave Rebellions, The Proslavery Argument, Baseball, Hunting and Gambling in the Old South* (Princeton, NJ, 2002), pp. 81–82.

47 References to these duels come from *The Times*, 9 February 1818; Hippisley, *Narrative of the Expedition to the Rivers Orinoco and Apure*, p. 136; Weatherhead, *An Account of the Late Expedition Against the Isthmus of Darien*, p. 6; 'Diary of Robert James Young', p. 13; Hippisley, *Narrative of the Expedition to the rivers Orinoco and Apure*, p. 555; Pérez Vila, *Vida de Daniel Florencio O'Leary*, p. 76; *Belfast Chronicle*, rpd. in *CMP*, 11 February 1820; Chesterton, *A Narrative of Proceedings in Venezuela and South America*, p. 107; Adam, *Journal of Voyages to Marguaritta, Trinidad and Maturín*, p. 85; Howell (ed.), *The Life of Alexander Alexander*, Vol. 2, p. 139; *DEP*, 15 July 1820; [Cowley], *Recollections of a Service of Three Years*, p. 83.

48 Peter Linebaugh and Marcus Rediker, *The Many-Headed Hydra: The Sailors, Slaves, Commoners and the Hidden History of the Revolutionary Atlantic* (London, 2000), pp. 145–67.

49 M'Mahon, *Jamaica Plantership*, p. 11.

50 Howell (ed.), *The Life of Alexander Alexander*, Vol. 2, p. 113.

51 Adam, *Journal of Voyages to Marguaritta, Trinidad and Maturín*, p. 11; Chesterton, *Peace*,

War and Adventure, p. 107.

52 Howell (ed.), *The Life of Alexander Alexander*, Vol. 2, p. 31; Joseph, *Warner Arundell*, p. 253.

53 Howell (ed.), *The Life of Alexander Alexander*, Vol. 2, p. 113; [Anon], *Narrative of a Voyage to the Spanish Main*, p. 36.

54 Howell (ed.), *The Life of Alexander Alexander*, Vol. 2, p. 131.

55 *Black Dwarf*, 18 April 1821. See also Alan Smith, *The Established Church and Popular Religion, 1750–1850* (London, 1971), p. 52.

56 Stephen Brumwell, *Redcoats: The British Soldier and War in the Americas, 1755–1763* (Cambridge, 2002), pp. 88–89; Holmes, *Redcoat*, pp. 284–88.

57 For examples of these accusations see Joseph, *Warner Arundell*, pp. 179–82.

58 Kiernan, *The Duel in European History*, pp. 210–22; Kelly, 'That Damn'd Thing Called Honour', pp. 223–25.

59 Christopher J. Wheatley, '"I hear the Irish are naturally brave": dramatic portrayals of the Irish soldier in the seventeenth and eighteenth centuries', *Irish Sword*, 19:77 (1995), pp. 187–96. See the interesting comments on the subject in John Besant, *Narrative of the Expedition under General MacGregor against Porto Bello: Including an Account of the Voyage; and of the Causes which Led to its Final Overthrown (by An Officer who Miraculously Escaped)* (London and Edinburgh, 1820), p. 14.

60 Declaration of Alexandro Rulo, 30 October 1818, translated from the original French to Spanish in AGI Cuba, Legajo 906.

61 Anonymous fragment of a letter from La Guayra, 13 October 1820, in AGNC R GYM, Vol. 325, fo. 916.

62 Paul Verna, *Robert Sutherland: Un amigo de Bolívar en Haiti*, pp. 60–62. Some Spanish officers also duelled. In Puerto Cabello on 23 April 1822, Colonel Tomás García was wounded by Pascual Churruca, Marshall La Torre's aide-de-camp. See Tomás Pérez Tenreiro, 'Tomás García', Fundación Polar, *Diccionario de Historia de Venezuela*.

63 Howell (ed.), *The Life of Alexander Alexander*, Vol. 2, p. 303.

64 General Antonio Nariño (b. 1766 Bogotá, d. 1823 Leiva) returned from imprisonment in Spain in the 1810s, and was named Vice-President of Colombia.

65 Bolívar to Santander, 10 July 1821, Valencia, in Germán Arciniegas (ed.), *Cartas Santander – Bolívar 1820–1822*, Vol. 3 (Bogotá, 1988), p. 119. Thomas Manby agreed in a letter to Baron Von Eben, 10 December 1821, Cali, translated into Spanish (without English original) in *MOL*, Vol. 12, pp. 350–51. For a different and compelling perspective on the affair see Scott, *Mary English*, p. 90.

66 Nariño to Bolívar, 28 June 1821, Rosario, in Guillermo Hernández de Alba (ed.), *Archivo Nariño, Vol. 6, 1816–1823* (Bogotá, 1990), p. 169.

67 Nariño to Congress, 12 July 1821, Rosario, in Hernández de Alba (ed.), *Archivo Nariño, Vol. 6, 1816–1823*, pp. 187–90.

68 Nariño to Bolívar, 31 May 1821, Rosario, in *Archivo Nariño, Vol. 6, 1816–1823*, pp. 131–33.

69 Nariño to Bolívar, 31 May 1821, Rosario, in *Archivo Nariño, Vol. 6, 1816–1823*, pp. 131–33.

70 Diego Bautista Urbaneja to Soublette, 8 June 1821, Rosario, in José Felix Blanco and Ramón Azpúrua, (eds), *Documentos para la vida pública del Libertador de Colombia, Perú y Bolivia*, Vol. 7 (Caracas, 1875–77), fo. 611. Urbaneja (b. 1782 Barcelona, Venezuela, d. 1856 Caracas) was a lawyer and administrator who occupied most of the principal positions in Colombian and later Venezuelan government.

71 John Keegan, *The Face of Battle* (London, 1991), p. 190.

72 Carlos Diego Minchin to Congress, 1 February 1854, Bogotá, AGNC HDS, Vol. 62, ff. 504–6.

73 O'Leary, *Narración de O'Leary,* Vol. 2, p. 82.
74 Thomas Manby, 23 March 1835, Bogotá, AGNC HDS, Vol. 30, fo. 979. For Mackintosh's own account, see Mackintosh, 20 March 1835, Bogotá, AGNC HDS, Vol. 30, fo. 976.
75 For 'individual honour', I am working from the definition presented by Lyman L. Johnson, in 'Dangerous Words, Provocative Gestures and Violent Acts', in Johnson and Lipsett-Rivera, (eds), *The Faces of Honor*, p. 129. 'In Buenos Aires, as elsewhere in the Spanish Empire, the successful assertion of personal honour depended upon an individual's inherited characteristics, such as European birth or descent, legitimacy, family social status, and personal attainments such as social influence, wealth, education, reputation for honesty, courage and restraint. ... Few social historians of colonial Spanish America would deny that a desire to protect individual honour defined in essential ways relations among members of the élite.'
76 My thanks to Reuben Zahler for his perceptive comments on this section.
77 Johnson, 'Dangerous Words, Provocative Gestures and Violent Acts', p. 149.
78 Twinam, 'Las reformas sociales de los borbones: una interpretación revisionista', in Victor M. Uribe Urán and Luis Javier Ortiz Mesa, (eds), *Naciones, gentes y territorios: Ensayos de historia e historiografía comparada de América Latina y el Caribe* (Medellín, 2000), pp. 73–102.
79 Stern, *Secret History of Gender,* p. 161.
80 Use of Mary Louise Pratt's concept in this sense comes from Charles F. Walker, 'Crime in the Time of the Great Fear: Indians and the State in the Peruvian Southern Andes, 1780–1820', in Ricardo Salvatore, Carlos Aguirre, and Gilbert Joseph, (eds), *Crime and Punishment in Latin America: Law and Society since Late Colonial Times* (Durham, NC, 2001), p. 35.
81 See for example Stern, *Secret History of Gender,* pp. 161–68.
82 Ana Rooke to James Hamilton, 26 October 1818, Barbados, AL, Vol. 14, Roll 45, fo. 9.
83 For a typical dispute revolving around the 'insulting' confiscation of property see 'Memorial to the Honourable Members of the Council of Government of the Republic of Venezuela', 14 January 1819, Angostura. AL, Vol. 14, Roll 45, fo. 17.
84 Santiago España, 1 October 1820, Nueva Guayana, AGNV GDG, Vol. 12, ff. 167–84. For Hand's career see José Rafael Fortique, *Dos legionarios irlandeses en el ejército de Bolívar* (Maracaibo, 2001), pp. 13–36.
85 Fernando Mendoza, 15 September 1820, Soledad, AGNC R, AC, Legajo 76, fo. 131.
86 Santiago Mariño, 26 September 1820, Angostura, AGNC R, AC, Legajo 76, fo. 143. A Loyalist *hacendado*, imprisoned in Angostura at the time, reported that the rebellion took place because the troops were drunk. 'Copia de la declaración tomada a Don Feliciano Pérez benido de Guayana', 19 February 1819, La Bannosa, AGI Cuba, Legajo 898A, 'Asuntos pertenecientes a la comandancia de los llanos'.
87 Private John Jones, 23 September 1820, Ciudad de Guayana, AGNC R, AC, Legajo 76, fo. 146.
88 Collective representation of 'All the English Troops', 25 September 1820, Ciudad de Guayana, AGNC R, AC, Legajo 76, fo. 143.
89 Of around two hundred soldiers, 47 were listed as being in hospital or absent on missions. Therefore, around 150 were involved in the rebellion, and either 15 or 16 were shot. The list of those not involved is in AGNC R, AC, Legajo 76, ff. 160–61; there is no surviving list of those involved, or of those executed.
90 Private James Haworth, 6 October 1820, AGNV GDG, Vol. 12, fo. 177.
91 These insults appear in the Spanish translation of John Taylor and Rupert Hand's (English) testimonies, 15 September 1820, Soledad, as *'pícaro, ladomismo, y ladrón'.* AGNC R, AC, Vol. 76, fo. 136, fo. 147.
92 Rupert Hand, 6 October 1820, Angostura, AGNV GDG, Vol. 12, fo. 179.

93 Santiago de España, 17 October 1820, Angostura, AGNV GDG, Vol. 12, fo. 183.
94 Urbaneja to Comandante General, 18 October 1820, Angostura, AGNV GDG, Vol. 12, fo. 184.
95 Creole fear of possible rebellions amongst the British troops is made clear in 'Declaración de Cristóbal Ricaus', 11 April 1819, Puerto Cabello, AGI Cuba, Legajo 911A.
96 William Lyster, 20 July 1820, Angostura, AGNV GDG, Vol. 12, ff. 207–22.
97 Arthur Jones, 27 July 1820, Angostura, AGNV GDG, Vol. 12, f. 216.
98 FitzThomas, 29 July 1820, Angostura, AGNV GDG, Vol. 12, ff. 218–19.
99 José Martínez, 29 July 1820, Angostura, AGNV GDG, Vol. 12, f. 220.
100 Doroteo Vélez, 14 December 1818, Angostura, AGNV GDG, Vol. 3, fo. 126.
101 AGNV GDG, Vol. 3, f. 152.
102 Asunción Ferrera, 2 January 1819, Angostura, AGNV GDG, Vol. 3, fo. 156
103 Juan José Conde, 19 December 1818, Angostura, AGNV GDG, Vol. 3, fo. 153.
104 The case is discussed in some detail in Matthew Brown, 'Scots in South America', pp. 139–43.
105 Seferino Sarmiento, 13 August 1820, Angostura, AGNV GDG, Vol. 12, fo. 140.
106 Domingo Mancino, 13 August 1820, Angostura, AGNV GDG, Vol. 12, fo. 142.
107 María Andrea de la Gardera, 13 August 1820, Angostura, AGNV GDG, Vol. 12, fo. 144. This was the only accusation of rape against an adventurer discovered in the archives; other scholars of the period have emphasised how such behaviour was covered by the umbrella of 'indiscipline' and was rarely explicitly addressed by the authorities. Rape could be a means of bringing shame and degradation to families, communities, fathers and brothers, as well as the women themselves. The sources consulted simply do not reveal if or how often this occurred. See Earle, 'Rape and the Anxious Republic: Revolutionary Colombia, 1810–1830', in Elizabeth Dore and Maxine Molyneux, *Hidden Histories of Gender and the State in Latin America* (Chapel Hill, NC, 2000), pp. 134–42; Lipsett-Rivera, 'A Slap in the Face of Honor: Social Transgression and Women in Late Colonial Mexico', in Johnson and Lipsett-Rivera, (eds), *The Faces of Honor*, pp. 194–95; Esdaile, *The Peninsular War: A New History*, p. 151, p. 198.
108 Tomás José, 13 August 1820, Angostura, AGNV GDG, Vol. 12, fo. 143.
109 Peter Grant, 13 August 1820, Angostura, AGNV GDG, Vol. 12, ff. 143–4.
110 Diego Bautista Urbaneja, 21 August 1820, Angostura, AGNV GDG, Vol. 12, fo. 146.
111 Chesterton, *A Narrative of Proceedings in Venezuela*, p. 26.
112 Carlos Arbeláez Urdaneta, 'Dos Wilson en la guerra de independencia', *BANH*, 94 (1944), pp. 237–42; Matilde Moliner de Arévalo, 'Ingleses en los Ejércitos de Bolívar: El coronel Enrique Wilson', *Revista de indias*, 51 (1953), pp. 89–111.
113 John Brown, 4 August 1818, Angostura, AGNV GDG, Vol. 4, fo. 475.
114 Thomas Simpson, 11 August 1818, AGNV GDG, Vol. 4, fo. 481.
115 Declaration of the War Council, 15 October 1818, Angostura, AGNV GDG, Vol. 4, fo. 484.
116 José Olivares, 15 October 1818, Angostura, AGNV GDG, Vol. 4, fo. 484.
117 Declaration of Court of Enquiry, June 1819 [no date], Angostura, AGNV GDG, Legajo 12, fo. 88. In contrast to the other court documentation discussed above, all the documents referring to this court of enquiry were only written in English (hence Sergeant rather than Sargento Delany). Gustavus Butler Hippisley (dates unknown) was the son of Gustavus Mathias Hippisley. After leaving Venezuela in 1820 he wrote several articles and poems including *Hours of Idleness* (undated, co-published with his wife) and *Siege of Barcelona* (London, 1842).

118 George Evans, June 1819 [no date], Angostura, AGNV GDG, Vol. 12, fo. 90.
119 William Mahony, June 1819 [no date], Angostura, AGNV GDG, Vol. 12, fo. 96. Note that for sargentos and sargentos-mayor like Delany and Harrison there was no prohibition against such association.
120 Stern, *Secret History of Gender*, p. 161.
121 'Inventario a abaluo de los bienes que quedaron por fallecimiento del Capitan Inglés', November 1819, AGNV GDG, Legajo 9, ff. 143–44.
122 For an example see J.D. Farrar to 'Most Excellent Sir' [Bolívar], in English, n.d. [1821], AGNC R GYM, Vol. 325, fo. 204.
123 Chambers, *From Subjects to Citizens*, p. 246.
124 Chesterton, *Peace, War and Adventure*, Vol. 2, p. 129. Also on the balls hosted by Hamilton, see *Correo del Orinoco*, 21 July 1821, and Adam, *Journal of Voyages to Marguaritta, Trinidad and Maturín*, p. 135.
125 Adam, *Journal of Voyages to Marguaritta, Trinidad and Maturín*, p. 69, p. 80. Adam did not record the name of his pardo benefactor.
126 Urdaneta to English, 1 May 1819, Norte [Margarita], EP, HA157/6/74.
127 Julio Hoenigsberg, *Influencia revolucionaria de la masonería en Europa y América. Esbozos históricos* (Bogotá, 1944), pp. 151–78.
128 Tomás Polanco Alcántara, *Simón Bolívar: Ensayo de una interpretación biográfica a través de sus documentos* (Caracas, 1994), p. 417. For another example see Rafael Sevilla, *Memorias de un oficial del ejército español; campañas contra Bolívar y los separatistas* (Madrid, 1916), p. 195.
129 On hunting and masculinity, see John M. Mackenzie, 'The Imperial Pioneer and Hunter and the British Masculine Stereotype in late Victorian and Edwardian times', in J. A. Mangan and James Walvin, (eds), *Manliness and Masculinity: Middle Class Masculinity in Britain and America, 1800–1940* (Manchester, 1987), pp. 176–95, and also Greenberg, *Honor and Slavery*, pp. 115–31. Hunting does not emerge from the sources consulted as an important constituent of Creole masculinity.
130 Green, *The Adventurous Male*, p. 65; see also Joseph, *Warner Arundell*, p. 253.
131 Macaroni, *Memoirs of the Life and Adventures of Colonel Macaroni*, pp. 293–94; Griffith Dawson, *The First Latin American Debt Crisis*, p. 40.
132 Anon., *The Soldiers of Venezuela*, Vol. 1., pp. 55–57.
133 Adam, *Journal of Voyages to Marguaritta, Trinidad and Maturín*, p. 110.
134 Chesterton, *A Narrative of Proceedings in Venezuela and South America*, p. 41, Anon. [Cowley], *Recollections of a Service of Three Years*, pp. 89–90.
135 Robert Sutherland to Canning, 5 July 1824, Maracaibo, TNA FO 18/8, fo. 103.
136 *CMP*, 17 December 1819.
137 See C. S. Cochrane, *Journal of a Residence and Travels in Colombia*, p. 220; Anon., *Narrative of a Voyage to the Spanish Main*, p. 116; Richard Clough Anderson Jr, *The Diary and Journal of Richard Clough Anderson Jr., 1814–1826*, ed. Alfred Tischendorff and E. Taylor Parks (Durham, NC, 1964), p. 148, p. 224, p. 230, p. 251, p. 265; John Potter Hamilton, *Travels Through the Interior Provinces of Colombia*, Vol. 2, p. 18, p. 61; Anon. [Cowley], *Recollections of a Service of Three Years*, p. 242; Lowe, 'A Brief Sketch of Operations', EP, HA157/6/28, fo. 7.
138 'Desafío de caballos' in Museo Bolivariano, Caracas, repr. in Pedro Grases, (ed.), *Impresos de Angostura* (Caracas, 1969), p. 91 and in Brown and Roa, (eds), *Militares extranjeros*, p. 83.
139 D. G. Egan to Anon., 20 May 1820, repr. in *DEP*, 29 July 1820.
140 Guenther, *British Merchants in Nineteenth-Century Brazil*, p. 98.
141 As in Cochrane, *Journal of a Residence and Travels in Colombia*, p. 473.
142 Luis Perú de la Croix, *Diario de Bucaramanga; o Vida pública y privada del Libertador, Simón Bolívar* (Paris, 1912), p. 182.

143 O'Connor, *Independencia americana*, p. 105. Arthur Sandes died a bachelor in Cuenca in 1834.
144 Sucre earlier competed with O'Leary for the attention of a woman in Guayaquil in 1823, as cited in Pérez Vila, *Vida de Daniel Florencio O'Leary*, pp. 140–41.
145 This is the argument of Cannadine in *Ornamentalism*.
146 José Manuel Restrepo, *Diario político y militar: Memorias sobre los sucesos importantes de la época para servir a la Historia de la Revolución de Colombia y de la Nueva Granada, desde 1819 para adelante*, 4 Vols (Bogotá, 1954), p. 125, entry for 14 October 1821.
147 For discussion of this dispute, see Brown, 'Adventurers, Foreign Women and Masculinity', pp. 45–46. Santander accused O'Leary of challenging him to a duel in 1827; O'Leary denied this. Pérez Vila, *Vida de Daniel Florencio O'Leary*, p. 342. The duel was only slowly incorporated into New Granadan political life in the 1830s and 1840s, probably in imitation of the contemporary resurgence in France in the same period. For one example see Botero Herrera, *Estado, nación y provincia de Antioquia*, p. 123.

CHAPTER FIVE

Nations and Armies

No one saw him disembark in the unanimous night, no one saw the bamboo canoe sinking into the sacred mud, but within a few days no one was unaware that the silent man was from the South and that his *patria* was one of the infinite villages upstream on the violent mountainside, where the Zend tongue is not contaminated by Greek and where leprosy is infrequent.

(Jorge Luis Borges, 1945)[1]

In Gran Colombia, nations were much more the consequence of the wars of independence than they were their cause.[2] Race-based identities and caste hierarchies were also substantially reconceptualised in this period, as Indians and free blacks went from being subjects to citizens, even though many critics detect little long-term change once the dust had settled and arms had been laid down. As Aline Helg has observed, race was absolutely fundamental in negotiating and constructing collective identities (and often in preventing the successful survival of such identities) in Caribbean Gran Colombia in this period.[3] This and the subsequent chapter outline the argument that having foreigners in the midst of a 'national' army of 'liberation' catalysed the formulation of national Gran Colombian identity out of the institution of the military, an identity which was delineated upon race and shaped by the continued prevalence of slavery across the region. In 1830 the Gran Colombian state fell apart, causing problems for the national identities of Bolivarian loyalists (many of them European by birth) who still considered themselves to be *colombianos*.

The presence of the 'nation' in discussions about sovereignty and representation was common throughout the Hispanic world at the end of the eighteenth century.[4] The Spanish empire was divided into the *'república de los españoles'* and the *'república de los indios'*, each with their own legal jurisdictions and exclusive membership. Both of these legal groups were often talked of as *naciones*, although, as Mark Thurner has demonstrated, they were far from equal. Social and racial hierarchies shaped colonial society, and were determined to a large extent by 'schisms' which ran on through post-colonial nations.[5] In the Americas, Spanish colonial rule was constituted by a plurality of kingdoms (*reinos*) just as it was in the Iberian peninsula. As Jaime Rodriguez put it concisely, 'Spanish Americans considered their *patrias* to be kingdoms in the worldwide Spanish monarchy, and not colonies.'[6] When in 1808 Napoleon replaced King Ferdinand VII with his own brother, Joseph,

the Spanish state was not able to prevent the American territories from frag-
menting into the various kingdoms and triggering the formation of nations
which competed for representation, sovereignty and authority.[7] François-
Xavier Guerra argued that the Wars of Independence were neither national
nor anti-colonial but rather an arena for competition between multiple over-
lapping identities and loyalties to nations and *pueblos* (towns) which, as Brian
Hamnett pointed out, had been politicised during the late colonial period.[8] It
was the extended period of warfare against Spain that triggered the new and
now political 'self-definition of nation' on the part of the Creole élites who
directed the conflict.[9] In many ways these conflicts were the fruits of decades
of tension over the meaning of *patria* and nation based upon the political ideals of the Enlightenment.[10]

In the Viceroyalty of New Granada, the Captaincy-General of Venezuela,
and the Presidency of Quito, the Loyalist reconquest after 1815 put an end to
the first period of warfare with its mobilisation based on towns and cities and
the colonial militia system.[11] From 1816, with his expedition from Aux Cayes
in Haiti, Simón Bolívar began the process of constructing a larger ideological
basis for the struggle against Spain, drawing on notions of an American nation. The new political entities that eventually replaced the rule of the Spanish Crown were the result of outright military conflict on a continental scale,
the experience of which branded new notions of collective identity on to the
warring parties.[12] In the face of mass desertion, deaths through disease and
wounds received in battle, the remaining soldiers developed close bonds of
loyalty and identity based on the obstacles they had overcome. In this way,
'Gran-Colombianness' developed primarily as an identity held by veteran soldiers who had taken part in patriotic endeavours.[13] It was thus open to all
men regardless of their ethnic or national origin. It was no coincidence that
Bolívar opened up his idea of the Colombian nation at the same time – 1816 –
as he began to recruit foreign mercenaries and renewed his efforts to bring
slaves and indigenous peoples into his depleted armies. The arrival of British
and Irish soldiers and sailors to Gran Colombia made questions of collective
identity more pressing because, by their explicit and acknowledged 'foreignness', they served as a marker for the nation that was now, in the transition
from colony to republic, 'emotionally plausible and politically viable'.[14]

Building on Guerra's insights, the Wars of Independence in Gran Colombia can be seen as a period of foundational fighting, lasting over a decade in
many parts of the continent, which catalysed thinking about national identities. These wars were shrouded in a culture of adventure that provided the
necessary heroes, symbols, myths and legends upon which national identities
could be constructed in subsequent decades.[15] This was as much a conscious
experiment on the part of leaders such as Bolívar who wished to create nations to support the new state as it was the result of unintended and unexpected consequences. The outcome of military campaigns against colonial
armies was not, as C. A. Bayly put it, 'pseudo nations'.[16] Rather, the ebbs and
flows of military campaigning, the realities of large-scale military mobilisation

and the large distances covered by 'armies of liberation' served in themselves
to trigger thinking about nations, *patrias* and loyalty to political institutions.[17]
As military mobilisation and campaigning – and resistance to them – involved
virtually all sections of society, the growth of national identities (and the difficulties they faced in becoming established) was more organic and complicated than a simple 'top-down' imposition or invention.[18]

National sentiment initially remained the preserve of relatively small political and military groups because military service was largely unpopular outside of the Gran Colombian élites (and often within them) because of forced
conscription and the vast distances recruits had to travel away from their
homes. National identity differed from loyalty to the state in that it was primary experienced, in this period, through the military. Military leaders claiming to be loyal to the nation often expressed discontent with the state and its
civilian leaders.[19] Outside the military therefore, across all of Gran Colombia
– but particularly outside its Andean heartland, as Alfonso Múnera has argued – local and regional identities were much more important for men in
this period than any national loyalty: the *patria chica* of town, province, regiment or political grouping all held strong attractions.[20] For New Granada a
consensus has arisen which sees a nation debilitated by regional fragmentation, a nation that was born 'in spite of itself'.[21] As in Ecuador, geographical
obstacles and communication difficulties prevented the development of a 'national economy' or a successful national identity in this period.[22] In comparison, Venezuela emerged as a more 'integrated' nation, based on its export
economy orientated towards the Caribbean colonies.[23] During the Gran Colombian period, however, collective identities were still subject to the unpredictable flux of war. The rupture in the colonial relationship with Spain and
the spread of Enlightenment ideas of liberalism, virtue and republicanism,
served to encourage new ways of thinking about collective identities which
were increasingly based upon understandings of the franchise and a more secu-
lar state. As Simon Collier showed for the Independence of Chile, fractures in
traditional political relations caused by the upheaval of military conflict and
encounters between previously unconnected groups of people all contributed
to moulding the development of collective identities.[24] National identities
formed only a small part of such changes.

The development of a British national identity is a useful point of comparison when considering the national sentiments of the adventurers as they
encountered this situation in Gran Colombia. Linda Colley argued that war
against France in the eighteenth century provided the circumstances for the
'forging of the British nation'. France was a Catholic, foreign 'Other' against
which Britain, its component parts brought together by the experience of war,
could constitute and conceptualise itself.[25] Colley argued that only by understanding the processes and realities of this warfare could British national identity be comprehended. Throughout the eighteenth century the British Army
was a 'military melting-pot' that provided opportunities for soldiers to meet
others from elsewhere in Britain and Ireland, and to redefine themselves against

each other and against the enemy, producing a new and peculiar sense of 'Britishness'.[26] Thibaud proposed that these processes also took place in Bolívar's army, producing a new sense of 'Gran-Colombianness' throughout its ranks, but predominantly amongst the officer corps.[27] Thibaud also explored how military leaders understood what it meant to be in opposition to Spanish rule, and henceforth how they came to define Gran Colombia according to the territories won on the battlefield.[28] Thus during the long years of war the allegiances and identities of people in Gran Colombia – national and otherwise – were in flux, continuously being defined and redefined, 'sometimes advancing, sometimes regressing, but never static', as was the national territory until the mid-1820s.[29] The key members of the Gran Colombian nation were the men who took part in the military victories that would bring Independence.

Bolívar's conception of 'Gran-Colombianness' was deliberately broad. He proclaimed in 1821 that 'for us, everyone is Gran Colombian, and even our invaders, if they wish, can be Gran Colombians'.[30] He proposed a military melting pot out of which everyone would emerge as Gran Colombians. 'Everyone' included all the adventurers serving in his army, but their Gran Colombian identity had to be crafted on top of a diverse selection of collective and national identities brought with them across the Atlantic. These identities are studied in the next sections, dealing in turn with the British Legion, the Irish Legion, the legions raised by Gregor MacGregor, and the Hanoverian Legion.

The British Legion

The British Legion, which left London between 1817 and 1819, was made up of men from across Britain and Ireland, although many of its officers were Anglo-Irishmen, including the leader, James Towers English. He emphasised the 'British' nature of the expedition at key moments, such as when they embarked upon campaign in 1819. Addressing himself to the 'Soldiers of the British Legion', English proclaimed:

> The long expected Moment has arrived. You are about to Embark, to fight in support of that glorious cause for which you have engaged yourselves; Remember you are Britons, Remember the Eyes of your Country are fixed upon you, and wish for your Success. That Success is certain, if you cheerfully obey the Commands of your superiors, only observe strict discipline and unanimity and your national valor will overcome every obstacle. You are already Hail'd by those brave and suffering People the Liberators of their long oppressed Country. They are prepared to open their arms to receive you: all that Tyranny and Oppression have left them (Their Country), the Richest and most fertile in the world, they offer to share with you.[31]

To conclude his speech, English recognised the heterogeneous nature of his British Legion, men whom he felt to be united by shared bonds of national honour, avarice and alcohol:

> I trust you will ere long return to your Native Countrys covered with Honour and abounding in Riches. I have with difficulty been able to procur for you, a small sum as a gratuity to drink success to the British Legion during their operations on the Main.[32]

When in Venezuela, English repeatedly stressed the British nature of his enterprise, which he saw as continuing the struggle against tyranny that Britain had fought in Spain (regardless of the fact that neither he nor very many of his men had actually been in Spain, as shown in Chapter 1).[33] English saw his troops' British identity as key to their role in the ongoing conflict between liberty and tyranny in Gran Colombia.[34] The Independent General Arismendi echoed this, declaring that 'born freemen, you detested tyranny and tyrants alike'.[35] In this way, officers' continual preoccupation with honour was reconciled with the need to feel patriotically British while serving in the forces of another state. The fight against 'tyranny' in the name of 'liberty' was deemed honourable, no matter where it took place.[36] In the words of Mary English, presenting the British Legion with its colours at a ceremony at Pampatar, 'you are employed in a glorious cause, the cause congenial to the hearts of Britons, the support of Liberty and Independence against Tyranny and Oppression'.[37] There was a paradox here in the nature of the perception of Britain as the defender of liberty and the foe of tyranny, when it had also been a bulwark against Napoleon's attempts to spread the French version of liberty across Europe. British adventurers repeatedly claimed to be continuing the fight against tyranny that they had begun in the Napoleonic Wars, arguing that 'the same reverence of virtuous liberty which thus in the Old World restored [Spain's] freedom ... now animates [them] in the New'.[38] For these Britons, tyranny was embodied not by Spain itself but by Spanish imperialism, which was understood as 'acquisitive, cruel, state-sponsored, exploitative' in contrast to Britain's own imperialism which was 'vigorous, hard-working, entrepreneurial, honest and free'.[39] In Gran Colombia, the adventurers presented themselves as 'the champions of liberty' responding to 'the pleadings of humanity'.[40] The struggle to free weaker individuals and nations from unjust and dishonourable dependence on the rule of others was presented as equal, whether liberating Spain from French rule, or Gran Colombia from Spanish rule. The question of monarchical, republican or imperial rule did not enter the equation, and was only rarely mentioned in the sources. Tyranny was understood as the opposite of liberty and, as such, something that the free-born Briton was duty-bound to fight against wherever it was found. Britons embraced the cause of liberty.

James English was keen to stress that his men would rival any unit from the regular British Army. In a diary extract published in Dublin, English wrote that he had embarked for Barcelona on the Venezuelan coast with 'one thousand British troops attached to me with feelings of ardour and respect that might have raised the envy of any General in the British service'.[41] The other principal organiser of the British Legion, Coronel George Elsom, defined Britishness in terms of the manly feats of his men in Venezuela. He emphasised their great physical achievements, marvelling that

> mountains have been marched over, of which the summits joined the clouds; rivers and torrents have been crossed; savannahs and forests have been penetrated which before had been considered impenetrable by man; in truth they have accomplished a task so truly gigantic, as to astonish every native who is acquainted with the country they have succeeded in traversing ... [it] will be a tale of glory for every person who has had the honour of being concerned in it.[42]

With the arrival of the first contingents of the Irish Legion to Venezuela in early 1820, there was increasing differentiation between British and Irish, as indicated by the horse-racing competitions held in Angostura discussed above. An influential commentator compared English's 'well-disciplined and seasoned troops, inured to fatigue and danger of every description' with Devereux's 'confused, heterogeneous mass, varying from the peasant fresh from the plough share, to the artisan, whose close, sedentary occupation rendered him sickly, and altogether unfit for the active duty of a soldier'.[43] The Irish Legion had its own identity, rooted in evolving Romantic nationalism and affected by the Irish experience of suppressed rebellion in 1798.

The Irish Legion

The Irish Legion was recruited by John Devereux in Dublin, Cork and Belfast in 1819 and early 1820. Devereux and his associates proudly proclaimed the Irishness of the Irish Legion. The revival of romantic Irish nationalism and its symbols – revolving around language, harps, the colour green and an ostensible love of liberty – was an integral part of the Irish Legion's recruitment and activities.[44] Some contemporaries claimed that Devereux was a veteran of the 1798 rebellion of the United Irishmen, and as such epitomised in his person the patriotic Irish love of liberty. There was an element of conscious myth-making about this, as surviving archival documents in Ireland indicate that if he was involved in 1798, it was either as a (very) young sympathiser of negligible importance, or he was lucky enough to escape detection by the authorities.[45] Beyond the figure of Devereux, commentators portrayed the expeditions as an opportunity for Irishmen to display their identity on the world stage. One orator noted that the Irish Legion was 'the electric communication' of Irishmen united. Inspired by 'the graves of your brave countrymen, trampled by tyranny, ... [who] died for freedom and are clamorous of Revenge', Charles Phillips exhorted Irishmen to

> Go! Plant the banner of green on the summit of the Andes. If you should triumph, the consummation will be liberty; and in such a contest should you even perish, it will be as martyrs perish – in the blaze of your own glory. Yes, you shall sink, like the Sun of the Peruvians, who you seek to liberate, amid the worship of a

people, and the tears of a world; and you will rise reanimate, refulgent, and immortal.[46]

Devereux acted in full accordance with Phillips's call. His green flag had an Irish harp emblazoned upon it, as did the ceremonial stamp he carried with him.[47] He ordered a sword to be forged, and later presented it to Simón Bolívar, decorated with harps and imitation Celtic script. Daniel O'Connell supported the expedition and told Devereux that he hoped the Legion would 'give glory to Ireland'.[48] O'Connell sent his son Morgan to join the struggle, telling Bolívar of his hopes that 'my son may be enabled to form one link in that kindly chain which, I hope, long binds in mutual affection the free people of Colombia and the gallant but unhappy natives of Ireland'.[49] As such, the Irish Legion drew on the eighteenth-century growth in Irish Catholic consciousness identified by Thomas Bartlett but, because it was an expedition designed to operate outside of the confines of British imperialism, it could also openly include men of all religious and political affiliations. Indeed, several of the officers were Protestants, for example William Lyster and William Aylmer.[50] One adventurer described the Irish Legion as 'a glorious crusade in the cause of liberty'.[51] Whilst the Irish Legion was not wholly Catholic, neither can it be conclusively linked to the radical politics of the 1798 rebellion of the United Irishmen. As in the case of Devereux, attempts to cross-reference the names of adventurers with those of United Irishmen prisoners do not convince.[52] Military service played an important role in strengthening and diffusing Irish national and regional identities, and experience gained in the British or Spanish empires could make them feel more (or less) Irish, depending on the circumstances of their service.[53] The heir to various political and military traditions, from the Wild Geese to the British Army, the Irish Legion should be seen in this light, providing an opportunity and outlet for individuals to seek adventure abroad, largely regardless of creed or political ideology.[54]

The Irish Legion was raised in the name of liberty by the Irish. In stark contrast to the British Legion, which incorporated men born in England, Ireland, Scotland and continental Europe, the Irish Legion was almost entirely formed from men born in Ireland. Nevertheless, the Union between Britain and Ireland was not yet two decades old. Identities were not fixed. Irish Catholics were still generally loyal to the Crown, and Irish and British identities were complementary rather than antagonistic.[55] As is shown below, adventurers often chose when they wished to be British, Irish, or indeed Gran Colombian. In the early 1820s, the cause of liberty was an essential component of all three.

Gregor MacGregor's Legions

In contrast to the strong Irish identity of the Irish Legion, there was very little Scottishness about the legions raised by Gregor MacGregor in 1818 and

1819.[56] Many Scots regarded themselves as 'North Britons' in this period, and Scotland was essentially content with its status within the Union with England. Scots were motivated to enlist in military service by socio-economic factors and local or regimental (not national) loyalties.[57] It was in this period that the British empire, according to John M. Mackenzie, began to provide Scots with the opportunity 'to establish a distinctive identity which reflected back upon the survival of her religious, intellectual, legal and ethical civil culture'.[58] The expeditions to South America do not really bear out this argument. MacGregor's expeditions were often perceived as being made up of men 'without nation'.[59] This was perhaps because they operated almost entirely in the Caribbean Sea and its coastline, rather than in the Gran Colombian interior, and thereby recruited reinforcements from the mobile community of Caribbean soldiers and sailors during visits to Jamaica, Haiti and other islands. MacGregor himself made little attempt to apportion a national identity to his men, placing their actions instead within the transatlantic struggle for liberty and Independence, regardless of national origin.

A look at the members of MacGregor's expedition who were executed by Loyalists at Riohacha in 1819 reflects its overall composition. Out of 56 people named, the grim list revealed a predominantly Catholic expedition with just two Protestants. Two were said to come from Germany and two from England. Twenty-seven came from Ireland, and twenty from Scotland. Like the British Legion, MacGregor's legions were not nationally homogenous – they contained members from all parts of the new Union. Yet MacGregor did not apply the term British to his legions. Perhaps their Catholicism explains this. In contrast to the Protestant Anglo-Irishman James Towers English, MacGregor was Catholic himself, proud of his uncle who had been involved in the 1745 Jacobite rebellion. In 1811 MacGregor married a Catholic Venezuelan, a cousin of Simón Bolívar.[60]

If religion can explain why MacGregor did not consciously describe his expeditions as British, it is less clear why he avoided mention of Scotland. In fact, during the wars very few of the adventurers in Gran Colombia were positively identified in any text as Scottish.[61] This may have been because of links often made in the Caribbean between Scots and slavery, which were uncomfortable during an age of revolution and emancipation. One adventurer wrote, 'to the dishonour of our national character, abroad our countrymen have none of that sympathy so distinguishable in the people of other nations; we are in fact denationalised'.[62] Because of this, Scots such as Alexander Alexander made no effort to challenge the social convention that allowed them to pass as *inglés*. Others identified themselves as North Britons.[63] Certainly MacGregor did not feel that Scottish national identity was sufficiently established or attractive for him to be able to recruit adventurers by playing on it often, as Devereux did in Ireland. Instead, in his recruitment, Gregor MacGregor offered land and freedom, selling potential soldiers and colonists the vision of a better life in the New World.[64] Only occasionally did he remind Scots of their history in Darien, suggesting that his own forebears had been involved and his aim was the 'reestablishment of the Scotch Darien Company ... [to] colonise the bay of Caledonia'.[65]

MacGregor did not recruit men by appealing to their Scottish identity, as Devereux did for the Irish, but, like Devereux, MacGregor recruited families of colonists as much as soldiers. At least twenty named women accompanied MacGregor's expeditions, and in 1820 he turned his attention to the colonisation of the Mosquito Coast. Like Devereux's men, MacGregor's put great importance on the fulfilment of what they had been offered – pay, land and food. Whilst all the legions attracted potential emigrants encouraged by such 'New World' propaganda, MacGregor's case was unique in that he did not attach this to rhetoric of any national or regional identity, as the British and Irish Legions did.[66] His expeditions therefore occupied an ambiguous place with regard to the way in which Gran Colombians viewed foreign intervention in their Wars of Independence.

The Hanoverian Legion

The Hanoverian Legion was integrated and incorporated within the British Legion, exemplifying the way that contrasting cultural and, in this case, linguistic identities could be complementary within a wider context. While George IV, the elector of Hanover, was still on the British throne, Hanoverian soldiers served in distinct regiments of the British Army in the American Wars of Independence and the Napoleonic wars.[67] Some of these veterans joined the expeditions to Gran Colombia after demobilisation, and they were joined by other adventurers without military experience. The Hanoverian Legion included men describing themselves as Germans, Poles, Englishmen, Irishmen and Prussians.[68]

During the Wars of Independence, the Hanoverian Legion gained the reputation of being the best-behaved, most disciplined group of foreign soldiers. Their loyalty was contrasted with the 'extraordinary indiscipline' of the British Legion troops at Barcelona in 1819, and with the rebellion of the Irish Legion at Riohacha in 1820.[69] Frustrated by lack of pay, and drunk on plundered rum, British officers and soldiers alike had ransacked shops and houses in Barcelona, ignoring orders to remain in their barracks outside the town.[70] During these events, the Hanoverians were reputed to have remained aloof from the rioting, standing firm in their barracks while chaos reigned around them, and eventually being instrumental in restoring order.[71] The reputation of German troops remained good in Latin America throughout the century.[72] The Hanoverians were also remembered because of the high-ranking and influential descendants they left in Venezuela, such as Juan Uslar.[73] In contrast, the Welsh adventurers, who also fitted into the British Legion, left very little record of their contribution. The Welsh only rarely asserted any difference of identity from the British, were relatively few in number, and were predominantly private soldiers or non-commissioned officers.[74] The foreign adventurers carried these diverse identities with them across the Atlantic. In Gran Colombia, their experiences in the service of the cause of liberty turned some of them into *colombianos*.

Colombianos

In Margarita in late 1819, Morgan O'Connell described a banquet organised for the officers of the Irish Legion on their arrival. He managed to recall some of the toasts at the end of the evening:

> To The President (three times),
> To Brion, D'Evereux, and the foreign volunteers,
> To Arismendi,
> To long-lasting friendship between Ireland, England and Colombia,
> To Daniel O'Connell.[75]

The variety of the toasts show that the Irish Legion was neither conceived of, nor presented as, an anti-British enterprise. In Riohacha in 1820 the Irish Legion's band played 'Rule Britannia' and 'God Save the King' as well as 'St Patrick's Day'.[76] Daniel O'Leary described the British and Irish Legions as 'twin sisters ... which provided worthy servants for America and for freedom'.[77]

While they recognised the difference between *inglés* and *irlandés*, most Creoles tended to use *ingleses* as a catch-all term for foreigners, at least before 1820. Much of the documentation from military archives used *inglés* to refer to any Northern European or North American. In 1818, Francisco Zea welcomed the first units of the heterogeneous British Legion, proclaiming 'let's show them what an army of *ingleses* and *venezolanos* can do!' He explicitly linked Englishness with military prowess, in his hope and expectation that the newcomers would improve the quality of the Independent army.[78] This was not unusual, nor was it offensive to either side. Even as late as 1840 many Catholics in Ireland were content to see themselves as West Britons.[79] There was no predetermined or inevitable split between Britishness and Irishness, and the expeditions provide an excellent example of the way that the two identities could co-exist. At the same time though, the British and Irish Legions were compared and contrasted as a means of asserting one or other identity. This first happened in the wake of the rebellion of the Irish Legion at Riohacha in May 1820, when several hundred Irishmen refused to continue in the Independent service, and were transported to Jamaica. When news of what they termed 'black proceedings' reached the British Legion stationed in the Venezuelan interior, officers and men fired off a joint letter to Santander. They felt that 'abandoning the cause of Independence' was 'an embarrassing flaw for a European soldier'. They dissociated themselves from 'these mutineers' who had committed a 'sin' which meant that they would 'carry with them the double ignominy of having disgusted their Compatriots as well as those they were supposed to be fighting for'.[80] From this moment on, the image of the Irish as cowardly, mutinous and 'void of principle'[81] spread across the circum-Caribbean and Gran Colombia. In contrast, their 'compatriots' the British – *ingleses* – were held to be honourable, loyal and brave.

The negative image of the Irish which developed in post–1820 Gran Colombia was a far cry from that constructed by the organisers of the Irish Legion back in Dublin. They had emphasised the innate heroism of the Irish and their love of liberty; according to William Aylmer, this was 'but the common virtue of every Irishman'.[82] Deserters who returned home without seeing active military combat were now derided in the press as 'feather-bed soldiers'[83] who lacked 'manly fortitude' and had 'forgotten the honourable principle which they would have the world believe first moved them in the Cause'.[84] This desire to base an Irish identity on love of liberty remained constant amongst those who remained in Gran Colombia, and facilitated the survivors taking on the identity of *colombiano*. In 1822 Arthur Sandes wrote to Daniel O'Connell, informing him that his nephew Maurice O'Connell had died from fever after two years' service and constant campaigning. Sandes emphasised that O'Connell's character was 'truly Irish, uniting in it all those virtues for which the sons of our country are so justly celebrated, being always worthy of his ancient and honourable name and of that love of liberty which had engaged him in the defence of an oppressed people'.[85] However, even a devote love of liberty foundered upon practical difficulties in Gran Colombia. Fever and other illnesses killed many. As Teniente Nicholas White observed, the Riohacha rebellion was catalysed by the troops' constant fear of being attacked by an unseen enemy while they were out marching near Riohacha.[86] The unknown landscape of the Goajira peninsula, and the potentially murderous Indians who populated it, produced an anxiety and, ultimately, a rebellion, which overcame all other considerations and which prejudiced the reputation of the Irish in the Gran Colombian region for many years to come.

The Irishmen who did not leave Gran Colombia in 1820 had to struggle to re-affirm their own reputations now that Irishness had become synonymous with mutiny and indiscipline.[87] Santander described 'the god-damned Irish, who would rob us of everything and set such a terrible example for our troops'.[88] The *Correo del Orinoco* depicted the Irish as 'the most insubordinate in the world'.[89] In early 1823 the Caracas newspaper *El Colombiano* published a series of jokes at the expense of stereotypical Irish simplicity.[90] By making such distinctions, Gran Colombian élites were able to reflect upon their own feelings of patriotism, loyalty and identity. Collective identities, therefore, were further grounded in conduct and ideology, rather than origin or ethnicity. Creole officers developed a pre-existing argument that foreign adventurers should not be given special privileges based on identity. Rafael Urdaneta argued that 'the British Legion is, and should be considered, as a Venezuelan unit'.[91] In 1822 Pedro Briceño Méndez argued that there was 'no difference between' Gran Colombian and 'foreign' troops.[92] General Arismendi was reported as saying that 'it would be a great pleasure for him to expel prejudice from these lands and to cultivate Religion's social virtues; that he would sweep away all the different nationalities so that Englishmen, Irishmen and Americans can become one family – the Sons of Colombia'.[93] This was in effect what happened. Previous nationalities were temporarily swept under the carpet, and foreign adventurers became *colombianos*.

This change was possible because during 1819 and 1820, events had changed Creoles' and Spaniards' understandings of what their *patria* was, and what the nature of its government should be. By the time of the armistice talks in 1820, even at the highest levels of the Loyalist army there was some sympathy for the Independents' cause,[94] but also heightened determination in certain 'Loyalist' areas to maintain allegiance to their own understanding of the *patria*.[95] This was the result of experiences in Gran Colombia as well as the political situation in Spain. Key to the Gran Colombian element was the involvement of foreigners in the Independent service, especially on the Caribbean coast where nineteenth-century 'pirates' such as Brion and MacGregor were supported by new national bodies and authorities rather than the traditional Old World powers.[96] For other people who lived far from the coast, the presence of the *ingleses* in the conflict probably had little effect on collective identities. A pardo farmer from San Jayme on the llanos, Felipe Suarez, served for one year with the Independents without seeing a single *inglés*.[97] Francisco Linares, who was born, raised and married in Villa de Ospino near Santa Lucia also in the llanos, was forcibly recruited to the Independent army in early 1819, and he did not distinguish between the *ingleses* he heard were serving with Bolívar and the *forasteros* he served alongside.[98] The *forasteros* (strangers or foreigners) who came from the next town, and the *ingleses* who came from across the ocean, were equally foreign to Linares. In coastal regions, however, identities were reformulated as a result of foreigners' incursions. In Riohacha, the incursions of Gregor MacGregor and the Irish Legion resulted in all sectors of society having to reconsider their loyalty to King, Governor, *patria* and town.[99] These changes were not straightforward: Aniseto Rodriguez, a local who MacGregor charged with organising the Independents' defence of Riohacha, was unsuccessful in his attempts to persuade his old colleagues that 'just as you used to serve the King, now you can serve the *patria*'.[100] In their testimonies, several residents of Riohacha claimed that they had replied that they 'could not serve the *patria*, because [they] did not want to fight against their brothers'.[101]

In the early 1820s, once Gran Colombia had been established by military means, honourable foreigners were gradually accepted into the Gran Colombian family as brothers. Service records reveal that it was in the early 1820s when both *inglés* and *irlandés* adventurers began to hispanify their first names (from John to Juan, from William to Guillermo, from Thomas to Tomás). This can be explained as an attempt to achieve a certain degree of 'acceptance' and 'assimilation' into Gran Colombian society, at the same time as making communication a little easier. In the words of Trinh T. Minh-ha, 'foreignness is acceptable once I no longer draw the line between myself and the others. First assimilate, then be different within permitted boundaries.'[102]

After 1820, Irish adventurers in the army emphasised that their love of liberty existed regardless of their Irishness. One of them, John Johnston, wrote to the Gran Colombian government in 1823, noting, 'when I was in France in 1817 and I heard favourable talk of a Heroic Bolivar and his glorious struggle … against the tyranny and despotism of Spain … at that moment my heart inflamed with the ardent desire to join such a noble cause'.[103] In order to assure an honourable reputation in the eyes of Creole leaders, such individuals transferred their loyalties to the 'banners of Colombia', for which they would be prepared to sacrifice their lives.[104] This process, which we might call the Gran-Colombianisation of individuals, was not total, and residual loyalties to Britain, Ireland, region and town remained. But, after the all-encompassing military mobilisation against Spain was over, Creole élites increasingly demanded that the adventurers became Gran Colombian if they wished to remain in the new republic. The integration of foreigners into the nation was an uncertain and ambiguous process, explored further in Chapters 7 and 8. The adventurers' collective identities were flexible, negotiable and rooted in the historical circumstances of their departure from home. The Gran-Colombianisation of the remaining adventurers was possible because the love of liberty was a core element of Britishness, Irishness and Gran-Colombianness in this period. Liberty provided a firm basis for a collective identity that grew out of the war against Spain.

An integral part of Gran-Colombianisation was the formation of the Albion Battalion in Bogotá from the remnants of the British, Irish and MacGregor Legions. Formed of a wide cross-section of the remaining adventurers, the Albion battalion of *ingleses colombianos* epitomized the 'military melting pot'.[105] When Bolívar named the Albion Battalion as such in 1820, he accepted a degree of foreignness as part of the larger Gran Colombian identity. All of the battalion's documentation referred to the *ingleses* with hispanified first names, even in the listings transcribed by officers who spoke little Spanish. Amongst the private soldiers there were foreigners as well as local men recruited in the areas through which the battalion passed. For the next few years the Albion Battalion was the adventurers' own *patria chica*, to correspond with the loyalties to Pasto, Cali and Popayán held by local people.[106] Such loyalties fitted into the larger provincial, Gran Colombian or even 'American' identities also held by Independent soldiers, and which Independent leaders such as Bolívar attempted to superimpose onto pre-existing regional, local, racial and social identities.[107] The Albion Battalion was the natural home for *ingleses colombianos* and symbolised the way in which previous loyalties had been subsumed – for the duration of military conflict at least – into the new Gran Colombian nation.

Gran Colombian élites were at pains to present their rebellion against Spain as 'national' to the outside world. At home they foraged for the basis of a national history and a national culture that would support the new national identity being created and imagined by military veterans. This search was an essential companion to military victory and recognition abroad. In the words of Mauricio Tenorio Trillo, 'historically there seemed to be no option but to craft a national image'.[108] José Manuel Restrepo wrote the first narrative of Gran Colombian history while he was Minister of the Interior in the 1820s. Emphasising the heroism of such peers as Bolívar and Santander, Restrepo also brought out the unique geographical and cultural characteristics of the region. As Germán Colmenares commented, 'by means of Restrepo's narrative, the fathers of the *patria* seem to have constructed their own myths'.[109] The attempt to identify a 'national culture' was more problematic. With considerable indigenous, black and mixed-race populations, Gran Colombia's regional, social, linguistic and geographical diversity tended to thwart nation-building attempts grounded in any claims to common culture. As Hans-Joachim König has argued, the creation of Gran Colombia in 1819 by Bolívar was an 'artificial nation' that broke with the late-colonial processes in which collective identities coalesced around the colonial administrative divisions of viceroyalties, captaincy-generals and presidencies.[110] For König, Gran Colombia had no deeper meaning than its political and military immediacy.[111] But in the late 1810s and early 1820s, Gran Colombia was more than an artifice or pseudo-nation. In Luis Castro Leiva's words, the Gran Colombian nation was a 'telling illusion' that remained after the practical military necessity that created it had evaporated.[112] During the 1820s there were a considerable number of people who believed in Gran Colombia, and who felt they were *colombianos*.

These individuals included some of the adventurers. Bolívar wrote of John Illingworth in 1822 that 'he knows the country very well, and he knows what its men are like. He is married to a rich woman there. He is talented and honourable. He is very *colombiano*, and it seems that he doesn't lack the British talent for leadership either. Above all, he enjoys a very high-standing among Colombians'.[113] In Bolívar's view, high-status foreigners such as Illingworth could be the cement to hold Gran-Colombianness together, without any local or regional identities to pull them away from the overarching Gran Colombian identity that had won the War of Independence against Spain.

When Gran Colombia began to disintegrate after 1826, foreigners were gradually excluded from the formational New Granadan, Venezuelan and Ecuadorean identities that political élites came to see as the basis for the new, post–1830 republics. Foreigners had become so identified with the Gran Colombia project that when it fell apart they struggled to reconfigure their identities once again to the new political reality. The continued existence of foreigners in civilian and military circles, from serving military personnel to politicians and fishermen, acted as a catalyst to the resurgent local and regional patriotisms from which they were excluded. Whereas in the late 1810s and early 1820s patriotism could be demonstrated by anybody showing loyalty in the service of the cause of liberty in the Gran Colombian army, during the 1820s ideas of birth (and of being in some way culturally located in the territory of the republic) began to regain importance. When Gran Colombia disappeared in 1830, the *ingleses colombianos* veterans of the Albion Battalion and others who remained in the territory struggled to convince the authorities that they had in fact long been Venezuelan, New Granadan, or Ecuadorean. Such claims rested on more localised and ethereal ideas of the *patria* from which they were unavoidably excluded. In response, adventurers sought to ground their claims to patriotism in their military service, honour and bravery. Indeed, as Chapter 7 explores in more detail, this was all they were left with. One Hanoverian volunteer wrote in 1832, 'once I am away from the bosom of my country, Germany, I am nothing more than a New Granadan Colombian [*colombiano granadino*], and I will shed my blood in the defence of Independence and Liberty'. His patriotism was founded in the cause of Independence, but post–1830 this was often not enough to convince the authorities.[114]

Jaime Jaramillo Uribe argued that internal socio-economic, political and ideological changes in nineteenth-century New Granada all had their roots in the colonial period.[115] The sources examined here support the argument that the arrival of foreign adventurers helped to hasten these changes. Arriving as an apparently homogeneous whole, often categorised simply as *ingleses* by all social groups, in a short period of time they revealed themselves to be composed of a variety of collective identities, British, English, Irish, Scottish, German and foreign. In military service, where Creoles, pardos, *mestizos* and blacks served and lived alongside foreigners and fought alongside them, there was a unique opportunity for comparison and assessment.[116] Such encounters served to undermine any conception that, as Halperin Donghi has suggested was the case elsewhere in Latin America, all foreigners were seen as 'almost members of a higher humanity rather than mere mortals'.[117] In addition, foreign adventurers were among the most strident supporters of what Collier called Bolívar's Gran Colombian 'supranationalism'.[118] Many of them, such as Daniel O'Leary, William Ferguson and Belford Hinton Wilson, stayed loyal to Bolívar during his attempts to extend his rule well beyond the Equator. In many ways he was 'their' caudillo, having recruited them and in many cases promoted them to positions of authority and prestige. But these were exceptional figures. During the Wars of Independence, local circumstances and regional and regimental loyalties were far more important in shaping men's identities. These identities were constructed from national origins on the other side of the Atlantic, but also from conceptions of honour which evolved out of their situation as adventuring mercenaries in a new environment.

The Albion Battalion made this clear in their 1820 letter to Santander. They claimed that 'the English soldiers in Venezuela ... will never stain their character with such acts of atrocity and murder. They will always respect the rules of warfare, and the rights of humanity, and they will always despise those savage principles which, until now, have prevailed in this melancholy struggle.'[119] The members of this group sought publicly to redefine themselves with relation to three events: first, the departure of the Irish Legion from the Independent service, destroying the town of Riohacha as they went; secondly, the spread of the perception among Gran Colombian élites that such behaviour from auxiliary troops was not acceptable; and thirdly, the continuing 'War to the Death', in which no quarter was to be given to prisoners. The members of the Albion Battalion tried to define themselves as honourable outsiders with regard to this type of warfare (in which they had long taken, and continued to take, an active part).[120] They attempted to express a non-Hispanic, European superiority, in which brave men respected the rule of law, whilst remaining part of the Gran Colombian nation. What Creole officers thought of such claims is unclear, although they could justifiably have perceived them as rather disingenuous, given the adventurers' recent history of rebellion, mutiny and claims for preferential treatment. The presence of proclamations from such foreigners in the heart of the Independent army was an integral part of the ongoing political debates about collective identities.

For those adventurers who remained in Gran Colombia after 1821, distinctions between English, Scottish, British or Irish lost their relevance. It is no coincidence that the sources used in this chapter have predominantly been public ones such as newspaper articles, proclamations, and speeches. Collective identities, whether national, regional, local or regimental, were negotiated in public arenas, whereas more individualistic notions of honour were discussed in private correspondence and in conversation. Groups of adventurers sought to stress their honour and love of liberty, to which end their foreign origins were immaterial to their good conduct as *colombianos*. An unspoken element of this honour was their whiteness.

Notes

1 Jorge Luis Borges, 'Las ruinas circulares', *Ficciones* (Madrid, 1993, first pub. 1945), p. 61.
2 Simon Collier, 'Nationality, Nationalism and Supranationalism in the writings of Simon Bolivar', *JLAS*, 63:1 (1983), pp. 37–64.
3 Helg, *Liberty and Equality in Caribbean Colombia*, p. 8.
4 François-Xavier Guerra, *Modernidad e independencias. Ensayos sobre las revoluciones hispánicas* (Madrid, 1992).
5 Mark Thurner, *From Two Republics to One Divided: Contradictions of Post-Colonial Nation-making in Andean Peru* (Durham, NC, 1995). The argument is refined with relation to the subsequent writing of national history in Thurner, 'Peruvian Genealogies of History and Nation', in Mark Thurner and Andrés Guerrero, (eds), *After Spanish Rule: Postcolonial Predicaments of the Americas* (Durham, NC, 2003), pp. 141–76.
6 Jaime E. Rodríguez O., 'The Emancipation of America', *AHR*, 105:1 (2000), p. 142.
7 Charles Minguet, 'El concepto de nación, pueblo, estado, patria en las generaciones de la independencia', in Jean-René Aymes (ed.), *Recherches sur le Monde Hispanique au dix-neuvième siècle* (Lille, 1973), pp. 57–73.
8 François-Xavier Guerra, 'De lo uno a lo múltiple: Dimensiones y lógicas de la independencia', in Anthony McFarlane and Eduardo Posada-Carbó, (eds), *Independence and Revolution in Spanish America* (London, 1999), pp. 43–68; Brian Hamnett, 'Process and Pattern: A Re-examination of the Ibero-American Independence Movements', *JLAS*, 29:2 (1997), p. 286.
9 Hamnett, 'Process and Pattern', p. 303.
10 McFarlane, 'Identity, Enlightenment and Political Dissent in late-Colonial Spanish America', *TRHS* (1998), pp. 309–37.

11 Thibaud, *Repúblicas en armas*, pp. 152–212.

12 König, 'Nacionalismo y nación en la historia de Iberoamérica' in Tristan Platt, König and Colin Lewis, eds., *Estado-nación, comunidades indígenas, industria: Series cuadernos de historia latinoamericana, viii* (Ridderkerk, 2000), pp. 17–46.

13 Thibaud, *Repúblicas en armas*, p. 517. This is an awkward translation of *(gran) colombianidad*.

14 For the nation defined in this way, see Benedict Anderson, *Imagined Communities: Reflections on the Origin and Spread of Nationalism* (London and New York, 1991), pp. 51–52.

15 J. Leon Helguera showed how military experience shaped national identity in Colombia, in 'The Changing Role of the Military in Colombia', *Journal of Inter-American Studies*, 3 (1961), pp. 351–58.

16 C. A. Bayly, *The Birth of the Modern World, 1789–1914: Global Connections and Comparisons* (Oxford, 2003), p. 126.

17 David Bushnell, *The Santander Regime in Gran Colombia* (Westport, CT, 1970), pp. 249–54.

18 For similar arguments dealing with Mexico, Peru and Argentina, see John Tutino, *From Insurrection to Revolution in Mexico: Social Bases of Agrarian Violence, 1750–1940* (Princeton, NJ., 1986); Florencia Mallon, *Peasant and Nation: The Making of Post-Colonial Mexico and Peru* (Berkeley, CA, 1995); Peter Guardino, *Peasants, Politics and the Formation of Mexico's National State: Guerrero, 1800–1857* (Stanford, CA, 1996); José Carlos Chiaramonte, *Nación y estado en Iberoamérica: Lenguajo politico en tiempos de las independencias* (Buenos Aires, 2004).

19 Anthony P. Maingot, 'Social Structure, Social Status, and Civil–Military Conflict in Urban Colombia 1810–1858', in Stephen Thernstrom and Richard Sennett, (eds), *Nineteenth Century Cities: Essays in the New Urban History* (New Haven, CT, 1969), pp. 297–355.

20 Múnera, 'El caribe colombiano en la república andina, pp. 29–50.

21 Bushnell, *The Making of Modern Colombia: A Nation in Spite of Itself* (Berkeley, CA, 1993). See also McFarlane, *Colombia before Independence*, p. 346; Safford and Palacios, *Colombia: Fragmented Land, Divided Society*, pp. 102–10; Ots Capdequi, 'The Impact of the Wars of Independence', pp. 111–98.

22 Chiriboga, 'Las fuerzas del poder durante el proceso de la independencia y la Gran Colombia', pp. 267–306.

23 Elías Pino Iturrieta, *Las ideas de los primeros venezolanos* (Caracas, 1993); John V. Lombardi, 'La invención de Venezuela en el marco mundial: El siglo de transición 1750–1850', *BANH*, 83:332 (2000), pp. 8–31. On Venezuela's economy in this period, see Izard; 'Política y economía en Venezuela 1810–1976: Período de la independencia y la Gran Colombia 1810–30', in Izard (ed.), *Política y economía en Venezuela 1810–1976* (Caracas, 1976), pp. 1–30; and McKinley, *Pre-Revolutionary Caracas*, pp. 35–73.

24 Simon Collier, *Ideas and Politics of Chilean Independence, 1808–1833* (Cambridge, 1967).

25 Linda Colley, *Britons: Forging the Nation, 1707–1837* (New Haven, CT, 1992).

26 Peter Way, 'The Cutting Edge of Culture: British Soldiers Encounter Native Americans in the French and Indian War', in Martin Daunton and Rick Halpern, (eds), *Empire and Others: British encounters with indigenous peoples, 1600–1850* (London, 1999), pp. 15–19. Stephen Conway, 'War and National Identity in the mid-Eighteenth-Century British Isles', *English Historical Review*, 116:468 (2001), pp. 863–93, emphasised the transatlantic and imperial nature of this Britishness.

27 In *Repúblicas en armas* Thibaud built upon the interpretation of Hermes Tovar Pinzón, 'Guerras de opinión y represión en Colombia durante la independencia 1810–1820', *ACHSC*, 11 (1983), pp. 187–232.

28 Thibaud, *Repúblicas en armas*, p. 212, p. 286, p. 479.
29 John Elliott, 'Introduction', in Nicholas Canny and Anthony Pagden, (eds), *Colonial Identity in the Atlantic World 1500–1800* (Princeton, NJ, 1987), p. 13.
30 Bolívar, in *Correo del Orinoco*, 19 May 1821. Here I have translated Bolívar's use of Colombia and *colombiano* as 'Gran Colombia' and 'Gran Colombian' for the purpose of consistency. For Bolívar's use of the Colombian state and national identity as a means of maintaining the war effort, see David A. Brading, 'Classical Republicanism and Creole Patriotism: Simon Bolívar (1783–1830) and the Spanish American Revolution', in Brading, *Prophecy and Myth in Mexican History* (Cambridge, 1984), p. 50; Carrera Damas, 'Simón Bolívar, el culto heroica y la nación', *HAHR*, 63:1 (1983), p. 117. Salvador de Madariaga saw Colombia as the means that enabled Bolívar's desire for increased personal power, in *Bolívar* (London, 1952), p. 594.
31 James Towers English, 'Speech to the Soldiers of the British Legion on the eve of embarkation', EP, HA157/6/33.
32 English, 'Speech to the Soldiers of the British Legion'.
33 James Towers English, 'Reply of the British Officers and Soldiers of the Independent Army of Venezuela to General Morillo', *The Times*, 24 April 1819; and *Correo del Orinoco*, 27 November, 1819; repr. in Spanish and English in Brown and Roa, (eds), *Militares extranjeros*, pp. 70–71 and pp. 272–74.
34 Francisco de Miranda (b. 1750 Caracas, d. 1816 Cadíz, Spain) had argued this a decade before when trying to encourage British intervention in Venezuela, in William Burke, *Additional Reasons for our Immediately Emancipating Spanish America* (London, 1808), p. 37. Miranda was the principal instigator of schemes for the Independence of Venezuela until his capture by Loyalists in 1812.
35 Arismendi, 'Proclamation to the British Legion', repr. in Anon., *Colombia: Being a Geographical, Statistical, Agricultural, Commercial and Political Account of that Country*, Vol. 2, pp. 436–38.
36 Edward Costello wrote expansively on this theme, having served in the British Legion during the Carlist Wars in Spain in the 1830s. Costello, *The Adventures of a Soldier; Or, Memoirs of Edward Costello, Formerly a Non-Commissioned officer in the Rifle Brigade, and Late Captain in the British Legion, Comprising Narratives of the Campaigns in the Peninsular under the Duke of Wellington, and the Recent Civil Wars in Spain* (London, 1841), p. 320.
37 Mary English's speech was reported in an anonymous letter [probably from her correspondent Richard Jaffray], *London Weekly Dispatch*, 4 July 1819, repr. in Scott, *Mary English*, p. 69.
38 English, 'Reply of the British Officers and Soldiers'.
39 Porter, *The Absent-Minded Imperialists*, p. 70.
40 English, 'Reply of the British Officers and Soldiers'.
41 'Copy of a Journal of General English from his arrival in the Island of Margarita to his return from the expedition to Barcelona and Cumaná', in *FDJ*, 12 May 1820.
42 Letter from Elsom, undated and unaddressed, repr. in *DEP*, 2 November 1819.
43 Anon., [Cowley], *Recollections of a Service of Three Years*, p. 174.
44 On Irish nationalism in this period see R. F. Foster, *Modern Ireland 1600–1972* (London, 1988), pp. 259–89; for the roughly contemporary hopes of 'the Irish love of liberty warming [North] America', see Noel Ignatiev, *How the Irish Became White* (London, 1995), pp. 1–38.
45 Devereux is not mentioned in any history of the United Irishmen, the most prominent of which is Thomas Pakenham, *The Year of Liberty: The Story of the Great Irish Rebellion of 1798* (London, 1997 edn., 1st edn. 1969). For an example of talk of Devereux's United Irish heritage, see John Hambleton, *Diario del Viaje por el Orinoco*,

p. 63. His relation, John Corish Devereux, was already in the US by 1798, in correspondence with another family member from Wexford, Walter Corish Devereux. See Kerby Miller, Arnold Schrier, Bruce D. Boiling and David N. Doyle, (eds), *Irish Immigrants in the Land of Canaan: Letters and Memoirs from Colonial and Revolutionary America, 1675–1815* (Oxford, 2003), pp. 39–44. The 'Memorial of John Devereux', dated Wexford, 1802, may well be John Devereux the adventurer. NAI, Rebellion Papers, 620/61/82.

46 *Fairburn's edition of the speech of Chas. Phillips*, pp. 4–6.
47 The flag was planted on the fort of Riohacha in 1820. O'Connor, *Independencia Americana*, p. 28.
48 *Correo del Orinoco*, 2 October 1819. Daniel O'Connell (b. 1775 Co. Kerry, d. 1847 Genoa) was a prominent Irish Catholic lawyer who campaigned for Catholic Emancipation, passed in 1829. In the 1840s he founded and led the Repeal Association, and like Bolívar was known as 'The Liberator'. His son Morgan O'Connell (b. 1804 Dublin, d. 1885 Dublin) later served in the Austrian Army and was MP for Meath between 1832 and 1840. Eric T. D. Lambert and F. Glenn Thompson, 'Captain Morgan O'Connell of the Hussar Guards of the Irish Legion', *Irish Sword*, 14:53 (1979), pp. 280–82.
49 Daniel O'Connell to Bolívar, 17 April 1820, Dublin, in Maurice O'Connell, (ed.), *TCDOC* (Dublin, 1972), Vol. 2, p. 257. O'Connell's first draft of this letter is in NLI, MS 13645, fo. 22. A Spanish version appears in O'Leary, *MOL*, Vol. 12, p. 263.
50 Lambert, *Voluntarios británicos e irlandeses*, Vol. 2, p. 35, p. 421; Richard John Aylmer, 'The Imperial Service of William Aylmer 1800–1814', *Irish Sword*, 20:81 (1997), pp. 208–16.
51 Coronel Sampson, *DEP*, 3 February 1820.
52 For a little circumstantial evidence see Aylmer, 'The Imperial Service of William Aylmer 1800–1814', pp. 208–16; Gregor MacGregor, 'Autobiographical Segment', John MacGregor Papers, NAS, GD 50/184/104. The collection of 'Prisoners' Petitions and Cases 1791–1826, Official Papers, Registered Papers', held in the NAI, contains 386 named United Irishmen. 33 have the same first name and surname as an adventurer who travelled to Venezuela, but owing to reservations about a similar method expressed earlier, it would be extremely hazardous to argue that any more than 1–2 per cent of United Irishmen did drift from imprisonment, to the British Army (or a life of crime or other employment) and then into the expeditions two decades later.
53 See, for example, Karsten, 'Irish Soldiers in the British Army 1792–1922', pp. 31–64; Keith Jeffrey, 'The Irish Military Tradition and the British Empire', in Jeffrey, (ed.), *An Irish Empire? Aspects of Ireland and the British Empire* (Cambridge, 1996), pp. 94–118; Ian McBride, *Scripture Politics: Ulster Presbyterians and Irish Radicalism in the late Eighteenth Century* (Oxford, 1998), pp. 214–30; David Fitzpatrick, 'Ireland and the Empire', in Porter, (ed.), *The Oxford History of the British Empire*, Vol. 3 (Oxford, 1999), pp. 494–521.
54 On the Wild Geese, see R. A. Stradling, *The Spanish Monarchy and Irish Mercenaries: The Wild Geese in Spain 1618–68* (Dublin, 1994); Harman Murtagh, 'Irish Soldiers Abroad 1600–1800', in Thomas Bartlett and Keith Jeffreys (eds), *A Military History of Ireland* (Cambridge, 1996), pp. 294–314; and numerous essays collected in Enrique García Hernán, Miguel Angel de Buenes, Oscar Recio Morales, and Bernardo J. García García, (eds), *Irlanda y la monarquía hispánica: Kinsale 1601–2001, Guerra, política, exilio y religion* (Madrid, 2002).
55 Even Canning's secretary at the Foreign Office had to be reminded when, in the first draft of his letter accompanying the first British commissioners to Colombia in 1823, he forgot to mention that His Majesty was King of Ireland as well as of Great Britain. Canning to the Secretary of the Government of Colombia, undated, October 1823, TNA FO 80/1 fo. 1.

56 For more detail on MacGregor, see Matthew Brown, 'Inca, Sailor, Soldier, King'.

57 Janet Fyfe, 'Scottish Volunteers with Garibaldi', *Scottish Historical Review*, 57 (1978), pp. 168–96; Andrew McKillop, 'Military Recruiting in the Scottish Highlands, 1739–1815: The Political, Social and Economic Context', Unpub. Ph.D., University of Glasgow, 1995. See also Brown, 'Scots in South America'.

58 John M. Mackenzie, 'Empire and National Identities: The Case of Scotland', *TRHS*, 6th Series, 7 (1998), p. 229.

59 Proclamation of Luis Aury, undated, *Correo del Orinoco*, 7 February 1819; editorial comments in *Correo del Orinoco*, 27 March 1819; Rafter, *Memoirs of Gregor M'Gregor*, p. 145.

60 Gregor MacGregor, *Autobiographical Segment*, John MacGregor Papers, NAS, GD 50/184/104, p. 1.

61 For a list of them, see Brown, 'Scots in South America', pp. 131–34.

62 Anon., *Narrative of a Voyage to the Spanish Main*, p. 51.

63 'Descriptive Roll of the B.L, Achaguas 20 December 1820', AHG G, Actas 1–6. On the prevalence of ideas of 'North Britishness', see Colin Kidd, 'Sentiment, Race and Revival: Scottish Identities in the Aftermath of Enlightenment', in Brockliss and Eastwood, (eds), *A Union of Multiple Identities*, pp. 117–23.

64 See G. A. Low, *The Belise Merchants Unmasked: A Review of their late proceedings against Poyais; From Information and Authentic Documents Gained on the Spot, During a Visit to Those Parts in the Months of August and September 1822* (London, 1822), p. 2; MacGregor, 'Autobiographical Segment', p. 18.

65 'Petition of Officials held Prisoner', to Governor Solís, October 1819, AGI Cuba, Legajo 745. Original in English, repr. (with some transcription errors) in Friede, 'La expedición de Mac-Gregor', p. 74.

66 For this reason, MacGregor the 'adventurer' was contrasted unfavourably with Devereux 'the Irishman' in *Freeman's Journal*, repr. in *DEP*, 6 July 1819.

67 Holmes, *Redcoat*, p. 59; Brumwell, *Redcoats*, p. 97.

68 For the German adventurers, see Gunter Kahle, *Bolívar y los alemanes* (Bonn, 1980) and José Angel Rodriguez, 'Viajeros alemanes a Venezuela en el siglo XIX', *Jahrbuch für Geschichte Lateinamerikas*, 38 (2001), pp. 234–41. On the adventurers from other European countries, see María Wielopolska, 'Polacos en la Independencia de Venezuela', *Revista de la Sociedad Bolivariana de Venezuela*, 331:103 (1974), pp. 69–74; Sergio Elías Ortiz, *Franceses en la independencia de la Gran Colombia* (Bogotá, 1949); Russell H. Bartley, *Imperial Russia and the Struggle for Latin American Independence 1808–1828* (Austin, TX, 1978); and references throughout Filippi, (ed.), *Bolívar y Europa*.

69 Tomás Cipriano de Mosquera, *Memoria sobre la vida Simón Bolívar*, p. 276. See also *Correo del Orinoco*, 24 April 1819, 5 August 1820.

70 Urdaneta, *Memorias del general Rafael Urdaneta*, p. 230; [Cowley], *Recollections of a Service of Three Years*, p. 77; Young, 'Diary of Robert James Young', p. 53.

71 Urdaneta, *Memorias del general Rafael Urdaneta*, p. 230.

72 See Marshall, *English, Irish and Irish-American Pioneer Settlers*, p. 146, p. 152.

73 For Johannes Uslar-Gleichen, Juan Uslar, (b. 1779 Lockum, Hanover, d. 1866 Valencia), see Vicente de Amezaga, 'El General Juan Uslar', *Boletín histórico*, 11 (1966) pp. 117–48; and Juan Uslar Pietri, *Historia de la rebelión popular de 1814, contribución al estudio de la historia de Venezuela* (Caracas, 1962), p. 200.

74 The very few references to Welsh soldiers came only from documents where they had to name their place of birth, for example the 'Descriptive Roll of the B.L. 20 December 1820, Achaguas', AHG G, Actas 1–6. In addition, two sailors listed their national origin as *Galés* (Welsh) while serving on *La Venezuela* in 1824, in AGNC R GYM, Legajo 363, ff. 850–936. For Welsh identity this period see Prys Morgan, 'Early

Victorian Wales and its crisis of identity', in Brockliss and Eastwood, (eds), *A Union of Multiple Identities*, pp. 93–109.

75 Morgan O'Connell to Daniel O'Connell, repr. in *CMP*, 23 and 27 August 1820.

76 Robert Parsons, 15 March, 1820, Riohacha, repr. in *DEP*, 6 July, 1820.

77 Daniel F. O'Leary, *Correspondencia de extranjeros notables con el Libertador*, Vol. 1 (Madrid, 1920), p. 1.

78 Francisco Zea, 'A los jefes, Oficiales, y Soldados de la brigada de artillería. Y de los 4 regimentos ingleses alistados baxo nuestras banderas, 6 de marzo, 1818', in Grases, (ed.), *Impresos de Angostura*, p. 67. See also Juan Germán Roscio (b. 1763 San José de Tiznados, Venezuela, d. 1821 Cúcuta) 28 May 1819, Margarita, repr. in *DEP*, 7 August 1819.

79 S. J. Connolly, 'Varieties of Britishness: Ireland, Scotland and Wales in the Hanoverian state', in Alexander Grant and Keith Stringer, (eds), *Uniting the Kingdom? The Making of British History* (London, 1995), pp. 193–208.

80 John Mackintosh and others to Santander, 26 December 1820, Popayán, repr. in Spanish in *Correo del Orinoco*, 31 March, 1821.

81 Howell (ed.), *The Life of Alexander Alexander*, Vol. 2, p. 126, p. 257.

82 William Aylmer's speech at Morrison's Hotel, 29 May 1819, rpd. in *DEP*, 1 June 1819. Aylmer re-iterated this point of view in a letter to Frank Burdett O'Connor, dated 6 May 1819, a copy of which was kindly given to me by James Dunkerley.

83 Adam, *Journal of Voyages to Marguaritta, Trinidad and Maturin*, p. v.

84 *DEP*, 2 November 1819.

85 Sandes to Daniel O'Connell, 10 September 1822, Quito, O'Connell Papers, UCD, P12/3/110. Only the first paragraph of this letter is reproduced in *TCDOC*, Vol. 2, p. 410. O'Connell's biographer followed Sandes' analysis in his treatment of the period, Oliver Macdonagh, *The Hereditary Bondsman: Daniel O'Connell 1775–1829* (London, 1988), p. 169.

86 *CMP*, 4 December 1820.

87 Bolívar to Santander, 14 November, 1819, Soata, in *Cartas Santander – Bolívar 1813–1820*, Vol. 1, p. 216, was still referring to 'Devereux's 1,500 *ingleses*'.

88 Santander to Bolívar, 13 August, 1820, Bogotá, in *Cartas Santander – Bolívar, 1820*, Vol. 2, p. 270.

89 Compare *Correo del Orinoco*, 1 January 1820 with 5 August 1820. The *Correo del Orinoco* itself was often published in bilingual (English and Spanish) editions.

90 'A young Irish soldier having obtained leave to exchange from the Regiment in which he was serving, into the 31, was questioned respecting the cause of his anxiety to effect this. His reply was "that he had a brother in the 30, and he wished to be near him"', *El Colombiano*, 14 January 1823. See other jokes at Irishmen's expense, 4 February 1824.

91 Rafael Urdaneta, 'Observaciones a la contestación que ha dado el Mayor Low en nombre del General English sobre la orden que se le comunicó para enviar los artilleros de la Legión Británica a hacer un servicio temporal, por no ser suficientes los artilleros existentes para el Servicio de las piezas destinadas a la División Expedicionaria', 20 July 1819, El Norte, EP, HA157/6/77.

92 Briceño Méndez to Morales, 28 November 1822, Bogotá, repr. in *Gaceta de Colombia*, 10 December 1822. Pedro Briceño Méndez (b. 1792 Barinas, d. 1835 Curacao) was later Minister of War.

93 Cited in Morgan O'Connell to Daniel O'Connell, dated 14–15 June, 1820, Margarita, repr. in *CMP*, 23 August 1820.

94 Earle, *Spain and the Independence of Colombia*, p. 159.

95 María Antonieta Martínez Guarda, *La región histórica de Coro y su articulación en tres*

momentos de la historia de Venezuela: 1528–1824 (Caracas, 2000), p. 69.

96 Described as 'pirates' in Sámano to Solis, 30 March 1820, Cartagena, AGI Cuba, Legajo 745; José Cienfuegos to Marques de Casa Trufo, 24 May 1819, Havana, AGI Estado, Legajo 12, N. 13, ff. 1–2. On these changes see Manuel Lucena Salmoral, *Piratas, bucaneros, filibusteros y corsarios en America: Perros, mendigos y otros malditos del mar* (Madrid, 1992), p. 13.

97 'Declaración de Felipe Suarez', 23 April 1819, Puerto Cabello, AGI Cuba, Legajo 911A, 'Declaraciones de pasados y aprehendidos'.

98 'Declaración de Francisco Linares', 23 April 1819, Puerto Cabello, AGI Cuba, Legajo 911A.

99 Matthew Brown, 'Rebellion at Riohacha 1820: Local and International Networks of Revolution, Cowardice and Masculinity', *Jahrbuch für Geschichte Lateinamerikas*, 42 (2005), pp. 77–98.

100 'Declaración de Bartolo Moreno', 19 January 1820, Riohacha, AGI Cuba, Legajo 745, 'Causa criminal seguida contra José Aniseto Rodriguez, por delito de infidencia, y por admisión del empleo de coronel y comandante de las tropas que intentaron poner sobre las armas los insurgentes'.

101 'Declaración de Mateo Bermúdez', 20 January 1820, Riohacha, AGI Cuba, Legajo 745, 'Causa criminal seguida contra José Aniseto Rodriguez'.

102 Trinh T. Minh-ha, 'Other than Myself/My Other Self', in George Robertson, Melinda Mash, Linda Tickner, Lisa Bird, Jon Curtis and Tim Putnam, (eds), *Travellers' Tales: Narratives of Home and Displacement* (London, 1994), p. 9.

103 Johnson, Bogotá, 11 November 1822, AGNC R GYM, Vol. 35, fo. 884.

104 *FDJ*, 7 December 1820.

105 Conway, *The British Isles and the War of American Independence* (Oxford, 2000), pp. 186–202.

106 On regimental identities, see also Frey, *The British Soldier in America*, pp. 112–32.

107 Demetrio Ramos Pérez, 'Nación, supernación y nación local en Hispanoamérica en la época bolivariana', in Ingle Buisson, Gunter Kahle, Hans-Joachim König and Horst Pietschmann, (eds), *Problemas de la formación del estado y de la nación en Hispanoamérica* (Bonn, 1984), p. 175.

108 Mauricio Tenorio Trillo, 'Essaying the History of National Images', in Thurner and Guerrero (eds), *After Spanish Rule*, p. 59.

109 Colmenares, '*La Historia de la Revolución*, por José Manuel Restrepo', p. 11.

110 Hans-Joachim König, *En el camino hacia la nación: Nacionalismo en el proceso de la formación del estado y de la nación de la Nueva Granada 1750–1856* (Bogotá, 1994), pp. 234–65.

111 König, *En el camino hacia la nación*, p. 327.

112 Luis Castro Leiva, *La Gran Colombia. Una ilusión ilustrada* (Caracas, 1985).

113 Bolívar to Santander, 27 October 1822, Cuenca, in *Cartas Santander – Bolívar 1820–1822*, Vol. 3, p. 273. See also Cochrane, *Journal of a Residence and Travels in Colombia*, Vol. 2, p. 187.

114 Tomás Reber, 20 June 1832, Mompox, AGNC HDS, Vol. 38, fo. 166.

115 Jaramillo Uribe, *La personalidad histórica en Colombia y otros ensayos*, pp. 131–54. For the long-term features of these changes in Colombia, see Garrido, *Reclamos y representaciones*, pp. 355–60.

116 In this sense I discuss a series of hospital entry forms from Caracas in 1822 in Matthew Brown, 'Not Forging Nations but Foraging for Them: Uncertain Collective Identities in Gran Colombia, *Nations and Nationalism*', 12:2 (2006), pp. 223–40.

117 Tulio Halperin Donghi, *Hispanoamérica después de la independencia*, p. 146, pp. 153–54.

118 Collier, 'Nationality, Nationalism and Supranationalism', pp. 37–64.

119 John Mackintosh on behalf of the Albion Battalion to Santander, 26 December 1820, Popayán, in *Correo del Orinoco*, 31 March 1821.
120 For British and Irish involvement in the repression of Pasto in 1822, see Guerrero Vinuenza, *Pasto en la guerra de independencia*, Vol. 2, p. 144.

CHAPTER SIX

Race, Slavery and Abolitionism

Race was an integral component of honour in Gran Colombia, for adventurers and Creoles alike, although it was seldom explicitly invoked. The white adventurers saw themselves to be inherently more honourable than blacks, Indians, pardos and *mestizos*. Because their independence and freedom were constricted, slaves were held to be the least honourable of all. This chapter explores the ways in which race and slavery affected the adventurers as they fought for the cause of liberty and Independence, and then on into the 1820s. Adventurers only rarely embraced the call for slaves to be freed, regardless of their rhetoric of liberty. They were much more concerned with asserting their own honour as white men. When it was in their interest, some even managed slave plantations or purchased their own slaves. With some exceptions, their dealings with slaves and people of colour reveal the great extent to which the adventurers' honour, and the nature of their adventuring in Gran Colombia, depended on their position and identity as white men.

At an 1822 City of London dinner held in honour of the Gran Colombian representative Francisco Antonio Zea, the anti-slavery campaigner William Wilberforce spoke of the need for 'the entire and speedy abolition of the slave trade', and thanked 'the Congress of Colombia for its efficient exertions towards that object'.[1] Wilberforce announced that 'the darkness of slavery was receding – the light of freedom was already beaming with brilliancy, and they would shortly be enabled to hail a glorious day in its full meridian lustre'.[2] He concluded his speech by reflecting that it was 'delightful' for him to see the culmination of his own campaigning work in the abolitionist tendencies of the South American Independents.[3] To various extents, Wilberforce's sentiments were shared, developed and contradicted by the adventurers who fought in the Wars of Independence. They encountered slavery across Gran Colombia, reaching as far south as Esmeraldas on the Ecuadorean Pacific coast. The British government had formally abolished its own slave trade in 1807. A decade later campaigning against the institution of slavery was superseding indignation at the continuing trading of slaves by other powers.[4] Hispanic American élites recognised that they had to prove their 'abolitionist' credentials to gain the political recognition they so desired from Great Britain.[5]

Just as in the attitudes towards national identity discussed in the previous chapter, the years 1820 and 1821 were a turning-point in the Independents' attitudes to slavery.[6] Before the 1821 Cúcuta Congress, freeing slaves was seen as a military necessity that provided manpower to debilitated armies, and these men contributed both to the Independents' military success and to shaping the discourse surrounding Independence.[7] With the establishment of the Republic of Colombia in 1819, and its subsequent institutionalisation at Cúcuta, fears of losing the war against Spain gradually became less acute. Concerns about regaining control of the labour force and enabling economic recovery, added to anxiety regarding the prospect of inter-ethnic warfare, led Independent leaders to revert to their original ambivalence about freeing slaves. They preferred to focus on what they saw as more pressing liberties: freedom to trade, freedom of expression, and political freedoms for those who had fought for Independence. Similarly, by 1821 many adventurers had left the continent to pursue other interests, some finding employment in the British colonies where slavery remained important. Those who stayed and integrated themselves into Gran Colombian societies tended to adopt the dominant local attitudes, accepting slavery as an integral part of economic relations.[8] As shown in Chapter 2, however, slavery was not an issue in all regions. Numbers of slaves were limited in highland and forest areas and more common on coastal plantations and in mining regions. This meant that the propertied classes across Gran Colombia were not united in their attitude to slavery, unlike their counterparts in Santo Domingo, Cuba or Brazil, where slavery was fundamental to their economies, and where British abolitionism caused significant diplomatic and political tensions.[9] In the Hispanic Caribbean islands, slaves made up at least one third of the population; on the Hispanic American mainland, the figure was just 2 per cent.[10] For this reason, in contrast to Cuba and Puerto Rico, slavery was not defended staunchly by Creole élites except

Table 6. 1   *Distribution of Slaves across Gran Colombia, c. 1820.*[11]

Region	Slaves as percentage of regional population
Venezuelan Coast	26. 29
Venezuelan Coastal Range	21. 57
Segovia Highlands	9. 65
Venezuelan Andes	3. 20
Venezuelan Llanos	7. 94
Guyana	9. 60
New Granadan Caribbean Coast	8. 67
New Granadan Eastern Cordillera	2. 29
Upper Magdalena	6. 38
New Granadan Central Cordillera	19. 26
Upper Cauca Valley	20. 76
New Granadan Southern Highlands	0. 69
New Granadan Pacific Lowlands and Coast	48. 82
New Granadan Eastern Llanos	0. 57
Ecuadorean Highlands	2. 00
Ecuadorean Coast	25. 00

in very specific locations and circumstances, such as Cartagena or the Pacific Coast. Elsewhere it was not a core institution underpinning the social order.

The next section analyses the adventurers' encounters with slavery and people of colour across these Gran Colombian regions. It is first worth noting that the expeditions did not consist solely of white men. There were a substantial number of black adventurers, perhaps in the region of 2–3 per cent of the total, just as in the British Army at the time. In the late eighteenth century the British Army's West India garrisons had increasingly recruited slave soldiers and other British Army units contained black men, generally in their musical corps, as black men were perceived to be particularly good musicians.[12] By the end of the Napoleonic Wars around one quarter of the British Navy was black.[13] There are limited sources for this subject, but several individual records point to a wider prevalence. Gregor MacGregor's expedition on Portobello contained black seamen, and Gustavo Hippisley's Hussars had several black trumpeters and cooks.[14]

Black adventurers generally occupied subordinate positions in the expeditions, and they were seldom recorded in surviving documentation. Any attempt to break out of that role was strictly limited, and relations between black and white British were not always convivial. On one occasion in 1818 a 'black West Indian British subject' in Maturín was 'hauled into the patriot ranks' by a Creole officer. Whilst white British officers looked on, he was repeatedly beaten by an Independent officer who did not believe that that the man was British. One of the officers who watched the beatings, 'averse to interfering with the native troops', remembered that the 'unfortunate black called [out], "Shame!"'[15]

The Rhetoric of Slavery

The rhetoric of slavery in the early nineteenth century was applied to a much wider variety of conditions than just the chattel slavery of black Africans. John Devereux wrote in 1824 of 'the dark and heavy chain of Slavery which had so long palsied the energies' of Gran Colombia. Devereux was talking of Spanish colonial rule rather than the system of forced labour.[16] Other adventurers who became disillusioned with their treatment in South America often employed the rhetoric of slavery to describe their situation. One, upon his return to London in 1820, described the expeditions as 'this traffic in human blood' of a nature 'as black and barbarous as the SLAVE TRADE'.[17] Merchants also used the language of slavery to emphasise their own difficult situations. In 1824, British merchants in Cartagena complained about 'the shackles imposed' on their mercantile transactions.[18]

The semantics of slavery had long been loose enough for soldiers and merchants to appropriate them, but when they encountered its reality in the Caribbean, the transition from rhetoric to reality was complicated.[19] All of the adventurers would have had some contact with slave societies as they passed through the West Indies, and around two thousand of them later dispersed into the islands looking for work after leaving the Independents.[20] When they encountered slavery in reality, the first impression of many was simply shock: 'the heart was moved to pity by the condition of the slaves'.[21] Whether these were easy, throwaway expressions of sympathy is difficult to ascertain. For every adventurer who criticised slavery, or hoped for its rapid disintegration, there was another who lambasted slaves themselves for their idleness or savagery. Describing a Venezuelan maroon community he visited, one officer commented that they were 'fit for nothing but beasts of burden or slaves'.[22] The foreign adventurers, often reaching Gran Colombia via the Caribbean, were exposed to the widespread fear of slave insurrection, with white settlers permanently 'on the defensive'.[23] The memory of the Haitian Revolution and War of Independence remained with the anxious Caribbean planters, and refugees took their scare stories with them to Cuba, Louisiana, Venezuela, and back to Europe.[24] The encounter with slavery underscored the ways in which the adventurers thought about race in their relationships with other Gran Colombians.[25]

Indigenous Peoples, Racial Diversity and British Civilisation

Chapter 2 described how adventurers on military campaigns passed through diverse regions of Gran Colombia populated by a large number of different indigenous peoples. In similar fashion to the way they looked at slaves, on the whole the adventurers' attitudes towards Indians were fearful, patronising and ignorant. The fear of ambush by 'savages' was omnipresent amongst the adventurers, and stories relating to the death of Donald MacDonald reinforced anxiety about race, status and personal safety. Brief encounters with, or views of, indigenous peoples served to perpetuate stereotypes about 'wild and savage' and 'uncivilised' Indians.[26] On the eve of the Irish Legion attack on Riohacha, a Creole observer noted that 'the attackers are scared to death of the Indians'.[27] Most commentators made superficial general comments about entire communities; just sailing past the village of Sanchapá in Guayana was enough confirmation for Charles Brown to label the inhabitants as 'a timid and cowardly people'.[28]

As David Cannadine has observed for the British empire, Britons thought of the peoples they encountered 'in *individual* terms rather than in collective categories, [and] they were more likely to be concerned with rank than with race'.[29] This was also the case in Gran Colombia. British and Irish observers explicitly formulated hierarchies of civilization: the Indians around Bogotá were 'hard-working' and 'passive', whereas Indians in Guayana, Goajira and Pasto were especially 'savage' and threatening.[30] Bernard Porter labels this ranking of peoples according to their perceived progress towards British ideas of civilisation as 'culturism'.[31] This category is also applicable to the adventurers who, like Richard Vowell, tried to look beyond their 'imperial eyes'.[32]

In one travel narrative and two novels, Vowell commented on the indigenous peoples that he encountered according to a scale of civilisation based around 'manners', 'religion' and military capacity.[33] Vowell's outlook was explicitly hierarchical and comparative. Indians resident on the Páramo de Pisba were 'short, and compare[d] unfavourably to the llaneros'.[34] Civilisation was understood as implying sedentary living, rather than any particular political or cultural outlook. In Patía, where many Creoles saw savage and hostile opponents, Vowell observed 'a nation of civilised Indians who have always been inveterate enemies to the patriots'.[35] Personal experience was paramount: adventurers most often encountered Indians when they marched through their territory, the forms of interaction varying between the hostile (ambush, resistance), the positive (provision of assistance, food, drink, shelter) or, most commonly, the neutral, interpreted as 'passive' (where communities made themselves scarce until the armies had passed by). Vowell's attempts at compassion and understanding were conditioned by his own experience; like several other adventurers, Vowell's life was saved by the assistance of Indians when he was straggling through unknown territory.[36]

Race was an important consideration for adventurers in Gran Colombia, principally for the pragmatic reason that their whiteness provided access to higher status in the new republic than that of the people of colour they served alongside. In a similar fashion to the Irish in North America described by Noel Ignatiev, and the Britons in Cuba described by Jonathan Curry-Machado, they 'became white' as a result of their encounters with subordinate people of colour.[37] Race became an increasingly important part of identity while they were in Gran Colombia. Adventurers seldom mentioned their own whiteness but they constantly observed and detailed the skin colour of Gran Colombians, and the customs and characteristics that they presumed could be attributed to particular groups. Their way of thinking was influenced by Enlightenment ideas of 'natural' cultural characteristics of Indian races and castes as described by Alexander von Humboldt and commonly held by many Creoles.[38] Broadly categorising the various indigenous 'tribes' was more or less manageable for the chronicler with patience and good informants, but when it came to the rest of society the adventurers found the extent of *mestizaje* (miscegenation) bewildering and the number of layers in caste hierarchies difficult to comprehend. Ignorance, error and over-generalisation abounded. Steiner A. Saether has shown how the very meaning of 'indianness' was being negotiated and changed during the independence period; but foreign adventurers were not able to observe such subtle evolutions in identity.[39] Their categories were crude and often inaccurate. Many adventurers labelled any non-white or non-black as 'Indian'. The mixed-race llaneros in Venezuela were brave 'guerrilla Indians'.[40]

Civilisation was a means of categorising peoples, and it was also an aspiration. When indigenous peoples were praised or admired in adventurers' writings, the subtext was still that the 'savages' needed the expertise and discipline provided by British officers to improve and civilise them. Observing a unit of men raised from the Caroní missions by Coroneles Pigott, Sandes and Peacock in 1818, one writer commented that 'the perfect state of discipline into which these men were brought, and the valiant services which they rendered the republic, showed that Bolivar had formed a proper estimate of European discipline upon the raw materials of the most uncivilised of his countrymen'.[41] The juxtaposition of 'uncivilised' people and broad racial diversity with the language of equality was unsettling for many adventurers. Alexander Alexander suffered 'melancholy dreams ... [and] when [he] saw ... the negroes, Creoles and Indians, dressed [in their second-hand British Army uniforms] it looked as if they had returned from ransacking Britain, and [he] was prisoner to a horde of barbarians'.[42] This is what Catherine Hall refers to as discovering that one's 'pre-existing map was not quite adequate to the task' for thinking about the complex, layered societies that Britons encountered in the colonial world.[43] Adventurers hoped to spread civilisation as they fought for the cause of liberty, but practical obstacles thwarted these aims.

Another group who complicated the ways in which adventurers thought about caste and race in Gran Colombia were neither slaves nor Indians, but Creoles. For many, all of the 'natives' of Hispanic America (which included Creoles) were condemned by climate, culture and religion to be 'chained in ignorance'.[44] This meant that, despite their shared whiteness with Creoles, adventurers could deride all the 'natives' of Gran Colombia as 'indolent' (and all the women as 'slovenly').[45] The Creole llanero José Antonio Páez was 'a wild herdsman utterly devoid of education ... an active and indefatigable savage'.[46] It was only in the 1820s and beyond that British and Irish veterans acknowledged Creoles' claims to equality with them on the basis of race; during the Wars of Independence, many adventurers were not prepared to accept such equality. The concepts of status, honour and equality were profoundly racialised themselves, bearing the marks of three centuries of colonial rule and *mestizaje*.[47] Influential new formulations of social hierarchies relied heavily on colonial ideas of racial difference, which were only in theory flattened by the discourse of liberty and equality.[48] These matters were further accentuated by the existence of slavery, albeit in varying intensity, throughout Gran Colombia.

Freeing Slaves and Fighting with Them

The ideological focus on 'liberty' that underpinned the expeditions meant that slavery, rather than the condition of the indigenous peoples, was one of the adventurers' key concerns in Gran Colombia. The reality of slavery, and the experience of living and serving alongside slaves and freed slaves, was therefore particularly poignant for many adventurers and especially relevant to the British imperial experience. This section explores the ambiguous position of slavery for the adventurers in the Wars of Independence, and then discusses the career of John Runnel, an adventurer whose career and posthumous reputation were both closely linked to his association with slaves and men of colour.

When the expeditions were first being recruited in London in 1817, some radicals did see the abolition of slavery as an integral part of the movement for 'liberty'. A dramatised version of Aphra Behn's anti-slavery novella *Oroonoko* was shown in London's West End in February 1817, and was favourably reviewed in the radical newspaper *The Black Dwarf*.[49] The *Correo del Orinoco* continued the explicit link between political emancipation and the freedom of slaves in 1820, arguing that 'nature, justice and religion reprove man being converted into simple merchandise. All nations are agreed that this horrible traffic must be suppressed. Only the oppressive Spaniard resists the voice of nature, of justice, and of religion: the unanimous voice of nations. So America, in emancipating itself, will have also to break the chains of the African.'[50] The claims of 'the chains of the African' were still secondary priorities for radicals who felt that political emancipation and the introduction of constitutions and rational law codes would 'naturally' lead to social change. Yet it was an integral part of the rhetoric, and one that adventurers chose to give as much weight to as they saw fit. Some adventurers saw the abolition of slavery as a logical extension of 'liberty', while others did not.

Radicals who read papers such as *Black Dwarf* sympathised with the slaves, but had other priorities. Those who wished to fight in the name of liberty were urged to support the British labouring poor before worrying about the freedom of others. Contemporary black radicals in London such as Robert Wedderburn and the 'radical underworld' of which they formed part may have secretly hoped for the two causes to be united, but even they were not explicit.[51] Any radicals yearning to contribute to the abolition of slavery came up against firmly entrenched interests in the Caribbean. In the British West Indian islands where many ships arrived before heading to Venezuela, influential traders and planters sought to undermine the expeditions. They perceived the adventurers as a threat to their interests. Many adventurers recalled that upon their arrival in the Caribbean islands they had been told that their cause was 'hopeless' and that they should return home.[52] More tangibly, British West Indian newspapers such as the *Jamaica Gazette* waged campaigns to damage the reputation of Gregor MacGregor, whose operations were supported by the government of Haiti and who freed slaves where it was a political or military necessity.[53]

Adventurers who were in favour of freeing slaves have been excluded from most histories of the Wars of Independence. John Runnel, for example, was not discussed by either Hasbrouck or Lambert, despite his appearance in a wide variety of published sources relating to the Independence period. The key to Runnel's exclusion from the conventional narratives lay in the nature of his relationship with slaves and other non-whites in the Wars of Independence in Gran Colombia. An exploration of Runnel's career illuminates hitherto hidden aspects of the ways in which race and slavery underscored the careers of all the mercenaries.[54] Runnel left no written documents of his presence in Gran Colombia. Like the majority of seamen and soldiers in the ranks who came from Britain and Ireland in this period, he was probably illiterate. Even his name is ambiguous – although many documents referred to him as 'el inglés Juan Runnel', there is no obvious Anglicisation of Runnel.[55] Runnel's brief Gran Colombian career can be sketched as follows. He arrived in Buenaventura as a crewman under the Irish corsair William Brown flying the Independent flag of Buenos Aires in 1816, but was left on shore when Brown departed in a hurry.[56] He remained in the Cauca region, perhaps joining the Spanish army and then finding work as an overseer on slave plantations.[57] When the Independent armies arrived in 1819, Runnel was one of several men already leading guerrilla groups of black slaves, robbing mail coaches and 'disturbing the peace and public morals'.[58] After taking a decisive part in the victory over Loyalist forces at the battle of San Juanito in September 1819, his forces took control of the town of Cali when it was threatened with reconquest in early 1820.[59] In March 1820 he was again leading guerrilla bands in the Cauca region, when Loyalist operations forced him 'into hiding in the mountains' with 'two hundred fugitives'. When he was on the verge of being captured, Runnel was alerted by local sympathisers and managed to escape.[60] In April that same year he was finally persuaded to enlist, with his men, in the regular Independent army.

Runnel's followers were not necessarily all slaves. The labour system in Cauca and the surrounding area was flexible and irregular; around Popayán at least, indigenous people worked on haciendas as often as black slaves. During the Independence period, the temporary collapse of the plantation economy gave even greater freedom to these workers, many of whom joined mobile guerrilla groups such as that led by Runnel, which was therefore probably a racially-mixed group of workers, some previously enslaved, some with other types of relationship to the haciendas.[61] This meant that when he was successfully taking the fight to the Loyalists, sympathetic commentators such as Ricaurte, Castrillón and Mosquera overlooked the freed slaves he commanded. Indeed, Runnel's leadership of the civilian resistance in Cali was widely praised at the time.[62] The opposing side, in particular the Loyalist commander General Basilio García, recognised Runnel's success in harnessing the latent power of freed slaves in the region.[63] The man directly responsible for pursuing Runnel, General Sebastián de la Calzada, was more explicit, describing Runnel as 'the English leader of the villains'.[64]

High-ranking Creole officials in the region, such as José Concha, welcomed Runnel's victories and encouraged his gradual incorporation into their fold in 1820.[65] Based on what Concha told him, Vice-President Santander dismissed allegations of pillaging and violence, writing that 'fear and terror produce these visions'.[66] Local mercantile and land-owning élites in Cali, however, regretted that Runnel had brought confusion and anarchy to Cali. The cabildo voted to replace Runnel with Antonio Cifuentes in charge of the defence of the town. Cifuentes's principal virtues were his 'honour, ability and good conduct' and that he knew how to 'contain the disasters caused by the blacks of the haciendas and the other evil people led by the Englishman Juan Runel [sic]'.[67] Implicitly, what Runnel suffered from in the eyes of the *cabildo* was a lack of honour. This derived from his association with the slaves from the haciendas and the other 'villains'. Most of the members of the *cabildo* were hacienda (and therefore slave) owners and so Runnel's bands directly affected their interests, in addition to threatening the established social and racial orders.

The first historian to mention Runnel, Demetrio García Vásquez writing in the 1920s, followed this interpretation by accusing Runnel of 'stirring up hatred amongst the slaves so that they would engage in the most terrible rampaging'.[68] Germán Colmenares, writing a generation later and more sympathetic to Runnel's concerns, wrote admiringly that Runnel 'had his own version of the revolution ... fighting alongside the lower orders and escaped slaves'.[69] As Colmenares suggested, Runnel was an integral part of the conflict in Cauca. The men who followed him were an effective guerrilla/bandit force, as proved by their participation at San Juanito and their successful resistance to Loyalist attacks on Cali. Runnel's links to newly freed slaves determined his fate, however. After his departure from Cali, Runnel and his guerrilla forces were formally incorporated into the Independents' Army of the South in Popayán. Runnel was entrusted with men and mules – but no arms – and instructed to 'surprise Spaniards and their companions, and to defeat them so as to pacify the Cauca Valley'.[70] Runnel followed these orders throughout June, when he was recalled to Popayán.

The Independent leader in Popayán was Coronel Manuel Valdés, an ageing Venezuelan soldier who was increasingly exhausted by the task of organising an army in the Cauca.[71] His orders from Bolívar were to liberate the Presidency of Quito from Loyalist control, but he was hindered by the tropical climate which caused frequent illness and extremely high rates of desertion. Runnel's incorporation into the army was an indication of how desperate things were – soldiers were required to replace those who had died or left. Even Runnel's guerrillas, who had so disconcerted the Cali élites just months previously, were welcome. Surviving letters written by Valdés reveal a little about his state of mind in the weeks when he had Runnel under his command. He described Loyalists as 'these barbarous enemies, whose intention is to destroy humanity, [who] should no longer be allowed to exist within Colombian territory'. In order to succeed, he demanded that every soldier 'pursue those traitors' who weakened his army by deserting.[72] Valdés thought himself surrounded by disloyal cowards who were unable to comprehend the sacrifices demanded by the war effort. Having lived through several years of the War to the Death in his native Venezuela, Valdés's thinking was full of paranoia, arbitrary punishments and unwillingness to compromise. At this point, with these concerns uppermost in Valdés's mind, Juan Runnel re-entered the scene. On 14 July, Runnel was sent, wearing handcuffs, from Cali to Valdés at Popayán. The reasons given by the military authorities in Cali were that Runnel had tried to resist marching orders by pretending to be ill. In the light of the 'terrible desertions' suffered by the 4th and 5th companies of the Cauca Battalion under Runnel, it was held 'that Runnel was subversively encouraging this desertion'. He was therefore 'so prejudicial to this province, and could well bring [them] worse problems, that he simply must be punished'.[73]

Ten days later, armed with these suspicions about the previous conduct of the newly arrived Runnel, Manuel Valdés wrote to José Concha to complain of 'uncontrollable and scandalous desertions'.[74] The previous night he had locked his new recruits in a barn so that they could not desert in the night, but 18 of them had still managed to jump out of a window. Those he managed to recapture were executed by firing squad, to 'set an example to the others'. He then explained to Concha that desertion would continue to plague the Independents whilst those who did not obey orders went unpunished. At the end of a lengthy exposition on how to combat desertion, came one apparently unrelated paragraph, reporting 'the Englishman Runel [sic] is leaving today for Bogotá, so that the Vice-President [Santander] can expel him from the country, if he sees fit. A man like this does not deserve to be in our country, nor in this army, under my command'.[75]

The two subjects were in fact intimately linked. The context for Runnel's expulsion from the Independent army was Valdés's continuing anxieties over his own leadership, along with allegations linking Runnel to the subversive incitement of soldiers to desert, presumably for them to join separate bandit groups under Runnel's own command. As was suggested above in Chapter 3, desertion was one of the few means that subordinate groups possessed of registering their aversion to the Wars of Independence. In the Cauca region many of the soldiers enlisted into the armies were black; for Valdés, then, their desertion became directly linked to race, and any encouragement of their insubordination became furthermore a threat to the established racial hierarchies which could lead towards *pardocracia*. Valdés found that he could not even prevent overnight desertions, and his authority was consistently undermined by the escapes of the new recruits he desperately needed to fill the ranks. Runnel was accused of two of the most dishonourable acts Valdés could imagine: encouraging the equality of coloured people and fomenting desertion. The prisoner was therefore to be sent to the capital 'with all the appropriate security measures'.[76] The same day Valdés wrote to Santander. He explained that he feared Runnel would 'set an example of insubordination', and that all the troops would desert to become bandits, warning, 'you should not keep him a moment longer than you have to, for reasons you are well aware of'.[77]

Santander did not mention receiving the prisoner in any of his subsequent letters.[78] Runnel's name never appeared again in the military diaries written in Bogotá or the towns between Popayán and the capital. None of the official or unofficial newspapers that were published in Bogotá featured Runnel's arrival there, his exile or any exemplary punishment that he received. Once Valdés had sent Runnel from Popayán, the prisoner disappeared. On 29 July, a simple note recorded that the authorities in Popayán were to dispose of any possessions which the prisoner had left behind.[79] This is an unsatisfactory

end to Runnel's story. His activities in the Cauca had attracted much comment from contemporaries up to this point. He could not have travelled up
to Bogotá and then on to one of the Caribbean ports and into exile without
being noticed. Perhaps he rejoined the Loyalist army. Possibly he escaped
his captors and fled into the mountains to earn a subsistence living, as so
many locals did in this period. One further explanation would be that Runnel never arrived in Bogotá, but that upon his departure from Popayán, Valdés
verbally ordered Runnel to be executed. Such an interpretation is supported by
José Manuel Restrepo's diary entry for 9 October 1820, commenting that 'Valdés
has committed many rigorous acts against the disaffected and the deserters,
and he has made a terrible mess of the Southern Campaign, of which we hoped
so much.'[80]

The partial reconstruction of Runnel's career reveals that at least some of
the foreign adventurers did form effective relationships with non-whites which
involved a certain degree of loyalty and respect, as shown by Runnel's success
in guerrilla warfare in Cauca. Runnel's activities, however, were not univer-
sally approved of by those in charge of the Independent armies. In areas such
as Cauca with high black and slave populations, it was easier, cheaper and,
many Creoles thought, more secure, to base these white–black relationships
on physical force. If slaves were to be allowed liberty through enlisting in the
army, it must be enforced by severe discipline. Runnel's unorthodox relations
with his guerrillas made other Independent leaders uncomfortable, and led to
his expulsion from the Gran Colombian army. His career reveals how the dis-
ruption of war could lead some subaltern white soldiers to form relationships
approaching equality and solidarity with similar groups in Gran Colombia.
Nevertheless, by leading (rather than following) groups of escaped slaves, he
avoided undermining his own position in the racial hierarchy. Runnel's 'insubordination' implicitly questioned the social and racial orders and produced
anxiety amongst military leaders.

Overseeing Slavery

Runnel was very much an exception. Many adventurers did not question or
subvert the system of slavery in the New World. Some claimed that when
they enlisted they had been promised 'six slaves each' to work the land they
would be granted in Venezuela.[81] Slave plantations were so prevalent in some
regions of the circum-Caribbean that most adventurers saw no reason to
question them. Indeed, faced with the alternative of mendicancy or returning home having made no discernable gains in currency or honour, many
adventurers found work on slave plantations as overseers, book-keepers or
labourers. One of those who worked in such a capacity in Jamaica after re-
belling at Riohacha, Benjamin M'Mahon, stressed that as an Irishman who
'abhor[hed] slavery in [his] very soul', this work was extremely unpleasant.
Nini Rodgers' work on Ireland and the 'Black Atlantic' concurs with

M'Mahon's position, awarding Irishmen a unique antipathy to the institution of slavery, because of their own colonial past and interdependent position in the Atlantic economy.[82] However the sources relating to the adventurers' encounters with slavery, M'Mahon included, do not bear out such an interpretation.

M'Mahon recorded his initial reaction upon encountering slavery as incomprehension followed by disgust. When he first arrived at Margarita in 1818, every black person he saw was 'covered with scars' which he could not understand.[83] Nevertheless, a few months working in Jamaica meant that '[his] feelings became a good deal blunted by seeing these things so often, and [he] could not help himself, being poor and unprotected, and [his] remarks never did any good'.[84] M'Mahon worked on plantations in Jamaica until 1837, and even served in the militia against slave rebels in 1832.[85] For all his shared humanity with blacks and slaves – expressed throughout his memoir, *Jamaica Plantership* – M'Mahon's loyalty to other whites came before any supposed solidarity with the unfree. M'Mahon came to hold an uncomfortable position in what Gordon Lewis called 'an accidental society composed of different groups alienated from each other, each understanding Jamaica in different terms', although he did not openly acknowledge it.[86] M'Mahon did not advocate racial equality; rather he sought to make white rule in Jamaica more benevolent and secure.

M'Mahon's *Jamaica Plantership*, published 20 years after he travelled to the Caribbean in search of adventure, honour and riches, was a story of thwarted ambition. Racial hierarchies in Jamaica provided him with employment as an overseer of slave labour; they also provided him with the tools with which to understand and explain his own unfulfilled dreams. In the conclusion to *Jamaica Plantership* he wrote 'I record it to the eternal disgrace of humanity, that treachery, fraud, cruelty and bestiality were the only stepping stones to preferment.'[87] By carefully blaming slavery's excesses on those just above him in the white social hierarchy, he hoped to preserve his honour, threatened by the abolition of the institution that had supported him for almost two decades. Like the lower-class white men and women described by Colley in *Captives,* M'Mahon was largely impotent in the face of the social, economic and political institutions that governed Britain's empire.[88] Whilst his desire to abolish slavery may have been as genuine as he claimed, M'Mahon's priorities were always his own thwarted advancement and honour. The writings of subordinate adventurers such as M'Mahon suggest that they were the victims of an inversion of the natural order. The constant evocation of the language of slavery, as noted above, carried the implicit suggestion that it was people of colour who should be in this situation, and not whites. The association of slavery with blackness meant that M'Mahon and other adventurers considered themselves to be reduced to the status of racially inferior people by virtue of their failed adventures.

Pragmatism over Idealism

M'Mahon's early career in Jamaica suggests that anti-slavery sentiments could exist quite peacefully with the willingness to preserve slavery, or at least an acknowledgement that abolition would be slow and gradual. The *Correo del Orinoco,* in the same edition that it announced Bolívar's convocation of the Congress of Angostura in late 1818, reported the escape of five slaves from an English ship anchored in the port.[89] This section explores the case of another adventurer, Alexander Alexander, to reveal the pragmatic concerns that underpinned adventurers' relations with slaves in Gran Colombia.

Alexander Alexander was one of several adventurers who joined the Independents after having spent time working on slave plantations in the British colony of Demerara. In contrast to M'Mahon and many of the Irish Legion, who were visiting the New World for the first time, Alexander had much experience of slavery, having worked on several plantations before enlisting. Indeed, Alexander found that slaves in Demerara were allowed too much freedom for his liking, and he travelled to Venezuela precisely because he had had enough of showing leniency towards them when they questioned his authority. He was therefore dismayed when he discovered that in reality Bolívar's army was a mixture of colours and social groupings.[90] Alexander served for just two years with the Independents, and then left to seek alternative employment. He found it easy to re-enter the slave economy, which survived in altered form despite the ravages of the wars and the recruitment of slaves into both Independent and Loyalist armies along the Caribbean littoral. He first found work on a plantation near Santa Marta, owned by a Spaniard who had fled to the Caribbean islands. Upon arrival, Alexander discovered that he was the only white man there. He was surprised to find that the estate was 'watched and clung to by the negro slaves, who in vain strove to protect the property of their masters', but soon he resigned his position because he feared being attacked in his sleep by the slaves.[91]

Alexander had a complex relationship with the slave system. At first, he was shocked at the brutality of the punishments employed to maintain slave discipline. After wide experience of the system, however, he became increasingly worried by the idea of black insurrection, and seriously discomforted by having to serve alongside freed slave soldiers in the Independent army. He joined with those who hoped to learn from 'best practice' to ameliorate conditions for slaves in the British colonies. Rather than arguing for the abolition of slavery, Alexander Alexander wished it to be more humane, so that the threat of insurrection would be lessened and white superiority could be assured. He had absolutely no qualms about profiting from slavery himself. This had in fact been his original motive for travelling to the Caribbean.

Newspapers published in Gran Colombia throughout the 1820s illustrate this paradox. The very first edition of Bogotá's *El Constitucional* newspaper was published on 27 May 1824, and expressed its aims as being 'to promote [Gran Colombia's] prosperity. ... the improvement of our native land'. Right at the top of the first column of the first page of the first edition, appeared the following advertisement: 'FOR SALE – A YOUNG MAN, about 20 Years of Age, without any natural defect, and will be sold cheap. For particulars apply at this Office.'[92]

Owning Slaves

El Constitucional's first edition demonstrates how, for the commercial élites at least, the existence of slavery by no means diminished the value of the liberty that had been achieved with political Independence. By the mid-1820s this liberty was a highly flexible concept that could mean more or less what any author or reader wanted it to mean. As the intended readership of bilingual newspapers such as *El Colombiano* and *El Constitucional* included retired adventurers, it is possible that some were the unnamed sellers or buyers of the slaves advertised. The papers of the *Comisiones de Repartimiento de Bienes Nacionales* show that foreign officers such as Edward Stopford, Charles W. Smith, John Benjamin Hubble and Daniel Maclaughlin were able to buy up many small amounts of *haberes militares* (assets given by the state to those who served in key periods of the Wars of Independence, or their dependants, literally, 'military fortunes'), and when they had collected enough of these, they could apply to the Commission to grant them a house, or even an estate.[93] All those named above chose to take land on or near the Caribbean coast, where many of the large sugar- or cacao-producing estates also contained slaves. So when the Polish-born adventurer Felipe Mauricio Martin asked in 1826 to be granted the Calabozo estate in northern Venezuela, he knew that over one third of the total value of the estate was made up of slaves, who were listed by name (and price) in the documents he received.[94] Adventurers such as Stopford, who spent several years consciously accumulating *haberes militares* in order to purchase confiscated Loyalist estates from the Gran Colombian government, would have been well aware that they were buying slaves along with the estates.[95]

Adventurers who settled in Ecuador also owned and managed slaves. The case of Coronel Brooke Young reveals the extent to which adventurers became incorporated into pre-existing slave-owning societies. After serving in the Irish Legion, in 1826 Young was appointed to a civilian position as the Political Judge of Esmeraldas, on the Pacific coast of the Department of Ecuador.[96] Esmeraldas was a minor port in this period, administered from the Departmental capital, Quito, from which, for the want of a direct road, Young felt extremely detached.[97] Young observed that Esmeraldas suffered from a 'complete lack of trade or commerce', and was populated by 'simpletons'.[98] Young felt that the local population was naturally inferior to him, alarmingly uneducated and potentially dangerous. The majority of the population of Esmeraldas was (and is) black.[99] Esmeraldas was surrounded by slave plantations and, early on in his tenure, Young assured the Intendant in Quito 'here not a single slave has been manumitted'.[100] By early 1827, Young was increasingly worried about his situation. He saw no hope of getting black men to work effectively on road construction projects without employing physical force, he used them as a bargaining tool in his negotiations over budgets with the authorities in Quito, and he feared that they would rebel against the government unless it paid 'someone who would never let them out of his sight'.[101]

In the same region, Sargento Mayor Charles Richard Rudd was awarded the ownership of a mine and its slaves in 1824 in lieu of payment of his unpaid officer's wages.[102] When Rudd died some years later and the estate and the slaves were returned to their original owner, Young and the Governor of nearby Buenaventura disputed the allocation.[103] Two years later, Young claimed to have discovered a conspiracy amongst the slaves at Cachaví, admitting with some embarrassment that two of the rebellious slaves were actually his own personal property.[104] This conspiracy was caused by the 'most terrible state of abandon and disorder' that the absence of the Cachaví mine owner had brought about. The mine did not have 'a resident Administrator, or even a white person who [would] look after it'. For this reason, Young believed, it had 'become the asylum of all the vagrants of Barbacoas and the Sierra' and the whole region was threatened by the 'contagious evil of the Cachaví blacks'. Young reported that they planned to 'kill all the whites' and so he sent 'an expedition of thirty-five soldiers under Teniente Gómez to the mine' to suppress the conspiracy 'using all necessary means'.[105] Physical force was the only way that Young could think of to maintain racial hierarchy.

Later in 1829, Brooke Young left Esmeraldas. As he explained, he was called back to Quito 'to respond for the death of a murderer Mr Anselmo Arroyo, who I ordered to be killed'.[106] Brooke Young's post-war career reveals much about the Gran Colombian state. The new republican authorities in Bogotá chose a foreigner to govern a peripheral coastal town in Ecuador. Young had never set foot in Ecuador before he was posted there. The extent to which Young's whiteness defined his honour and his identity meant that, upon arrival, he felt increasingly isolated from the rest of the republic and infuriated with what he saw as the simple, lazy and rebellious people it was now his duty to govern. Once in Esmeraldas (and much like Manuel Valdés in Cauca), Young was worried at being surrounded by potentially murderous slaves. He used markedly similar language to the stories told about the death of Coronel MacDonald on the Apure in 1818. In order to secure his own personal situation (and safety), he chose to continue the system of slavery which used physical force to suppress slaves' claims to liberty. In the light of the highly contingent and pragmatic attitudes to slavery taken by adventurers already studied, Young's position should not be surprising. He demonstrated a marked willingness to perpetuate the system – he owned slaves himself and he sent military expeditions to suppress suspected slave rebellions. The installation of a white outsider as governor did not go unnoticed by the slave communities in the Esmeraldas region who, according to that same governor, planned to take power and 'kill all the whites'.[107] Adventurers such as Rudd and Young saw no place for black slaves in the liberty that they had fought to give to Gran Colombia. No doubt Young's opinion was influenced by his own experiences – by the time he took up his position in Esmeraldas, he had lived in Gran Colombia for over five years, and had travelled to the Southern regions of the United States. Whatever his view of slavery had been upon arrival in Gran Colombia in 1819, it was tempered (or reinforced) by the experiences of military service and by his subsequent travels. His colleague Francis Hall, one of the most prominent radicals in Independent Ecuador, also owned slaves on the coast.[108]

The first British Commissioners to Gran Colombia circulated the interpretation that the impetus given to the abolition of slavery was one of the major achievements of Independence.[109] Some high-ranking adventurers such as Belford Hinton Wilson agreed with this assessment, and took the moral high ground on subsequent trips to the United States.[110] Daniel O'Leary believed that the decline of slavery demonstrated the growth of a new civilised culture in Gran Colombia, writing 'the weight of tyranny has been removed. The universal right to freedom has been recognised.' O'Leary, however, also noted the practical reality behind such a claim, adding, 'admittedly in practice the freedom is often abused or misunderstood'.[111] Adventurers such as Alexander, Young and Rudd were part of this process of abusing or misunderstanding freedom.

By the 1830s, the situation regarding slavery had changed further. Reduced armies no longer required slave recruits, and the propertied classes were too poor to buy new slaves. Many men and women were still slaves across the region, but other working relations were becoming increasingly common. Slave labour was increasingly recognised as untenable. A long-term change was under way, variable across regions and economic sectors, from slave labour to other forms of retained or dependent labour. By 1835 there was a growing recognition that 'liberty' should also apply to black slaves. Formal abolition had by then been reduced to the matter of finding the political will and finance to pay compensation to the owners.[112] Some slave-owners in Trinidad made overtures to the Venezuelan authorities in Guayana in order to circumvent the new British laws, but Venezuelan laws prohibiting the import of slaves into the republic were invoked to prevent 'English' slaves being brought into the country.[113] Some retired adventurers resisted the trend by continuing to own slaves – and one, George Woodbine, was reportedly murdered along with his family by his own slaves near Cartagena in 1833.[114]

Whilst some men such as Alexander Alexander had worked in slave plantations in the Caribbean before, most adventurers encountered a slave economy and environment whose physical reality was previously unknown to them. Abolition was easily contemplated in London or Dublin, but it was much more problematic in the reality of the Gran Colombian heartland, and even more so in areas such as Cartagena and Esmeraldas where the economy relied on slavery. Adventurers found themselves in an unfamiliar and insecure world where their primary concerns were to gain sustenance and employment, and to demonstrate their individual sense of honour and worth to other adventurers and to local people. Fundamental to their understanding of honour was their identity as white men. In seeking employment and serving in a republican army that included free black, *mestizo* and indigenous troops and officers, adventurers struggled to retain what they felt should be their natural position near the apex of social and racial hierarchies which were often rigidly stratified. By 1821 Alexander and M'Mahon, as well as the majority of the Irish Legion, had left the Independent army to seek employment in the slave economy of the littoral and Jamaica. By the same time, John Runnel had been expelled from the Independent army because of his 'subversive' relationships with escaped slaves. Renegades such as Runnel were no longer welcomed by Independent Creole élites who were anxious to assert their control over subaltern groups, and Runnel received no support or recognition from any of the other adventurers. Some officers such as Brooke Young remained in the Independent service but, once the liberty of Gran Colombia had been achieved, they tended to share Creole concerns about giving liberty to black slaves.

These examples show that the expeditions can not be interpreted as an offshoot of the Clapham Sect and the abolitionist movement in Britain. Neither can an argument be made that the Irish were in some way predisposed to be hostile towards slavery. The rhetoric of slavery might have been integral to the language of campaigners and radicals when the expeditions left home, but it was often just rhetoric, used by journalists, soldiers, labourers and merchants alike. Louise Guenther found in Bahia that overt British abolitionism often antagonised local élites, and that many Britons profited personally from slavery anyway.[115] When they encountered the reality of chattel slavery in the Caribbean and beyond, adventurers re-thought their rhetoric in practical terms, and they did so in highly pragmatic ways. John Runnel showed that it was possible for white adventurers to live and work with freed slaves and other ethnic groups. Most, however, expressed anti-slavery sentiments when it seemed convenient, and then attempted to integrate themselves into slave economies when these offered employment or security. They focused their struggles on bettering the condition of lower-class whites like themselves. The intellectual arguments against slavery may have been won by the 1820s but economic and personal interests easily overrode these concerns, both for local élites and for adventurers.[116]

When William Wilberforce described a Gran Colombia in which 'the darkness of slavery was receding – the light of freedom was already beaming with brilliancy' he was not personally acquainted with the region. Men who encouraged the liberty of slaves were increasingly seen as renegades, and by the early 1820s these had largely left the Independent service. Foreign adventurers, concerned primarily with preserving their individual honour and advancement in society, often shared the same personal interests as Creole élites, and, as in the West Indies, slavery was 'taken for granted as part of the immutable order of things'.[117] These interests prevented anti-slavery sentiments from being converted into formal abolition for several more decades. Race and slavery continued to underpin social relations and collective identities in the post-war period.

Notes

1 Anon., 'Account of the Public Dinner In Honour of Francisco Antonio Zea', 10 July 1822, repr. as an appendix to *Colombia – Being a Geographical, Statistical, Agricultural, Commercial and Political account of that country*, p. 741 and in Brown and Roa, (eds), *Militares extranjeros*, pp. 92–110.

2 William Wilberforce, quoted in Anon., 'Account of the Public Dinner', p. 739.

3 William Wilberforce, quoted in 'Account of the Public Dinner', p. 740.

4 John Pocock, *Wilberforce* (London, 1976), p. 283; Roger Anstey, *The Atlantic Slave Trade and British Abolition, 1760–1810* (London, 1975). The literature on the abolition of slavery is vast. See Christopher Schmidt-Nowara, 'Big Questions and Answers: Three Histories of Slavery, the Slave Trade and the Atlantic World', *Social History*, 27:2 (2002) pp. 209–17.

5 Humberto Triana y Antorveza, 'La abolición del comercio de negros de Africa en la política internacional de la Gran Colombia 1821–30', *BHA*, 82:788 (1995), pp. 9–73; and Margarita González, 'El proceso de manumisión en Colombia' in her *Ensayos de historia colombiana* (Bogotá, 1975), pp. 222–25.

6 John Lombardi, 'Los esclavos negros en las guerras venezolanas de la independencia', *Cultura universitaria*, 93 (1966), pp. 153–66.

7 In addition, see Nuria Sales de Bohigas, *Sobre esclavos, reclutas y mercaderes de quintos* (Barcelona, 1974) and Peter Blanchard, 'The Language of Liberation: Slave Voices in the Wars of Independence, *HAHR*, 82:3 (2002), pp. 499–523.

8 For the abolition of slavery in Colombia, see Harold A. Bierck, 'The Struggle for Abolition in Colombia', *HAHR*, 33 (1953), pp. 365–86. For Venezuela, see John V. Lombardi, *The Decline and Abolition of Negro Slavery 1820–1854* (Westport, CT, 1971).

9 These tensions are explored in Leslie Bethell, *The Abolition of the Brazilian Slave Trade: Britain, Brazil and the Slave Trade Question 1807–1869* (Cambridge, 1970) and in microdetail in Guenther, *British Merchants in Nineteenth-Century Brazil*.

10 Robin Blackburn, *The Overthrow of Colonial Slavery 1776–1848* (London, 1988), p. 5. Figures are estimates for the late eighteenth century.

11 Figures taken from Lombardi, *People and Places* and McFarlane, *Colombia Before Independence*. The figures given for Ecuador are estimates based on Sherwin K. Bryant, 'Enslaved Rebels, Fugitives, and Litigants: The Resistance Continuum in Colonial Quito', *CLAH*, 13:1 (2004), pp. 7–46. Most slaves in the Ecuadorian highlands were in the Chota valley; see Coronel Rosario Feijoo, 'Indios y esclavos negros en el Valle del Chota', *Sociedad Amigos de la Genealogía* (Quito), 38 (1988), pp. 171–87.

12 Holmes, *Redcoat*, pp. 124–27; Duffy, *Soldiers, Sugar and* Seapower, pp. 363–67; Buckley, *The British Army in the West Indies*, pp. 119–22.

13 Linebaugh and Rediker, *The Many-Headed Hydra, p. 311*.

14 Black adventurers are mentioned in Rafter, *Memoirs of Gregor M'Gregor*, p. 422; Weatherhead, *An Account of the Late Expedition Against the Isthmus of Darien*, p. 104; Hippisley, *Narrative of the Expedition*, p. 205, pp. 366–39;.Adam, *Journal of Voyages*, p. 84; 'Review of Rifles under John Mackintosh', 1 March 1819, in AL, Vol. 14, fo. 37. At least one black adventurer, John Lewis, had probably previously served in the British Army: see WO 97/389/12, WO 97/97/1133/226. In addition, a small number of adventurers from 'Bermuda', 'The West Indies' and 'Jamaica' were listed in 'Descriptive

Roll of the B.L, Achaguas, 22 December 1820', AHG G, Actas 3–5. Comparatively, see George Reid Andrews, *The Afro-Argentines of Buenos Aires, 1800–1900* (Madison, WI, 1980) which contains some astute observations on the historical invisibility of black soldiers in the Independence period.

15 Adam, *Journal of Voyages to Marguaritta, Trinidad and Maturín*, p. 84.

16 Devereux to Daniel O'Connell, 22 August 1824, London, O'Connell Papers, UCD, P12/3/148.

17 Chesterton, *A Narrative of Proceedings in Venezuela and South America*, p. vi, original emphasis.

18 Petition of Robert McFarlane, James A. Brush, George Still, James G. Simpson, W. Simpson, and Robert Cartmell to Edward Watts, 16 February 1824, Cartagena, TNA FO 18/6, ff. 204–20.

19 Comparatively, see Christopher Brown, 'Empire without Slaves: British Concepts of Emancipation in the Age of the American Revolution', *William and Mary Quarterly*, 3rd Series, 56 (1999) p. 286.

20 This figure is based on the statistical analysis in Chapter 2. See also Buckley, *The British Army in the West Indies*, p. 180.

21 Chesterton, *Peace, War and Adventure*, p. 170, p. 216, p. 243. See also Anon., *Travels in South America* (Dublin, 1824), p. 36; Hackett, *Narrative of the Expedition which sailed from England in 1817*, p. 36.

22 Robinson, *Journal of an Expedition*, p. 185.

23 Gad Heuman, 'The Social Structure of the Slave Societies in the Caribbean', in Knight (ed.), *UNESCO General History of the Caribbean: Vol. 3: The Slave Societies of the Caribbean*, p. 162.

24 William J. Callahan Jr, 'La propaganda, la sedición y la revolución francesa en la capitanía-general de Venezuela, 1789–1796', *Boletín histórico*, 14 (1967), pp. 182–205.

25 Comparatively, see the analysis of Andrew Jackson O'Shaughnessy, *An Empire Divided: The American Revolution and the British Caribbean* (Philadelphia, PA, 2000), p. 244.

26 Brown, *Narrative of the Expedition*, p. 7, p. 33.

27 Miguel José Gómez to Solis, 15 March 1820, Riohacha, AGI Cuba, Legajo 745.

28 Brown, *Narrative of the Expedition*, p. 67.

29 Cannadine, *Ornamentalism*, p. 123. (Original emphasis.)

30 Good examples are Vowell, *Campaigns and Cruises*, p. 167, p. 223, and Rafter, *Memoirs of Gregor M'Gregor*, pp. 326–67.

31 Porter, *The Absent-Minded Imperialists*, pp. 78–79.

32 Brown, 'Richard Vowell's Not-So-Imperial Eyes', pp. 95–122

33 [Vowell], *Campaigns and Cruises*, p. 20.

34 [Vowell], *Campaigns and Cruises*, p. 161, also p. 22 and pp. 59–62.

35 [Vowell], *Campaigns and Cruises*, p. 223.

36 Brown, *Narrative of the Expedition*, p. 59; Adam, *Journal of Voyages To Marguaritta, Trinidad and Maturin*, p. 61; [Vowell], *Campaigns and Cruises*, p. 90.

37 Ignatiev, *How the Irish Became White*, p. 59; Curry-Machado, 'Contradiction, Exclusion and Disruptive Identities'.

38 Frank Safford, 'Race, Integration and Progress: Elite Attitudes and the Indian in Colombia 1750–1870', *HAHR*, 71:1 (1991) pp. 1–33.

39 Steiner A. Saether, 'Independence and the Redefinition of Indianness around Santa Marta, 1750–1850', *JLAS*, 37 (2005) pp. 68–74, p. 80.

40 Brown, *Narrative of the Expedition*, p. 88.

41 Anon., *Present State of Colombia*, p. 92.

42 Howell (ed.), *Life of Alexander Alexander*, Vol. 2., p. 96.

43 Hall, *Civilising Subjects*, p. 413.
44 Robinson, *Journal of an Expedition*, p. 163.
45 Robinson, *Journal of an Expedition*, p. 101.
46 Chesterton, *Peace, War and Adventure*, Vol. 2, p. 153.
47 Twinam, 'Las reformas sociales de los borbones', pp. 73–102.
48 For a synthesis of the literature on race in Colombia, see Peter Wade, *Blackness and Race Mixture: The Dynamics of Racial Identity in Colombia* (Baltimore, MD, 1993), pp. 6–25; also useful is Helg, 'Raices de la invisibilidad del afrocaribe', pp. 222–24.
49 *Black Dwarf*, 12 February 1817, p. 48. For Aphra Behn, see David Brion Davis, *The Problem of Slavery in Western Culture* (New York, 1966), p. 473. *Oroonoko* itself can be found in Paul Salzman, (ed.), *Oroonoko, and Other Writings* (Oxford, 1994).
50 *Correo del Orinoco*, 29 July 1820. The travel writers who shared this opinion were few. One was Carl August Gosselman, a Swede who travelled in Colombia in 1825–26 and 1837–38. See his *Informes sobre los Estados Sudamericanos en los años de 1837 y 1838*, ed. Magnus Mörner (Stockholm, 1962), p. 21, and *Viaje por Colombia, 1825 y 1826* (trans. Ann Christien Pereira, Bogotá, 1981), p. 333.
51 Iain McCalman, (ed.), *'The Horrors of Slavery' and Other Writings by Robert Wedderburn* (Edinburgh, 1991), pp. 17–18. Iain McCalman, *Radical Underworld: Prophets, Revolutionaries and Pornographers in London, 1795–1840* (Cambridge, 1988), especially pp. 233–37, argued strongly for the existence of a 'small but continuous revolutionary-republican "underground" which runs from the mid 1790s to early Chartism'. Neither McCalman nor his underground made any mention of the expeditions to Colombia.
52 For example, on St Thomas. Anon., *Narrative of a Voyage to the Spanish Main*, p. 42.
53 Brown, 'Inca, Sailor, Soldier, King', pp. 61–66.
54 I have reconstructed Runnel's career in some detail in 'Castas, esclavitud y extranjeros', pp. 109–25. The following section develops material from this article, and I am grateful to the editors of *Historia y Sociedad* for their permission to do so.
55 In the other sources used to compile the database there were no references to any John Runnel, or John Ronald, which seemed the most obvious translation. For discussion of his possible origin see Brown, 'Castas, esclavitud y extranjeros'.
56 'Un documento que parece ser un anexo de actas de cabildo', in Latin American Manuscripts Collection, Lilly Library, Indiana University, Bloomington, Indiana, repr. in Francisco Ramírez Zuluaga, *Guerrilla y Sociedad en el Patia: Una relación entre clientelismo político y la insurgencia social* (Cali, 1993), p. 113. For Brown, see De Courcey Ireland, *The Admiral from Mayo: A Life of Almirante William Brown of Foxford, Father of the Argentine Navy* (Dublin, 1995).
57 A Loyalist document dated 28 June 1816 mentioned 'three Englishmen who have come [from Buenaventura to Cali] to join the army', ACC, Sala Independencia, C1-5f, Sig. 507.
58 Mosquera, *Memoria sobre la vida del General Simón Bolívar*, p. 305; Pérez Ortiz, *Guerra irregular en la independencia de la Nueva Granada y Venezuela*, pp. 201–54; Diego Castrillón Arboleda, (ed.), *Memorias de Manuel José Castrillón (Biografía y memorias)* Vol. 1 (Bogotá, 1971), p. 175.
59 José Manuel Saavedra Galindo, *Colombia libertadora: La obra de la Nueva Granada y especialmente del Valle del Cauca, en la campaña emancipadora del Ecuador y del Perú* (Bogotá, 1924), pp. 29–30; Joaquín de Ricaurte, 29 September 1819, Buga, in AGNC R GYM, Vol. 323, fo. 909; Restrepo, *Diario político y militar*, Vol. 1, p. 29.
60 'Estado Mayor, División del Reyno, Resumen Histórico, 1r Quincena del mes de marzo de 1820', 3–5 March 1820, AGI Cuba Legajo 906.
61 For Cauca in the Wars of Independence see Brian R. Hamnett, 'Popular Insurrection and Royalist Reaction in the Colombian Regions 1810–1823', in Fisher, Kuethe and

McFarlane, (eds), *Reform and Insurrection in Bourbon New Granada and Peru*, pp. 313–22. On the labour system in Cauca see Díaz de Zuluaga, 'La fuerza de trabajo en el Cauca grande 1810–1830', pp. 27–67.

62 Letter from José Concha, Ibagué, 22 January 1820, copied in 'Diario de operaciones del Exercito de Cundinamarca desde 1º de enero de 1820', AGNC R GYM, Vol. 325, fo. 536; *Correo del Orinoco*, 3 June 1820; Restrepo, *Diario político y militar*, 8 April 1820, p. 53; *Gazeta de Santa Fe de Bogotá*, 12 March 1820.

63 Basilio García to President of Quito, Popayán, 16 April 1820, ANE, Fondo Especial, Caja 230, 1820 Legajo 2, fo. 24.

64 *'inglés caudillo de los malvados'*. 'Diario del Estado Mayor de la División del Reyno al mando del señor comandante don Sebastián de la Calzada, en enero a abril de 1820', entry for 3 March 1820, repr. in Elías Ortiz, (ed.), *Colección de documentos para la Historia de Colombia*, pp. 186–88.

65 José Concha to Domingo Caycedo, 7 March 1820, Popayán, in Hernández de Alba et al., *Archivo epistolar del General Domingo Caycedo*, Vol. 1, p. 86.

66 Santander to Domingo Caycedo, 13 February 1820, Bogotá, in Hernández de Alba et al., *Archivo epistolar*, Vol. 1, p. 86, an interpretation supported by Colmenares, 'Castas, patrones de poblamiento y conflictos sociales', pp. 143–46.

67 *'malvados acaudillados'*. *Cabildo* minutes, 17 April 1820, AHC, Fondo Consejo, Actas Capitulares, Vol. 42, ff. 6–8. The Director of the Archivo Histórico de Cali, Amanda Caicedo, kindly provided me with copies of these documents when I was unable to travel to Cali.

68 Demetrio Garcia Vasquez, *Revaluaciones Históricas*, Vol. 1 (Cali, 1924), pp. xxix–xliii.

69 Colmenares, 'Castas, patrones de poblamiento y conflictos sociales', p. 147. How Runnel fits in to the 'bandit' theses developed by Hobsbawm, Slatta and Izard is debatable. In the absence of any documentary sources giving further details as to who the *'malvados'* that followed him actually were, any judgement would be premature. See Eric J. Hobsbawm, *Bandits* (London, 1998, third edn); Slatta, (ed.), *Bandidos*, and Gilbert M. Joseph, 'On the trail of Latin American bandits: A Re-examination of Peasant Resistance', *LARR*, 25:3 (1990), pp. 7–53.

70 'Continuación del diario de la comandancia General de la Provincia del Cauca, desde 9 de junio de 1820', signed by Estado Mayor Juan Nep.o Aguila, AGNC R GYM, Vol. 324, ff. 274–95.

71 General Manuel Valdés (b. 1780 Trinidad, d. 1845 Angostura) was active in post-Independence political life in Venezuela but was isolated by his opposition to Páez's rule, and spent much time in exile.

72 Valdés, Proclamation, 2 May 1820, Neyva, ACC, Sala Independencia, M1-4-c, Vol. 1, Sig. 6379, fo. 8.

73 'Continuación del diario de la comandancia General de la Provincia del Cauca, desde 9 de junio de 1820', AGNC R GYM, Vol. 324, fo. 316.

74 Valdés to Concha, 24 July 1820, Popayán, ACC, Sala Independencia, M1-4-c, Vol. 1, Sig. 6379, ff. 39–40.

75 Valdés to Concha, 24 July 1820.

76 Manuel Valdés to 'Sr Gobernador interino de esta plaza', 22 July 1820, Popayán, ACC, Sala Independencia, M1-4-c-1, Sig. 6532, fo. 18.

77 Valdés to Santander, 24 July 1820, in García Vásquez, *Revaluaciones históricas*, Vol. 1, p. xliii.

78 Santander's correspondence has been comprehensively published by the Fundación para la conmemoración del Bicentenario del Natalicio y el Sesquicentenario de la muerte del General Francisco de la Paula Santander (Bogotá, 1988–1990).

79 Manrique, 'Oficio del Estado Mayor del Ejército del Sur', 29 July 1820, Popayán, AGNC

R GYM, Vol. 326, fo. 209.

80 Restrepo, *Diario politico y militar*, p. 76, entry for 9 October 1820.

81 'Declaración de Jayme Powling', 12 April 1819, Puerto Cabello, AGI Cuba, Legajo 911A, 'Declaraciones de pasados o aprehendidos'.

82 Nini Rogers, 'Ireland and the Black Atlantic in the Eighteenth Century', *Journal of Irish Historical Studies*, 32:126 (2000), pp. 175–92. Henrice Altink has used M'Mahon as an example of a fervent abolitionist, ignoring the fact that he wrote some six years after abolition was enacted. Henrice Altink, '"An Outrage on all Decency": Abolitionist Reactions to Flogging Jamaican Slave Women, 1780–1834', *Slavery and Abolition*, 23:2 (2002), p. 100, footnote 20.

83 M'Mahon, *Jamaica Plantership*, p. 13.

84 M'Mahon, *Jamaica Plantership*, p. 18.

85 M'Mahon, *Jamaica Plantership*, p. 107. For the rebellion see Mary Turner, *Slaves and Missionaries: The disintegration of Jamaican Slave Society 1787–1834* (Urbana, IL, 1982).

86 Gordon K. Lewis, *Main Currents of Caribbean Thought: The Historical Evolution of Caribbean Society in its Ideological Aspects, 1492–1900* (Baltimore, MD, 1983), p. 321.

87 M'Mahon, *Jamaica Plantership*, p. 214.

88 Colley, *Captives*, Ch. 7.

89 *Correo del Orinoco*, 24 October 1818.

90 Howell (ed.), *The Life of Alexander Alexander*, Vol. 2, p. 96.

91 Howell (ed.), *The Life of Alexander Alexander*, Vol. 2, pp. 216–18.

92 *El Constitucional*, 27 May 1824, original emphasis. *El Constitucional* was a bilingual Spanish-English publication. Editorials such as that quoted here seem to have been translated from fluent Spanish into more juddering English. The original Spanish version of 'For Sale: A Young Man' was '*De venta: un negro o mulato*', so the colour-specific noun had been replaced with the generic 'Man' in English.

93 Charles William Smith (b. 1793 Ireland, d.c.1850 Bogotá) settled in Zulia in the late 1820s, and then in Bogotá between 1829 and 1835, remaining unmarried. AGNC HDS Vol. 42, ff. 543–64.

94 Estate documentation in CDM, Db4681, Db4719. For Felipe Mauricio Martín (b. 1786 Warsaw, d. 1854 Bogotá) see Angel María Galán, *Biografía del Coronel de la Independencia, Felipe Mauricio Martin, escrita para el 'Papel Periódico de Bogotá'* (Bogotá, 1882).

95 For the *haberes militares* collected by Edward Stopford in the 1820s, see CDM, Db0204, Db0475, Db2183, Db2408, Db2820, Db2927, Db4720.

96 For Young's career see *DEP*, 29 June 1820; Notes of John D'Evereux, 'Head-Quarters', 14 July 1820, AL, Vol. 14, Roll 45, fo. 65; Lambert, *Carabobo*, p. 43; Devereux to Daniel O'Connell, 24 November 1824, Caracas, NLI, Fitzsimmon Papers, Microfilm 2718 p. 1. 622; AGNC R GYM, Vol. 16, ff. 418–21; Winifred Scott to Páez, Fort Monroe, 28 May 1823, repr. in *El Colombiano*, 6 August 1823; José Contreras to Juez Político del Canton, Popayán, 27 February 1826, ACC, Sala Independencia, M1-1-c, Vol. 4, Sig. 3003, f. 3; AGNC R GYM, Vol. 1447, fo. 172; and Carl August Gosselman, *Viaje por Colombia, 1825 y 1826*, p. 361.

97 Young to Intendant of the Department of Ecuador, 18 February 1827, Esmeraldas, ANE, Fondo Especial, Caja 256, Legajo 3, fo. 42. The Intendant of Ecuador, based in Quito, was one of three Intendants of the District of the South in this period (the others were the Intendants of Guayas and Azuay, based respectively in Guayaquil and Cuenca). It was a three-year position, appointed by the central government in Bogotá, whose function was to transmit orders from the central government to regional authorities. See Vela Witt, *El Departamento del Sur en la Gran Colombia*, pp. 35–39.

98 Young to Intendant of the Department of Ecuador, Esmeraldas, 17 May 1827, ANE,

Fondo Especial, Caja 257, Legajo 4, fo. 245.

99 The institution of slavery in the region had long been contested by slaves themselves, either through physical means as discussed here, or through the courts. See Bryant, 'Enslaved Rebels, Fugitives, and Litigants', pp. 7–46.

100 Young to Intendant of the Department of Ecuador, 14 May 1827, Esmeraldas, ANE, Fondo Especial, Caja 257, Legajo 4, fo. 226. For the laws of manumission passed by the Colombian Congress, see Margarita González, 'El proceso de manumisión en Colombia', pp. 222–50.

101 Young to Intendant of the Department of Ecuador, 18 February 1827, Esmeraldas, ANE, Fondo Especial, Caja 258, Legajo 8, fo. 54.

102 Rudd to Comisión Principal de Repartimento de Bienes Nacionales, 1 April 1824, Bogotá, CDM, Db4693.

103 Young to Intendant of the Department of Ecuador, 18 February 1827, Esmeraldas, ANE, Fondo Especial, Caja 258, Legajo 8, fo. 58.

104 Young to Principal Municipal Mayor, 6 July 1829, Esmeraldas, ANE, Fondo Especial, Caja 263, Legajo 4, fo. 11.

105 Young to General Prefect of the Department of Ecuador, 21 July 1829, Esmeraldas, ANE, Fondo Especial, Caja 263, Legajo 4, fo. 60.

106 Young to General Prefect of the Department of Ecuador, 5 December 1829, Esmeraldas, ANE, Fondo Especial, Caja 264, Legajo 6, fo. 155.

107 Although using the governor's own testimony is not the ideal way of considering these 'slave voices', it is apparently the only one recorded in documents preserved in the ANE.

108 Torres, Corregidor de Esmeraldas, 10 January 1832, Esmeraldas, ANE Fondo Especial, Caja 271, Legajo 1, fo. 43. See also the official disposal of Hall's estate after his death in 1833, Juan García del Río to Sr Prefecto Departamental, 24 October 1833, Quito, ANE Fondo Especial, Caja 276, Legajo 7, fo. 165, and Caja 276, Legajo 8, fo. 123.

109 Campbell to Planta, 6 November 1824, London, TNA FO 18/3, fo. 164. The argument is also made in John Lynch, *Latin American Revolutions 1808–1826, Old and New World Origins* (Norman, OK, 1994), p. 379, and Lombardi, *The Decline and Abolition of Negro Slavery*.

110 Wilson to Bolívar, 10 February 1829, Washington, repr. in O'Leary, (ed.), *Correspondencia de extranjeros notables con el Libertador*, Vol. 1, p. 116.

111 O'Leary, *MOL: Narración*, Vol. 1, p. 13. See also William Duane, *A visit to Colombia in 1822 and 1823, by Laguayra and Caracas, over the Cordillera to Bogota, and thence by the Magdalena to Cartagena* (Philadelphia, PA, 1826), p. 354.

112 Lombardi, The *Decline and Abolition of Negro Slavery*, pp. 137–38.

113 Statement of Antonio Guevara, n.d., 1835, Angostura, AHG CB, 1835, Sig. 2. 1. 37.

114 FO documents repr. in Malcolm Deas and Efrain Sánchez, (eds), *Santander y los ingleses 1832–1840* (Bogotá, 1991) Vol. 2, pp. 176–84.

115 Guenther, *British Merchants in Nineteenth-Century Brazil*, pp. 40–59.

116 Jaime Jaramillo Uribe, *Ensayos de historia social* (Bogotá, 1989), Vol. 1, pp. 240–44.

117 Cannadine, *Ornamentalism*, p. 14.

CHAPTER SEVEN

Veteran Soldiers and the State

This chapter examines the changing relations between foreign veterans and the Gran Colombian state in the 1820s. During the Wars of Independence and the early 1820s, as was shown in Chapter 5, patriotism was conceived of as roughly the same thing as belief in liberty. This meant that foreigners who fought for liberty alongside Gran Colombians were justifiably seen and recognised as Gran Colombians themselves. Around the middle of the decade, however, with the receding threat of Spanish invasion, and political and economic considerations coming to the fore, these two threads of patriotism and liberty began to unravel. Foreigners who still believed in liberty now found themselves to be held as lacking in patriotism and correspondingly having to change the ways in which they related to the state and nation.

This chapter explores these processes by examining how the state proposed to indemnify foreign veterans for their services through the distribution of *haberes militares* and the award of citizenship. Towards the end of the decade a public debate arose in which foreigners' rights to be considered as *colombianos* were questioned. Foreigners stressed their status as veterans of patriotic fighting, and claimed recognition and recompense from the state using the language of honour and virtue that had been used during the Wars of Independence. Ultimately they found themselves to be excluded from the *patria* by the renewed emphasis on the 'national family' by the end of the 1820s. The investigation of themes of *haberes militares*, citizenship and the place of the foreigner, in combination, will show how gradually emerging notions of national identity came, towards the end of the 1820s, to hinder the ability of some veterans to integrate into post-war Gran Colombian society. Those adventurers who did settle permanently in Gran Colombia were admitted into the nation on terms that stressed kinship and affective bonds, and their experiences are explored in Chapter 8.

Rewarding the Soldiers of Independence

The *haberes militares* laws institutionalised the award of pay and land to veterans of the Wars of Independence. Just two scholarly works have examined them. Germán Carrera Damas's study focused on Venezuelan agrarian matters.[1] Francisco Miguel López's research stressed the social content of the *haberes militares* laws, and described how Bolívar's redistributive intentions to create a nation of propertied citizens were thwarted by self-interested politicians, landowners and military chiefs.[2] The guidelines for rewarding the Republic's soldiers were set down well before the majority of the foreign adventurers had even thought about leaving Europe. The 'Law of Distribution of National Property in Recompense to Officers and Soldiers', signed by Bolívar in October 1817, considered that 'the Government's first duty is to recompense the services of the Republic's virtuous defenders, who have generously sacrificed their lives and property for the liberty and happiness of the *patria*'.[3] From the start, honourable characteristics such as generosity and sacrifice were central to interpretations of what made a good soldier. The law's second article set out clearly that 'the distribution of property will be made in accordance with the promotions obtained on campaign, which are definitive proof for the merits of each individual'. The law set up a special Commission to deal with the distribution of goods and properties confiscated from Loyalists, and this was the foundation of the subsequent commissions that dealt with requests for *haberes militares* throughout the 1820s.[4]

One week after establishing the 1817 law, Bolívar published a modification that was specifically aimed at the foreign component of the Independent army. Foreigners were not given preferential treatment, as the amendment stated that 'no foreigner admitted to the service of the Republic, whether officer or soldier, will be able to claim the amount assigned to their rank, if they have not served under Venezuela's flag for two years'.[5] Unlike locally born soldiers, foreigners would have to prove that they had served for at least two years, or had performed some 'very distinguished action', in order to be eligible. With the arrival of much larger numbers of mercenaries from early 1819, the authorities re-assessed the situation. In October 1819 Arismendi decreed 'the foreign troops, who have come to Venezuela in virtue of the contracts celebrated with the Supreme Government's commissioners, constitute part of the Republic's army. As such they enjoy the same *fueros*, privileges and rights as the country's *naturales*'.[6] Arismendi promised foreign troops the best of both worlds – they were to be included in the laws of the Republic, as well as having their original contracts completely fulfilled. In the years 1817–20, therefore, the *haberes militares* laws were used to mollify complaints about delays in payments to officers and troops, and to postpone crucial questions until an unidentified future time when the state was established and institutionalised enough to sort out all of the pending claims. This stored up problems for subsequent years.

The *haberes militares* laws began to be put into action after the 1819 capture of Bogotá and the great expansion in the territory of the republic that followed. On 6 January 1820 the Angostura Congress passed its 'Law on the Redistribution of National Property to the Servants of the *Patria*'. Two weeks later an amendment noted that *haberes militares* would only be awarded for the period encompassed between 1816 and the installation of Congress on 15 February 1819, 'when formal wages began to be paid to soldiers and civil employees'.[7] Nevertheless, a special clause was to apply to foreigners, whose service up to 1 May 1820 would be included, so as to give them more chance to have served the full two years required by the law. Another modification enabled adventurers to claim for a fraction of the *haberes* if they had served less than two years.[8] This was a pragmatic modification of Arismendi's proclamation that the adventurers would be treated as regular soldiers as well as having their original contracts fulfilled. Henceforth, the Congress intended *haberes militares* to be the only recompense for all officers and soldiers, regardless of their place of origin. The small concession was made in recognition of the fact that the foreigners had generally arrived on the scene quite late, but strict adherence to the letter of the law meant that some received derisory amounts. Private John Mackay, for example, requested his *haberes* in Bogotá in 1825 after five years' service. He received just ten pesos because his late arrival meant that he had served only 15 days in the required period back in 1820.[9] At the end of 1820 a further amendment to the law was published. Very few soldiers or officers retained their original dispatches or indeed any paper records of their service, owing to the 'extraordinary circumstances of the war'. Officers, therefore, were required to vouch for the dates and location of service of their subalterns. The amendment demanded certification from 'trustworthy people who [were] certain of the facts' before any awards could be made.[10] Such conditions meant that notions of honour, trust and respect were at the centre of all petitions to the commissions.

These changes were formalised in September 1821 when the Gran Colombian Congress assembled at Cúcuta passed a new law on the distribution of *bienes nacionales* (national resources). The time had finally come for the republic to discharge its 'most sacred obligations' and 'to reward the great sacrifices of its servants who contributed to its freedom and Independence'.[11] *Haberes militares* were to be paid out of confiscated goods, land, and cash (when available). *Vales* (promissory notes) were explicitly prohibited (although speculators were to have their *vales* honoured). A national commission was to be set up in Bogotá, with subaltern commissions in other towns and cities around the Republic as necessary. Military men were to be favoured over civilians, 'in consideration of the fact that it was the armed forces that renewed and extended the lands of the Republic'. Nevertheless, these and subsequent reforms could not prevent the majority of the estates confiscated from Loyalists from 'passing into the hands of merchants who had bought up *vales* from soldiers'.[12] The rank-and-file veterans rarely prospered from the 'distinctly inadequate' way in which the state dealt with their *haberes militares*.[13]

The Cúcuta Congress also decreed on the memory of those men who had died for the *patria*. There were to be three levels of honourable death. First, those '*Colombianos* who died on the fields of honour, defending the Independence of their *patria*', deserved 'eminent and faithful' remembrance. Secondly, those who 'perished at the hands of firing squads' were named 'illustrious martyrs' whose memory should be 'transmitted to posterity with the due glory'. Thirdly, those who had served the Republic with honour and died naturally in its service would merit 'grateful remembrance'.[14] The Congress therefore formally ratified the importance of honourable service and honourable death in determining the degree of recognition that the Gran Colombian state would grant to those who had served it.

Foreigners immediately began to petition the commissions for their *haberes militares*.[15] Probably there were more than the 100 cases that survive in the archives, as the commissions' documentation has only recently been catalogued, and much of it has been restored from a deplorable state. Some records may have been lost in the intervening period.[16] The vast majority of the over a thousand Hispanic American petitioners were assigned their *haberes militares* with little ado. Most llaneros received their allocated 500 pesos for two years' service with a simple statement from their Coronel that 'they had served much more than two years'.[17] Proving the identity and services of foreign mercenaries involved more complicated and often problematic bureaucracy, which provoked the criticism that by putting so much effort into organising these 'paltry sums', the government had lost sense of its priorities.[18] Even when land was on offer (rather than currency), most adventurers preferred credit notes or cash in order to settle the debts which they had incurred during the Wars of Independence. This was the first sign that future promises had already been used up during the wars themselves – for most individuals the *haberes militares* system became a way of paying old debts rather than reaping new fortunes.

Foreign veterans seldom qualified for their full allocation of *haberes*. The maximum award for a capitán with two years' service was 6,000 pesos; on average the foreign capitanes received 3,431 pesos. For tenientes the maximum award was 4,000 pesos; on average they received 2,461 pesos. For sargentos the figures were 1,000 pesos and 619 pesos; for cabos 700 pesos and 455 pesos; and for private soldiers 500 pesos and 303 pesos.[19] In summary, commissioned officers were awarded eight times the *haberes* of their non-commissioned counterparts. Soldiers and non-commissioned officers waited for their award on average seven months longer than commissioned officers.

The commissions' correspondence casts light on the workings of early republican Gran Colombia. The Wars of Independence ravaged the economies of Venezuela, New Granada and Ecuador, disrupting communication, dislocating labour markets, and sending many of the principal landowners and merchants into exile. For this reason, currency was especially coveted as a means of assuring (or obtaining) status and honour, which in turn was increasingly linked to 'the authority of wealth'.[20] The commissions' correspondence brings out the diverse ways in which adventurers viewed the state and their honour, and the ways in which the state and its administrators perceived the adventurers.

The commission was a newly created national body and it suffered even more from the difficulties of nation-building than did institutions with substantial colonial antecedents such as the Church or customs offices. The structure and workings of the Commissions reveal some of the tensions which eventually led to the disintegration of the Republic of Gran Colombia in 1830. The principal commission operated out of Bogotá, and subaltern commissions were set up in Barinas, Caracas, Maracaibo and Cumaná, to where many of the Venezuelan soldiers (and several foreigners) had returned when the focus of warfare moved south. The geographical distance between the commissions, and the time it required for the principal commission to approve the decisions of its subalterns, caused conflict common to other national institutions.[21] Distance combined with bureaucracy to cause delay and frustration. James Constant, a musician in the British Legion, first applied to the subaltern commission in Caracas in October 1825. Owing to frequent requests for more documentation, Constant was awarded 372 pesos only in February 1827. But it was not until January 1828 that the Principal Commission in Bogotá authorised the decision, and therefore Constant probably did not receive his *haberes militares* until three years had passed from the time of his original submission.[22] The commissions adopted a punctilious regard for the correct presentation of documents by applicants.[23] Officials frequently requested that foreigners provide more validation of their careers. Often this meant proving on which date they had entered the service, or at what rank, or that they had been 'valiant and loyal'.[24] In some cases extra verification was avoided because of practical and insuperable difficulties, such as 'all of the officers from that time now being dead'.[25] The commission repeatedly requested adventurers to prove their foreign origin, questioning the foreignness of surnames such as Ashford and Hubble.[26] These practical obstacles meant that the *haberes militares* system only rarely fulfilled the hopes and needs of the foreign veterans.

The few who truly profited from *haberes militares* were well-connected officers. Both Carrera Damas and López concluded that the *haberes militares* system was exploited by élites to strengthen their hold on power in the post-war period. Neither mentioned the involvement of foreigners in this process, yet it is clear that, at least initially, foreign officers and their associates bought up *haberes militares* from soldiers, and amassed considerable collections for themselves. Experienced foreign officers took advantage of their own relative economic security and friendship with members of the commissions. They purchased the rights to the *haberes militares* of lower-ranked officers and soldiers who needed ready currency immediately and could not wait for the commission's bureaucracy to deal with their cases.[27] Merchants such as Richard Illingworth and Joseph Clark took advantage of the opportunities offered to networks of individuals who could lobby the commissions across Gran Colombia.[28] They profited from their links and friendships with adventurers such as Coronel Edward Stopford in order to speculate on the *haberes militares* of llaneros and their relatives. In Caracas in May 1826, a group of llaneros sent a petition to the subaltern commission explaining that they had asked Illingworth to represent them: 'it is not easy for us to cash in our *haberes,* because the necessary separation from our place of work and residence is impossible. So we have chosen together to give our powers to a person of trust who is resident in the city of Bogotá.'[29] Taking advantage of his mobility and networks across Gran Colombia, from the llanos to the capital, Illingworth eventually claimed a total of 67,099 pesos in *haberes militares* – by far the largest amount claimed by any one individual. The operation worked on the basis that Illingworth's contact in Caracas, Edward Stopford, paid the soldiers a minimal amount for the *haberes militares* in ready cash, which Illingworth would later recoup with profit from the awards made by the central government in Bogotá. While in theory Stopford and then Illingworth were 'representing' the llaneros in their claim, in reality the original holders of the *haberes* were paid off early on in the transaction.

Stopford was the classic example of an adventurer who exploited his links to British merchants and his position as a nexus between Creole authorities and poorer soldiers. Throughout the 1820s Stopford occupied prestigious positions of authority in Caracas as well as editing *El Colombiano* for the commercial elite. He harvested the trust formed in military comradeship and the shared masculine experience of good times (military victory, celebrations, romances) and bad times (privations, deaths of friends, illness). During the wars he had cemented bonds of trust and reciprocity, which often provided the basis for long friendships and understandings, such as those he shared with figures such as Carlos Soublette and Juan José Conde.[30] In the immediate post-war years Stopford sat on the subaltern commission in Caracas, whilst simultaneously purchasing *haberes militares* at knock-down prices from the soldiers and non-commissioned officers who appeared before him. In some cases, Stopford's conflict of interest went so far that he represented a soldier and then immediately crossed the floor to deliberate as to whether his submission should be approved.[31] In May 1828 Stopford represented eight cabos and nineteen private soldiers in their claims for long-overdue *haberes militares*. All of the men were from the village of San Rafael de Onoto in the llanos, and their claim had been organised by another speculator, Miguel Ledesma. Although none of the men could sign their names, Ledesma drew up a contract which they approved, under which Ledesma was empowered to follow their claims through the relevant authorities in the departmental capital.[32] Three weeks later Ledesma transferred this duty over to Stopford in Caracas, and the resulting correspondence revealed a chain of speculators and middle-men operating a system in which little if any of the *haberes militares* actually made its way back to the residents of villages such as San Rafael. A list of *haberes militares* being passed from the Caracas Subaltern Commission to the Principal Commission in Bogotá in 1822 indicated the extent of this speculation. A total of 325 *haberes* were held in just 25 pairs of hands, with only 13 belonging to the 'original creditor'. Most had been bought by intermediaries.[33] Over one third (132, with a total value of 38,073 pesos) belonged to Edward Stopford.[34]

These high-status networks of officers and merchants also reached into political circles. In several cases a friendship with an influential Independent officer such as Rafael Urdaneta could resolve any difficulty or bureaucratic obstacle. Similarly, high-ranking officers such as John Mackintosh and John Johnston received their *haberes militares* within days of returning to Bogotá from the Campaign of the South in 1822, in marked contrast to the months and sometimes years that subordinate officers and soldiers had to wait. In 1825 in Caracas, Coronel Thomas Richards had his *haberes militares* claim rushed through in just one day by his friends and acquaintances on the subaltern commission, granting him a coffee- and cacao-producing hacienda in Ocumare.[35] In 1827 Daniel O'Leary's *haberes militares* were awarded promptly after Bolívar submitted a personal testimony.[36] Adventurers who settled far from the administrative centres reluctantly acknowledged that this was how the system worked. As James Fraser wrote from his coffee plantation in the north of New Granada, 'it is evident that nothing can make up for our absence from the spot where anything interesting is to be done'.[37]

Low-ranked adventurers sometimes resorted to extraordinary methods in order to exploit the bureaucratic system that frustrated them. In 1825 Private George Meates and Private John Wilton left Maracaibo for Bogotá to petition the government over their unpaid wages, at the end of their five-year period of service. Wilton died on the passage over the cordillera. Once in Bogotá, George Meates claimed his own *haberes militares*, and then impersonated John Wilton so as to claim those pertaining to the deceased as well. He quickly sold on both of these entitlements to pay for food and lodging in Bogotá.[38] Meates's deception was only discovered one year later, when the Bogotá speculator Manuel Escovar petitioned the Ministry of War for compensation for the fake papers.[39] Some confusion was perhaps understandable given that several hundred soldiers were petitioning the Ministry in this period, most of whom had lost their original papers whilst campaigning in the mountains or on the marshy plains. For men such as Manuel Escovar, the foreign soldiers were not so rare as to be individually distinguishable, and this highlighted the importance of trust and honour in the transactions. Low-ranked foreign veterans suffered from their relative lack of prestige and their isolation from social networks encompassing officers, merchants, politicians and administrators. Where there was no personal acquaintance, governmental approval was sometimes impossible to obtain.[40]

Foreigners and Citizenship

The difficulties that foreigners encountered in the ways in which *haberes militares* were allocated were symptomatic of a wider discomfort in Gran Colombian society about the place that foreigners occupied within the new nation. During the 1820s this became a matter of public debate as part of a wider evaluation of the scope of citizenship.[41] The way in which private soldiers such as John Mackay were treated should make it clear that there was little interest in rewarding and incorporating low-status adventurers into the nation.

They were to be paid off and got rid of. The offer of Gran Colombian citizenship to all foreigners was hedged with sharply defined property qualifications which excluded most of the soldiers and even many officers.[42] The newly 'naturalised' foreigners who were listed in newspapers were few in number and were as likely to be merchants for whom citizenship facilitated special commercial treatment as they were to be serving or retired adventurers.

This was not how the government initially envisaged naturalisation. The official government publication the *Gaceta de Colombia*, announced with great rhetoric the granting of citizenship to foreigners in 1821: 'Thanks to the heroic triumphs won in bloody combats by our soldiers worthy of the justice of our cause ... the time for reward and rest is approaching ... '[43] Citizenship was to be the reward of the veterans who had contributed to winning Independence for the nation. From the beginning, the language used combined the metaphor of the family, in which foreigners were welcomed as brothers. The 'Ley sobre naturalisación de estranjeros' (1821) declared, 'We consider it necessary to introduce a uniform rule of naturalisation for those individuals born outside of Colombia who wish to come and establish themselves in its territory and to take advantage of the opportunities offered them by a liberal government, and wanting to encourage them to form one single family with the *naturales* whose fraternity has been denied them until now.' Individuals desirous of naturalisation had to give up all titles of nobility and the 'relationships that linked them to another government'.[44]

When a man was naturalised, his wife and children under 21 years of age also became Gran Colombians by default. The conditions for eligibility, however, were extremely strict. Applicants needed to register their desire to naturalise before the local *cabildo,* and then reside in the country for three years. This requirement was modified for men of property:

> Those who acquire a rural property in Colombia worth more than one thousand pesos will need only two years residency before they can obtain their *carta de naturaleza;* proprietors of estates worth two thousand pesos need only wait for one year; and those individuals who marry a women born in Colombia will have the right to naturalisation after six months of continuous residence.[45]

For those foreigners who bought an estate worth 6,000 pesos, there was no residency requirement at all. This meant that property or patience were the most important qualifications for naturalisation. The inclusion, however, of the potential for naturalisation by means of marriage marked the foundation of a new criterion for entry into the nation – kinship.

Given the requirements noted above, it is no surprise that most of those foreigners who became naturalised Gran Colombians were wealthy merchants. The first batch consisted entirely of merchants who qualified under the property requirement. The *Gaceta de Colombia* recognised that granting of citizenship rights to these individuals did not alter their national identities in the slightest. Welwood Hyslop, the Jamaica merchant who had assisted Bolívar during his exile in the West Indies, was listed as 'English of birth'; others were 'of the English nation'.[46] James Henderson, the British Consul in Bogotá, noted that 'several British merchants … [had] become citizens of Colombia, in order to avoid the effects of the … regulations' affecting their foreign trade, and they continued to appeal to him, as British subjects, requesting his assistance.[47]

In the first five months of 1823, just 13 foreigners were naturalised. There were five Britons amongst them: two merchants and three veterans. The veterans who received *cartas de naturaleza* (naturalisation certificates) were the commanding officers of the Albion Battalion. Even the award of citizenship took place according to strict hierarchies of rank: commanding officer Coronel John Mackintosh became a naturalised Gran Colombian citizen on 13 March 1823; and his deputy John Johnston on 10 April 1823. Teniente Coronel John Bendle became a naturalised Gran Colombian citizen on 12 May 1823, and Mayor Thomas Manby joined him later in the year.[48]

By July 1823 Congress recognised that the naturalisation law 'had not had the effects [they] hoped for because of the strict conditions imposed upon those individuals who aspired to a *carta de naturaleza*'. The requirements were softened a little in recognition of the fact that great numbers of new colonists were unlikely to arrive and that the veterans already present would have to be catered for.[49] Very few veterans took up the offer.[50] This suggests that foreign veterans, in general, did not aspire to full active citizenship to the extent that the government hoped they would. There are two possible and interlinked explanations for this. One is that the veterans continued to think of themselves as British subjects and that this identity was superior to being a Gran Colombian citizen, even when resident in Gran Colombia. Crucially, they also believed that their participation in the Wars of Independence and in the cause of liberty entitled them to rewards, in terms of *haberes militares* and, later, state pensions, regardless of their citizenship status. That is to say, the veterans viewed citizenship as largely immaterial to their belonging to the nation to whose foundation they had practically contributed. In contrast, the Gran Colombian government had purposefully set out strict criteria for active citizenship based around property, residency and marriage. Gran Colombian élites hoped to shape the nation around these values through the strict control on access to citizenship. At this early stage in the nation-building process, élites were still cautious as to which foreigners they should invite to join them.[51]

The disjuncture between the ways in which Creole and foreign veterans treated the issue of citizenship was full of ambiguities. Being a high-status, white, married veteran did not assure a foreigner of citizenship, or recognition of 'Gran-Colombianness', no matter how much this was desired. The case of Edward Stopford bears this out, and is discussed below. The scope of national Gran Colombian identity was a matter of debate throughout the 1820s, revolving around notions of gender, birth and virtue. What did it mean to be a Gran Colombian? Many 'foreigners' attempted to hold on to their 'Gran-Colombianness', which they felt they had earned by fighting in the Wars of Independence. Some local élites in Bogotá and Caracas, however, saw the presence of foreigners as unnecessary and unhelpful to the process of active nation-building in which they were involved. They were also suspicious of the links between some adventurers, such as Stopford, and the British merchant community. As such the press debate over the place of foreigners in the new republic was particularly fervent in the bilingual outlets that foreigners tended to read. From its inception in 1818, Bolívar's *Correo del Orinoco* (published in Angostura) regularly featured English translations of its principal reports and editorials. In 1822 the bilingual newspaper *El Anglo-Colombiano* was published in Caracas under the editorship of an adventurer, Francis Hall, who went on to edit *El Quiteño Libre* in 1833.[52] Within a few months of Hall leaving Caracas *El Anglo-Colombiano* had become *El Venezolano* and its editorial policy became correspondingly less accommodating towards foreigners. Between 1823 and 1826 Edward Stopford edited *El Colombiano*, another bilingual paper, in Caracas. From 1825 Leandro Miranda (the English-born son of Francisco de Miranda and friend of many adventurers) edited *El Constitucional* in Bogotá, devoting one-third of each issue to material in English.[53]

By tracing the gradual closing-up of Gran Colombian identity to veterans not born in its territory, unless they could fulfil certain social criteria, such as marriage into the national family and fathering children born in Gran Colombia, we can detect some of the shifting ideas about collective identity that underpinned the disintegration of Gran Colombia in 1830. The debate over the place that people of foreign birth should occupy in the nation began in *El Anglo-Colombiano* in 1822 just after an editorial team made up entirely of Venezuelans replaced the British editor, Hall. An editorial immediately argued that *ingleses* had excessive confidence in their perceived rights in Gran Colombia.[54] High-ranking military officials, bound by their loyalty to friends and colleagues, initially withstood this challenge. In late 1822 Pedro Briceño Méndez ridiculed anyone making a distinction between 'Colombian' and 'foreign' troops. He claimed that 'either they are foreigners, or they are Colombians. There is no middle way between these two.'[55] The official government paper the *Gaceta de Colombia* made clear its position in an editorial, probably written by Briceño Méndez himself: 'In Colombia there is no distinction between classes, slavery is disappearing and people are only differentiated by their services, their virtues or authorities.'[56] José Manuel Restrepo, Minister of the Interior, made it clear that the veterans' decision to 'link their fortune to that of Colombia, even when the cause of Independence was uncertain' was crucial in assuring them of rights in the eyes of government. 'You must be confident that your fate is closely identified with the honour of the republic', he told them.[57]

Restrepo's comment was prescient. As people's identification with Gran Colombia was slowly undermined by political challenges and separatist ideas during the 1820s, the foreign veterans' relation to the nation became an important touchstone for nascent collective identities. In subsequent years the argument moved on to the terrain of 'rights'. In an editorial in 1823 *El Colombiano* argued that foreigners and citizens had 'equal protection' under

the law for their 'persons and properties'.[58] Liberals who wished to exclude
foreigners from the nation argued that foreigners could have equal rights, but
they would have to earn them. The debate had shifted again into a purely
utilitarian mode. *El Colombiano* asked, 'what is it to us, under what name the
foreigner benefits the state, provided he does benefit it? – does he not pay his
taxes, grant contributions, serve in our militia, submit to our laws equally
with the citizen?'[59]

The argument put forward in *El Colombiano* recognised that the foreigner
was not implicitly imagined as part of the community, but rather was included
contingent upon his perceived utility. This perceived utility declined with
each year's distance from the time of Independence, when the nation's very
existence seemed to be in the balance and every possible support was encouraged. The foreigners' motivations for being in Gran Colombia were now irrelevant or, worse, suspicious. *El Colombiano* hoped, but did not assume, that all
foreigners would be tied affectionately to Gran Colombia, pleading, 'if he gives
us but the benefit of his hands and head, let us not examine matters too closely,
nor dispute about his heart'.[60] The automatic link between patriotism and
republican virtue – in this instance the taking up of arms against Spain in the
name of liberty – had been broken without repair. The hope remained that 'it
[was] the property of human nature to be more attached to the scenes around
one, to the immediate objects of one's hopes and affections, than to a distant
country, from whence the foreigner may be supposed to have withdrawn all
his interests and sympathies'.[61] Returning to its preference for utility over
patriotism, *El Colombiano* asked,

> Where is the mighty danger to the state from his cherishing in secret the love of
> his native country? Does it render his benefits to ours less substantial? His
> taxes any less welcome? His services in our militia, and in the hour of common
> danger, less zealous? Or his industry, capital and example less profitable to the
> state? If there be even cause for alarm or mistrust, it dies with the object of it,
> whilst the fruits of his industry still continue to enrich our country, and his
> children are incorporated within the family of Colombia.[62]

This last point was absolutely fundamental. As Chapter 8 shows, marriage
and producing children became the principal criteria for accepting foreigners
into the national family. It can be argued that incorporating foreigners' off-
spring into the national 'family' was seen as useful to development, on racial,
social and cultural grounds. The children of such foreigners would by birth
become citizens, and the American environment would make them patriots
so that they would henceforth contribute to 'improving' the nation's racial
and moral composition, and hence its civilisation.

This formulation, however, left those remaining adventurers who did not
marry into local families as still open to the charge of lacking patriotism. In
1824 Edward Stopford, who at the time was the editor of *El Colombiano*,
explained why he thought of himself as *colombiano*. He harked back to the
'risks' that he had taken in 'defending the cause' of Independence.[63] He

contrasted his own services among 'those who came from Guayana' against those who served the Loyalists or sought refuge in the Caribbean during warfare. Stopford argued for a conceptualisation of patriotism based not on family but on a collective journey – the adventure of independence in 1819–21, which travelled from Guayana to Caracas. This enabled Stopford to side-step questions of birth, race, culture and language, while consistently claiming not to be one of 'those newcomers'.[64]

Stopford's interpretation of Gran Colombian national identity, as based on a communal military expedition across the national territory, fell apart during the 1820s. As the military threat from Spain receded, birth and culture returned to the fore in considerations of national identity. *El Venezolano* accused Stopford of being 'the tool of a faction – [a] mercenary writer'.[65] This newspaper accused many individuals of factionalism during the 1820s, but in Stopford's case the claim was strengthened by reviving the charge of mercenary, once the epithet aimed at the adventurers by the Loyalist propagandists. In Bogotá the same charge was made of Leandro Miranda, who was born in London and was strongly associated with the British merchant élite resident in the capital.[66] In June 1827, Miranda launched a ferocious defence of his position in his editorial columns.[67] Miranda claimed that his patriotism was completely unaffected by the coincidence of his English birth. Like Stopford, he believed and felt himself to be *colombiano* and was astounded that such a thing could be disputed. However, Miranda had a more convincing argument because he could point to his father's disinterested actions in the cause of Independence. Leandro Miranda's own efforts to cement the Independence of Gran Colombia were buttressed by his patriotic family honour and his father's sacrifices for the cause. This patriarchal link to the struggle against Spain was completely unavailable to foreign adventurers such as Stopford, and its successful use by Miranda illustrates the increasing importance of kinship and affectionate bonds in conceptualisations of patriotism and national identity throughout the 1820s.

Contemporary events and commentaries in the 1820s revealed that belonging to the nation was increasingly contingent upon political loyalty and public demonstrations of patriotism. At the same time, foreigners' claims to patriotism and Gran-Colombianness were under threat from the resurgent importance of birth in conceptions of collective identities. The threat to foreign Gran Colombians accelerated as part of the wider reaction to the rebellions against Bolívar's rule in 1828, and the renewed processes of self-definition that followed. *El Colombiano de Guayas*, for example, was relaunched stressing that its editors were 'Colombians in origin and in heart', which was an implicit though obvious contrast to foreign Gran Colombians such as Hall, O'Leary, and Miranda.[68] During the battle of El Santuario in 1829, José María Córdoba proclaimed that his opposing general, O'Leary, was 'a vile foreigner and a mercenary'.[69] By the time Gran Colombia disintegrated the following year, foreignness had become a controversial political issue and many foreign adventurers were forced into exile.[70]

This chapter has shown how foreign veterans' relations with the Gran Colombian nation evolved dramatically during the 1820s. The early *haberes militares* legislation promised them the same rewards as their colleagues who were born in the Gran Colombian region, and treated them as *colombianos* within the same administrative institutions. Yet at the same time amendments were made to these laws in order to allow for the different conditions of foreign involvement, most notably their later arrival on the scene than most other veterans. When peace came, and soldiers and officers came to petition the state for their *haberes militares,* they encountered a lengthy and laborious process which often resulted in only minimal recompense – a far cry from the adventurers' original dreams of wealth and fortune. The few who did benefit from the system were the officers who had forged friendship and kinship links with political and administrative élites. These élites were in the process of creating a nation in the aftermath of warfare, and the way in which they dealt with foreign veterans revealed how their thoughts about the nation were changing. Military service in the cause of liberty was no longer enough to be assured of patriotism. The press debates throughout the 1820s instead illustrate an increasing emphasis on the Gran Colombian family. Only the foreign veterans who could demonstrate that they were now linked to the nation by kinship and affectionate bonds – who could prove that that they truly loved the *patria* – were assured of a warm welcome into the nation. These relationships are explored further in the next chapter.

Notes

1 Germán Carrera Damas, (ed.), *Materiales para el estudio de la cuestión agraria en Venezuela, 1800–1830,* Vol. 1 (Caracas, 1964).

2 Francisco Miguel López, *Contribución al estudio de la ley de haberes militares y sus repercusiones* (Caracas, 1987).

3 'Ley de repartición de bienes nacionales como recompensa a los oficiales y soldados', 10 October 1817, repr. in Grases and Pérez Vila (eds), *Las fuerzas armadas de Venezuela,* Vol. 2, pp. 295–96.

4 The commission was to reside in Angostura until the occupation of Caracas, and initially consisted of General Manuel Cedeño, Francisco Zea, and Fernando Peñalver. 'Repartición de Bienes Nacionales: Comisión encargada', 1 November 1817, repr. in Grases and Pérez Vila (eds), *Las fuerzas armadas de Venezuela,* Vol. 2, pp. 323–24.

5 'Repartición de Bienes Nacionales: Modificación de la ley', 17 October 1817, repr. in Grases and Pérez Vila (eds), *Las fuerzas armadas de Venezuela,* Vol. 2, pp. 297–98. See also 'Repartición de Bienes Nacionales: Reglamento de la ley', 1 November 1817, repr. in Grases and Pérez Vila (eds), *Las fuerzas armadas de Venezuela,* Vol. 2, pp. 320–23.

6 Vice-President Arismendi, 'Decreto sobre fueros, preeminencias y derechos de las tropas extranjeras', 11 October 1819, repr. in Grases and Pérez Vila (eds), *Las fuerzas armadas de Venezuela,* Vol. 3, pp. 116–26. Bolívar was absent, campaigning in New Granada.

7 'El Congreso modifica la ley de repartición de bienes nacionales', 21 January 1820, rpd. in Grases and Pérez Vila (eds), *Las fuerzas armadas de Venezuela,* Vol. 3, pp. 177–80. The exemption for foreigners was Article 4.

8   The exemption was not always applied; see Juan Gerbat, 21 February 1821, Caracas, CDM, Db0134, fo. 10.
9   Documents relating to Juan Mackey, 29 August 1825, Bogotá, CDM, Db0689, fo. 9.
10 'Reglamento sobre repartición de bienes nacionales', 31 July 1820, repr. in Grases and Pérez Vila (eds), *Las fuerzas armadas de Venezuela*, Vol. 3, pp. 204–7.
11 'Ley haciendo asignaciones de bienes nacionales a los que sirvieron a la República desde el año 6 hasta el 9', 28 September 1821, repr. in Carrera Damas, *Materiales para el estudio de la cuestión agraria*, Vol. 1, pp. 304–7.
12 López, *Contribución al estudio*, pp. 20–24.
13 Bushnell, *The Santander Regime in Gran Colombia*, pp. 275–81.
14 'Decreto sobre memoria de los muertos por la patria, y consideraciones y recompensas a que son acreedores sus viudas, huérfanos y padres', 11 October 1821, Cúcuta, repr. in Grases and Pérez Vila (eds), *Las fuerzas armadas de Venezuela*, Vol. 3, pp. 312–14. For a discussion of the implications of this hierarchy of honourable death in later nineteenth-century Colombia, see Tovar Zambrano, 'Porque los muertos mandan', pp. 125–69.
15 Not all of the petitions contain complete records, and those which are incomplete have been omitted from the statistical analysis that follows.
16 The commission's papers are collected in the CDM section of the Biblioteca Luis Angel Arango in Bogotá. I am extremely grateful to Jorge Orlando Melo for suggesting this source to me, and to Martha Jeanet Sierra for her continual efforts and assistance in tracking down my requests. It may be possible to cross-reference some of these figures with a document referenced by López, AGNV, Sección Intendencia de Venezuela, Legajo 128, fo. 115, 'Relación de haberes militares al Batallón Carabobo', 1822, which I was unable to consult because the volume was being restored.
17 See as a good example the papers of Private Gregorio Andrade, CDM, Db0589.
18 *El Constitucional*, 3 June 1824.
19 Non-commissioned officers are defined here, as elsewhere, as sargentos and cabos. These calculations are made based on analysis of documentation held in the CDM. The figures for Standard Awards are taken from 'Ley de repartición de bienes nacionales como recompensa a los oficiales y soldados', 10 October 1817, rpd. in Grases and Pérez Vila (eds), *Las fuerzas armadas de Venezuela*, Vol. 2, pp. 295–96.
20 Uribe Urán, *Honorable Lives*, p. 158.
21 On occasions (and, increasingly as time went on) the Principal Commission made minor amendments to regional decisions. See the increase in Sargento George Cox's *haberes* made in 1823, in CDM, Db0430, ff. 4–5. Equally, the Subaltern Commission in Caracas questioned arrangements made by its counterpart in Barinas. See for example CDM, Db0328, ff. 6–10.
22 Documentation regarding James Constant, CDM, Db0978, ff. 1–6.
23 Commissioner José Joaquín Gori once raged at General Carlos Soublette that 'in future informal papers such as these do not reach my desk'. Gori, 18 August 1825, Bogotá, CDM, Db1217, fo. 6. Gori was one of Gran Colombia's principal civilian officials. In 1828 he was elected to the Ocaña Convention.
24 See, for example, papers relating to Archibald Dunlop, CDM, Db0567, or Julian Bunn, CDM, Db0110.
25 Briceño Méndez, 24 October 1822, Bogotá, CDM, Db0335, fo. 6.
26 Teniente John Benjamin Hubble's *haberes* were delayed by 18 months because Bolívar's secretary transcribed his name as Bubble, not Hubble, on his original contract in 1820. CDM, Db2222. The officer who became known as Enrique López also suffered this problem when requesting his *haberes* in 1827. A mass of documentation, including a letter from Bolívar, was required to prove to the Bogotá authorities that Heinrich

Loeper, a Hanoverian, was in fact a foreigner who had hispanised rather too success-fully. CDM, Db0510, ff. 1–8.

27 An example: in 1825 Fernando Sirakowski claimed *haberes militares* totalling 16,750 pesos, which he had bought from soldiers of Venezuelan and foreign origin. Capitanes Francisco Sedeño and Archibald Dunlop were among his 'clients', as were Sargento Diego Renedi and Private James Flinn. Fernando Sirakowski, 1 May 1825, CDM, Db2917, fo. 1.

28 For Richard Illingworth (John Illingworth's cousin) see CDM, Db5494. For Clark, see Db0363.

29 Submission of Vicente Hernández, Francisco Mosquera, soldados Miguel Rivera, Jo-seph María Mesa, Pantaleón Serpa, Simón Gómez, 3 May 1826, Caracas, CDM, Db0134, fo. 20. Illingworth's final bill is fo. 49.

30 Juan José Conde (b. 1793 Caracas, d. 1848 Caracas) was a civilian administrator who occupied several important positions in post-war Caracas.

31 Submission relating to Capitán Eugenio Díaz, 11 February 1827, Caracas, CDM, Db0475, ff. 10–11.

32 Empowerment of Miguel Ledesma, San Rafael, 5 May 1826; Empowerment of Stopford, Caracas, 26 May 1826; Stopford presentation to Commission, 7 May 1828, Caracas, CDM, Db2813, ff. 1–3.

33 'List of twenty-five vales emitted by the Guayana Commission, being sent by the Caracas Commission to Bogotá', signed by Manuel Ruiz (b. 1763 Valladolid, Spain, d. 1834 Caracas), Fernando Key Muñoz (b. 1768 Tenerife, d. 1845 Caracas), Juan Pablo Ayala Soriano (b. 1768 Caracas, d. 1855 Caracas) and Thomas Richards (Secretary), 6 September 1822, Caracas, CDM, Db0046, fo. 1.

34 Stopford seemed not to benefit financially in the medium term – by 1827 Sir Robert Ker Porter's diary was full of references to Stopford's economic distress. For example, Ker Porter, *Diario de un diplomático británico en Venezuela*, p. 230.

35 Documents relating to Thomas Richards, 11 February 1825, Caracas, CDM, Db4971.

36 *Haberes militares* of 3,000 pesos granted to O'Leary, 23 December 1827, cited in Pérez Vila, *Vida de Daniel Florencio O'Leary, p. 346*. The original letter does not survive.

37 Fraser to Mary English, 18 April 1845, Salazar, EP, HA157/3/177.

38 Documents relating to George Meates and John Wilton, CDM, Db0598, Db0696, Db01467, Db4805.

39 Manuel Escovar to Minister of War, 10 June 1826, Bogotá, CDM, Db4805, fo. 1. The forged signature was certainly in the same hand; see CDM, Db0696 for Wilton; Db0147 for Meates.

40 Exemplified in the case of María Bachelor, 15 July 1823, Bogotá, CDM, Db1269, fo. 12.

41 For this debate see Véronique Hebrard, 'Patricio o soldado: ¿Qué uniforme para el ciudadano? El hombre de armas en la construcción de la nación (Venezuela, primera mitad del siglo XIX)', *Revista de Indias*, 225:62 (2002), particularly p. 443, p. 450, and Armando Martínez Garnica, 'El debate legislativo por las calidades ciudadanas en el régimen representativo del Estado de la Nueva Granada (1821–1853)', *BHA*, 90:821 (2003) pp. 241–63.

42 The 'Ley sobre la naturalisación de extranjeros' was reproduced in the *Gaceta de Co-lombia*, 20 September 1821. This law was amended to relax the residence qualification on 13 July 1823. For a later view of the naturalisation of foreigners as 'unnecessary', see the editorial of *El Constitucional*, 12 January 1826. The government was slower to recognise the services of sailors than soldiers; see 'Decreto mandando despachar cartas de naturaleza a los extranjeros que hayan servido en buques nacionales', 3 May 1825, repr. in Grases and Pérez Vila (eds), *Las fuerzas armadas de Venezuela*, Vol. 5, p. 29.

43 *Gaceta de Colombia*, 6 September 1821.
44 *Gaceta de Colombia*, 20 September 1821. This meant resigning any commissions retained in the British Army or Navy.
45 *Gaceta de Colombia*, 20 September 1821.
46 *Gaceta de Colombia*, 22 September 1822. Hyslop received his on 17 December 1821; Guillermo Linch, who had been a Capitán in the British Legion and was now a merchant settled in Mompox, received his on 21 March 1822. Antonio Elías Martín 'francés de nación, residente en Guayana', received his on 18 May 1822. Juan Atalaya 'español residente en Maracaibo' received his on 4 July 1822. Nicolás Lamoetie 'de nación francesa' received his on 8 August 1822. Juan Dousdebes 'francés de nación' received his on 19 September 1822.
47 Henderson to Planta, 4 April 1824, Bogotá, TNA FO 18/4 fo. 51.
48 *Gaceta de Colombia*, 15 June 1823. The others were five Frenchmen, two Italians and one Spaniard.
49 *Gaceta de Colombia*, 13 July 1823. Residence previous to the petition to the *cabildo* could now be included.
50 The sources available for the later period are less comprehensive. Major Julius August Reinholdt and Capitán Brownlow became naturalised Colombian citizens in 1824. Naval capitán Thomas Brown became a naturalised Colombian citizen in 1825. See AGNV IP Vol. 72, ff. 222–38; TNA FO 18/4 fo. 100; AGNV IP Vol. 13, fo. 157.
51 For the rise and fall of European immigration to Colombia in the later nineteenth century, see Martínez, 'Apogeo y decadencia del ideal de la inmigración europea en Colombia', pp. 3–45, and at greater length, in Frédéric Martínez, *El nacionalismo cosmopólita: La referencia europea en la construcción nacional de Colombia, 1845-1900* (Bogotá, 2001). The principal source on the first immigration schemes is 'Colección de documentos sobre inmigración de extranjeros, reimpresos de la *Gaceta de la Nueva Granada*, no. 611, del 13 de septiembre de 1847' (Bogotá, 1847).
52 *El Quiteño Libre* has been analysed in excellent detail in Diego Pérez Ordóñez, '*El Quiteño Libre': El más espectacular periódico de oposición de la República* (Quito, 1999), and is not considered here.
53 The standard introduction to the Colombian press is David Bushnell, 'The Development of the Press in Great Colombia', *HAHR*, 30:3 (1950), pp. 432–52, which built on Gustavo Otero Muñoz, *Historia del periodismo en Colombia* (no date), BNC, Fondo José María Quijano Otero.
54 *El Anglo-Colombiano*, 20 July 1822.
55 Briceño Méndez to Morales, undated, Bogotá, repr. in *Gaceta de Colombia*, 28 November 1822.
56 Editorial, *Gaceta de Colombia*, 27 October 1822.
57 Restrepo, in *Gaceta de Colombia*, 10 December 1822.
58 *El Colombiano*, 8 October 1823.
59 *El Colombiano*, 15 October 1823.
60 *El Colombiano*, 15 October 1823.
61 *El Colombiano*, 15 October 1823.
62 *El Colombiano*, 15 October 1823.
63 *El Colombiano*, 10 March 1824.
64 This is consistent with Thibaud's conclusions in *Repúblicas en armas* on the evolution of a national 'Colombian' identity based primarily upon territorial expansion grounded in military success.
65 *El Colombiano*, 24 March 1824.
66 *El Constitucional*, 9 August 1827.
67 *El Constitucional*, 14 June 1827.

68 *El Colombiano de Guayas,* 6 August 1829.
69 Cited in Pérez Vila, *Vida de Daniel Florencio O'Leary*, p. 438.
70 These are listed in Jaime Duarte French, *América del Norte al Sur: ¿Corsarios or Libertadores?* (Bogotá, 1975), p. 520.

CHAPTER EIGHT

Settling In

Chapter 7 showed how the strict criteria demanded by Gran Colombian élites meant that the question of citizenship or naturalisation was principally a matter for veteran officers or merchants. Lower-status officers and rank-and-file soldiers were excluded from active citizenship and were integrated into society in other ways. This chapter explores the practical details of how many adventurers settled in Gran Colombia and its successor states, examining which regions they lived in, what occupations they exercised, and whom they married. The final part discusses the different aspects of honour, service and allegiance that were articulated by the adventurers, and examines how they reacted to their treatment by the state in the decades that followed Independence. The chapter demonstrates that veteran soldiers gradually changed the way they conceived of themselves and their roles in the Wars of Independence, and that to some extent they were correspondingly assimilated into society.[1] The way that they thought about identity, honour and belonging changed as a result of being denied the rewards that they felt entitled to as a result of their adventures in the Wars of Independence. Veterans repeatedly claimed that, as a result of their experiences, they felt that they were Gran Colombians, and later Venezuelans, New Granadans and Ecuadoreans. These repeated claims to national belonging contributed over the course of the nineteenth century, to the gradual broadening of scope of the nation in the Gran Colombian region.

In the post-Independence years, people in Gran Colombia accepted the British and Irish into social relationships based around trust, friendship and mutual benefit, in similar fashion as occurred across the British empire in the same period.[2] This was especially apparent in, although not exclusive to, élite circles.[3] According to Alan Knight, leisure activities were part of the way in which Britons attempted to 'create congenial collaborating élites [by converting] them to the British way of life'.[4] The adventurers observed with pleasure the social ascent of those Creoles who associated with them.[5] This was a two-way process – in 1825 Santander reported that 'the *ingleses* in Bogotá [were] now crazy with happiness' as a result of his attention.[6]

Leisure activities were integral to the formation of these relationships between Creoles and foreigners. One arena was horse-racing, just as it was during the Wars of Independence.[7] Diplomats complained about it, but Creoles and foreigners gambled together on the horses, and, according to the British

Commissioner John Potter Hamilton, lower-status adventurers and their Bogotano peers did so too, with festival days providing another focus for drinking, partying and comradeship.[8] Aside from memoirs such as Hamilton's, though, there is a lack of first-hand evidence for such events, and the only way to gain insight into the way that the less-celebrated foreigners settled in Gran Colombia in the 1820s is to examine where they lived, with whom they associated, and what their occupations were. The subsequent analysis is used to draw out general trends about the ways in which foreigners were incorporated into society in the Gran Colombian region.

Occupations

Table 8. 1   *Principal post-war occupations of adventurers in Gran Colombia post-1822[9]*

Occupation	Number of Adventurers	%
Accountant	1	0. 26
Administration	12	3. 07
Arms dealer	1	0. 26
Army	140	35. 81
Bricklayer	1	0. 26
Diplomacy	6	1. 53
Doctor	9	2. 30
Evangelist	1	0. 26
Farming	3	0. 77
Fishing	1	0. 26
Housewife	1	0. 26
Jockey	1	0. 26
Journalist	1	0. 26
Landowner	5	1. 28
Merchant	7	1. 79
Mining	5	1. 28
Navy	14	3. 58
Newspaper agent	1	0. 26
Novelist	1	0. 26
Security guard	1	0. 26
Printer	1	0. 26
Retired	165	42. 20
Servant	3	0. 77
Shop owner	1	0. 26
Trader	2	0. 51
Student	1	0. 26
Tailor	1	0. 26
Teacher	3	0. 77
Translator	2	0. 51
Total in Selection	*391*	*100*

Table 8. 1 allows a few general remarks to be made, even though it is constructed from fragmentary documentation such as pension records and casual
references in correspondence and newspapers. First, very few of the adventurers recorded here became permanently involved in farming, or in skilled occupations such as those of muleteers, masons, blacksmiths and inn-keepers.
Despite the number who claimed to have been artisans in Britain or Ireland
(see Chapter 1), there is little documentary evidence to show that they went
on to exercise these trades in Gran Colombia. Perhaps they found no demand
in the post-war economy of what was still a predominantly rural region or
perhaps they discovered that even soldiering assured them of a better income.
Possibly it was a case of supply outstripping demand, or of artisans dying or
deserting at a higher rate than labourers. Bogotá, Socorro and Quito already
had a plentiful supply of artisans in the late colonial period, so incomers with
skills such as carpentry, tailoring or shoemaking were not required anyway.[10]
It is possible that some artisan adventurers who did settle were not recorded
in archival documents. Sir Robert Ker Porter recorded that in the 1820s in
Caracas some adventurers worked in artisan trades, for example as butchers
and cobblers; these individuals do not appear in other sources.[11]

The army was by far the most prevalent occupation, along with the navy,
medicine and political administration (all of which, in the sense that they did
not involve adventurers having to learn new roles, were extensions of their
military service).[12] Several years after they 'retired' from the service, many
adventurers rejoined the army, either because the government called them up
in an emergency, or, as in the case of financially stricken James Fraser, because they 'had to take whatever [they] could'.[13] Table 8. 1 includes 165 'retired' soldiers for whom no further profession has been detected. What exactly this 'retirement' consisted of is less clear. Certainly many of them cashed
pensions at the same time as taking up other types of employment, but given
the small size of most urban population centres, it is possible that when these
adventurers retired from military service they also left the regional capitals
(hence going beyond the reach of much of the archival documentation) and
entered semi-autonomous rural trading and a semi-subsistence farming existence. This is the picture that emerges from the correspondence between Mary
English and James Fraser, who took over neighbouring cacao and coffee plantations around Cúcuta.[14] The prospect of such a precarious agricultural existence probably deterred many potential farmers. An 1827 book promoting agricultural emigration from Britain recorded that 20 adventurers had turned to
farming in Gran Colombia, while Table 8. 1 records no more than ten named
individuals as owning land or farming.[15] There is little evidence to suggest
that foreign settlers were in the vanguard of improvements in farming, live-
stock or irrigation.[16] Overall, perhaps because of their difficult experiences in
long years of rural campaigning, adventurers preferred to settle in towns rather
than the countryside. Some adventurers sought work in their previous trades.
Hugo Hughes petitioned the government for work in copper mining, stating,
'I have been brought up in one of the most considerable copper mines in

England, and ... I have a complete knowledge of all the different operations of the Smelting and Refining of Copper Ores as practised in the most extensive works in England'.[17] Private Daniel Dowd advertised his services as a 'gardener, bricklayer or tiler of houses' in *El Colombiano*.[18] Other adventurers were unable to find paid labour and drifted into criminality. Ker Porter described the 'useless, invalid, drunken English soldiers' who lived in Caracas, thieving money and jewellery from more affluent individuals.[19] Peter Grant epitomised the failure of some adventurers to settle into society. He was accused of attempted rape in 1820 in Angostura, of assault in June 1826 in Bogotá, and then a month later of the murder of the US Consul.[20] Ker Porter described him as a 'negative, useless type ... an infamous thief'.[21]

Very few adventurers became successful entrepreneurs after retirement. Probably many practised more than one occupation, in addition to receiving a military pension and taking whatever seasonal work came to them, combined with an occasional return to military duties in times of crisis. One of the merchants examined in Chapter 1, James Hamilton, continued to live and trade in Angostura, and was awarded British consular positions as a reward. Capitán Guillermo Lynch established himself as a merchant in Mompox.[22] But in the 1820s many foreign merchants were bankrupted, and success stories were rare even before the 1826 crash that triggered the withdrawal of much foreign investment.[23] There were only limited opportunities for adventurers once warfare was over, and this meant that the adventurers settled all across Gran Colombia. Those adventurers who did earn a comfortable existence from their adventuring in Gran Colombia were limited to those who married into established families, and other senior officers who profited from their links with the important figures running the new republics.

Where to Settle

Table 8. 2 shows that, of the 384 named individuals featured, 38 per cent settled in Venezuela, 5 per cent in Ecuador and 57 per cent in New Granada, with a marked emphasis towards major urban centres. The fragmentary documentation upon which Table 8. 2 is based means that it can do no more than suggest general trends in conjunction with other sources. The apparent statistical preference for New Granada over Venezuela or Ecuador can largely be attributed to the number of soldiers who were last documented in Bogotá before disappearing from the historical record. Alternatively, Frank Safford has argued that the Bogotá élites admired foreigners for their financial aptitude, and therefore facilitated their rise from humble employee or artisan to capitalist within just ten years.[1] This could explain why so many veterans chose to remain in Bogotá. It is possible that many of these individuals subsequently left Gran Colombia entirely, but Table 8. 2 indicates the existence of a Bogotá–Caracas axis that was most welcoming to the retired adventurers. This may have been as a result of the colonial pasts of these cities as seats of *audiencias*, which gave them a more direct link with Europe than other urban or rural centres. The better communications with Europe, in addition to the opportunities provided by greater economic activity, may also explain the relatively high number of adventurers who settled in major ports such as Cartagena and Guayaquil. Many of the adventurers did not stay in just one place. Peter Grant spent over five years in Caracas, in Bogotá and in Tocaima. Edward Brand lived for two decades in Bogotá, and another two in Caracas. Francis Hall ran newspapers in Caracas and Quito, and was involved in a lengthy topographical survey on the Magdalena river.

Table 8. 2 *Geographic distribution of adventurers across Gran Colombia post-1822*

Places settled	Number of individuals	%
Angostura	5	1. 30
Barinas	1	0. 26
Barquisameto	1	0. 26
Barrancas	1	0. 26
Barranquilla	2	0. 52
Bogotá	166	43. 23
Buenaventura	1	0. 26
Caracas	100	26. 04
Cartagena	10	2. 60
Citera	1	0. 26
Coro	1	0. 26
Cúcuta	1	0. 26
Cuenca	6	1. 56
Esmeraldas	2	0. 52
Guayaquil	5	1. 30
La Guaira	1	0. 26
Maracaibo	21	5. 47
Margarita	1	0. 26
Medellín	5	1. 30
Mérida	3	0. 78
Mompós	2	0. 52
Pamplona	2	0. 52
Panama	1	0. 26
Pasto	1	0. 26
Popayán	11	2. 86
Puerto Cabello	12	3. 13
Quito	8	2. 08
Santa Marta	2	0. 52
Socorro	1	0. 26
Sogomoso	1	0. 26
Tocaima	1	0. 26
Valencia	4	1. 04
Vélez	1	0. 26
Zipaquirá	3	0. 78
Total in selection	*384*	*100*

Cosmopolitan ports were favoured over isolated mountain towns and villages. As has been documented by Townsend, Guayaquil families married their daughters to foreign businessmen in the late-colonial period, and this continued into the 1820s.[25] A change had occurred, however, in that these foreigners were now more likely to be British, Irish, North American or German, rather than Spanish, as they had generally been in the past. This openness was reciprocated by the adventurers, who appreciated the tolerance they found in the ports in contrast to the often conservative interior. As Thomas Manby wrote to a friend in 1821, 'you will like Guayaquil. If you have a bit of money, it is better than anywhere I have visited in Colombia (but if you do not have any, it could be hellish). No one pays much attention to army officers, except the women, which is exactly as it should be, as far as I am concerned.'[26] Saether's work suggests that the Wars of Independence occasioned a change in relations with foreigners on the New Granadan Caribbean coast. Despite (or perhaps because of) their colonial contact with foreign smugglers and pirates, local élites had married amongst themselves until Independence. Saether's study of their marriage patterns demonstrated that the local élite in Santa Marta now actively sought alliances with foreigners after 1821.[27] This desire was fulfilled by the influx of white foreign veterans of the Wars of Independence, who therefore fitted neatly into the new hierarchies of republican society.[28] In contrast, more isolated mountainous areas attracted fewer adventurers. Perhaps a town such as Popayán was too conservative and too Catholic to encourage retired adventurers to settle there. Even Quito had few foreign residents – just one Briton served in the Quito militia in 1823 less than a year after the Albion Battalion passed through.[29]

Some adventurers settled away from the capitals or principal ports, mainly where their services were in demand by the local population, or as political administrators appointed from Bogotá. Hugo Hughes settled in Medellín, from where he worked on various mining projects. Doctors settled in Barquisameto and Santa Marta, areas where their services were required by foreign traders as well as local people. Thomas Murray was a political administrator in Vélez, as were Brooke Young in Esmeraldas and Arthur Sandes in Cuenca. The relationships they formed during warfare subsequently allowed these veterans to find employment within local ambits. Those who did not have such immediate and remunerative employment often stayed in the capital cities, close to the seats of the governments that they perceived as their best source of employment, honour and financial assistance. Urban centres were also the principal arenas for public sociability, and therefore the best place for meeting and marrying local women.[30]

Marriage

Table 8. 3:   Adventurers' marriages in Gran Colombia[31]

Name	N	Spouse	Year	Place	Wife's relations
Ashdown, Charles William	BI	María del Carmen Landaeta	1824	Valencia	Daughter of Ignacio Landaeta and Teresa Hidalgo
Blair Brown, Hugo	I	Eduviges Gaviria	c. 1828	Medellín?	Daughter of F. A. Zea's cousin
Brigard, Juan de	P	Unknown	1824	Unknown	
Brown, Thomas	S	María Francisca Ruiz	1828	Cumaná	Daughter of Francisco Ruiz and María del Carmen Ruiz
Brun, Jayme	SP	Unknown	n/a	Cartagena?	
Burton, David Adolph	BI	Unknown	c. 1823	Angostura	
Caballi, Carlos	IT	Unknown	c. 1831	Popayán?	
Castelli, Clemente	NA	Unknown	n/a	Unknown	
Chamberlayne, Charles William	B	Eulalia Ramos	<1817	Venezuela	
Collins, Samuel	E	Unknown	n/a	Unknown	
Council, Daniel	BI	Dominga Alvares	<1820	Caracas?	She later married Daniel Maclaughlin
Cox, George	E	Unknown	1822–42	Caracas?	
Curtis, Javier Francis	M	Antonia España	c. 1821	Angostura	Widow of Francisco Antonio de Orellana
D'Cross, Frederick	I	Unknown	c. 1831	Popayan	
de Adlercreutz, Fredrik Thomas	SW	María Josefa Diaz Granados	1821	Cartagena?	Daughter of Spanish officer
Finlay, Edward	BI	Eliza Barres	<1818	Trinidad	
Flegel, Ludwig	P	Ursula de Liendo	1822	Caracas	Daughter of Independent Coronel Juan José Liendo
Fraser, James	S	María Ignacia Marquez	c. 1830	Cúcuta?	
Gregory, Edward	I	Carlota de Castro Jimeno y Collantes	1825–30	Santa Marta	
Hallowes, Miller	E	Unknown	n/a	Unknown	

Name	N	Spouse	Year	Place	Wife's Relations
Hands, John	E	Trinidad Páez Lobera	1823	Pto Cabello	
Harris, William	I	Unknown	c. 1830	Cuenca	
Hill, John	E	Unknown	c. 1825	Coro?	
Illingworth, John	B	Mercedes de Decimavilla	1823	Guayaquil	Daughter of Vicente Decimavilla from Cádiz, and Gertrudis Cosio also Spanish
Irwin, John	I	Josefa Joaquina Vale Mijares	c. 1827	Maracaibo	
Jeampierre, Francisco	F	Mercedes Mauricia Bruzual	1825	Sta Marta	Daughter of Antonio Bruzual of Caracas
Joly, Nicholas	F	Unknown	<1824	Margarita	Sister of Juan Bautista Arismendi
Kean, Francis	I	Unknown	1821	Maracaibo	
Klinger, Adolfo	H	María Cabrera	c. 1826	Quito	
Lecumberry, Ignacio	F	Rita Robles	c. 1826	Quito	Sister of Francisco Robles, future President of Ecuador
Lee, Robert	BI	Leonor Franco	c. 1840	Bogotá	
Luzon, Henrique	G	Unknown	<1828	Unknown	
MacGregor, Gregor	S	Josefa Lobrera de Bolívar	1811	Valencia	Cousin of Simón Bolívar
Maclaughlin, Daniel	S	Dominga Alvares	c. 1828	Caracas?	She had been married previously to Daniel Council
MacPherson, John	S	Unknown	n/a	Unknown	
Manby, Thomas	E	María Josefa Fortoul	1836	Bogotá	Daughter of General Pedro Fortoul
Martin, Felipe Mauricio	P	Francisca Gaitán	1823	Bogotá	Daughter of Carmen Rodriguez de Gaitán
Mayne, Henry	E	Rita Paris	1824	Bogotá	Daughter of General Joaquín Paris
Meyer, Johannes	R	Unknown	c. 1832	Bogotá	

Name	N	Spouse	Year	Place	Wife's Relations
Minchin, Charles	I	Unknown	1827	Coro	
Minuth, John	P	María Genovera Bitaude	c. 1840	Cartagena	
Murphy, Richard	I	María de la Natividad Landaeta Codecido	1830	Valencia	Daughter of militia capitán
O'Connor, Francisco Burdett	I	Francisca Ruyloba	1827	Bolivia	
O'Hara, N	B	Unknown	<1819	Caribbean	Josefa MacGregor's servant
O'Leary, Daniel Florence	I	Soledad Soublette	1828	Bogotá	Sister of Carlos Soublette
Rasch, Frederick	H	Francisca Granados	c. 1830	Cartagena	
Von Reimboldt, Julius Augustus	H	Ana María Salina	1824	Maracaibo	Daughter of Independent officer Fabián Salina and Antonia Miranda
Richards, Thomas	E	María Vergara	c. 1825	Caracas	
Rooke, James	BI	Ana Tucker Rooke	1815	St Kitts	Daughter of Governor of St Kitts
Russian, Giuseppe	I	Ana Flex	1819	Margarita	
Server, Thomas	NA	Francisca Antonia González de Goursac	1834	Angostura	Daughter of María de la Cruz González
Sirakowski, Ferdinand	P	María Infanta Rusiano	1822	Bogotá	
Smith, Julian	BI	Unknown	c. 1825	Bogotá	
Smith, William	S	Mercedes Vera	c. 1828	Caracas	
Smith, William Porter	BI	Unknown	1822	Sta Marta	
Stagg, Leonard	BI	Unknown	1830s	Quito	Daughter of Juan José Flores
Stopford, Edward	I	Laura Margarita	<1818	n/a	
Thomas, Alexander	BI	Soledad Pérez	1818	Angostura	

Name	N	Spouse	M	Married	Wife's Relations
Uslar, Juan	H	Dolores Hernández	1823	Valencia	
Vernon, George	B	Barbara Muñoz	1843	Barrancas	
Voigt, Louis	F	Unknown	c. 1825	Cartagena?	
Wallace, George	E	Baltasara Caldas	c. 1800	Popayán	Relative of scientist Francisco José de Caldas
Weir, Henry	E	Dolores Salina	1826	Maracaibo	Daughter of Independent officer Fabián Salina and Antonia Miranda
Woodbine, George	BI	Unknown	n/a	Unknown	
Wright, Thomas	I	María de los Angeles Victoria Rico y Rocafuerte	1832	Guayaquil	Daughter of Vicente Rocafuerte

Table 8. 3 lists the 66 marriages firmly documented to have taken place between named foreign adventurers and Gran Colombian women.[32] References to these marriages were found in fragmentary fashion across a range of primary and secondary sources and they cannot be taken as comprehensive. Nevertheless, they reveal some illustrative trends. Most of the men in Table 8. 3 were officers; matrimony was expensive and may have been neglected by soldiers from the rank and file, but more likely their marriages escaped the documentary record. Before 1821 very few adventurers married local women: perhaps the attitude of Daniel O'Leary was typical. His commanding officer, Antonio José de Sucre, described him as having 'such a consistent heart, which you give to the first beauty you meet wherever you go'.[33] One of the exceptions was Private Francis Kean, who married in 1820 during a break in fighting at Altagracia on the Venezuelan coast.[34] The failure officially to ratify relationships in this early period was perhaps caused by the crisis of ordination in the Catholic Church, which meant a huge shortage of priests who could otherwise have officiated at weddings.[35] Just one priest was recorded as travelling with the expeditions. Father Cornelius O'Mullan accompanied John Devereux, and he died of fever less than one year after his arrival in Gran Colombia.[36] There were no Protestant churches and there were no possibilities for civil marriage.

Adventurers were more likely to marry in the later 1820s, once their military careers were over and they looked to settle into domestic life. Many married the daughters of principal military figures from the Independent army and navy. Others married the cousins of civilian politicians or members of

traditional land-owning families, who were the principal dispensers of patronage in a new and uncertain period. This was a sharp divergence from the
practices of Britons elsewhere in Latin America in the same period. Britons
in Bahia, Buenos Aires and Santiago de Chile followed a 'pattern of social
integration as a separate community within the local society'.[37] In these places,
where most Britons were engaged in some form of commercial activity, there
was barely any intermarriage at all between Britons and Latin Americans;
Britons remained 'a small group of people who saw themselves as separate
from the local community, and made a concerted effort to remain that way,
raising their children with the expectation that they would not marry out'.[38]

Thomas Manby is a good example of one of the ways in which integration
through marriage worked. Manby was exceptional amongst the adventurers
because he did naturalise as a Gran Colombian at an early stage (1825), but his
extensive surviving private correspondence is revealing of the ways in which
local women were perceived as the best way of assuring a permanent link to
the adopted *patria*. Reflecting, 'I dearly love women (not civil wars) and wine',
Manby felt that becoming a *padre de familia* would best cement his position in
post-colonial New Granadan society.[39] In 1833 Manby revealed his dilemma
to Tomás Cipriano de Mosquera: 'I am 34 years old and still single. I do not
have enough to return to Europe, and here there are hardly any young women
with money. I could not lower my standards and marry a penniless woman!'[40]
Manby hoped that his dreams of financial security would be fulfilled with an
honourable marriage to a upper-class Creole woman, but his hopes of one
such possibility were shattered when 'the young lady broke off the match,
because some kind friends told her I was fond of Women – and what man of
taste is not? – that I was a bad temper, and intended to cut the family altogether after our marriage'.[41] Manby was devastated by being turned down by
the 'young lady', especially on the grounds that his previous reputation as a
womaniser had reached his betrothed. Manby claimed, 'the damsel has fallen
100 per cent in public opinion', but in fact it was Manby himself whose public
reputation was incompatible with marriage to a daughter of the Bogotá élite.
His whiteness and considerable military honour were not enough for a Creole
woman more concerned with his apparent reputation for womanising, his temper and his disrespect for her family.[42] After this setback, Manby resolved
that his prime concern in any future marriage would be 'the cash – if we can
ever get hold of it'.[43] Such a possibility arose when Mary English proposed
General Pedro Fortoul's daughter as a potential bride. Manby made it clear
that the marriage would have to be on his terms, and stated, '[It] would be
dependent on Fortoul meeting my wishes in a manner which I flatter myself
I have an unquestionable right to expect, according to the true spirit and meaning of Rank, respectability, etc., etc. conceded in cases of marriages.'[44]

Economic concerns underpinned the emotional ties that came to bind the
adventurers to Creole élites. Manby wished to assure his financial security,
but he was also anxious that his concern with the wealth of his bride's family
should not be thought to be 'mercenary'.[45] The correspondence of the Fortoul

family, however, shows that they shared Manby's pragmatic concerns.[46] Eduardo Fortoul noted that now he was *padrino* (godfather) to one of the Manby children, 'in this way our relationship is deepened further'. Fortoul used Manby to enlarge his circle of business contacts and to expand his commercial networks, as is evidenced by the correspondence on these matters between the two.[47] Use of godparents as a means of broadening kinship relations within 'our children's *patria*' was widely used in 1830s New Granada.[48] There was a political dimension to the union too: Fortoul was a cousin of Santander, president of New Granada between 1837 and 1841.

The marriage strategies of élite Gran Colombian women and their families are also revealed by Table 8. 3. Manby's first proposed bride's rejection of him hints at the way foreigners were selected by Creole families, and not necessarily the other way round. Manuel Pérez Vila wrote that Soledad Soublette married Daniel O'Leary 'because of his very condition as a foreigner, come from far-away lands: a circumstance that tends to seduce the feminine imagination'.[49] Karen Racine claimed that the same was true of Francisco de Miranda and Andrés Bello's 'fondness for daughters of blond Albion' during their time in London.[50] But if this pattern held generally true, perhaps rather more mercenaries would have formed permanent relationships with smitten Gran Colombian women. More usefully, the type of adventurer that these women married must be considered. Soledad Soublette could have married any of the adventurers if she had been seduced by the idea of marrying a foreigner, but she ended up with General O'Leary, a close confidant of Bolívar and by 1828 one of the highest-ranked volunteers. Soublette herself was the sister of General Carlos Soublette, a Bolivarian loyalist who would later become President of Venezuela. Other adventurers who married, such as John Illingworth and Thomas Richards, had links to foreign traders or British investors. The O'Leary–Soublette, Wright–Rocafuerte, Stagg–Flores and MacGregor–Lobera marriages joined highly ranked and relatively prestigious (at the time of marriage) adventurers to families who had considerable political influence. Some linked adventurers to prominent colonial families, as in the case of the Illingworth–Décimavilla and Ashdown–Landaeta marriages. Most marriages were with Creole women; there is little in the documentation to suggest otherwise.[51]

The marriages of lower-ranking foreign adventurers were not so well documented. Possibly, as suggested by several studies, marriage to a low-ranking foreigner was a source of prestige to women in rural villages.[52] Investigations into a similar group, British migrants to Cuba later in the nineteenth century, show that lower-class Britons did not engage in stable sexual relationships with locals. Whatever lay behind this non-occurrence, while merchants and officers were assimilated into Cuban society, lower-class individuals remained outsiders.[53]

The position for the female members of the original expeditions is less clear. Faced with the reluctance of the government to provide them with sustenance, foreign women either left the region or discovered new ways of supporting themselves. In the absence of any comprehensive evidence, some isolated examples must suffice. In May 1823 there were still 18 foreign women resident in Angostura. Catalina Peterson and Isabel Negard were widows of members of the British Legion, and when asked for a census both described their present occupation as 'trader'. Other foreign women were listed as servants or 'domestics'.[54] Another woman who settled in Gran Colombia, Ann Hodgkins, had travelled to Venezuela with her parents in the Irish Legion back in 1820, survived the climatic extremes of military campaigning, and then settled in Bogotá. In 1825 she was 19 years old, and spoke and wrote fluent Spanish. She travelled regularly between Bogotá and Mompox, two of the principal towns in the republic, and received money from a foreign military officer, Henry Macmanus, although she denied in court that she had had 'any social contact or intimacy' with him.[55] One widow of a member of the Irish Legion, Mary Helen Lawless, lived in Bogotá and ran her own shop in the 1820s.[56] Also in Bogotá, Mrs Nowlam supported herself, her retired husband and their young child until 1831, when she 'drop[ped] down dead while standing at the table washing'.[57] There is no evidence that any of these women married in Gran Colombia, apart from Mary English who was widowed in 1819 and married a British merchant, William Greenup, in Bogotá in the mid–1820s. English's biographer described her as the 'belle of Bogotá' in this period, with all the major figures in society competing for her hand in marriage.[58] In general, foreign women's integration into Gran Colombian society was severely limited by gender codes and economic hardship, but the examples cited above suggest that there was some opportunity for working outside the home and forming new relationships.

The sources available indicate that the men and women who left Britain and Ireland as adventurers changed the way they looked at Gran Colombia during the 1820s and 1830s. They may have found a region they liked, or someone to marry. Some were appointed to positions of political or military authority, and subsequently settled in the area having formed personal or business relations. They had played a part in the region's Independence from Spain, and now lived alongside the very people to whose 'liberation' they had contributed. They were ten years older and some had fathered children. As a result of these experiences, the way they imagined their relation to the state and the nation evolved. Political institutions also began to view them in a new light – as patriotic veterans rather than as adventurers. The articulation of these changes is the subject of the next sections of this chapter.

Looking Back on Foundational Fighting

Changing conceptions of honour and identity were integral to the processes of settling and assimilation. Chapter 4 demonstrated how adventurers sought to assert and protect their individual honour in their new circumstances in Venezuela as a means of first demonstrating and then negotiating their position with regard to the new social groups that surrounded them. This individual

honour was founded on class and race distinctions and on ostentatious bravery and loyalty in military service. The first three decades after political Independence saw an extensive reworking of the 'myriad standards of legitimacy'
and the 'dense thicket of loyalties' upon which the new republican states rested
precariously, as Reuben Zahler has shown.[59] These new ideas were illumi-
nated in court room discussions of corruption, in newspaper and congres-
sional debates of political heresy and in threats and challenges to central
government.[60] The recognition of the role of foreign soldiers in the Wars of
Independence was a fundamental part of the reconceptualisation of post-colonial society. Those adventurers who remained in the region after 1830 were
affected by these developments more than they influenced any changes themselves. Their adventurous ideas of individual honour became subsumed into
deeper conceptions of the honour of the nation, the state, and race and class
groups, and in particular they absorbed the value ascribed to the national
family and the consequent emphasis placed on kinship ties to the *patria*.

Military men of all backgrounds looked back on the Wars of Independence
as a period of foundational fighting that had brought the nation into being.
Having been a good soldier was, for high-ranking Independent officers such
as Briceño Méndez and Páez, enough to make a foreigner a good patriot. When
Briceño Méndez spoke of a 'good soldier', he meant one who 'always behaved
himself, and had shown loyalty and courage under duress'.[61] In exalting the
Wars of Independence as the foundational patriotic myth of the new republics, Creoles praised these qualities in the adventurers, and also their selfless-
ness and devotion to the cause – their republican virtue. This devotion was
sometimes imbued with religious intensity. General Julián Castro described
Capitán William Ashdown 'as one of the brave men who made up that Crusade for Liberty that left the Old World to fight in the New for the cause of
humanity. They sacrificed their interests, and lent their bravery to support
the Independence of Colombia.'[62] Casting the adventurers as 'Crusaders of
Liberty' set them above religious distinctions and beyond political factions.
Tomás Cipriano de Mosquera praised John Mackintosh for 'coming here to
fight for liberty, not as an adventurer like some others ... he experienced misery and poverty, all in the name of a *patria* that was not his own'.[63] These
values of sacrifice, abnegation and faith in the cause were consistent with all
the Christian denominations, and were employed to side-step the vexed question of patriotism which was intertwined with, but not the same as, republican virtue. Thomas Manby articulated the shared roots of adventure, patriotism and sacrifice in 1832.

> For fourteen years I have had the honour of belonging to the Colombian family,
> to this heroic family born out of the ruins of despotism at the cost of our most
> dear sacrifices.
>   The burning plains of Apure and the frozen mountains of Pisba can testify
> that I crossed them barefoot in order to fight the tyrants and throw them from
> this country in the memorable battles of Vargas and Boyacá.[64]

Those adventurers still loyally serving in the armed forces in the 1830s, even more than those such as Mackintosh who retired after the foundational fighting was over, provided a difficult question for those seeking to set out the meanings of nation and patriotism. When General Diego (James) Whittle was murdered by his rebellious troops near Quito in late 1831, obituaries recorded that Ecuador had 'lost a pillar of its military and a fine servant of the nation',[65] and that Whittle had 'sacrificed himself for a *patria* which he served with honour and constancy ... the *patria* will forever remember his name'.[66] Yet unlike James Rooke's patriotic death at Pantano de Vargas in 1819 at the height of the Wars of Independence, Whittle's demise occurred at the end of an extended period during which notions of foreignness had been extensively debated, as discussed in the previous chapter. Whittle would not pass into the *historia patria* because by 1831 Gran Colombia, the republic which Whittle had loyally served for a decade, no longer existed, and the Wars of Independence were over. Whittle was a virtuous republican who believed in liberty, certainly, but he was not a patriot. The weakness of any sense of Ecuadorean national identity in this period meant that heroism and patriotism became ambiguous characteristics, particularly because the President himself, Juan José Flores, was of Venezuelan birth. The elision between patriotism and belief in liberty that was a fundamental component of the Gran Colombian decade fell apart along with the disintegration of the state that it sustained.

During the 1830s the post-Gran Colombia states struggled to come to terms with the ramifications of the coming apart of the twin threads of liberty and patriotism. The example of post-1830 Ecuador provides a useful case study for exploring these changes. The Ecuadorean population was overwhelmingly of indigenous roots and still unrepresented in government. As such, it was difficult to employ birth or ethnicity as a base for national identity alongside the Gran Colombian discourse of liberty and equality. White foreigners therefore continued to occupy an ambiguous position between patriot and enemy. Patriotism was defined by President Flores and his allies purely in terms of virtue and duty. According to an editorial in the *Gaceta de Gobierno de Ecuador,*

patriotism is a virtue for which a man will sacrifice all his personal interests for the wider good without limit. Patriotism is the cooperation of the individual with the well-being and prosperity of the society to which he belongs. It is one of man's most sacred duties, indeed without patriotism there is neither probity nor virtue in the whole world. A man who does not love the *patria* is ignorant of the duties of society, and natural feelings. ... he is inhuman because his heart does not contain the sweet sensations produced by loving one's fellow man. ... There is no greater danger in the world than a man dispossessed of feelings of patriotism. ... It is also necessary to distinguish the true from the false patriot. A man who serves society so as to be personally rewarded is not a patriot. A soldier who fights in order to be promoted above others, without feeling for the public good, is not a patriot. A man who has served the *patria,* but then becomes offended by some perceived injustice caused by its leaders, is not a patriot. A man who complains that the government favours the merit and virtue of others instead of recognising his own nobility or greatness, is not a patriot.[67]

The way that Flores defined patriotism only in terms of virtue meant that his political opponents were therefore derided as 'unpatriotic'.[68] Honour and patriotism had become closely related to political loyalty, which in Flores' eyes equated to civic virtue. His friends, such as Whittle, were therefore commemorated as honourable and heroic servants. His political enemies, such as Coronel Francis Hall, were lambasted as unpatriotic. Hall was hung as a traitor after leading an unsuccessful attempt to overthrow Flores' government and died unlamented.[69] In the chaotic and uncertain 1830s following the disintegration of Gran Colombia, political loyalty had to be an important constituent of reconfigured national identities. Foreigners had to learn to adapt to this reality or they were excluded from the patriotic and honourable communities – this could end in exile, or death as in the case of Hall. The Colombian archives abound with accusations that one or another foreigner was partial to a particular faction, and as such was unpatriotic. These accusations were almost always denied. After the failed assassination attempt on Bolívar on 25 September 1828, Capitán Charles Wilthew (who was directly implicated in the plotting) was forced into exile. Wilthew claimed, 'I was expelled from the country because of the upheavals of that time, and because of my liberal principles.'[70] This emphasis on political loyalty in patriotism worked both ways, however, and when Wilthew returned to Bogotá in 1833 to request back-dated pay and pensions, another of the conspirators, Joaquín Posada Gutiérrez, now in political office, welcomed him with open arms and vouched for his 'honourable conduct and good services' as a patriot.[71]

The principal reference point for these discussions throughout the 1830s was the battle of El Santuario in Antioquia on 17 October 1829, in which a foreign adventurer was widely blamed for the death of the popular Gran Colombian General José María Córdoba.[72] Rupert Hand was accused of committing the 'homicide' under the orders of Daniel O'Leary, while Córdoba lay wounded and defenceless.[73] During the battle, Córdoba had directly contrasted himself, as a patriot born just a short distance from the battlefield, with O'Leary as a 'vile foreigner'.[74] In 1830 Bolívar saw that 'antipathy towards foreigners grows every day'.[75] The governments of Bolívar and Urdaneta that followed the battle of El Santuario were seen by subsequent administrations as 'dictatorships'.[76] When they failed to maintain Gran Colombia's unity and three new republics were created, those adventurers who had been involved in the unrest came under detailed scrutiny. Acutely conscious of the precarious legitimacy of the new republican regimes, government authorities and civil society engaged in lengthy periods of self-justification and denial of any involvement in supposedly 'revolutionary' uprisings. Foreign veterans were now obvious targets for the politically disenchanted, and they were at pains to 'reproach the conduct of some *ingleses* who were at El Santuario, and who were Friends of Despotism'.[77] Veterans had to strive not to be tarred with the same brush as 'the men of El Santuario … who had plunged their fists into the bosom of the *patria*'.[78]

In this context, adventurers clung to the old Gran Colombian identity in which patriotism and the love of liberty were interlinked. They repeatedly claimed that they had 'always belonged to the cause of Liberty' rather than any political faction.[79] In 1835 John Mackintosh called the events of El Santuario 'a disgrace' and united a string of friendly witnesses to deny that he 'was involved in anything at all' in 1830.[80] There was ample evidence that Mackintosh had in fact commanded a paramilitary force of 60 men at the Zipaquirá salt mines in 1830 under the orders of Urdaneta's dictatorship.[81] According to one witness, Mackintosh asked, 'why would I support an illegitimate military government, when I have fought and spilt my blood to see a government established in Colombia that could equal the best in Europe, and when I am waiting for the government to pay its recognised debts to my brother?'[82] Thus Mackintosh and his associates linked their political neutrality back to an original belief in liberty, attempting to bypass charges of unpatriotic behaviour by evoking both honour and interest. Such arguments were generally successful when supported by ample testimony from friends in government circles. Astute foreigners avoided making political comment in public places (unlike Henry Mayne, accused in 1831 of 'calling Obando a whore' in the street and hence 'subversively undermining the established order').[83] Despite much evidence attesting to political involvement, foreign veterans reiterated that they 'never got mixed up in politics', and stressed their ideological links back to the cause of liberty and Independence.[84]

Political loyalty, however, was only one aspect of honour and patriotism in the 1830s. Issues of race, subordination and age were all important in mapping honour and identity in the immediate post-war, post-colonial, post-Gran Colombia period, just as they were during the Wars of Independence. Analysis of a 1832 court case in Ecuador illustrates the ways in which these categories intermeshed post–1830. The case involved a 24-year-old Caracas-born officer, Comandante Pascual Guedes, who was accused of striking an English naval officer, Capitán Jaime Williams. The events took place on the frigate *Colombia* which was anchored outside the port of Guayaquil. Both Guedes and Williams were in the pay of the Ecuadorean state, and the case was heard by the Ecuadorean authorities. The lengthy court documentation does not reveal any conflict based on national origin, but rather a dispute between ranks, personalities and generations. The two men clashed during the daily distribution of rum to sailors, and theirs was therefore a highly public confrontation which observers warned could set a bad example to the rank and file. The crux of the issue was the two individuals' refusal to recognise each other as honourable.[85] There was some confusion as to whether Guedes' terrestrial rank of Comandante was in fact superior to Williams's naval rank of Capitán. Guedes 'knew himself to be superior'.[86] Williams asserted that he 'was nobody's slave, and certainly not yours'.[87] The terms used indicate a confrontation loaded with the language of masculinity: after the scuffle Williams shouted, 'I could have killed you or broken your balls, but I chose not to.'[88]

The case was reviewed by the General Commander of the Maritime Department (Guayaquil) who was an Irish *colombiano*, Tomás Wright. His initial response to the events was to side with Williams, to sack Guedes from active service and to try him in a civilian court.[89] Nevertheless, the authorities in Quito under President Flores considered that Wright had 'greatly misunderstood' the law, and that Guedes was entitled to be judged by a military court.[90] In this exchange between the authorities in Quito and Guayaquil, the *fuero* (colonial military court) became the site upon which new republican understandings of honour and collective identity were negotiated.[91] In his defence, Guedes focused attention on both Williams's private and public behaviour, alleging corruption and misuse of navy resources for personal use, and that Williams had neglected to wear insignia indicating his rank.[92] As with many colonial debates over honour, much of the debate in court focused on the precise detail of which part of the body had been infringed upon, and to what degree.[93] For many hours they discussed whether Guedes had inflicted a 'slap', a 'strangle', a 'neck-grip', a 'smack' or a 'whack' on Williams.[94] The eventual compromise was that it had been an unacceptable 'blow in the face' against a subaltern, not an officer, because Williams was not wearing a public symbol indicating his rank at the time of the clash.[95] This technicality allowed Guedes to escape with no further punishment than dismissal from the army. Allegations of impropriety against Williams were ordered to be investigated.[96]

The trial and conviction of Pascual Guedes demonstrates the extent to which the European birth of foreign veterans was gradually losing importance as a result of the mass mobilisations of the Wars of Independence. Foreigners such as Tomás Wright, Juan Illingworth and Juan Lannigan had been assimilated into the Creole élite, and in Ecuador in 1832 they were just as foreign as Venezuelans such as Flores or Guedes. On no occasion throughout the heated and often aggressive confrontation and subsequent legal battle were any national or regional origins used against (or in favour of) the contenders. Men disputed hierarchies of rank based on authority, conduct and physical force, employing the rhetoric of slavery and possession familiar to Creoles and adventurers alike. In the absence of a successfully forged Gran Colombian identity, veterans retreated to conventional ideas of honour, based on respect for social hierarchies and personal loyalties. These ideas were so important that men fought each other over them.

Petitioning for Honour and Patriotism

In the military sphere after 1830 individual honour was still closely related to public demonstrations of service, loyalty and bravery. For those veterans who had left the service and entered civilian life, however, such public manifestations of masculinity were not enough to secure them recognition from the state. Post-war society increasingly valued those veterans who gave up their manly independence, got married and became respectable *padres de familia* with sons and daughters born in Gran Colombia. Veterans' petitions to the post-war states reveal how they gradually and reluctantly adapted to the demands placed upon them by the prevalent local concepts of honour, patriotism and service.

Veterans claimed their rights from the new republics according to the new laws enacted after Independence. Throughout their petitions, foreign private soldiers and non-commissioned officers had recognised that in applying for rewards from the government they should stress their loyalty, constancy, heroism and bravery.[97] They contrasted themselves with the supposed disloyalty, insubordination and treachery of deserters, complaining officers and the rebellious Irish Legion. Men such as John Gardiner, an illiterate English tailor who lived in Caracas until his death in 1856, emphasised that they had earned the respect of their superiors through long campaigns, in contrast to the several hundred foreigners who had died or deserted.[98] Thomas Scott claimed to have 'lent [his] services wherever they were needed, and wherever the Chiefs sent [him]'.[99] Others soldiers emphasised the honourable wounds they had received on campaign, such as Private James Flannigan who lost his left leg.[100] The submissions of commissioned officers were generally longer, more wordy and paid more attention to honourable conduct than the testimonies of private soldiers. Foreign officers measured their services against an ideal standard of honour, bravery and loyalty.[101] The operative verb used was always *portarse* (to conduct oneself) and emphasis was not so much on where they had been or what they had done (although these aspects were important because of the specifications of the law), but on how the individual had behaved whilst doing these things.[102] Because they were increasingly excluded from the patriotic discourse of the new states, as shown in Chapter 7, foreign officers emphasised the nobility and honour of their original enlistment or 'calling', and their great sacrifices in the name of liberty. When this was not described in financial or physical terms (the sacrifice of property, health or limbs), adventurers claimed to have given 'the best times of [their] life'.[103] Others said that their 'brilliant youth was consumed by the fight against oppression'.[104] Essential to the idea of sacrifice was that it had been given voluntarily and without complaint.[105] They cast themselves as 'volunteers' for liberty rather than mercenaries.

Adventurers' post-war petitions to the state reveal how they gradually realised that honour now emanated from a functioning republican state and court system, and that public demonstrations of honour were of decreasing value. Because of the years spent campaigning together, officers built up strong relationships of trust and loyalty to each other, and veterans used these relationships to further their claims on the state. Like Venezuelan political leaders such as Páez and Bermúdez, they employed the language of shared sacrifice in the name of the *patria*.[106] When testifying to each others' qualities, they used familiar tropes to cement bonds of shared experiences and interest.[107] If an officer's behaviour fell below the standards expected, as was the case of Capitán Henry Hugo Macmanus, then this honour was forfeited. Macmanus was accused of drinking and gaming with his subalterns in Bogotá in the mid-

1820s, displaying 'familiarity with his inferiors', and abusing the trust and 'fraternity' of a fellow officer.[108] Non-commissioned officers occupied a middle ground between those of commissioned officers and private soldiers. Like Cabo Jacob Teeson, with whom Macmanus fought in Bogotá in 1826, they defended their honour through physical prowess when challenged, at the same time as they petitioned the state for recognition of their service through bureaucratic means.[109]

Foreign veterans' claims to honour and patriotism in the 1820s and 1830s were always placed on top of their previous identities and loyalties. As they got older they looked back on the Wars of Independence as a time of ideal heroism when their youthful selves were dedicated to a noble cause in stark contrast to the subsequent political wrangling and factionalism. As the wars became more distant, their memories of the key battles of Carabobo and Pantano de Vargas (discussed in Chapter 2) hardened and developed established patterns. The same motifs and events recurred in their letters and petitions.[110] From the 1840s onwards, the focus of national memory in New Granada and Venezuela increasingly emphasised the foundational period of the Wars of Independence, from 1818 to 1821, rather than the less glorious political situation of the late 1820s and early 1830s.[111] These individual, collective and national memories were deeply interlinked and were complicated at times when diplomatic relations between Britain and the republics were fraught.[112] Nevertheless, the idea of a peculiarly 'British' bravery remained integral to the ways in which some adventurer officers considered their honour throughout the period.[113] They remembered John Mackintosh's call at Pantano de Vargas that 'nothing [was] impossible for British bayonets'[114] which was held to typify their courage, determination and uniquely British resolution. Others recalled acts of heroism and endurance, climbing the highest mountains or being drenched by 'the fiercest rains ever seen'.[115] Correspondingly, the charge of cowardice was the ultimate insult for the active or retired soldier, such as when Jacob Teeson accused Henry Macmanus of 'hiding behind a rock during the battle of Genoy'.[116]

Family and Affective Bonds

Increasingly throughout the 1830s and 1840s, it was not the strongest or bravest or most loyal veterans who were regarded as honourable by Creole élites, but rather those adventurers who formed family ties with Creole families. Political leaders considered the family to be the essential bedrock of the nation in New Granada, Venezuela and Ecuador.[117] William Ashdown was recognised as 'distinguished in the eyes of his chiefs because of his bearing, and since his retirement, he has been in the eyes of society a good husband and good father' to his two daughters.[118] The *padre de familia* was husband, home-owner and father, and had a multitude of dependants that consequently reinforced his masculinity and honour.[119] Because of these testimonies

Figure 8.1   *Daniel O'Leary*

Ashdown was recognised by the state and received a pension. Over two decades after Independence, being a good *padre de familia* was just as important
as any military achievements in the 'crusade of liberty'. In 1844 Daniel O'Leary
wrote, 'my family is now the State for which I labour'.[120]

Retired adventurers who did not have children born in Gran Colombia
increasingly recognised that in a period of 'nation-building' in the new republics, they also needed to stress some affective bonds linking them to their
'adopted *patrias*'.[121] Edward Stopford claimed 'deep attachment to the *patria*'.[122]
Edward Brand claimed to have 'a thousand pleasant memories' of Venezuela.[123] Creoles were most impressed when these affectionate bonds produced
real ties to 'the Colombian family': children.[124] In 1832 Thomas Manby claimed
to belong to the 'heroic family born out of the ruins of despotism', founded on
its members' 'love of liberty', but it was only once his children were born in
later years that he began to convince the New Granadan authorities of his
veracity.[125] In 1840 Manby published a pamphlet that set out in public the key
constituents of his honour and identity: being a loving husband and father, a
loyal friend, and a patriotic officer without politics.[126] He used his children as
the principal motif of the pamphlet in order to tie himself to the 'national
family' in the minds of his readers.

Veterans emphasised the affective ties that bound them to the nation when
they turned to the authorities as a last resort, precisely because those children
were an excessive burden upon their limited resources without assistance from

a patron or the state. Those who had achieved the desired independence, of course, had no reason to petition the state and therefore only rarely left a trace in the archives. Private John Hill lived in Coro from 1825, and he did not write to the authorities until 1842, when he requested to be registered as an invalid, claiming that '[my wounds] prevent me from exercising any profession in order to sustain myself and my large family'.[127] He explained that he would much rather exercise an independent profession than live off the munificence of the state, but asked for assistance 'so as to buy a crust to feed myself and my wife and six tiny children'.[128] In 1854 Charles James Minchin claimed in a petition to the government that his love of liberty and his love of his Venezuelan wife were born from the same part of his heart, resolving that he would 'never leave the country that [he] had bathed in my blood, and whose liberty had come at such a cost to [him] and [his] family'.[129] Liberty, family and sacrifice became merged into the love of *patria*.

Adventurers who settled in Gran Colombia throughout the 1830s, 1840s and beyond stressed above all other considerations these affectionate bonds that tied them to their adopted *patrias*. In the cases of Manby, Minchin and many others, the birth of New Granadan or Venezuelan children facilitated the progression from rhetoric to reality. In other instances, the claims were tortuous and convoluted. Rupert Hand enlisted medical experts in 1839 to prove that his damaged reproductive organs were caused by a 'severe groin strain' he suffered while dragging heavy artillery in 1822 rather than (as was really the case) a 'severe gunshot wound to the left testicle' received in a duel in 1820.[130] An injury gained in a duel – the ultimate defence of individual honour, rather than the *patria* – would not have gained Hand state recognition. He therefore skilfully and successfully marshalled evidence and testimonies in order to compensate for the rather unpatriotic loss of his reproductive capacity.

The testimonies of their widows also illustrate the extent to which the foreign veterans had been assimilated into society by the 1840s and 1850s. These women emphasised how their husbands' deaths endangered their own honour by threatening them with poverty. Francisca Granados told the New Granadan government that her husband's honour and reputation were worth nothing to her: 'when my husband died he left me no more patrimony than the decorations on his chest. ... I have eight innocent children who ask me for bread to eat, and I have nothing.'[131] María Francisca Ruíz of Cumaná was widowed on the death of Thomas Brown in 1832 and was consequently 'reduced to a state of the most extreme poverty, almost blind because of [her] sufferings, only surviving because of the occasional beneficence of [her] aunt'.[132] Mary English described her life as a widow post–1819 as 'one long misadventure', a difficult and unhappy period and the exact opposite of her husband's military adventures.[133] In addition to asserting their own 'decency', 'morals' and 'honesty' in their petitions, widows such as Trinidad Páez appropriated much of the language of honour from their husbands, laying heavy emphasis on the adventurers' decision to 'abandon their own *patria*' and the blood they had

nobly shed on Venezuelan battlefields.[134] Adventurers' dreams of 'manly independence' had gradually been subsumed into the honourable identity of a
patriotic *padre de familia*. In subsequent years it was the Gran Colombian-
born widows and children of these retired adventurers who petitioned the
state for pensions and rewards such as the *Ilustres Próceres*.

Most of the adventurers were dead or had disappeared from the historical
record by 1860. As the remaining adventurers became fewer and fewer, their
very survival and perseverance became part of their claim for honour and
recognition.[135] The new republics now valued them more for their decision to
settle in Gran Colombia, to marry local wives and to establish themselves as
patriarchal *padres de familia*, rather than for their original military service. In
fathering new generations of New Granadans, Venezuelans and Ecuadoreans,
they were finally acknowledged as performing a collective (rather than individual) service. They could now present themselves, in old age at least, as
both honourable *and* patriotic. A few lived into the 1870s, when Hispanic
America was rapidly being incorporated into the international economy and large
numbers of migrants from Europe were crossing the Atlantic once again. The
British representative in Cuenca observed the local military unit in mourning for
three days after the death of John Talbot, a papermaker from Maidenhead in Berk-
shire who settled in Cuenca in 1830 and died there in 1891, aged 90.[136]

The foreign veterans were few in number and geographically dispersed
across Gran Colombia. Too few traces of them remain in historical archives
for generalisations about them to be made with too much confidence. The
detailed study of their own representations and the observations of Creoles
who knew them presented in this chapter reveal, when taken in conjunction
with a wider appraisal of social change, that they were part of, as well as symptomatic of, longer-term changes in the first half-century after Independence.
They contributed to the reintroduction of military honour – glory, endurance, manly exertion and physical strength – into a region that had witnessed
a very limited military presence since the times of the *conquistadores*. The Wars
of Independence gave a large number of people the experience of military
service. When these veterans returned to civil society – like the adventurers
examined in this chapter – they struggled to realign their military concerns
with the respect given to *padres de familia* in colonial times and with the new
importance ascribed to virtue and patriotism.

Chapter 7 found that in the post-war Gran Colombian region, citizenship
and belonging to the nation were increasingly tied to élite ideas of practical
utility to the *patria*, and also conditional upon public demonstrations of patriotism. The two threads of patriotism and the cause of liberty that underpinned Gran Colombian Independence had unravelled by the late 1820s, leaving the foreign veterans in a curious middle position, neither entirely foreign
nor completely *colombiano*. In turn, patriotism was increasingly tied to a record
of military service, sacrifice, residency, a sedentary lifestyle, family life and a
work ethic. Foreigners could access all of these criteria and therefore be considered patriotic. Those veterans who married Creole women became linked

to the national family through affection and love and through their children who were *naturales* of the *patria*. Compared to the almost seven thousand adventurers who left Europe in the 1810s, these survivors were few, but they were part of the Gran Colombian family and were commemorated as such in *historia patria* in the post-1830 successor states. The factors that shaped these memories are explored in Chapter 9.

Notes

1 See for example Véronique Hebrard, 'Ciudadanía y participación política en Venezuela 1810–1830', in Anthony McFarlane and Eduardo Posada-Carbó (eds), *Independence and Revolution in Spanish America: Perspectives and Problems* (London, 1999), pp. 122–53; Elías Pino Iturrieta, *Fueros, civilisación y ciudadanía* (Caracas, 2000), pp. 42–55.

2 As described in Cannadine, *Ornamentalism*.

3 Uribe Urán, *Honorable Lives*, pp. 3–6, pp. 14–18; Deas, *Vida y opinión de Mr William Wills*, Vol. 1, pp. 22–27.

4 Alan Knight, 'Britain and Latin America', in Andrew Porter (ed.), *The Oxford History of the British Empire, Vol. 3 The Nineteenth Century* (Oxford, 1999), p. 125. Knight shared the perspective elaborated in Jaime Jaramillo Uribe, 'Bentham y los utilaristas colombianos del siglo XIX', *Ideas y valores*, 4:13 (1962), pp. 11–28, and Bushnell, *The Making of Modern Colombia*, pp. 57–60.

5 Reflecting on the social rise of Juan Galindo, Thomas Manby observed 'so much for the man who translated papers for Mr Henderson and others'. Manby to Mary English, 6 March 1836, Bogotá, EP, HA157/3/213. For Galindo representing adventurers as an *apoderado*, see for example CDM, Db0676, Db4583, Db4696. For his later career as an administrator in Guatemala see Robert A. Naylor, *Penny Ante Imperialism: The Mosquito Shore and the Bay of Honduras, 1600–1914: A Case Study in British Informal Empire* (London and Toronto, 1989), p. 109.

6 Santander to Bolívar, 21 April 1825, Bogotá, *Germán Arciniegas, Cartas Santander-Bolívar 1823–1825*, Vol. 4, p. 349.

7 Scott, *Mary English*, p. 134; Gosselman, *Viaje por Colombia, 1825 y 1826*, p. 275. TNA FO 357/12 fo. 28 is an undated sheet from a sketchpad, upon which the British Consul in Bogotá scrawled odds and proposed bets with other foreigners.

8 Hamilton, *Travels Through The Interior Provinces of Colombia*, Vol. 2, pp. 240–41. Official British criticism of gambling in Colombia can be found in Consul Edward Watts to George Canning, 27 March 1824, 'Carthagena de Colombia', TNA FO 18/6 fo. 18.

9 Table constructed from the database including only named individuals, which inevitably leads to the neglect of many lower-status adventurers, who are discussed below.

10 McFarlane, 'The Rebellion of the "Barrios". Urban Insurrection in Bourbon Quito', pp. 197–218; McFarlane, *Colombia Before Independence*, pp. 43–56.

11 Diary entry for 5 March 1828, Ker Porter, *Diario de un diplomático británico*, p. 307. These comments were atypical. Porter generally ignored the presence of lower-status foreigners in Caracas, recording only the activities of his acquaintances among officers and British merchants.

12 Note that the term 'occupation' is used in preference to 'profession' because in early republican Colombia (as is abundantly demonstrated by this table) individuals occupied multiplex, non-specialised roles, and were not 'professional' in the current sense.

13 Fraser to Mary English, 1 August 1845, Salazar, EP, HA157/3/189.

14 Fraser to Mary English, 1844–46, Salazar, EP, HA157/3/166–98.
15 Anon., *The Present State of Colombia*, p. 177.
16 Family tradition reveals that Walter Chitty took to growing coffee in his retirement. José de Armas Chitty, 'Walter Dawes Chitty', in Fundaciá Polar, *Diccionario de Historia de Venezuela*.
17 Hugo Hughes, original in English, 31 August 1824, Bogotá, AGNC R GYM, Vol. 56, fo. 183.
18 Daniel Dowd, Advertisement, *El Colombiano*, 14 January 1823, in both Spanish and English. Two British sargentos were working as domestic servants in Angostura in 1823, although it is not clear whether that was their occupation before travelling to Colombia. 'Padrón de todos los Extranjeros de ambos sexos que se encuentran en esta Capital, con distinción de sus oficios, motivo de su permanencia, y los que están, o no, naturalizados en Colombia', AHG CB, Sig. 1. 3. 4. 103. 5.
19 Diary entry for 5 March 1828, Ker Porter, *Diario de un diplomático británico*, p. 307.
20 For a discussion of this case, see Pablo Rodriguez, 'Noche sangrienta en San Vitorino: Asesinato de un consul norteamericano en Bogotá', *Credencial historia*, 169 (2004), pp. 3–6.
21 Ker Porter, *Diario de un diplomático británico*, p. 605.
22 For Lynch see Hamilton, *Travels Through The Interior Provinces of Colombia*, Vol. 2, p. 75, *El Constitucional*, 12 January 1826; AL Vol. 14, fo. 55; *Gaceta de Colombia*, 22 September 1822; CDM Db4664.
23 Banko, *El capital commercial en La Guaira y Caracas (1824–1848)* (Caracas, 1990), pp. 42–56.
24 Frank Safford, 'Foreign and National Enterprise in Nineteenth Century Colombia', in *Business History Review* 39:4 (1965), pp. 503–26, p. 47. See also David Sowell, *The Early Colombian Labor Movement: Artisans and Politics in Bogotá, 1832–1919* (Philadelphia, PA, 1992), pp. 1–20.
25 Townsend, *Tales of Two Cities*, p. 80.
26 Manby to Baron Von Eben, 10 December 1821, Cali, translated into Spanish (without English original) in *MOL*, Vol. 12, pp. 350–51. See also Sandes' comments in a letter to Flores, 9 June 1828, Guayaquil, *MOL*, Vol. 12, p. 410.
27 Saether, 'Identities and Independence', pp. 307–9.
28 Saether, 'Identities and Independence', p. 325.
29 'Santiago Blanco' (Private James White) from London was not mentioned in any other archival documents consulted. 'Filaciones de los individuos del Cuerpo de Notables de Honor de la Ciudad de Quito, Segunda Compañía, 1824', ANE Fondo Especial, Caja 247, Legajo 7, ff. 130–48.
30 On the links between urban networks and marriage patterns in late-colonial Spanish America see many chapters collected in Luis Navarro (ed.), *Las élites urbanas en Hispanoamérica*, (Seville, 2005)
31 This table includes all adventurers who married into Gran Colombian society. National Origin (N) key: B = British; BI = British or Irish; E = English; F = French; H = Hanoverian; I = Irish; IT = Italian; M = Maltese; NA = North American; P = Polish; R = Russian; S = Scottish; SW = Swedish; SP = Spanish. My thanks to Claire Brewster for allowing me to cross-reference the women listed in this table with an early version of her database from the 'Gendering Latin American Independence: Women's Political Culture and the Textual Construction of Gender, 1790–1850' project. I owe the information regarding Edward Gregory to a personal communication from Luis Carlos Rodriguez Alvarez, for which I am very grateful.
32 In addition to those in Table 8. 3, another 50 named adventurers were recorded as having married in Britain before leaving for Colombia. Many of these wives

accompanied the expeditions, as discussed in Brown, 'Adventurers, Foreign Women and Masculinity'.

33 Sucre to O'Leary, 18 March 1825, Oruro, cited in Pérez Vila, *Vida de Daniel Florencio O'Leary*, p. 237.

34 See CDM, Db0010, Db0734.

35 On the shortage of priests see John Lynch, 'The Quest for the Millennium in Latin America: Popular Religion and Beyond', in Lynch, *Latin America between Colony and Nation: Selected Essays* (London, 2001), p. 99.

36 For O'Mullan see Anon. [Cowley], *Recollections of a Service of Three Years*, Vol. 2, p. 77.

37 See the historiographical review in Guenther, *British Merchants in Nineteenth-Century Brazil*, pp. 69–70.

38 Guenther, *British Merchants in Nineteenth-Century Brazil*, p. 69. Some adventurers did stay in Gran Colombia without marrying or having children. For the considerable material possessions of James Whittle when he died in 1831, see 'Inventario de bienes del difunto General Diego Whittle', 14 October 1831, Quito, ANE Causas Criminales, Caja 245, 1831, Expediente 20, ff. 1–3. See also the list of the property of the late Matthew Macnamara in Bogotá, as it was prepared for auction, repr. in *El Constitucional*, 20 October 1825.

39 Manby to Mary English, 3 March 1834, Bogotá, EP, HA157/3/206, also Manby to Mary English, 21 December 1835, Bogotá, EP, HA157/3/216 .

40 Manby to Mosquera, 21 October 1833, Bogotá, ACC, Sala Mosquera 1832, d. 6833.

41 He concluded, 'what was worse than all, [I] had made up my mind to love her as much as is necessary in such cases'. Manby to Mary English, 26 October 1835, Bogotá, EP, HA157/3/210 (Manby's emphasis). A decade earlier, on 3 April 1824, Manby had requested permission from the military authorities to marry 'Señorita Manuelita Lozano' – a copy of his request is held in AGNC R GYM, Vol. 56, fo. 328.

42 Manby to Mary English, 26 October 1835, Bogotá, EP, HA157/3/210. No correspondence from Manuelita Lozano has yet been found to give her version of events.

43 Manby to Mary English, 11 April 1836, Bogotá, EP, HA157/3/214.

44 Manby to Mary English, 23 November 1835, Bogotá, EP, HA157/3/211.

45 Manby to Mary English, 21 December 1835, Bogotá, EP, HA157/3/216; Manby to Mary English, 8 May 1836, Bogotá, EP, HA157/3/215.

46 For business dealings see Santiago Fortoul to Manby, 30 August 1838, Rosario de Cúcuta, in CDM, Sala de Libros Raros, Archivo de Cartas del Coronel Tomás Manby, fo. 12.

47 Eduardo Fortoul to Manby, n.d., 1838, Rosario de Cúcuta, Archivo de Cartas del Coronel Tomás Manby, fo. 11.

48 See Deas, *Vida y opinión de Mr William Wills*, Vol. 1, pp. 22–28.

49 Pérez Vila, *Vida de Daniel Florencio O'Leary*, p. 340.

50 Racine, 'Imagining Independence', p. 108.

51 For Guenther's comment that some Brazilian women were 'white-enough' for Britons to desire them, see *British Merchants in Nineteenth-Century Brazil*, p. 156.

52 See particularly Verena Martínez-Alier, *Marriage, Class and Colour in Nineteenth Century Cuba: A Study of Racial Attitudes and Sexual Values in a Slave Society* (London, 1974); and Eileen J. Findlay, 'Love in the Tropics: Marriage, Divorce, and the Construction of Benevolent Colonialism in Puerto Rico, 1898–1910', in Joseph et al., *Close Encounters of Empire*, pp. 139–72. For a complete bibliography on the subject, see Saether, 'Identities and Independence', pp. 14–15.

53 Jonathan Curry-Machado, 'Indispensable Aliens: The Influence of Engineering Migrants in Mid-Nineteenth Century Cuba', unpub. Ph.D., London Metropolitan University, 2003.

54 Census, AHG CB Sig. 1. 3. 4. 103. 5. This census is reproduced in Brown, 'La renovación de una élite', pp. 348–50.
55 AGNC R AC, Legajo 60, fo. 926.
56 EP, HA157/3/201.
57 EP, HA157/1/382.
58 Scott, *Mary English*, pp. 111–43.
59 Reuben Zahler, 'Honor, Corruption and Legitimacy: Liberal Projects in the Early Venezuelan Republic, 1821–50', unpub Ph.D., University of Chicago, 2005. I am extremely grateful to Reuben for allowing me to read early drafts of his work.
60 Zahler, 'Honor, Corruption and Legitimacy'.
61 Good examples are Briceño Méndez, CDM Db1011, fo. 3, and Db0657, fo. 3.
62 Julián Castro, 15 November 1856, Valencia, AGNV IP, Vol. 6, fo. 288. Castro (b.Petare 1805, d. 1875 Valencia) was President of Venezuela in 1858–59.
63 Mosquera, 21 March 1835, Bogotá, AGNC HDS, Vol. 30, fo. 981.
64 Manby, 21 November 1832, Bogotá, AGNC HDS, Vol. 31, fo. 164.
65 *Gaceta de Gobierno de Ecuador,* 13 October 1831.
66 *El Colombiano de Guayas,* 24 November 1831.
67 *Gaceta de Gobierno de Ecuador,* 1 June 1833.
68 *Gaceta de Gobierno de Ecuador,* 1 June 1833.
69 For Hall see Pérez Ordóñez, *'El Quiteño Libre': El más espectacular periódico de oposición de la República.*
70 Carlos Wilthew, 30 March 1833, Bogotá, AGNC HDS, Vol. 48, fo. 815.
71 Joaquín Posada Gutiérrez, [n.d., 1833], Bogotá, AGNC HDS, Vol. 48, fo. 812.
72 For El Santuario, see Enrique Otero d'Costa, (ed.), *Asesinato de Córdoba: Proceso contra el Primer Comandante Ruperto Hand* (Bogotá, 1942).
73 This term is used in much of the historiography, notably in Rafael Gomez Hoyos, *La independencia de Colombia* (Madrid, 1992), p. 299. A rare sympathetic interpretation of the accusations against Hand was Florentino González, *Memorias* (Bogotá, 1971), p. 165.
74 From O'Leary's own account, quoted in Pérez Vila, *Vida de Daniel Florencio O'Leary,* p. 438.
75 Quoted in Pérez Vila, *Vida de Daniel Florencio O'Leary,* p. 452.
76 RafaelUrdaneta only resigned the presidency of Gran Colombia on 28 April 1831.
77 Joaquín María Barrigas and Ramón Pérez, n.d. (probably 22 September 1832), Bogotá, AGNC HDS, Vol. 24, fo. 438.
78 John Mackintosh to 'Los honorables senadores y representantes', 2 April 1835, Bogotá, AGNC HDS, Vol. 30, ff. 990–95.
79 For a background to these disputes, see Safford and Palacios, *Colombia: Fragmented Land, Divided Society,* pp. 122–31. An example is William Keogh, 22 September 1832, Bogotá, AGNC HDS, Vol. 24, ff. 437–38.
80 According to Miguel Uribe Restrepo, 25 March 1835, Bogotá, AGNC HDS, Vol. 30, fo. 980.
81 Bernardino Tovar, 25 March 1835, Bogotá, AGNC HDS, Vol. 30, fo. 984.
82 Juan Granados, [n.d., probably March 1835, probably Bogotá], AGNC HDS, Vol. 30, fo. 997.
83 Cabo Gregorio Vargas, 7 December 1831, AGNC R, AC, Vol. 95, fo. 530.
84 Mackintosh testifying to the conduct of Charles W. Smith, n.d., AGNC HDS, Vol. 42, fo. 548.
85 James Parsons, on the Frigate *Colombia,* at Guayaquil, 27 December 1832, ANE Causas Criminales, Caja 247 (1832–33), Expediente 14, fo. 15.
86 Guedes, on the Frigate *Colombia,* at Guayaquil, 27 December 1832, ANE Causas

Criminales, Caja 247 (1832–33), Expediente 14, fo. 17.

87 Capitán Diego Salinas, on the Frigate *Colombia*, at Guayaquil, 27 December 1832, fo. 12.

88 Capitán Enrique Medina, on the Frigate *Colombia*, at Guayaquil, 27 December 1832, fo. 14.

89 Wright to Sr General Comandante de Armas y Director de Marina, 5 January 1833, Guayaquil, ANE Causas Criminales, Caja 247 (1832–33), Expediente 14, fo. 29.

90 Juan Antonio Ferrán [Chief of Staff] to Wright, 14 January 1833, Quito, ANE Causas Criminales, Caja 247 (1832–33), Expediente 14, fo. 31.

91 For the continuing relevance of the concept of the *fuero*, see Pino Iturrieta, *Fueros, civilisación y ciudadanía*, pp. 41–70.

92 General Juan Ignacio Pareja, Guedes's representative, undated testimony (probably early March 1833), Guayaquil, ANE Causas Criminales, Caja 247 (1832–33), Expediente 14, fo. 83.

93 Twinam, *Public Lives, Private Secrets*, pp. 28–33.

94 Enrique Medina, 9 February 1833, Guayaquil, ANE Causas Criminales, Caja 243 (1832–33), Expediente 14, fo. 55.

95 Supreme Court Martial Verdict, 25 February 1834, Quito, ANE Causas Criminales, Caja 243 (1832–33), Expediente 14, fo. 109.

96 Juez Fiscal Domingo Agustín Gómez, 9 March 1833, Guayaquil, ANE Causas Criminales, Caja 243 (1832–33), Expediente 14, ff. 97–103.

97 Matthew MacAllister, 9 February 1826, Bogotá, CDM, Db2248, fo. 2.

98 Juan Gardiner to Comandante de Armas, n.d. [1825], Caracas, CDM, Db1150.

99 Thomas Scott, 6 May 1839, Caracas, AGNV IP, Vol. 85, fo. 331.

100 Diego Flannigan, 15 June 1842, Caracas, AGNV IP, Vol. 29, ff. 137–41.

101 As in the claim of the Hanoverian adventurer Subteniente Juan Meyer, CDM, Db1271, ff. 4–6.

102 As in the documents of Capitán Jacinto Martel, CDM, Db0240, ff. 2–4.

103 Miller Hallowes, 13 September 1855, St Mary's, Georgia, USA, AGNC HDS, Vol. 23, fo. 453.

104 Juan Uslar, 14 November 1856, Valencia, AGNV IP, Vol. 6, fo. 289.

105 Daniel Malone, 7 November 1826, Maracaibo, CDM, Db0530, fo. 5. See also Arthur Sandes to Comandante Jefe de la Escuadra Peruana, Guayaquil, 1 December 1828, repr. in *El Colombiano de Guayas*, 6 December 1828.

106 Zahler, 'Honor, Corruption, Legitimacy, and Liberalism', Ch. 4, 'Secession and Rebellion'.

107 For example John Ferriar supporting Capitán Guillermo Ravenscroft, 16 February 1821, Achaguas, CDM, Db0337.

108 Felipe Fernando, 9 August 1826, Bogotá, AGNC R, AC, Legajo 96, fo. 968.

109 For Teeson see AGNC R, AC, Legajo 96, ff. 965–68, and CDM, Db0399.

110 Comparatively, see Michael Roper, 'Re-remembering the Soldier Hero: the Psychic and Social Construction of Memory in Personal Narratives of the Great War', *History Workshop Journal*, 50 (Autumn 2000) pp. 181–204.

111 Explicitly stated in 'Resolución de la Secretaría de Guerra a favor de los oficiales que sirvieron en las campañas de la independencia', 1 September 1848, repr. in Grases and Pérez Vila (eds), *Las fuerzas armadas de Venezuela*, Vol. 11, pp. 124–26.

112 Lucio Pabón Núñez, 'Colombia y Gran Bretaña al borde de la guerra', *BCB*, 20:1 (1983), pp. 236–44.

113 Eduardo Brand to the President of the Republic, 19 June 1850, Bogotá, AGNC HDS, Vol. 6, fo. 706.

114 Manby, 23 March 1835, Bogotá, AGNC HDS, Vol. 30, fo. 979.

115 Francisco Urdaneta, 25 March 1835, Bogotá, AGNC HDS, Vol. 30, fo. 1001; Manby to John Dover, 20 May 1836, Bogotá, cited by José María de Mier, 'Tomás Manby: Soldado en Europa y en América: Lectura del Ingeniero José M. de Mier, en la sesión del 18 de Septiembre de 1973 de la Academia colombiana de historia, al ser recibido como Miembro correspondiente de la Corporación', unpub. typescript provided by Martín Alonso Roa Celis, p. 11.

116 Teeson, 7 March 1826, Bogotá, AGNC R, AC, Legajo 60, fo. 902.

117 An evocative example of an officer talking of his relation to the Venezuelan nation in terms of the family is Subteniente Pedro Laura, 21 October 1821, Valencia, CDM, Db0651, fo. 3.

118 Juan Uslar, 24 December 1849, Valencia, AGNV IP, Vol. 6, fo. 301; also Trinidad Portocarrero, 15 March 1850, Valencia, AGNV IP, Vol. 6, fo. 308. In what follows, *padre de familia* is not translated into English. Its connotations of 'patriarch' and 'head of family' are too suggestive to translate simply as 'father', as discussed in Díaz, *Female Citizens, Patriarchs, and the Law*, pp. 24–29, p. 187.

119 Elias Pino Iturrieta, 'Caballeros, clérigos y hombres de armas: O por que los ciudadanos no existen en Venezuela', in Pino Iturrieta, *Fueros, civilisación y ciudadanía*, p. 46.

120 O'Leary, cited in Pérez Vila, *Vida de Daniel Florencio O'Leary*, p. 598.

121 Mary English to New Granadan Representatives and Senators, 1 April 1844, Pescadero, EP, HA157/6/45.

122 Stopford to President of the Republic, 30 April 1840, London, AGNV IP, Vol. 89, fo. 107.

123 Brand, 24 November 1834, Bogotá, AGNV IP, Vol. 12, fo. 24.

124 Tomás Manby, 21 November 1832, Bogotá, AGNC HDS, Vol. 31, fo. 164.

125 Manby, 2 May 1832, Bogotá, AGNC HDS, Vol. 31, fo. 170.

126 Manby, *A mis apreciados amigos de la Capital* (Popayán, 1840), BNC, Fondo Pineda, Sala Primera 12. 113, pza. 104. The proclamation is repr. in Brown and Roa (eds), *Militares extranjeros*, pp. 165–67.

127 John Hill, 22 July 1842, Coro, AGNV IP, Vol. 42, fo. 212.

128 John Hill to President of the Republic, 23 July 1842, Coro, AGNV IP, Vol. 42, fo. 214.

129 Carlos Diego Minchin, (Charles James Minchin, b. 1799 Tipperary, d. 1879 Caracas) to Congress, 1 February 1854, Bogotá, AGNC HDS, Vol. 31, ff. 504–49, repr. in Brown and Roa, (eds), *Militares extranjeros*, pp. 169–72.

130 Documents dated August to October 1839, Caracas, AGNV IP, Vol. 40, fo. 3–13.

131 Francisca Díaz Granados, 24 March 1859, Cartagena, AGNC HDS, Vol. 53, ff. 5–9.

132 María Francesca Ruíz de Brown, 8 October 1845, Cumaná, AGNV IP, Vol. 13, fo. 169. The law of Montepío in Venezuela, passed in 1845, granted financial recompense to widows of soldiers, conditional upon proof of their legitimate marriage.

133 Mary English to New Granadan Representatives and Senators, 1 April 1844, Pescadero, EP, HA157/6/45.

134 Trinidad Páez, 1 October 1869, Valencia, AGNV IP, Vol. 40, fo. 54.

135 For the pension, death and funeral of 'one of the few surviving British soldiers' in Caracas in 1842, Private George Cox, see AGNV IP, Vol. 21, ff. 73–85. For an emphasis on 'survival', see Hugo Hughes, 11 June 1855, Bogotá, AGNC HDS, Vol. 23, fo. 408.

136 St John to Foreign Office, 26 November 1891, Cuenca, TNA FO 25/88/42, ff. 98–99. My thanks to Nicola Foote who provided me with this reference.

CHAPTER NINE

After Adventure

This final section looks at how the adventures described above were remembered on both sides of the Atlantic. It looks to move on from Doreen Massey's formulation that 'the identity of places is very much bound up with the histories which are told of them, how those histories are told, and which history turns out to be dominant'.[1] In Gran Colombia national history writing led to particular types of adventurer being commemorated and the vast majority being forgotten. In Britain and Ireland, the considerable number of narratives written by disillusioned adventurers contributed to Gran Colombia coming to be seen as a place for extra-imperial adventure, and thereafter excluded from national history writing. During the rest of the nineteenth century, as a result of the commemorations studied, the region came to be seen as a place of failed adventure, and gradually excised from the British world view which increasingly concentrated on the responsibilities of the formal colonial possessions and moved away from the hope and optimism associated with Latin America during the Age of Revolution. These processes are explored first through an exploration of the commemoration of the adventurers in Britain and then by an examination of the Colombian sources.[2] The analysis of the commemoration of this transnational phenomenon reveals the contingent nature of national identity formation after independence. The presence of British and Irish adventurers in Wars of Independence in the Hispanic world was variously a point of pride, tension and embarrassment for Britons and Gran Colombians as they thought about their national histories in the subsequent century.

Commemoration in Britain and Ireland

In Britain and Ireland, commemoration of the adventures was shaped by the flood of books published immediately by returned and disillusioned adventurers. Colombia was cast as part of a brutish, savage and unwelcoming continent that they were glad to see the back of. The difficult journey back to Europe from Latin America was given a prominent position in their narratives of failed adventure. The sea voyage was often long, haphazard, 'tedious and disastrous'.[3] Some were delayed, diverted or shipwrecked by bad weather.[4] A disintegrating craft carrying three Irish soldiers was washed up on the beach at Santa Marta, where the adventurers begged the Loyalist authorities 'to allow them to go home' for they hated the insurgents they had deserted in Riohacha.[5] Besides those who wrote memoirs or who petitioned the new republics' governments, most adventurers who returned home went back to the historical anonymity from which they originated, and success stories were extremely rare. Private Jack Langan was one such individual. He was one of the rebels at Riohacha, but back home in Belfast he gained a reputation as a fist-fighter and was contracted to an agent who took him to London, where he fought several times for the Championship title.[6] Some soldiers enlisted in the British Army on their return from South America, although, as mercenary service did not appear on soldiers' service records, the evidence is necessarily fragmentary and uncertain.[7]

Documentation regarding those officers who returned home is slightly less sparse than for private soldiers. Many officers received passports or official permission to leave.[8] Often they returned to Dublin to publicly contest the conditions of their recruitment.[9] Sometimes there was sympathy, for example from Daniel O'Connell, who noted that 'there were dangers [even] a brave man would wish to escape from – famine and pestilence, together with a destructive climate, were enemies from which the stoutest need not be ashamed to effect their escape'.[10] It often took a while to become accustomed to European life again. Robert Young felt 'like a stranger' when he got home.[11]

Young men presented their Latin American adventure as a rite of passage that had initiated them into manhood. A difficult journey home only served to emphasise the feat of survival. As John Tosh has observed, nineteenth-century young, British, middle-class males had to perform a rite of passage 'involving detaching oneself from the home and its feminine comforts. It required a level of material success in the wider world which was so often represented in threatening and alienating terms ... a period of conflict, challenge and exertion.'[12] One such example was Morgan O'Connell, the second son of the Irish politician Daniel O'Connell.[13] The whole O'Connell family were saddened at their 'darling Morgan's imminent departure'.[14] Throughout his absence, his parents worried about his well-being and hoped for his safe return.[15] In 1821 Morgan returned to be 'safe in the bosom of [his] protecting family'.[16] His family were satisfied that the adventure had 'done him nothing but good'.[17] His younger sister felt that Morgan had become a man while he was away, and now he was 'an old Sailor, [as he had] been in South America and the West Indies, and shipwrecked on his way home'.[18] Shipwreck evoked literary adventurers such as Robinson Crusoe, and emphasised the brave endurance of the hardy individuals who survived it. Gran Colombia was presented as an obstacle which adventurers had overcome, rather than as a nation or society with which they had engaged and where they had lived.

Many adventurers remained only a short time in Britain or Ireland and then continued their travels elsewhere. Upon his return from Gran Colombia, Morgan O'Connell spent several years in the Austrian army before becoming

Member of Parliament for Meath.[19] Several veterans found status and an income through returning to South America in a diplomatic capacity, such as Daniel O'Leary in Bogotá, Richard Wright in Quito and Fredrik Adlercreutz in Caracas.[20] A handful of adventurers settled in France, British North America and the United States of America.[21] The relative lack of sources, however, means that it is not possible to argue – as Christine Wright has done for the British veterans of the Peninsular War who went on to form a colonial élite in New South Wales – that the Gran Colombian experience created bonds that survived into post-war life back in Britain and Ireland.[22] Most of those who returned had often spent less than two years away, and their complaints and letters to newspapers were quickly replaced in the public interest by more pressing matters such as the Queen Caroline affair, Catholic Emancipation and the agitation for parliamentary reform. After the 1826 stock market crash drastically reduced investment in South America, interest in the continent and those who had travelled through it was further diminished.

The most influential group of returnees were those who published their memoirs in London, Edinburgh or Dublin. Little is known about their post-Gran Colombia careers because most memoirs came out within a year or two of the author's return. George Laval Chesterton was unique in that he published two volumes of autobiography, in 1820 and 1853.[23] Back in Britain, Chesterton worked for a short time as a translator before taking employment as a prison governor in 1829.[24] W. Davidson Weatherhead published *A Medical and Philosophical Essay, on the Influence of Custom and Habit on the Human Economy* (1828) which confirmed that he had returned to his original medical profession, and made no reference to South America or his experiences there.[25] Another chronicler, Michael Rafter, went on to write a fictionalised account of British involvement in the Iberian Peninsula during the Napoleonic Wars, published in 1855, which again made no reference to his adventures in Gran Colombia.[26]

The adventurers' narratives published in the 1820s shaped the way in which Britons understood Gran Colombia for the rest of the century. The British 'imagined geography' of Latin America underwent a critical evolution in the period under study in this book; as Gareth Jones put it, 'a great deal about what we know about Latin America today derives from [nineteenth-century] travel writers who nevertheless gave preference to certain places and overlaid meanings onto landscapes according to the ideological and philosophical conventions of the day'.[27] They emphasised the difficulties of travel within Latin America itself, and also the struggle just to get there and back. As Ricardo Cicerchia points out for the case of Argentina, in 'all narratives organised from the perspective of a return, the predominant vision is a metropolitan one', emphasising 'the exhausting voyages, the majesty of the Andes, the barbarous customs of the peoples, [and] the disadvantages of the Spanish heritage' for the areas described.[28] Descriptions of the region stressed the 'sheer effort' of travel and claimed 'muscular exhaustion, boredom, disillusionment' at all times.[29] In *Imperial Eyes*, Mary Louise Pratt emphasised the importance of commercial travellers' insistence on recording distances, timetables and details of travel in Latin America. Pratt argued that by recording the practical obstacles to their journey the 'capitalist vanguard' was 'allegorising the lust for progress' linking Latin America to the modern world in this period.[30] Descriptions of difficult conditions were essential to the adventure narratives written by veterans returning home.

The epic of adventure in Latin America set out in the travel writing of the 1820s was designed for a metropolitan audience that saw the region as a 'brute new world',[31] and there was no room for the affectionate ties that bound settler–adventurers to the new nations that were studied in Chapter 8. Gran Colombia was cast off from the British world with the return and publications of these adventurers. The 1826 stock exchange crash effectively ended much British public interest in the region for half a century, and ushered in an era of 'misunderstanding and confrontation'.[32] Because they did not publish travel narratives, the many adventurers who stayed in Gran Colombia were largely forgotten back in Europe. Those adventurers who did settle in the region, marrying and establishing stable families and positions in society, such as Daniel O'Leary and Thomas Manby, were little spoken of in Britain or Ireland. The writings of those adventurers who wrote more nuanced and informed memoirs, such as Richard Vowell and Alexander Alexander, were discarded (if they were ever read at all) in favour of those which discussed Gran Colombia in conventional terms. The conclusions of the French traveller Gaspar Mollien neatly summarise the attitude towards the region that prevailed in much of Europe after the optimism of the mid–1820s had begun to die away. Mollien observed that 'lying, jealousy and ingratitude are the prevailing vices'; that 'the burning heat of the torrid zone' affects the mind too much for the correct functioning of 'mental faculties'; and that 'the government [of Gran Colombia, in 1824] is not yet powerful enough to rouse the inhabitants from their Asiatic indolence, and the people are not yet sufficiently fond of foreigners, to invite them with cordiality, and to favour them with all possible means'.[33] Even though this book has shown Mollien's assessment to have been far from correct, during the 1820s and 1830s Latin America passed in British eyes from being a landscape for adventure and optimism about the spread of commerce and civilisation to a region characterised by the failure of adventure and pessimism about its future.

If people in Britain thought about Gran Colombia at all, it was generally as a region which owed them money and where geography and climate inhibited both industry and liberty. Nevertheless, it was also still seen as a land rich in resources which could, if the conditions were right, be converted into a useful trading partner, providing opportunities to those down on their luck. The memoirs of the disillusioned adventurers who returned home early, such as Hippisley, Hackett and Robinson, fitted into the British world-view which dismissed the capacity of Gran Colombians. As Michael Mulhall wrote in 1878, summarising this interpretation, 'Our countrymen ... performed feats of valour worthy to rank with those of Greek or Roman history ... Yet their labours were not appreciated, and they were regarded as a set of needy adventurers, although several of them had sacrificed large fortunes, and all of them shed their blood freely, for the cause in which they had embarked.'[34] Great changes had taken place in the transition from colonies to republics in Gran Colombia, and these changes had been shared, witnessed and recorded by foreign adventurers. The risks taken by adventurers, however, were not perceived as having secured honour, status or sufficient glory. The inescapable conclusion was that it had all been a misadventure and was best forgotten. Only long after the historical interpretation of the adventures had been set in stone by disillusioned chroniclers such as Hackett, Hippisley and Chesterton in the 1820s were the accounts of those adventurers who settled in Gran Colombia first published. O'Leary's *Narración* appeared in 1879, Illingworth's writings in 1913 and O'Connor's *Independencia americana* in 1915. All three were published in Spanish and hence their experiences, and others like them, have taken their time to enter the British historiography and alter interpretations. The adventurers who returned home during and immediately after the Wars of Independence were the ones who shaped the prevailing interpretation of Gran Colombian independence in Britain.

Returned adventurers continued to exaggerate their services and difficulties once they were back home. The pursuit of claims for recompense from the new states was the principal avenue, but by claiming to love the *patria* without even residing there, let alone marrying into it, adventurers who petitioned from abroad were faced with many difficulties.[35] In trying to square the circle of patriotic loyalty from afar, they laid so much stress on personal sacrifice, selfless dedication to the cause and their own individual heroism that they exposed themselves to ridicule. In 1858 James Duff Paterson, writing from his home in Co. Kerry, claimed, 'when we entered Bogotá [in 1819] I was literally naked', and that in all his time in the army he did not receive 'any pay, not a single farthing'.[36] His story evolved so that ten years later, still petitioning the New Granadan government, he had apparently overcome suffering and privation that had 'no parallel in the annals of history'.[37] Expectations were also exaggerated. Gregor MacGregor's daughter, Josefa María MacGregor, who lived in Edinburgh, requested the Venezuelan government to inform her of 'any inheritance in Venezuela, or any other part of the American continent and its adjacent islands that might be [hers]', for example 'houses, lands, haciendas, inheritance and other effects or furniture'.[38] Similar was the letter sent by James Ryan of Tipperary, the brother of a private soldier of the Irish Legion, who hoped to inherit the estate of his brother 'who had remained in South America where he is supposed to have died, possessed of considerable property in Grenada [sic]'.[39] These exaggerated expectations were not met by the cash-strapped republics in Gran Colombia, which had other priorities and chose to commemorate and reward those adventurers who remained in the national territory and became part of the national family. Gran Colombia fell out of the British cultural world as the surviving adventurers died and politicians, thinkers and novelists concentrated on the formal empire.

The adventurers evoked in Joseph Conrad's 1904 novel *Nostromo: A Tale of the Seaboard,* one of the few works of British fiction that did consider Latin America, cast the region as a landscape of failed adventure. *Nostromo* was set in the fictional republic of Costaguana, much of which was based on what Conrad had heard about Colombia and Panama. As Conrad himself admitted, he 'had just a glimpse' of Latin America on a three-day visit 25 years before writing the novel.[40] Costaguana was an invented nation which epitomised the way in which Conrad imagined Latin America. One of the principal characters, Charles Gould, was the grandson of a British veteran of the Battle of Carabobo who inherited a mine in the interior of the country.[41] Conrad described the Gould family in the terms of conventional British expatriate behaviour rather than the integrated, assimilated experience described in Chapter 8. The Gould family was 'established in Costaguana for three generations, [but they] always went to England for their education and their wives'.[42] Conrad's interpretation of Latin American relations with Britain favoured typical British stereotypes of aloofness and straightforwardness when abroad:

> Uncle Harry [Gould] was no adventurer. In Costaguana we Goulds are no adventurers. He was of the country, and he loved it, but he remained essentially an Englishman in his ideas. He made use of the political cry of his time. It was Federation. But he was no politician. He simply stood up for social order out of pure love of rational liberty and from his hate of oppression. There was no nonsense about him. He went to work in his own way because it seemed right, just as I feel I must lay hold of that mine.[43]

Conrad's writing symbolised the way that adventure – and the embracing of risk and the unknown that it entails – was excised from the memory of the expeditions to Gran Colombia in the subsequent century in both Europe and the Americas. By mid-century liberal humanitarianism had been 'replaced by a more reactionary imperial discourse'.[44] Conrad sought to explore the imperial mindset behind British actions overseas. Later nineteenth-century Britons had become more sceptical, cautious and ungenerous towards other peoples than their counterparts had been in the 1810s. The adventurers to Gran Colombia were remembered, through figures such as Gould, as imperial Britons who faced up to the outside world as firm defenders of traditional freedoms and who always returned home to their domestic comforts and civilisation. Chroniclers of Britain's imperial activities passed over alternative histories such as those adventurers who served under Bolívar and settled in Gran Colombia. In Hispanic America, however, the adventurers were commemorated as volunteers in the cause of liberty who dedicated their lives to new nations and became part of the national family.

Commemorations in Gran Colombia

Gran Colombian chroniclers used the story of foreign adventurers to illustrate the original justice of the cause of liberty and national independence. With the consolidation of national states by mid-century, patriotic mythologising began to elevate the veterans and martyrs of the Wars of Independence into an 'entirely new pantheon of heroes' supported by the 'state cult of these *próceres*'.[45] In the 1840s, state-sponsored texts 'stressed the fundamental importance of the independence era to the status and legitimacy of the nation'.[46] Nations became 'inseparably associated' with the wars they had fought and the pro- tagonists of those wars therefore became national heroes.[47] The ambiguous place of foreign adventurers in these stories was often glossed over in favour of a straightforward emphasis on heroism and glory. Some voices recognised the peculiar mixture of economic, social and cultural factors that combined to send the adventurers across the Atlantic. Writing in 1867, José Antonio Páez reflected,

> One supposes that it was not mean ambition that persuaded these British officers
> to abandon their *patria* to fight for an oppressed people in America. Rather, it
> was their ambition to win military glory, their desire for new and dangerous
> adventures, and their passion for *excitement* which makes the Englishman seem
> sometimes like a madman, and sometimes like a hero.[48]

With their madness and heroism, foreigners were difficult to fit into the 'he- roic iconography' of independence.[49] Historical narratives only commemo- rated those few adventurers who were most appropriate for the nation to claim for itself. This generally meant those who died as heroes in the patriotic ser- vice or those whose figures were indelibly linked with Bolívar or other na- tional heroes.

For most chroniclers of the Wars of Independence, the substantial foreign participation in the conflict was a distraction from the *historia patria* which told how new nations had been born through their own strength, endeavour and application. Foreigners warranted only a walk-on, walk-off part in this process. José Manuel Restrepo's influential writings, for example, emphasised the bravery and loyalty of individual officers such as Rooke and O'Leary, demonised an errant few such as Wilson and Hippisley, and completely ig- nored the larger mass of adventurers.[50] For Restrepo, Páez and others, the interventions of foreigners were auxiliary in every sense. The 'natural' British love of glory and liberty and the participation of the 'worthy heirs to Richard the Lionheart' combined to confirm the justice of the cause of Independence, but the adventurers were deemed, to all intents and purposes, as irrelevant to its eventual success.[51] Other writers picked out particular instances of foreign heroism or villainy to illustrate their narratives. Manuel Antonio López re- called in 1878 the memory of James Rooke crying '*Viva la patria!*' on his death- bed after the battle of Pantano de Vargas.[52] José María Samper contrasted the Irish Legion's 'valiant volunteers' with the unfortunate embarrassments of other mercenaries.[53] Joaquín Posada Gutierrez reflected that 'English is freedom's language', and lambasted the foreigners involved in El Santuario for the 'cowardly betrayal' of their illustrious heritage.[54] The novelist Jorge

Isaacs was more sympathetic to the foreign veterans who settled in Gran Colombia, and less interested in heroic icons. In his 1867 novel, *María*, the heroine's doctor was modelled on Henry Mayne, a member of the expeditions who lived in Bogotá and then Cauca until his death in 1842.[55] In Doris Sommer's analysis, *María* is a mixed-up foundational fiction of Colombian nation-building which laments the racial and social divisions that divided Colombia in the nineteenth century. Mixed-up and complicated *María* may be, but Mayne was portrayed as a loyal and stable influence in a changing and confused society. In *María*, as in the histories written around the mid-century, foreign involvement in national society was acceptable and even desirable as long as it was subordinate to national policy and local élites. Later fictions took this process even further: foreigners were sidelined in Gabriel García Márquez's narrative of Simón Bolívar's last days, *El general en su laberinto*. Many of Bolívar's closest associates in the last year of his life were foreigners, including Daniel O'Leary and Belford Wilson, but they become peripheral figures in the novel, replaced by a Colombian servant, José Palacios, who García Márquez uses to draw out themes of internal Colombian conflict and tension rather than more complicated international networks.[56]

The history of the commemoration of the adventurers in Gran Colombia continues to be one of neglect, omission and half-truths. The public spaces cordoned off for remembrance of the dead adventurers and those who followed them – cemeteries created for foreigners – could conceivably have created a site for remembrance of this unique contribution to national independence, but two centuries of urban growth and neglect have left them dilapidated or indeed destroyed. The British cemetery in Caracas was built over in the early twentieth-century expansion of the urban centre; in Bogotá the British Cemetery survives, clinging to the side of a motorway flyover and under threat from redevelopers. According to a small sign, the inner fence was made out of the smelted down original bayonets and musket barrels of the British Legion. Some adventurers are noted as being buried there, including John Mackintosh, but no legible gravestones remain. Dwarfed by surrounding skyscrapers and urban noise, it is as vivid a picture of a historical cul-de-sac as Conrad's 'impious adventurers' hiding out in the mountainous mists.[57] In public society some chosen adventurers are commemorated in expected places. The bench on which James Rooke died gasping '*Viva la patria*' is on display in the National Museum of Colombia.[58] A plaque commemorating the sacrifices of the British Legion adorns a wall of the Colombian Senate, if you know where to look. The Museo Bolivariano in Caracas contains several important pieces of memorabilia relating to the adventurers, including the engraved sword donated by the Irish Legion to Simón Bolívar, which is kept underneath the Director's desk and rarely put on display.

There is ostentatious public commemoration of the adventurers on the battlefields themselves. A bust of Thomas Idlerton Ferrier – who died from his wounds at the Battle of Carabobo – forms part of a heroic ceremonial walk at the centre of the remodelled Carabobo battlefield. Each year the British

Legion is honoured by a military ceremony to commemorate their involvement in the Battle of Boyacá. There is a museum by the battlefield which contains original flags and standards, some of which feature the Union Jack.[59] In Venezuela since 1999 President Hugo Chávez's *república bolivariana* has aggressively asserted the importance of the *próceres* of the Wars of Independence, and works are constantly afoot to rehabilitate other monuments to their memory, including sections of the National Pantheon which commemorate several foreigners, including O'Leary.[60] In Colombia, foreign adventurers continue to take part in internal military conflict, with little awareness of their historical precedents. British mercenaries served in Colombia during the hunt for drug baron Pablo Escobar in 1989[61]; Irish Republicans visited FARC guerrillas in 2001 to share experiences and knowledge.[62] Both interventions conspicuously lacked either heroism or success, like the majority of their predecessors in the 1810s and 1820s.

In the United Kingdom, Ireland and the Gran Colombian region there are many people with access to the internet who show interest in tracing the adventurers' descendants. In contrast to the heirs of foreign agricultural colonists in Brazil who, according to Oliver Marshall, have no more than 'the faintest knowledge of (or interest in) their immigrant origins,' there is a broad awareness of this heritage in Colombia, Venezuela and Ecuador.[63] In an improvised and unscientific series of interviews with bartenders, taxi-drivers, coffee-salesmen, shoe-cleaners and archive administrators in Quito, Bogotá and Caracas, I learned that the descendants of Thomas Wright own the largest Ecuadorean supermarket chain and that 'half of the Bogotá élite' claims to be related to Daniel O'Leary; I heard numerous examples of 'my friend/colleague says he is related to one of those'. A browse through internet genealogy chatrooms reveals a number of unrelated individuals seeking confirmation that their unusual surname comes from one of the nineteenth century adventurers.[64] Hopefully online publication of the database from which much of this book is drawn will enable more people to discover the facts behind family legend, and will act as an interface that can draw together further as yet undocumented sources. More than statues, this ambiguous foreign involvement in a war now regarded as one of national liberation represents a hidden reference point for many people seeking to understand their own histories.

This chapter has explored the commemoration of the adventurers in Britain and in Gran Colombia, from the immediate aftermath of independence through to the present day. In Britain, the first narratives of failed adventure shaped subsequent commemorations and contributed to Latin America falling out of the British imperial mind. In Gran Colombia, contemporaries and subsequent chroniclers used foreign involvement in the Wars of Independence to enhance their own narratives of nation-building. By exploring the lives and adventures of the foreign individuals who served under Simón Bolívar in the Wars of Independence and by examining the way their stories have been used and manipulated by subsequent generations, we learn that misfortunes, mistakes and misunderstandings characterised this encounter between peoples just as much as heroism, idealism, love and friendship. The study of the diverse commemorations of the adventurers on both sides of the Atlantic shows how the histories of places are interlinked by the stories told by and about the peoples who travel through them, who fight over them, and who grow old remembering them.

Notes

1   Doreen Massey, 'Places and their pasts', *History Workshop Journal*, 39 (1995), p. 188.
2   Only recently has the Irish Legion been incorporated into narratives exalting Irish love of liberty, and for this reason the emphasis in this chapter is exclusively on Britain. See for example see Roy S. Carson, 'How Venezuelan Independence (and South America's) was won by the Irish!' (1996), www.vheadline.com/readnews.asp?id=27560.
3   Young, 'Diary of the Journey of Robert James Young', f. 37.
4   For Morgan O'Connell's shipwreck see Daniel O'Connell to Hunting Cap O'Connell, 5 January 1822, Cork, in *TCDOC*, Vol. 3, pp. 344–47.
5   Reported in Pedro Ruiz de Porras to Viceroy Sámano, 5 May 1820, Santa Marta, AGI Cuba, Legajo 745.
6   For Langan see Cochrane, *Journal of a Residence and Travels in Colombia*, p. 462 and Thomas Reynolds, *History of the Great Fight Between Spring and Langan, for the Championship of England, and One Thousand Sovereigns, on Tuesday, June 8, 1824: To Which is Added, The Whole of the Correspondence relative to the disputed points on their first battle; with their lives and portraits* (London, 1824).
7   For example, a tentative argument can be made for Private James Donohue, a butcher from Kilhogan who was invalided in Caracas in 1822. British Army records give a James Donohue of the same age, place of birth and profession, enlisting into the 17th Foot in York in April 1824, and deserting soon thereafter. After receiving corporal punishment, he served nine years in the East Indies and five in New South Wales, and retired in 1845. Lambert, *Carabobo*, p. 33; AGNC R GYM Vol. 16, fo. 576; TNA WO 97/378/30.
8   Angostura passports are in AGNV GDG, Vol. 4 fo. 182; Vol. 9, ff. 88–101; Vol. 12, ff. 60–124.
9   As in *Reply to the Letter of Adjutant General Kenny and the pamphlet of Mr Francis Hall, by the gentlemen who have returned from the Expedition to Margaritta* (Dublin, 1820).
10   *DEP,* 3 February 1820.
11   Young, 'Diary of the Voyage of Robert James Young', ff. 44–45.
12   John Tosh, *A Man's Place. Masculinity and the Middle-Class Home in Victorian England* (London, 1999), p. 110.
13   Morgan O'Connell's case is exceptional only because of the survival of intimate personal correspondence involving his father, brother, mother and sister.
14   Mary O'Connell to Daniel O'Connell, 4 January 1820, Dublin, in *TCDOC*, Vol. 2, p. 229.
15   Daniel O'Connell to Mary O'Connell, 12 October 1820, Tralee, in *TCDOC*, Vol., p. 285.
16   Devereux to Morgan O'Connell, 16 July 1822, Bogotá, NLI, Microfilm n.2718, p. 1622.
17   Daniel O'Connell to Hunting Cap O'Connell, 5 January 1822, in *TCDOC*, Vol. 2, pp. 344–47.
18   Ellen O'Connell, 'Narrative of a Residence in France, 1822–23', NLI, Microfilm n.2718, p. 1622, entry for 2 May 1822.
19   For Morgan O'Connell's later career, see '14 Letters and 1 copy to Daniel and Mary

O'Connell from Morgan O'Connell 1816–1846', NLI, MSS 13645 (1).

20 See the documents collected in Fredrik Thomas Adlercreutz, *Cartera del Coronel Conde de Adlercreutz: Documentos inéditos relativos a la historia de Venezuela y de la Gran Colombia Con introducción y notas de C. Parra Pérez* (Paris, 1928).

21 For Coronel Borrell in Paris see Maceroni, *Memoirs of the Life and Adventures of Colonel Maceroni*, p. 448; for Coronel Matthew Sutton in France see Thomas Sutton to Daniel O'Connell, 31 January 1824, Dublin, O'Connell Papers, UCD, P12/3/147. For officers Budd and Roberts in British North America see ACC, Sala Mosquera 1832, d. 6531.

22 Christine Wright, '"Really Respectable Settlers": Peninsular War Veterans in the Australian colonies, 1820s and 1830s', Unpub. Ph.D., Australian National University, Canberra, 2005. My thanks to Christine Wright for a fruitful interchange of information from her unpublished research, which as yet has not unveiled any networks of veterans encompassing Britain, Spain, Australia and Colombia.

23 Chesterton, *A Narrative of Proceedings* and *Peace, War and Adventure*.

24 Chesterton, *Revelations of Prison Life*, Vol. 1 (London, 1856), p. 104.

25 George Laval Weatherhead, *Account of the Late Expedition against the Isthmus of Darien*, and *A Medical and Philosophical Essay, on the Influence of Custom and Habit on the Human Economy* (London, 1828).

26 Michael Rafter, (author of *Memoirs of Gregor M'Gregor*), *Percy Blake, or the Young Rifleman*, 3 Vols (London, 1855).

27 Gareth A. Jones, 'Latin American Geographies', in Phillip Swanson, (ed.), *The Companion to Latin American Studies* (London, 2003), pp. 5–25.

28 Ricardo Cicerchia, *Journey, Rediscovery and Narrative: British Travel Accounts of Argentina (1800–1850)* (London, 1998), p. 14.

29 Cicerchia, *Journey, Rediscovery and Narrative*, p. 17.

30 Pratt, *Imperial Eyes*, p. 148.

31 The phrase and interpretation come from Desmond Gregory, *Brute New World: The Rediscovery of Latin America in the early Nineteenth Century* (London, 1992).

32 Dawson, *The First Latin American Debt Crisis*, p. 235.

33 Gaspar Mollien, *Travels in the Republic of Colombia in the Years 1822 and 1823* (London, 1824), pp. 361–69.

34 Michael Mulhall, *The English in South America* (New York, 1977, first edn, Buenos Aires, 1878), p. 15.

35 For recognition of these difficulties, see Turner to Palmerston, 14 January 1836, Bogotá, TNA FO 55/4 ff. 16–18, repr. in Deas and Sánchez, (eds), *Santander y los ingleses*, Vol. 1, p. 405; José Antonio Páez, 2 December 1857, New York, AGNV IP, Vol. 69, fo. 170; Fernando Bolívar, 24 December 1858, Valencia, AGNV IP, Vol. 69, ff. 173–5.

36 Paterson, 8 February 1858, Jarbert, Co. Kerry, AGNC HDS, Vol. 36, fo. 549.

37 Paterson, 8 February 1868, Queenstown, AGNC HDS, Vol. 36, fo. 567. Translated by V. S. Manrique. Once he had been awarded a pension from New Granada, Paterson turned his attention to Venezuela, as in Paterson, 8 August 1876, Plymouth, AGNV IP, Vol. 24, fo. 194.

38 Josefa María MacGregor, 24 February 1846, Edinburgh, AGNV IP, Vol. 49, fo. 63.

39 James Ryan to Aberdeen, 26 December 1845, Limerick, TNA FO 80/36 ff. 151–52, rpd. in Brown and Roa, (eds), *Militares extranjeros*, pp. 44–45.

40 Joseph Conrad to R. B. Cunninghame-Graham, 1904, cited in C. T. Watts, (ed.), *Joseph Conrad's Letters to R. B. Cunninghame Graham* (Cambridge, 1969), p. 37.

41 Joseph Conrad, *Nostromo: A Tale of the Seaboard* (Oxford, 1995, first edn London, 1904), p. 5.

42 Conrad, *Nostromo*, p. 46.

43 Conrad, *Nostromo*, p. 64.

44 Alan Lester, *Imperial Networks, Creating Identities in Nineteenth-Century South Africa*

and Britain (London, 2001), p. 189.

45 Rebecca Earle, 'Sobre heroes y tumbas: National Symbols in Nineteenth-Century Spanish America', *HAHR*, 85:3 (2005), p. 395.
46 Earle, 'Sobre heroes y tumbas', p. 396.
47 Michael Howard, *The Lessons of History* (Oxford, 1991), p. 40.
48 Páez, *Autobiografía*, pp. 246–47.
49 Earle, 'Sobre heroes y tumbas', p. 413.
50 Restrepo, *Historia de la revolución de la República de Colombia en la América Meridional* (Bogotá, 1942–50), Vol. 1, p. 299, Vol. 6, pp. 167–72.
51 Páez, *Autobiografía*, p. 240, p. 284. See also José Manuel Groot, *Historia eclesiástica y civil de Nueva Granada* (Bogotá, 1883), p. 119; Rafael María Baralt and Ramón Díaz Díaz, *Resumen de la historia de Venezuela desde el año de 1797 hasta el de 1830* (Bruges, 1939), Vol. 1, p. 381.
52 Manuel Antonio López, *Recuerdos históricos del coronel Manuel Antonio López, Colombia i Perú 1819–1826* (Bogotá, 1878), p. 12, see also p. 54, p. 82, pp. 133–34.
53 José María Samper, *Ensayo sobre las revoluciones políticas y la condición social de las repúblicas colombianas* (Bogotá, 1861), p. 195.
54 Joaquín Posada Gutiérrez, *Memorias históricas políticas* (Medellín, 1971), Vol. 1, p. 123, p. 190.
55 Jorge Isaacs, *María* (Bogotá, 1867); Doris Sommer, *Foundational Fictions: The National Romances of Latin America* (Berkeley, CA, 1991), pp. 172–204; Eduardo Posada, *Apostillas* (Bogotá, 1978), p. 261; AGNC HDS Vol. 31, ff. 791–98.
56 Gabriel García Márquez, *El general en su laberinto* (Bogotá, 1989); Jill E. Albada Jelgersma, 'Simón Bolívar en *El general en su laberinto* de Gabriel García Márquez', *Journal of Iberian and Latin American Studies*, 7:1 (2001), pp. 55–62.
57 Conrad, *Nostromo*, p. 5.
58 There is a photograph of this bench on display in Brown and Roa, (eds), *Militares extranjeros*, p. 234, and another of the entrance to the British Cemetery in Bogotá on p. 258.
59 It had been boarded up for some time when I visited, and the windows were dirty and hard to see through. The website relating to the battlefield continues to state (December 2005) that the museum is in the process of being modernised.
60 Germán Carrera Damas has criticised this as a return to the early twentieth-century historiography exalting heroes and deriding villains 'riding roughshod over the most basic historical understanding'. Carrera Damas, *Alternativas ideológicas en América Latina contemporanea (El caso de Venezuela: El bolivarianismo-militarismo)* (Gainesville, FL, 2001), p. 21.
61 Anthony Rogers, *Somebody Else's War: Mercenaries from the 1960s to the Present Day* (London, 1998), pp. 212–22.
62 Edgar Tellez, Oscar Montes and Jorge Lesmes, *Diario íntimo de un fracaso: Historia no contada del proceso de paz con las FARC* (Bogotá, 2002), p. 154. The FARC are the Revolutionary Armed Forces of Colombia, *Fuerzas armadas revolucionarias de Colombia*.
63 Marshall, *English, Irish and Irish-American Pioneer Settlers*, p. 209.
64 See http://genforum.genealogy.com/venezuela/page4.html#13 for a descendent of Guillermo Ashdown, and http://www.venezuelagenealogia.org/basededatos.html for others. The adventurers are largely absent from the excellent web resource 'Brits in South America' run by Neil Hampshire, www.bisa.btinternet.co.uk, which contains biographical information relating to over 20,000 Britons who travelled to South America in the nineteenth and twentieth centuries. Web pages referenced were correct on 15 October 2005. An edited version of my database can be consulted at www.bris.ac.uk/hispanic/department/resources.

Conclusion

This study of the British and Irish adventurers in the Wars of Independence in Gran Colombia brings out the social and cultural dimensions of their encounter with Hispanic American peoples, expanding upon the military focus of previous historiography. The diverse motives of individuals are revealed, alongside the variety of reactions that they provoked, ranging from admiration, respect and love, to neglect, disgust and pity. Chapter 1 explored the context for the adventurers' departure from Europe. Diplomatic, political, cultural and economic conditions combined to create pull factors attracting adventurers to Gran Colombia, push factors to take them away from Britain and Ireland, and commercial and imperial networks to carry them across the Atlantic. Over half of the adventurers were Irish, and only one third had any verifiable military experience. Some were inspired by the cause of liberty, whilst others were propelled by economic dislocation and sought new careers and fortunes. They were divided between officers and men and carried these class distinctions with them across the ocean.

The reality of military adventuring in Gran Colombia, discussed in Chapters 2 and 3, varied from region to region. The contrast between expectations and local conditions was sharp. Over half of the volunteers died or deserted within a few months of arrival. The heroism of some individuals at key battles was paralleled by a wider story of hunger, disease and debilitating fear of the unknown. These circumstances triggered loss of discipline, mutiny, desertion and pillaging. Disputes between officers concerned with their honour were often resolved through duelling. The high rates of death and desertion undermined any attempts to professionalise Bolívar's military forces through British influence. Over time, adventurers who remained in the Independent forces realised that acts of individual bravery were not enough to win recognition from Gran Colombians. New collective loyalties and aspirations began to take root. In 1820 two events – the rebellion of the Irish Legion at Riohacha, and Bolívar's creation of the Albion Battalion in Bogotá – combined to place the remaining foreign adventurers firmly under the banner of Gran Colombia. Shared difficulties in adversity, rather than a common political ideology, contributed to adventurers becoming some of Bolívar's most loyal allies and most fervent *colombianos*. Integral to their position in a society still sharply delineated according to race and slavery, was their whiteness. Most of the volunteers accepted slavery as a feature of local society and some went on to own slaves or work as overseers on slave plantations. There were others, such as John Runnel, who took an opposite path, associating themselves with people of colour and fugitive slaves.

Those adventurers who remained in Gran Colombia after the termination of the Wars of Independence chose to incorporate themselves into the new society, as discussed in Chapters 7 and 8. Veterans had to appeal to the state protesting their patriotism in order to receive back pay and pensions. Officers and merchants succeeded in settling into Gran Colombian society because they shared élite values, as Cannadine finds for Britain's empire later in the nineteenth century. Moreover, lower-status adventurers assimilated too; as fishermen on the Caribbean coast, for example, or as butchers in urban centres. Because of their participation in what became seen as a period of foundational fighting, retired adventurers had earned honour and prestige. If they started families and fathered *granadino, venezolano* or *ecuatoriano* children, veterans were welcomed into the heart of new national families. The prolonged encounter with foreigners in the midst of their new nations after 1830 caused Hispanic Americans to reassess their own concepts of honour, patriotism and citizenship. Identities matured with time; foreign adventurers adapted to Creoles' values and became patriotic citizens.

Gran Colombian Independence was shaped by its American and Atlantic contexts. Simón Bolívar was hailed as 'the Washington of South America'[1] and John Devereux's recruitment of the Irish Legion was compared to Lafayette's endeavours to bring French support to the War of Independence in North America.[2] In 1822 Lord Byron sailed to Greece on a boat named *Bolívar*, and rhapsodised that 'One common cause makes myriads of one breast,/ Slaves of the East, or helots of the West:/ On Andes' and on Athos' peaks unfurl'd,/ The self-same standard streams o'er either world.'[3] The subject has comparative ramifications for our understandings of the history of the British empire and the history of Latin American independence. This conclusion looks at both strands.

After 'Informal Empire'

The concept of 'informal empire' is insufficient to explain the activities of British subjects in Gran Colombia as described in this book. Gallagher and Robinson posited that in the nineteenth century Britain operated an 'imperialism of free trade' wherever it could, and that Latin America became the axiomatic fulfilment of the British empire's preferred method of operation. This was the extraction of trade and the exertion of influence across the world without recourse to formal colonial government unless this was absolutely necessary for strategic means. Historians of Latin America adopted the formulation of 'trade with informal control if possible, trade with rule when necessary' to argue that Latin America was gradually incorporated into Britain's 'informal empire' in the period leading to 1870.[4] In the last quarter of the century, when investment in railways and other infrastructure projects increased substantially in volume and importance, British policy became correspondingly 'belligerent, interventionist, and meddlesome'.[5]

Historians have shown 'informal empire' to have been a reality in parts of Brazil and the River Plate, where British interests were concentrated.[6] Elsewhere, the effectiveness of 'informal empire' was 'patchy', to say the least[7] Mexico and Central America witnessed varying degrees of 'informal imperialism', in which British demands and exhortations came up against entrenched and resilient local interests.[8] Gran Colombia was one step further removed from the periphery of the British imperial world. This book has shown that the ties that bound it to informal empire were as often based upon adventure, culture and kinship as they were upon commerce or threats of military force. It is doubtful whether the British Foreign Office was able to exercise or enforce any hegemony in Gran Colombia during the first half of the nineteenth century, or even whether it was particularly interested in doing so.[9] Debts owed to British investors were small by comparison with other regions, and the Venezuelan, New Granadan and Ecuadorean governments gradually moved towards repaying them. Political and cultural hegemony was not easily discernible either. Adventurers often adopted Gran Colombian cultural practices rather than imposing their own social mores. They were neither the willing agents of informal empire nor the unconscious pawns of Foreign Office machinations.

Certainly, cultural and commercial relations were mediated by the strong global geopolitical position held by Britain after 1815, but this was also a time of determined assertion of local and national identity in Gran Colombia. Several thousand British and Irish adventurers took part in foundational fighting and hundreds were incorporated into the new national families that arose after the wars. Like British subjects in the Cape colonies, Australia, India and the West Indies, the adventurers in Gran Colombia reimagined their identities in relation to the metropolis, whilst at the same time developing new allegiances and conceptions of belonging to the societies in which they now lived. In all senses they were a long way from official imperial policy. Cannadine argues that it was upon the basis of a hierarchy 'of civilization and achievement' rather than commerce that Britons tried to comprehend distant lands.[10] This league-table approach to ranking peoples, called 'culturism' by Bernard Porter, was complicated in Gran Colombia by the pre-existing presence of other settled, white, European, imperial peoples and their Creole heirs, who not only had been previously loyal to another imperial monarch, but had recently defined their new nations as independent republics. British and Irish adventurers struggled to assert their own identities in this environment and to gain recognition from local societies. Owing to the precarious nature of their day-to-day survival, their relatively small number, and the pre-existence of established colonial hierarchies (albeit ones which were in the process of fragmentation and disintegration), in Gran Colombia adventurers ended up fitting themselves into existing social and racial hierarchies. On the occasions when they were successful in negotiating themselves privileged positions, this was primarily the result of the prestige they had gained in the period of foundational fighting, their whiteness and their kinship connections to the new nations, and only tangentially related, if at all, to their Britishness.

Prolonged military service on the fringes of British imperial activity in Gran Colombia gave adventurers such as Alexander Alexander, Daniel O'Leary and Richard Vowell the chance to see outside the blinkers imposed by what Mary Louise Pratt termed their 'imperial eyes'. Despite their foreign birth, these adventurers took part in the military campaigns that brought independence to Gran Colombia. Soldiers and other adventurers experienced and described the world differently from the commercial travellers usually taken to be representative of the British in Latin America.[11] Foreign veterans of the Wars of Independence who settled in Gran Colombia became finely attuned to the political and social divides catalysed by military mobilisation. Gran Colombia was linked to Europe by means of transatlantic and continent-wide networks of politics, commerce, commemoration and migration. Carried upon these networks, foreign adventurers were in the thick of the struggles for independence and the writing of national histories.

After Spanish Rule

British imperial networks and other Atlantic connections enabled the transfer, distribution and diffusion of political ideologies during the Wars of Independence.[12] Liberty, republicanism and national identity took on new forms and trajectories in the post-colonial environment. In seeking to accommodate Hispanic American history 'after Spanish rule' with the literature on post-colonial studies elsewhere, Mark Thurner and Andrés Guerrero have observed that in many ways the relations between state, society and individuals were being re-imagined and reconceptualised in the half-century after Independence, although marked continuities from the colonial period remained.[13] The introduction of evidence relating to the role of external actors can enhance debates about identity formation during and after the Wars of Independence. The Gran Colombian identity was 'conceived in conflict, strengthened in battle, [and died] from a peace that could no longer unite its peoples'.[14] Members of the armed forces who occupied ambiguous positions in relation to the 'enemy', such as the foreign mercenaries, were therefore uniquely situated with regard to the formation of collective identities. Creoles and *mestizos* defined themselves not only in opposition to enemy forces but also in relation to the auxiliaries who served alongside them. The adventurers were the foreigners within the nation, and therefore acted as a touchstone for nascent national self-definition during the Gran Colombian period and beyond. The presence of foreigners made explicit the case that loyalty to Gran Colombia – for all groups – should be founded not on ethnic or cultural grounds, but upon military necessity and ideological belief in liberty. Thus when the need for manpower became less pressing during the 1820s, the remaining foreigners became an obvious incongruity highlighted by subsequent moves towards more local and regional allegiances. Detailed studies of other ambiguously placed groups, such as prisoners of war, deserters, and merchants, can further illustrate the ways in which identity formation was contingent not only upon military circumstance and its regional impact, but also upon the experiences of individuals as they moved within the networks of kinship, allegiance, rumour, commerce, vengeance, conspiracy and friendship that were the background to the Wars of Independence. Forging a national identity out of such networks was fraught with difficulties.

Gran Colombia's use of European auxiliaries to assist in its Wars of Independence was in sharp contrast to the experiences of other Hispanic American republics. Only Chile experienced a similar intervention, and its foreign adventurers were overwhelmingly naval-based and therefore had much less contact with society inland. Peru was 'liberated' by a combination of Gran Colombian, Chilean and Argentine troops, rather than Europeans who had crossed an ocean in order to join the conflict. In Argentina a formal British invasion in 1806–7 triggered the first moves towards Independence, which were eventually successful without recourse to troops from elsewhere. In one sense the Gran Colombian case was more similar to Central America, where profound regional variations across the territory, demographical diversity and the difficulties of communication all hastened the fragmentation of a great republic into smaller entities. The process of disintegration in Gran Colombia was ongoing well before Bolívar's death in 1830. The presence of foreign *colombianos* was tangential to the actual processes of secession from Gran Colombia, but the involvement of foreigners brought the Independents' Atlantic links into sharp relief, highlighting the international ideological context present in the cause of liberty. Discussions about national identity were catalysed, contributing to the collapse and fragmentation of the conceptual foundations of the Gran Colombian republic for which adventurers had sacrificed so much.

The analysis of the integration of foreigners into post-Independence Gran Colombian society presented here complements the rich vein of scholarly research that focuses on established 'immigrant communities' in Latin America in the nineteenth century. As Oliver Marshall points out for Brazil, these communities based their identities upon a sharp differentiation from local peoples: 'the British communities that came into being were close-knit, with every effort made to remain aloof from Brazilian society other than for the purposes of work'.[15] Adventurers in Gran Colombia, however, were not 'unable to overcome the formidable obstacles involved in establishing a self-sustaining [expatriate] community',[16] as was the case for the groups studied by Marshall in Brazil. The adventurers did not attempt to create such an isolated community. Their origins in adventure and the Wars of Independence thrust them into the midst of the birth of new nations and new societies of which they became an integral, if ambiguous, part.

In Gran Colombia, the integration of foreigners after independence was much deeper than elsewhere in Latin America and was primarily based upon the shared experience and sacrifices of a period of foundational fighting. Guenther remarks that the British merchants in Bahia in the same period 'who gradually developed closer ties with the local community' were extremely rare and were not following 'the typical British mode of operation' which was to remain aloof from society, 'proud of its superior status'.[17] In the Gran Colombian case, those who shut themselves off from society were the rarity. Adventure often took British and Irish individuals very far from the paths of diplomats and merchants, where their experiences, ideas and identities were shaped by unexpected local physical and social conditions, and by the people they lived alongside. Their adventures in Gran Colombia did bring new worlds into existence, but they had little to do with George Canning and his claim to have restored the balance of power in Europe.

Notes

1   For example Dermot Clinton to Bolívar, 25 April 1825, Albany, AL, Vol. 14, fo. 153; Hippisley to Bolívar, 29 October 1826, Guernsey, *MOL*, Vol. 12, p. 69, and most famously, the pamphlet attributed to Daniel O'Leary, discussed and reproduced in Robert F. McNerney, 'A Famous Paralelo Entre Bolivar y Washington and its Authorship', *Hispania*, 24:4 (1941), pp. 416–22.

2   Devereux to Daniel O'Connell, 16 July 1822, 'Palace of Bogotá', *TCDOC*, Vol. 2, p. 406; Bolívar to Lafayette, 20 March 1826, Lima, *MOL*, Vol. 30, pp. 187–88; Lafayette to Bolívar, 1 September 1825, Paris, AL, Vol. 14, fo. 187.

3   Lord Byron, 'The Age of Bronze', (1823) Stanza VI.

4   John Gallagher and Ronald Robinson, 'The Imperialism of Free Trade', *Economic History Review*, 6:1 (1953), pp. 1–15, p. 13. The historiography is fully summarised in Rory Miller, 'Informal Empire in Latin America', in Louis, (ed.), *The Oxford History of the British Empire, Vol. 5. Historiography*, pp. 437–48.

5   Knight, 'Britain and Latin America', p. 129. The final part of the nineteenth century is identified as a key transitional point in Charles Jones, '"Business Imperialism" and Argentina, 1875–1900: A Theoretical Note', *JLAS*, 12 (1980), pp. 437–44; and A. G. Hopkins, 'Informal Empire in Argentina: An Alternative View', *JLAS*, 26:2 (1994), pp. 469–84.

6   On informal empire in the River Plate, see Peter Winn, 'British Informal Empire in Uruguay in the Nineteenth Century', *Past & Present*, 73 (1973), p. 100–26, and David McLean, *War, Diplomacy and Informal Empire: Britain and the Republics of La Plata, 1836–1853* (London, 1995).

7   Knight, 'Britain and Latin America', p. 133.

8   Barbara A. Tenenbaum, 'Merchants, Money and Mischief: The British in Mexico, 1821–1862', *The Americas*, 35:5 (1979), pp. 317–39, also Will Fowler, 'Joseph Welsh: A British *Santanista* (Mexico, 1832), *JLAS*, 36 (2004), pp. 29–56.

9   This was the argument of D. C. M. Platt in 'Dependency in Nineteenth-Century Latin America: An Historian Objects', *LARR*, 15:1 (1980), pp. 113–30, which is followed in Fowler, 'Joseph Welsh', particularly pp. 40–55.

10 Cannadine, *Ornamentalism*, pp. 4–5.

11   Brown, 'Richard Vowell's Not-So-Imperial Eyes', pp. 95–122.
12   Hamnett, 'Process and Pattern', p. 294.
13   Thurner and Guerrero, (eds), *After Spanish Rule,* particularly p. 23. Relationships with foreigners had their own colonial precedents, as discussed in Chapter 2, particularly in terms of contraband and official commerce, with small numbers of foreigners serving in the Spanish colonial army in the eighteenth century, and considerable internal immigration within the colonies themselves. See Pearce, 'British Trade with the Spanish Colonies, 1788–1795', pp. 233–50; Tamar Herzog, *Defining Nations: Immigrants and Citizens in Early Modern Spain and Spanish America* (New Haven, CT, 2003); and specific examples in Allan Kuethe, *Cuba, 1753–1815, Crown, Military and Society* (Knoxville, TN, 1968), pp. 31–32; Peadar Kirby, *Ireland and Latin America: Links and Lessons* (Dublin, 1992), pp. 93–95.
14   Robert Louis Gilmore, *Federalismo en Colombia 1810–1858* (Bogotá, 1995), p. 99.
15   Marshall, *English, Irish and Irish American Pioneer Settlers,* p. 14.
16   Marshall, *English, Irish and Irish-American Pioneer Settlers,* p. 38.
17   Guenther, *British Merchants in Nineteenth-Century Brazil,* p. 17.

Glossary

alcalde	district magistrate or mayor
almirante	naval rank equivalent to admiral
audiencia	high court at the level of the colony, also a governing body, usually composed of a president and four judges (*oídores*)
cabildo	local government body, composed of figures notable for their social, ecclesiastical, political or economic influence
cabo	military rank roughly equivalent to corporal
caja	box
capitán	military rank roughly equivalent to captain
casta	various peoples of mixed racial heritage in colonial Latin America, generally applied (*las castas*) to all non-white peoples
consulado	local body or tribunal, formed to protect commercial interests
cordillera	mountain range, as in 'Cordillera de los Andes'
coronel	military rank roughly equivalent to colonel
criollo	Creole, generally a person of Spanish descent born in the Americas
encomienda	grant of labour initially awarded to the participants of the wars of conquest in the sixteenth century
forastero	stranger, or foreigner, usually applied to a newcomer to an indigenous community
fuero	corporate legal rights and privileges; in many cases included an exemption from prosecution in certain courts
haberes militares	assets given by the state to those who served in key periods of the Wars of Independence, or their dependants; literally, 'military fortunes'
hacienda	colonial estate, owned by a *hacendado*
historia patria	the history of the *patria*, written from a patriotic and favourable perspective
legajo	volume
mayor	military rank roughly equivalent to major
mestizo	in common usage, a person of mixed heritage, usually Indian/Spanish
moreno	usual Spanish word for person of dark skin, usually of African heritage (*mulato*, *pardo* also used)
padre de familia	father of the family, carrying connotations of domination of dependents including servants, also lord or master
pardo	of mixed race, with African ancestry; *mulato* or *moreno* also used

pardocracia	government by *pardos*
patria	country or homeland, literally fatherland
peón	generally an unspecialised day labourer, often tied to a hacienda by personal or economic dependency
pueblo	village, town or people
resguardo	reservation, generally land allocated to organised and sedentary indigenous peoples.
sargento	military rank roughly equivalent to Sergeant
teniente	military rank very roughly equivalent to Lieutenant
tertulia	regular informal discussion group, assembly or social club
vales	paper equivalents to government credits; literally IOUs

Bibliography

Primary Sources

Archives

ACC: Archivo Central del Cauca, Popayán.
Sala Independencia, Fondos C1, J1, M1, P1.
Sala Mosquera, Fondos 1818–1820, 1827–1829, 1832.

AGI: Archivo General de Indias, Sevilla.
Cuba, Legajos 745, 897–915.
Estado, Legajos 12, 48, 64, 69, 89.

AGNC: Archivo General de la Nación, Bogotá, Colombia.
Sección Academia Colombiana de Historia, Haberes militares, Legajo 1–2.
Sección Academia Colombiana de Historia, Eduardo Posada, Legajo 1.
Sección Academia Colombiana de Historia, Aquileo Parra, Caja 7.
Sección Colecciones, Fondo Enrique Ortega Ricuarte, Caja 82.
Sección República, Anexo Historia, Legajos 23–28.
Sección República, Asuntos Criminales, Legajos 15, 29, 32, 33, 37, 44, 60, 76, 78, 95–97.
Sección República, Fondo Negocios Administrativos, Legajo 11.
Sección República, Hojas de Servicio Vols. 4–6, 8, 11, 15–16, 23–31, 36, 38, 41–43, 47–
    48, 50–54, 57–58, 60–62.
Sección República, Secretario de Guerra y Marina, Vols. 1, 6, 13, 16, 35, 44, 56, 323–
    326, 330, 356, 363, 369, 408, 422, 480, 778, 779, 785, 1045, 1057–1062, 1078, 1083,
    1262, 1303, 1304, 1352, 1432, 1441, 1447, 1452, 1539.
Archivo Restrepo (available on microfilm in the AGNC), Vols. 22, 24, 28.

AGNV: Archivo General de la Nación, Caracas, Venezuela.
Sección Colonia, Comisos, Legajo 26.
Sección República, Blanco y Azpurúa, Vols. 4, 6, 7.
Sección República, Gobernación de Guayana, Vols. 1–13.
Sección República, Guerra y Marina, Vol. 49
Sección República, Ilustres Próceres, Vols. 2, 5–7, 10, 12, 13, 15, 18, 19, 21–24, 29, 33,
    40, 42–44, 49, 60, 64, 69, 72, 74, 75, 82, 85, 86, 88, 89, 94, 95, 99.
Sección República, Papeles de Dr. Julian Viso, Legajos 1, 4.
Sección Traslados Vols. 143, 415, 426.

AL: Archivo del Libertador, Caracas
Sección Juan de Francisco Martin, Vols. 14–15.

AHC: Archivo Histórico de Cali.
Fondo Consejo, Actas Capitulares, Legajo 42.

AHG CB: Archivo Histórico de Guayana, Ciudad Bolívar.
Fondo 1817–1839.

AHG G: Archivo Histórico de Guayas, Guayaquil.
Actas 1–6, Achaguas 1820.

ANE: Archivo Nacional del Ecuador, Quito.
Causas Criminales, Cajas 24, 245, 247.
Fondo Especial 1819–1830, Cajas 226–68.
Fondo Popayán 1818–1834, Cajas 303–6.
Ministerio de Gobierno, Gobierno de Guayas, 1823–1836.
Ministerio de Gobierno, Gobierno de Pichincha 1831–1835.

BLAA: Biblioteca Luis Angel Arango, Bogotá.
Archivo de Cartas del Coronel Tomás Manby, 1836–1840.
Papers of CDM (Casa de Moneda), Db0001–4708.

BNC: Biblioteca Nacional de Colombia, Bogotá.
Fondo Arciniegas.
Fondo José María Quijano Otero.
Fondo Pineda.

EP: James Towers English Papers, Suffolk County Record Office, Ipswich.
HA157/1–11.

FJB: Fundación John Boulton, Caracas.
Archivo Histórico, Legajos C–101, C–118, C–302, C–309, C–632, C–633, C–715, C–716, C–717, C–718, C–719, C–825, C–850.
Archivo del Libertador, Legajos C–072, C–073, C–074, C–076, C–104, C–109, C–110, C–143, C–168, C–287, C–428.
Archivo O'Leary (AOL), Sección Manuel Antonio Matos.
Archivo O'Leary (AOL), Sección Navarro.

NAI: National Archive of Ireland, Dublin.
Prisoners' Petitions 1791–1828.
Rebellion Papers.
Registered Papers 1819–1820.

NAS: National Archive of Scotland, Edinburgh.
John MacGregor Papers GD 50, GD 184.

NLI: National Library of Ireland, Dublin.
Microfilm 2718.
MS 5759, 8076.
MSS 13645, 13647.

NLS: National Library of Scotland, Edinburgh.
MS 15037.

PRO NI: Public Record Office of Northern Ireland, Belfast.
'Diary of the Voyage of Robert James Young, and of General Devereux's Expedition to Margherita with the Irish Legion, Bolivar', D/3045/6/3/2.

TNA CO: Public Record Office, London, Colonial Office Papers.
CO 137/148

CO 141/6, 14–17.

TNA FO: The National Archives, London, Foreign Office Papers.
FO 18/1–8.
FO 25/88, 90, 92.
FO 72/216.
FO 80/14, 36–38.
FO 97/114.
FO 357/1–2, 12.
FO 420/6.

TNA WO: Public Record Office, London, War Office Papers.
WO 97/28, 33, 45, 48, 50, 72, 102, 119, 165, 200, 250, 267, 273, 295, 326, 346, 366, 411,
    420, 444, 461, 497, 504, 550, 557, 585, 650, 758, 796, 808, 897, 927, 959, 965, 968,
    1035, 1049, 1061, 1112, 1116, 1121, 1122, 1131, 1133, 1137, 1143, 1156, 1210, 1227,
    1253, 1261, 1270.

UCD: University College Dublin Archive.
O'Connell Papers.

Newspapers

El Anglo-Colombiano (Caracas) 1822
Black Dwarf (London) 1817–24
Blackwood's Magazine (Edinburgh) 1829–33
British Monitor (London) 1818–19
Carrick's Morning Post (Dublin) 1819–20
Cobbett's Register (London) 1818–20
El Colombiano (Caracas) 1823–26
El Colombiano de Guayas (Guayaquil) 1827, 1828, 1833
El Constitucional (Bogotá) 1824–27
Correo del Orinoco (Angostura) 1818–22
Dublin Evening Post (Dublin) 1819, 1820
Edinburgh Review (Edinburgh) 1806–26
Faulkner's Dublin Journal (Dublin) 1819–20
Freeman's Journal, and Daily Commercial Advertiser (Dublin) 1820
Gaceta de Caracas (Caracas) 1819
Gaceta de Colombia (Cúcuta, Bogotá) 1821–24
Gaceta de Gobierno del Estado del Ecuador (Quito) 1830–34
Gaceta de Santafé de Bogotá (Bogotá) 1819–21
Jamaica Gazette (Port Royal) 1815, 1819, 1820, 1821
London Chronicle (London) 1818–19
Morning Chronicle (London) 1817–19
El Patriota de Guayaquil (Guayaquil) 1829
El Quiteño Libre (Quito) 1833
El Repertorio Americano (London) 1826–27
The Republican (London) 1819–26
Quarterly Review (London) 1814–26
The Times (London) 1818–21

Published Material and Documents

Adam, William Jackson, *Journal of Voyages to Marguaritta, Trinidad and Maturin; with the author's Travels across the Plains of the llaneros to Angustura, and Subsequent Descent of the Orinoco in the years 1819–1820; Comprising his Several Interviews with Bolivar, the Supreme Chief; Sketches of the Various Native and European Generals: And a Variety of Characteristic Anecdotes, Hitherto Unpublicised*, Dublin: R. M. Tims, 1824.

Adlercreutz, Fredrik Thomas de, *Cartera del Coronel Conde de Adlercreutz: Documentos inéditos relativos a la historia de Venezuela y de la Gran Colombia. Con introducción y notas de C. Parra Pérez*, Paris: Ediciones Excelsior, 1928.

Anderson, Richard Clough, Jr, *The Diary and Journal of Richard Clough Anderson Jr, 1814–1826*, eds. Alfred Tischendorff and E. Taylor Parks, Durham, NC: Duke University Press, 1964.

Anon., [An Officer Late in the Colombian Service], *The Present State of Colombia; containing an account of the Principal Events of its revolutionary war; the Expeditions fitted out in England to assist in its emancipation, its constitution, financial and commercial laws; revenue expenditure and public debt; agriculture; mines; mining and other associations; with a MAP exhibiting its mountains, rivers, departments and provinces*, London: John Murray, 1827.

Anon., [Gentlemen], *Reply to the Letter of Adjutant General Kenny and the pamphlet of Mr Francis Hall, by the gentlemen who have returned from the Expedition to Margaritta*, Dublin: J. Carrick, 1820.

Anon., [Hall, Francis], *Colombia: Its Present State, in respect of Climate, Soil, Productions, Population, Government, Commerce, Revenue, Manufactures, Arts, Literature, Manners, Education, and Inducements to Immigration, with an Original Map and Itineraries partly from Spanish surveys, partly from actual observation*, London: Baldwin, Cradock and Joy, 1824.

Anon., [Hankshaw, John], *Letters written from Colombia During a Journey from Caracas to Bogota and thence to Santa Martha in 1823*, London: G. Cowie and Co., 1824.

Anon., [Vowell, Richard], *Campaigns and Cruises in Venezuela and New Granada and in the Pacific Ocean from 1817–1830 containing Tales of Venezuela, Part 1, The Earthquake of Caraccas, and Part 2, The Savannas of Varinas*, 3 Vols, London: Longman and Co., 1831.

Anon., [Captain Cowley], *Recollections of a Service of Three Years during the War of Extermination in the Republics of Venezuela and Colombia, by An Officer of the Colombian Navy: Moving Accidents by Flood and Field*, London: Hunt and Clarke, 2 Vols, 1828.

Anon., [Francisco Antonio Zea and Alexander Walker], *Colombia – Being a Geographical, Statistical, Agricultural, Commercial and Political Account of that Country, Adapted for the General Reader, the Merchant and the Colonist*, London: Baldwin, Craddock and Joy, 2 Vols, 1822.

Anon., *The Narrative of a Voyage to the Spanish Main in the ship 'Two Friends'; The Occupation of Amelia Island, by McGregor, etc – Sketches of the Province of East Florida; and anecdotes illustrative of the habits and manners of the Seminole Indians: With an Appendix containing a detail of the Seminole War, and the Execution of Arbuthnot and Ambrister*, London: John Miller, 1819.

Anon., *Soldiers of Venezuela, A Tale in Two Volumes*, London: T. Egerton, 2 Vols, 1818.

Anon., *Travels in South America*, Dublin: John Jones, 1824.

Arciniegas, German, prologue to *Cartas Santander – Bolivar 1813–1820*, Vol. 1, Bogota: Fundación para la conmemoración del Bicentenario del Natalicio y el

Sesquicentenario de la muerte del General Francisco de la Paula Santander, 1988.

Arévalo, Juan Vicente, 'Cartas inéditas del General Francisco Burdett O'Connor, prócer irlandés, al coronel Juan Bautista Arévalo, olvidado prócer venezolano', *Boletín de la academia de la historia*, 72:325 (January–March 1999), pp. 137–46.

Aylmer, William, Unpublished letter to Frank [Francisco] Burdett O'Connor, 6th April 1819, Dublin, photocopy lent by James Dunkerley.

Bache, Richard, *Notes on Colombia Taken in the Years 1822–23; with an Itinerary of the Route from Caracas to Bogota, and an Appendix; by an Officer of the US army*, Philadelphia, PA: H. C. Carey and I. Lea, 1827.

Baralt, Rafael María and Ramón Díaz Díaz, *Resumen de la historia de Venezuela desde el año de 1797 hasta el de 1830*, Vol. 1, Bruges: Desclée de Brouwer, 1939, first pub. Paris, 1841.

Besant, John, *Narrative of the Expedition under General MacGregor against Porto Bello: Including an Account of the Voyage; and of the Causes which Led to its Final Overthrow (by An Officer who Miraculously Escaped)*, London and Edinburgh: C. and J. Ollier, and T. and J. Allman, 1820.

Blanco, Felix and Ramón Azpurúa (eds), *Documentos para la historia de la vida pública del Libertador de Colombia, Perú y Bolivia*, 14 Vols, Caracas: Imprenta de 'La Opinión Nacional', 1875–77.

Bolívar, Simón, *Cartas del Libertador*, 5 Vols, Caracas: Banco de Venezuela, Fundación Vicente Lecuna, 1964–67.

Brown, Charles, *Narrative of the Expedition to South America which Sailed from England in 1817, for the Service of the Spanish Patriots: Including the Military and Naval Transactions, and Ultimate Fate of that Expedition: Also the Arrival of Colonels Blosset and English, with British Troops for that Service, their Reception and Subsequent Proceedings, with Other Interesting Occurrences*, London: John Booth, 1819.

Burke, William, *Additional Reasons for our Immediately Emancipating Spanish America*, New York: AMS Press, 1976, first pub. London, 1808.

Bushnell, David (ed.), *El Libertador. Writings of Simón Bolívar*, Oxford: Oxford University Press, 2003.

Carrera Damas, Germán (ed.), *Materiales para el estudio de la cuestión agraria en Venezuela 1810–1830*, Caracas: Universidad Central de Venezuela, 1964.

Castillo, J. M., *Cuentas del empréstito de 1824, y de los resagos del de 1822, hasta fin de diciembre de 1825*, Bogotá: Manuel Marin Viller-Calderón, 1826.

Castrillón Arboleda, Diego (ed.), *Memorias de Manuel José Castrillón (biografía y memorias)* 2 Vols, Bogotá: Editorial Kelly, 1971.

Chesterton, George Laval, *A Narrative of Proceedings in Venezuela and South America in the Years 1819 and 1820; with General Observations on the Country and People; the Character of the Republican Government; and its Leading Members, etc. And also a Description of the Country of Caraccas; of the Force of General Morillo; the State of the Royalists; and the Spirit of the People under their Jurisdiction*, London: John and Arthur Arch, 1820.

Chesterton, George Laval, *Peace, War and Adventure: An Autobiographical Memoir*, London: Longman, Brown, Green and Longmans, 1853.

Chesterton, George Laval, *Revelations of Prison Life; with an Inquiry into Prison Discipline and Secondary Punishments*, 2 Vols, London: Hurst and Blackett, 1856.

Cochrane, Charles Stuart, *Journal of a Residence and Travels in Colombia during the years 1823 and 1824*, 2 Vols, London: H. Colburn, 1825.

Conway, Stephen (ed.), *The Correspondence of Jeremy Bentham*, Vols 9–10, Oxford:

Clarendon Press, 1989–94.

Costello, Edward, *The Adventures of a Soldier; Or, Memoirs of Edward Costello, formerly a Non-commissioned Officer in the Rifle Brigade, and late Captain in the British Legion, Comprising Narratives of the Campaigns in the Peninsular under the Duke of Wellington, and the Recent Civil Wars in Spain*, London: Henry Colburn, 1841.

Dauxion-Lavaysee, Jean François, *A Statistical, Commercial, and Political Description of Venezuela, Trinidad, Margarita and Tobago: Containing Various Anecdotes and Observations Illustrative of the Past and Present State of these Interesting Countries, with a Beautiful Map of the United and Independent Provinces of Venezuela and New Granada*, London: G. W. B. Whittaker, 1820.

de Mier, José María (ed.), *La Gran Colombia*, 7 Vols, Bogotá: Presidencia de la República, 1983.

Deas, Malcolm and Efrain Sánchez (eds), *Santander y los ingleses 1832–1840*, 2 Vols, Bogotá: Fundación para la conmemoración del Bicentenario del Natalicio y el Sesquicentenario de la muerte del General Francisco de la Paula Santander, 1991.

Duane (the Elder), William, *A Visit to Colombia in 1822 and 1823, by Laguayra and Caracas, over the Cordillera to Bogota, and thence by the Magdalena to Cartagena*, Philadelphia, PA: Thomas H. Palmer, 1826.

Dupouy, W. (ed.), *Sir Robert Ker Porter's Caracas Diary 1825–1842: A British Diplomat in a Newborn Nation*, Caracas: Instituto Otto y Magdalena Blohm, 1966; and the translation by Teodosio Leal, *Diario de un diplomático británico en Venezuela: 1825–1842*, Caracas: Fundación Polar, 1997.

Elias Ortiz, Sergio (ed.), *Coleccion de documentos para la historia de Colombia* (Epoca de la Independencia), III Serie, Bogotá: Editorial el Voto Nacional, 1966.

Fernández, Carmelo, *Memorias de Carmelo Fernández y recuerdos de Santa Marta – 1842*, Caracas: Biblioteca de la Academia Nacional de la Historia, 1973.

Flinter, George, *A History of the Revolution in Caracas: Comprising an Impartial Narrative of the Atrocities Committed by the Contending Parties, Illustrating the Real state of the Contest, both in a Commercial Point of View: Together with a Description of the llaneros, or People of the Plains of South America*, London: W. Glindon, 1819.

Fuller, Catherine (ed.), *The Correspondence of Jeremy Bentham*, Vol. 11, Oxford: Clarendon Press, 2000.

Gobierno de la Nueva Granada, *Cuestión Mackintosh: Historia de ella y documentos: Publicación oficial de la Nueva Granada*, Bogota, 1852.

González, Florentino, *Memorias*, Medellín: Editorial Bedout, 1971.

Gosselman, Carl August, *Informes sobre los Estados Sudamericanos en los anos de 1837 y 1838*, ed. Magnus Morner, Stockholm: Biblioteca e Instituto de Estudios Ibero-Americanos de la Escuela de Ciencias Económicas, 1962.

Gosselman, Carl August, *Viaje por Colombia, 1825 y 1826*, Bogotá: Banco de la República, 1981, translated by Ann Christien Pereira, first pub. Stockholm, 1830.

Graham, Gerald S. and R. A. Humphreys (eds), *The Navy and South America 1807–1823: Correspondence of the Commanders-in-Chief on the South American Station*, London: Publications of the Naval Records Society, 1962.

Grases, Pedro (ed.), *Impresos de Angostura 1817–1822: Facsimiles, Homenaje al Sesquicentenario del Congreso de Angostura*, Caracas: Ediciones de la Presidencia de la República, 1969.

Grases, Pedro and Manuel Pérez Vila (eds), *Las fuerzas armadas de Venezuela durante el siglo XIX (textos para su estudio)*, 12 Vols, Caracas: Biblioteca de la Academia de Historia, 1963–69.

Groot, José Manuel, *Historia eclesiástica y civil de Nueva Granada*, Bogotá: Ediciones de la Revista Bolívar, 1953, first pub. Bogotá: Imprenta Medardo Rivas, 1870.

Hackett, James, *Narrative of the Expedition which Sailed from England in 1817 to Join the South American Patriots*, London: John Murray, 1818.

Hall, Francis, *An Appeal to the Irish Nation on the Character and Conduct of General D'Evereux*, Dublin: W. Underwood, 1820.

Hambleton, John H., *Diario del Viaje por el Orinoco hacia Angostura (julio 11 – agosto 24, 1819) Con las instrucciones para el viaje dadas por el Secretario de Estado, John Quincey Adams*, Bogotá: Banco de la República, 1969.

Hamilton, John Potter, *Travels Through The Interior Provinces of Colombia*, 2 Vols, London: John Murray, 1827.

Harrison, William H., *Remarks of General Harrison, late Envoy Extraordinary and Minister Plenipotentiary of the United States to the Republic of Colombia, on Certain Charges Made against him by that Government, to which is added, an Unofficial Letter, from General Harrison to General Bolivar, on the Affairs of Colombia; with Notes, Explanatory of his Views on the Present State of that Country*, Washington, DC: Gales and Seaton, 1830.

Hernández de Alba, Guillermo (ed.), *Cartas íntimas del General Nariño 1788–1823*, Bogotá: Ediciones Sol y Luna, 1966.

Hernández de Alba, Guillermo (ed.), *Archivo Nariño*, 6 Vols, Bogotá: Biblioteca de la Presidencia, 1990.

Hernández de Alba, Guillermo, Enrique Ortega Ricaurte and Ignacio Rivas Putnam (eds), *Archivo epistolar del General Domingo Caycedo*, 2 Vols, Bogotá: Editorial ABC, 1943.

Hippisley, Gustavus, *Narrative of the Expedition to the rivers Orinoco and Apure in South America, which sailed from England in November 1817, and joined the patriotic forces in Venezuela and Caraccas*, London: John Murray, 1819.

Hippisley, Gustavus Butler, *The Siege of Barcelona, a Poem in Three Cantos*, London: W.J. Cleaver, 1842.

Hood, Miriam (ed.), *In Honour of Daniel O'Leary, Edecán and Historian of Simón Bolívar the Liberator*, London: Venezuelan Embassy in London, 1978.

Howell, John (ed.), *The Life of Alexander Alexander, written by himself and edited by John Howell*, 2 Vols, Edinburgh: William Blackwood, 1830.

Isaacs, Jorge, *María*, Bogota: José Benito Gaitán, 1867.

Lecuna, Vicente and Harold A. Bierck (eds), *Selected Writings of Bolivar*, Vol. 1 1810–1822, New York: Bolivarian Society of Venezuela, 2nd edn 1951.

López, Manuel Antonio, *Recuerdos históricos del coronel Manuel Antonio López, Colombia i Perú 1819–1826*, Bogotá: Imprenta Nacional, 1955, first pub. 1878.

Low, George Augustus, *The Belise Merchants Unmasked: A Review of their Late Proceedings against Poyais; From Information and Authentic Documents Gained on the Spot, During a Visit to those Parts in the Months of August and September 1822*, London: published by the author, 1822.

Maceroni, Francis, *Memoirs of the Life and Adventures of Colonel Maceroni, late aide-de-camp to Joachim Murat, King of Naples; Knight of the Legion of Honour, and of St. George of the Two Sicilies; Ex-General of Brigade, in the Service of the Republic of Colombia, etc, etc, with a portrait*, 2 Vols, London: J. Macrone, 1838.

MacGregor, Gregor, *Exposición documentada que el General Gregorio Mac-Gregor dirijió al Gobierno de Venezuela y resolución que a ella recayó*, Caracas: A. Damiron, 1839.

Mendoza, Cristóbal de and Francisco Javier Yanes (eds), *Documentos para la vida pública del Libertador,* Caracas: Fundación Diana Mendoza Ayala, 22 Vols, 1983, first published 1826–9.

M'Mahon, Benjamin, *Jamaica Plantership: A Description of Jamaica Planters viz Attorneys, Overseers and Book-Keepers, with several interesting anecdotes, compiled by the author during a residence of eighteen years on twenty-four properties, in the above capacity, situated in different parts of the island,* London: Effingham Wilson, 1839.

Mollien, Gaspar, *Travels in the Republic of Colombia in the Years 1822 and 1823,* London: C. Knight, 1824.

Montana, Andrés and Camilo Riano (eds), *Santander y los ejércitos patriotas 1811–1819,* 2 Vols, Bogotá: Fundación para la conmemoración del Bicentenario del Natalicio y el Sesquicentenario de la muerte del General Francisco de la Paula Santander, 1989.

Montilla, Mariano, *General de Division Mariano de Montilla: Homenaje en el Bicentenario de su Nacimiento 1782–1982,* Caracas: Presidencia de la República, 2 Vols, 1982.

Moreno de Angel, Pilar (ed.), *Correspondencia y documentos del general José María Córdoba,* Bogotá: Editorial Kelly, 3 Vols, 1974.

Morillo, Pablo, *Mémoires du General Morillo, Comte de Carthagene, Marquis de la Puerta, relatifs aux principaux événements de ses campagnes en Amérique de 1815 a 1821,* Paris: P. Dufart, 1826.

Mosquera, Tomás Cipriano de, *Memoria sobre la vida del General Simón Bolívar (1798–1878),* Bogotá: Instituto Colombiano de Cultura, 1977.

O'Connell, Maurice (ed.), *The Correspondence of Daniel O'Connell,* Dublin: Irish Manuscripts Commission, 7 Vols, 1972.

O'Connor, Francisco Burdett, *Independencia Americana: Recuerdos de Francisco Burdett O'Connor, coronel del ejército, libertador de Colombia y general de división de los del Perú y Bolivia. Los publica su nieto T. O'Connor d'Arlach,* Madrid: Sociedad Española de Librería, 1915.

O'Leary, Daniel F. (ed.), *Correspondencia de extranjeros notables con el Libertador,* Vol. 1, Madrid: América, 1920.

O'Leary, Daniel Florencio, *Narración: Memorias de O'Leary,* 3 Vols, Caracas: Imprenta Nacional, 1952.

O'Leary, Simón Bolívar (ed.), *Memorias del General Daniel Florencio O'Leary,* Caracas: Imprenta de la Gaceta Oficial, 32 Vols, 1879–87.

Ortega Ricaurte, Enrique (ed.), *Luis Brion de la orden de Libertadores, Primer Almirante de la República de Colombia y General en Jefe de sus ejércitos 1782–1821,* Bogotá: Minerva, 1953.

Ortega Ricaurte, Enrique (ed.), *Archivo del General José Antonio Páez,* Bogotá: Archivo Nacional de Colombia, 1957.

Ortiz, Sergio Elias (ed.), *Colección de documentos para la historia de Colombia (época de la Independencia),* Bogotá: Editorial El Voto Nacional, 3 Vols, 1964–66.

Páez, José Antonio, *Autobiografía,* Madrid: Editorial America, 1916.

Perú de Lacroix, Louis, *Diario de Bucaramanga; O Vida pública y privada del Libertador, Simón Bolívar,* Madrid: Editorial de América, 1924.

Phillips, Charles, *Fairburn's Edition of the Speech of Chas. Phillips, Esq., (the) Celebrated Orator, to General D'Evereux and the Regiments under his Command Previous to their Embarkation at Dublin to Join the Spanish Patriots in South America,* London: John Fairburn, 1819.

Posada Gutiérrez, Joaquín, *Memorias histórico-políticas,* 3 Vols, Medellín: Editorial Bedout, 1971.

Princep, John, *Diario de un viaje de Santo Tomé de Angostura en la Guayana Española a las Misiones Capuchinas del Caroní*, trans. Jaime Tello, Caracas: Ediciones de la Presidencia de la República, 1975.

Rafter, Michael, *Memoirs of Gregor M'Gregor; Comprising a Sketch of the Revolution in New Granada and Venezuela, with Biographical Notices of Generals Miranda, Bolivar, and Horé and a Narrative of the Expeditions to Amelia Island, Porto Bello, and Rio de la Hacha, Interspersed with Revolutionary Anecdotes*, London: Stockdale, 1820.

Rafter, Michael, *Percy Blake, or the Young Rifleman*, 3 Vols, London: Hurst & Blackett, 1855.

Restrepo, José Manuel, *Historia de la revolución de la república de Colombia en la América meridional*, 8 Vols, Bogotá: Ministerio de Educación Nacional, 1942–50.

Restrepo, José Manuel, *Autobiografía. Apuntamientos sobre la emigración de 1816 e índice del diario político*, Bogotá: Empresa Nacional de Publicaciones, 1957.

Restrepo, José Manuel, *Diario político y militar: Memorias sobre los sucesos importantes de la época para servir a la Historia de la Revolución de Colombia y de la Nueva Granada, desde 1819 para adelante*, 4 Vols, Bogotá: Imprenta Nacional, 1954.

Reynolds, Thomas, *History of the Great Fight Between Spring and Langan, for the Championship of England, and One Thousand Sovereigns, on Tuesday, June 8, 1824: To Which is Added, The Whole of the Correspondence Relative to the Disputed Points on their First Battle; with their Lives and Portraits*, London: Hodgson and Co., 1824.

Robinson, James H., *Journal of an Expedition 1,400 Miles up the Orinoco and 300 Miles up the Arauca; with an Account of the Country, the Manners of the People, Military Operations, etc*, London: Black, Young and Young, 1822.

Sevilla, Rafael, *Memorias de un oficial del ejército español*, Madrid: Editorial América, 1916.

Sowell, David (ed.), *Santander y la opinión angloamericana: Visión de viajeros y periódicos 1821–1840*, Bogotá: Fundación para la conmemoración del Bicentenario del Natalicio y el Sesquicentenario de la muerte del General Francisco de la Paula Santander, 1991.

Sutcliffe, Thomas, *Sixteen Years in Chile and Peru from 1822 to 1839 by the Retired Governor of Juan Fernández*, London: Fisher, Son and Co., 1841.

Urdaneta, Rafael, *Memorias del general Rafael Urdaneta (general en jefe y encargado del gobierno de la Gran Colombia)*, Madrid: Editorial América, 1916.

Von Humboldt, Alexander, *Personal Narrative of a Journey to the Equinoctial Regions of the New Continent*, London: Penguin, 1995, ed. Jason Wilson, first published 1814–5.

Waterton, Charles, *Wanderings in South America, the North West of the United States and the Antilles, in the Years 1812, 1816, 1820 and 1824, with Original Instructions for the Perfect Preservation of Birds, and for Cabinets of Natural History*, London: J. Mawman, 1825.

Watts, C. T. (ed.), *Joseph Conrad's Letters to R. B. Cunninghame Graham*, Cambridge: Cambridge University Press, 1969.

Weatherhead, W. Davidson, *An Account of the Late Expedition against the Isthmus of Darien under the Command of Sir Gregor McGregor; Together with the Events Subsequent to the Recapture of Porto Bello, till the Release of the Prisoners from Panama; Remarks on the Present State of the Patriot Cause and on the Climate and Diseases of South America*, London: Longman, Hurst, Rees, Orme and Brown, 1821.

Weatherhead, W. Davidson, *A Medical and Philosophical Essay, on the Influence of Custom and Habit on the Human Economy*, London, G. and T. Underwood, 1828.

Webster, C. K. (ed.), *Britain and the Independence of Latin America: Select Documents from the Foreign Office Archives*, Oxford: Oxford University Press, 2 Vols, 1938.

Wright, Alberto Eduardo, *Destellos de Gloria: Biografía Sintética de un Prócer de la Independencia, incorporando las 'Reminiscencias' del General de División Don Tomás Carlos Wright*, Buenos Aires: Castroman, Ortiz y Cia., 1949.

Yanes, Francisco Javier, *Relación documentada de los principales sucesos ocurridos en Venezuela desde que se declaró estado independiente hasta el año 1821*, Caracas: Editorial Elite, 1943.

Yanes, Francisco Javier, *Historia de Margarita, Observaciones del General Francisco Esteban Gomez*, Caracas: Ministerio de Educación Nacional, Dirección de Cultura, 1948.

Yanes, Francisco Javier, *Historia de la provincia de Cumaná en la transformación política de Venezuela, desde el día 27 de abril de 1810 hasta el presente año de 1821*, Caracas: Ministerio de Educación Nacional, 1949.

Secondary Sources

Acosta Ortegón, Joaquín, 'El doctor Andrés María Gallo y su época', *Boletín de historia y antigüedades*, 33:380 (June–August 1946), pp. 477–505.

Acosta Saignes, Miguel, *Vida de los esclavos negros en Venezuela*, Caracas: Hespérides, 1967.

Adams, William Forbes, *Ireland and Irish Emigration to the New World from 1815 to the Famine*, New Haven, CT: Yale University Press, 1932.

Albada Jelgersma, Jill E., 'Simon Bolivar en *El general en su laberinto* de Gabriel García Márquez, *Journal of Iberian and Latin American Studies*, 7:1 (2001), pp. 55–62.

Altink, Henrice, "An Outrage on all Decency': Abolitionist Reactions to Flogging Jamaican Slave Women, 1780–1834', *Slavery and Abolition*, 23:2 (August 2002), pp. 107–24.

Alvarez F., Mercedes M., *Comercio y comerciantes y sus proyecciones en la independencia venezolana*, Caracas: Tipografía Vargas, 1963.

Anderson, Benedict, *Imagined Communities: Reflections on the Origin and Spread of Nationalism*, London and New York: Verso, 2nd revised edn 1991, first pub 1983.

Anderson, Olive, 'The Growth of Christian Militarism in Mid-Victorian Britain', *English Historical Review*, 86 (1971), pp. 46–72.

Andrien, Kenneth J. and Lyman L. Johnson (eds), *The Political Economy of Spanish America in the Age of Revolution 1750–1850*, Albuquerque, NM: University of New Mexico Press, 1994.

Anna, Timothy, E., *Forging Mexico, 1821–1835*, Lincoln, NE: University of Nebraska Press, 1998.

Anstey, Roger, *The Atlantic Slave Trade and British Abolition, 1760–1810*, London: Macmillan, 1975.

Antei, Giorgio, *Los heroes errantes: Historia de Agustín Codazzi, 1793–1822*, Bogotá: Planeta, 1993.

Arbeláez Urdaneta, Carlos, 'Dos Wilson en la guerra de independencia', *Boletín de la academia de historia*, 94 (April–June 1944), pp. 237–42.

Arboleda Llorente, José María, *Catálogo general detallado del Archivo Central del Cauca*, Popayán: Universidad del Cauca, 1975.

Arcaya, Pedro M., *El Cabildo de Caracas*, Caracas: Ediciones del Cuatricentenario de Caracas, 1968.

Archer, Christon (ed.), *The Wars of Independence in Spanish America*, Wilmington, DE: Jaguar Scholarly Resources, 1999.

Arends, Tulio, *Sir Gregor MacGregor: Un escocés tras la aventura de América*, Caracas: Monte Avila Editores, 1988.

Ayala Mora, Enrique (ed.), *Nueva historia de Ecuador*, 15 Vols, Quito: Corporación Editora Nacional, 1988.

Ayala Mora, Enrique, *Historia, compromiso, y política: ensayos sobre historiografía ecuatoriana*, Quito: Planeta, 1989.

Aylmer, Richard John, 'The Imperial Service of William Aylmer 1800–1814', *Irish Sword*, 20:81 (Summer 1997), pp. 208–16.

Azpurúa, Ramón, *Biografías de hombres notables de Hispano-América*, 4 Vols, Caracas: Imprenta Nacional, 1877.

Banko, Catalina, *El capital comercial en La Guaira y Caracas (1821–1848)*, Caracas: Academia Nacional de la Historia, 1990.

Baron Ortega, Julio, *La campaña heroica: Pantano de Vargas*, Tunja: Academia boyacense de la historia, 1983.

Barraya, José María, *Biografías militares. Historia militar del país en medio siglo*, Bogotá: Gaitán, 1874.

Barrera Monroy, Eduardo, *Mestizaje, comercio y resistencia. La Guajira durante la segunda mitad del siglo XVIII*, Bogotá: Instituto colombiano de antropología e historia, 2000.

Bartlett, Thomas, 'A Weapon of War As Yet Untried: Irish Catholics and the Armed Forces of the Crown 1760–1830', *Historical Studies* 18 (Dublin 1993), pp. 66–85.

Bartlett, Thomas and Keith Jeffrey (eds), *A Military History of Ireland*, Cambridge: Cambridge University Press, 1996.

Bartley, Russell H., *Imperial Russia and the Struggle for Latin American Independence 1808–1828*, Austin, TX: University of Texas Press, 1978.

Bayly, C. A., 'Ireland, India and the Empire 1780–1914', *TRHS*, 6th Series, Vol. 10 (2000), pp. 377–98.

Bayly, C. A., *The Birth of the Modern World, 1789–1914: Global Connections and Comparisons*, Oxford: Blackwell, 2003.

Bermúdez Bermúdez, Arturo E., *Piratas en Santa Marta: Piratas que atacaron la Provincia de Santa Marta*, Bogotá, 1978.

Best, Geoffrey, *War and Society in Revolutionary Europe, 1770–1870*, London: Fontana, 1982.

Bethell, Leslie (ed.), *CHLA*, Vols 2–4, Cambridge: Cambridge University Press, 1985.

Bethell, Leslie, *George Canning and the Emancipation of Latin America* London: Hispanic and Luso-Brazilian Council, 1970

Bethell, Leslie, *The Abolition of the Brazilian Slave Trade: Britain, Brazil and the Slave Trade Question 1807–1869*, Cambridge: Cambridge University Press, 1970.

Bethell, Leslie, 'Britain and Latin America in Historical Perspective', in Victor Bulmer-Thomas, (ed.), *Britain and Latin America: A Changing Relationship*, Cambridge: Cambridge University Press and Royal Institute of International Affairs, 1989, pp. 1–20.

Bierck, Harold A., 'The Struggle for Abolition in Colombia', *HAHR*, 33 (August 1953), pp. 365–86.

Blackburn, Robin, *The Overthrow of Colonial Slavery 1776–1848*, London: Verso, 1996 edn., first pub 1988.

Blanchard, Peter, 'The Language of Liberation: Slave Voices in the Wars of Independence', *HAHR*, 82:3 (August 2002), pp. 499–523.

Botero Herrera, Fernando, *Estado, nación y provincia de Antioquia. Guerras civiles e invención de la región, 1829–1863*, Medellín: Hombre Nuevo Editores, 2003.

Brading, David A., *Prophecy and Myth in Mexican History*, Cambridge: Cambridge University Press, 1984.

Brading, David A., *The First America: The Spanish Monarchy, Creole Patriots and the Liberal State 1492–1867*, Cambridge: Cambridge University Press, 1991.

Brett, Edward M., *The British Auxiliary Legion in the Carlist War*, Dublin: Four Courts, 2005.

Brew, Roger, *El desarrollo económico de Antioquia desde la Independencia hasta 1920*, Bogotá: Banco de la República, 1977.

Brewster, Claire, 'Women and the Spanish–American Wars of Independence', *Feminist Review*, 79 (2005), pp. 20–35.

Brito Figueroa, Federico, *Las insurrecciones de los esclavos negros en Venezuela, 1777–1830*, Caracas: Editorial Cantaclaro, 1961.

Brockliss, Laurence and David Eastwood (eds), *A Union of Multiple Identities: The British Isles c. 1750–c. 1850*, Manchester: Manchester University Press, 1997.

Brown, Christopher, 'Empire Without Slaves: British Concepts of Emancipation in the Age of the American Revolution', *William and Mary Quarterly*, 3rd Series, 56 (1999), pp. 274–306.

Brown, Matthew, 'Castas, esclavitud y extranjeros en las guerras de independencia de Colombia', *Historia y Sociedad*, 10 (2004), pp. 109–25.

Brown, Matthew, 'Scots in South America', in Iain McPhail and Karly Kehoe (eds), *A Panorama of Scottish History: Contemporary Considerations*, Glasgow: Glasgow University Press, 2004, pp. 124–44.

Brown, Matthew, 'Richard Vowell's Not-So-Imperial Eyes: Travel and Adventure in Nineteenth-Century Latin America', *JLAS*, 38:1 (2006), pp. 95–122.

Brown, Matthew, 'Inca, Sailor, Soldier, King: Gregor MacGregor and the early Nineteenth Century Caribbean', *BLAR*, 24:1 (2005), pp. 44–71.

Brown, Matthew, 'Adventurers, Foreign Women and Masculinity in the Independence of Colombia', *Feminist Review*, 79 (2005), pp. 36–51.

Brown, Matthew, 'La renovación de una élite: Angostura, Venezuela, 1800–1830', in Navarro (ed.), *Las élites urbanas en Hispanoamérica*, 2005, pp. 341–53.

Brown, Matthew, 'Not Forging Nations but Foraging for Them: Uncertain Collective Identities in Gran Colombia', *Nations and Nationalism*, 12:2 (2006), pp. 223–40.

Brown, Matthew, 'Rebellion at Riohacha, 1820: Local and International Networks of Revolution, Cowardice and Masculinity', *Jahrbuch für Geschichte Lateinamerikas*, 42 (2005), pp. 77–98.

Brown, Matthew, 'Soldier Heroes in the Wars of Independence in Gran Colombia', *Hispanic Research Journal*, 7:1 (2006), pp. 41–56.

Brown, Matthew and Martín Alonso Roa Celis (eds), *Militares extranjeros en la independencia de Colombia. Nuevas perspectivas*, Bogotá: Museo Nacional de Colombia, 2005.

Brumwell, Stephen, *Redcoats: The British Soldier and War in the Americas, 1755–1763*, Cambridge: Cambridge University Press, 2002.

Brungardt, Maurice, 'Tithe Production and Patterns of Economic Change in Central Colombia, 1764–1833', University of Texas at Austin, unpub. Ph.D., 1974.

Bryant, G. J., 'Indigenous Mercenaries in the Service of European Imperialists: The Case of the Sepoys in the Early British Indian Army 1750–1800', *War in History*, 7:1 (2000), pp. 2–28.

Bryant, Sherwin K., 'Enslaved Rebels, Fugitives, and Litigants: The Resistance Continuum in Colonial Quito', *CLAH*, 13:1 (2004), pp. 7–46.

Buckley, Roger Norman, *The British Army in the West Indies: Society and the Military in the Revolutionary Age*, Gainesville, FL: University Press of Florida, 1998.

Buisson, Ingle, Gunter Kahle, Hans-Joachim König and H. Pietschmann (eds), *Problemas de la formación del estado y de la nación en Hispanoamérica*, Bonn: Bohlau, 1984.

Burnett, D. Graham, *Masters of All they Surveyed: Exploration, Geography and a British El Dorado*, Chicago: Chicago University Press, 2000.

Bushnell, David, 'The Development of the Press in Great Colombia', *HAHR*, 30:3 (1950), pp. 432–52.

Bushnell, David, *The Santander Regime in Gran Colombia*, Westport, CT: Greenwood Press, 1970, first pub. 1954.

Bushnell, David, 'The Last Dictatorship: Betrayal or Consummation', *HAHR*, 63:1 (1983), pp. 65–105.

Bushnell, David, *The Making of Modern Colombia: A Nation in Spite of Itself*, Berkeley, CA: University of California Press, 1993.

Bushnell, David, 'Vidas paralelas de dos pueblos hermanos: Venezuela y Nueva Granada después de la separación', *Boletín de la academia de la historia*, 83:330 (April–June 2000), pp. 289–300.

Bushnell, David, *Simón Bolívar: Hombre de Caracas, proyecto de América: Una biografía*, Buenos Aires: Editorial Biblios, 2002.

Bushnell, David (ed.), *El Libertador. Writings of Simón Bolívar*, Oxford: Oxford University Press, 2003.

Cain, P., and A. G. Hopkins, 'Gentlemanly Capitalism and British Expansion Overseas, I: The Old Colonial System, 1688–1850', *Economic History Review*, 39 (1986), pp. 501–25.

Callahan Jr., William J., 'La propaganda, la sedición y la revolución francesa en la capitanía-general de Venezuela 1789–1796', *Boletín histórico*, 14 (May 1967), pp. 182–205.

Camargo Pérez, Gabriel, 'Muerte y Sepultura de Jaime Rooke', *Boletín de historia y antigüedades*, 61:705 (July–August 1974), pp. 341–47.

Cannadine, David, *Ornamentalism: How the British Saw Their Empire*, London: Allen Lane, 2001.

Canny, Nicholas and Anthony Pagden (eds), *Colonial Identity in the Atlantic World 1500–1800*, Princeton, NJ: Princeton University Press, 1987.

Carl, George Edmund, *First Among Equals: Great Britain and Venezuela 1810–1910*, Ann Arbour, MI: Syracuse University UMI, 1980.

Carrera Damas, Germán, *El culto a Bolívar*, Bogotá: Universidad Nacional de Colombia, 3rd edn. 1987, first published Caracas, 1969.

Carrera Damas, Germán, *Boves: Aspectos socio-económicos de la guerra de independencia*, Caracas: Ediciones de la Biblioteca Universidad Central de Venezuela, 1972.

Carrera Damas, Germán, *La crisis de la sociedad colonial venezolana*, Caracas: Dirección General de Cultura, Gobernación del Distrito Federal, 1976.

Carrera Damas, Germán, *Una nación llamada Venezuela*, Caracas: Universidad Central de Venezuela, 5th edn. 1997, first published 1980.

Carrera Damas, Germán, 'Simón Bolívar, el culto heroico y la nación', *HAHR*, 63:1 (1983), pp. 107–45.

Carrera Damas, German, *Alternativas ideológicas en América Latina contemporanea (El caso de Venezuela: El bolivarianismo-militarismo)*, Gainesville, FL: University of Florida Press, 2001.

Castro Leiva, Luis, *La Gran Colombia. Una ilusión ilustrada*, Caracas: Monte Avila, 1985.

Chabaud-Arnault, Charles, *La Marine Pendant les Guerres d'independence de l'Amérique du Sud*, Paris: Libraire Militaire de L'Baudoin, 1894.

Chambers, Sarah C., *From Subjects to Citizens: Honor, Gender and Politics in Arequipa, Peru, 1780–1854*, University Park, PA: Pennsylvania State University Press, 1999.

Chambers, Sarah C., 'Republican Friendship: Manuela Saenz Writes Women into the Nation 1835–1856', *HAHR*, 81:2 (May 2001), pp. 225–58.

Cherpak, Evelyn May, 'Las mujeres de la Gran Colombia', *The Americas*, 39:2 (1987), pp. 32–37.

Chiaramonte, José Carlos, *Nación y estado en Iberoamérica: Lenguaje político en tiempos de las independencias*, Buenos Aires: Sudamericana, 2004.

Cicerchia, Ricardo, *Journey, Rediscovery and Narrative: British Travel Accounts of Argentina (1800–1850)*, London: Institute of Latin American Studies, 1998.

Colley, Linda, *Britons: Forging the Nation 1707–1837*, New Haven, CT: Yale University Press, 1992.

Colley, Linda, *Captives: Britain, Empire and the World 1600–1850*, London: Jonathan Cape, 2002.

Collier, Simon, *Ideas and Politics of Chilean Independence, 1808–1833*, Cambridge: Cambridge University Press, 1967.

Collier, Simon, 'Nationality, Nationalism and Supranationalism in the Writings of Simón Bolívar', *HAHR*, 63:1 (1983), pp. 37–64.

Colmenares, Germán (ed.), *La Independencia: ensayos de historia social*, Bogotá: Instituto Colombiano de Cultura, 1986.

Colmenares, Germán, *Las convenciones contra la cultura*, Bogotá: Tercer Mundo Editores, 1987.

Colmenares, Germán, *Ensayos sobre historiografía*, Bogotá: Tercer Mundo Editores, 1997.

Conde Calderón, Jorge, 'Poder local y sentimiento realista en la independencia de Santa Marta', *Historia caribe* 2:4 (1999), pp. 77–86.

Conde Calderón, Jorge, 'Provincias, ciudadanía y 'clase' social en el caribe colombiano, 1821–1855', Universidad Pablo de Olavide, Sevilla, unpub. Ph.D., 2001.

Conrad, Joseph, *Nostromo: A Tale of the Seaboard*, ed. Keith Carbine, Oxford: World's Classics, 1995, first pub. 1904.

Conway, Christopher Brian, *The Cult of Bolívar in Latin American Literature*, Gainesville, FL: University Press of Florida, 2003.

Conway, Stephen, *The British Isles and the War of American Independence*, Oxford: Oxford University Press, 2000.

Conway, Stephen, 'War and National Identity in the Mid-Eighteenth-Century British Isles', *English Historical Review*, 116:468 (September 2001), pp. 863–93.

Cookson, J. E., *The British Armed Nation 1793–1815*, Oxford: Clarendon Press, 1997.

Cookson, J. E., 'Service Without Politics? Army, Militia, and Volunteers in Britain during the American and French Revolutionary Wars', *War in History*, 10:4 (2003), pp. 381–98.

Cooper, Frederick and Ann Laura Stoler (eds), *Tensions of Empire: Colonial Cultures in a Bourgeois World*, Berkeley, CA: University of California Press, 1997.

Costeloe, Michael P., 'Spain and the Latin American Wars of Independence: The Free Trade Controversy, 1810–1821, *HAHR*, 61:2 (1981), pp. 209–34.

Costeloe, Michael P., *Bonds and Bondholders: British Investors and Mexico's Foreign Debt 1824–1888*, Westport, CT: Praeger, 2003.

Cuervo Márquez, Luis, *Independencia de las colonias hispano-americanas: Participación de la Gran Bretaña y de los Estados Unidos: Legión Británica*, 2 Vols, Bogotá: Editorial Selecta, 1938.

Cunninghame Graham, R. B., *José Antonio Páez*, London: William Heinemann, 1929.

Curry, Glen T., 'The Disappearance of the Resguardos Indígenas of Cundinamarca, Colombia, 1800–1863', unpub. Ph. D., Vanderbilt University, 1981.

Curry-Machado, Jonathan, 'Contradiction, Exclusion and Disruptive Identities: The Interaction of Engineering Migrants with Mid-Nineteenth Century Cuban Society', in A. Asgharzadeh, E. Lawson, K. Oca and A. Wahab (eds), *Diasporic Ruptures: Globality, Migrancy and Expressions of Identity*, Vol. 1, New York: Peter Lang Publishing, forthcoming, 2006.

Curry-Machado, Jonathan, 'Indispensable Aliens: The Influence of Engineering Migrants in Mid-Nineteenth Century Cuba', London Metropolitan University, unpub. Ph.D., 2003.

Curtin, Philip D., *Death by Migration: Europe's Encounter with the Tropical World in the Nineteenth Century*, Cambridge: Cambridge University Press, 1989.

Dávila, Vicente (ed.), *Diccionario biográfico de ilustres próceres de la independencia suramericana*, 2 Vols, Caracas, 1924.

Dávila, Vicente (ed.), *Hojas militares*, 2 Vols, Caracas: Tipografía Americana, 1930.

Davis, David Brion, *The Problem of Slavery in Western Culture*, Oxford: Oxford University Press, 1988 edn, first pub. New York: Cornell University Press, 1966.

Davis, Roger P., 'Ecuador Under Gran Colombia, 1820–1830: Regionalism, Localism and Legitimacy in the Emergence of an Andean Republic', University of Arizona, unpub. Ph.D., 1983.

Dawson, Graham, *Soldier Heroes: British Adventure, Empire, and the Imagining of Masculinities*, London: Routledge, 1994.

de Amezaga, Vicente, 'El General Juan Uslar', *Boletin Historico*, 11 (1966), pp. 117–48.

de Courcey Ireland, John, 'Irish Soldiers and Seamen in Latin America', *Irish Sword*, 1:4 (1952–3), pp. 296–302.

de Courcey Ireland, John, 'Thomas Charles Wright: Soldier of Bolívar, Founder of the Ecuadorian Navy', *Irish Sword*, 6:25 (Winter 1964), pp. 271–75.

de Courcey Ireland, John, *The Admiral from Mayo: A Life of Almirante William Brown of Foxford, Father of the Argentine Navy*, Dublin: Edmund Burke, 1995.

de Madariaga, Salvador, *Bolívar*, London: Hollis and Carter, 1952.

de Mier, Jose Maria, 'Tomás Manby: Soldado en Europa y en América: Lectura del Ingeniero José M. de Mier, en la sesión del 18 de Septiembre de 1973 de la Academia colombiana de historia, al ser recibido como Miembro Correspondiente de la Corporación'. Unpublished typescript provided by Martín Alonso Roa Celis.

de Mier, José María, 'Misión de López Méndez en Londres y Expedición de George Elsom', *Archivos de la academia colombiana de historia*, 3:4 (January–December 1971), pp. 2–83.

Deas, Malcolm, 'The Fiscal Problems of Nineteenth-Century Colombia', *JLAS*, 14:2 (1982), pp. 287–328.

Deas, Malcolm, *Del poder y la gramática: y otros ensayos sobre la historia, política, y literatura colombianas*, Bogotá: Tercer Mundo Editores, 1993.

Deas, Malcolm, *Vida y opinión de Mr William Wills*, 2 Vols, Bogotá: Banco de la República, 1996.

Demelas, M. D. and Y. Saint Geours, *La Vie quotidienne en Amerique du Sud au temps de Bolívar*, Paris: Hachette, 1987.

Denman, Terence, 'Ethnic Soldiers Pure and Simple? The Irish in the late Victorian British Army', *War in History*, 3:3 (1996), pp. 253–73.

Destruge, Camilo, *Biografía del Gral. Don Juan Illingworth*, Guayaquil: Imprenta Gutenberg, 1913.

Días Callejas, Apolinar, 'La solidaridad internacional y la regularisación de la guerra, dos aportes hispanoamericanos a la paz y al humanismo', *Boletín de historia y antigüedades*, 81:786 (June–September 1994), pp. 768–80.

Diaz, Arlene J., *Female Citizens, Patriarchs, and the Law in Venezuela, 1786–1904*, Lincoln, NE: University of Nebraska Press, 2004.

Díaz de Zuluaga, Zamira, *Guerra y economía en las haciendas, Popayán, 1780–1830*, Bogotá: Banco Biblioteca Popular, 1983.

Dickson, David, Daire Keogh, and Kevin Whelan (eds), *The United Irishmen: Republicanism, Radicalism and Rebellion*, Dublin: Lilliput Press, 1993.

Dominguez, Jorge I., *Insurrection or Loyalty: The Breakdown of the Spanish American Empire*, Cambridge, MA: Harvard University Press, 1980.

Donio Rios, Manuel Alberto, 'Sir Robert Ker Porter y los inicios del Protestantismo en Venezuela', *Boletín de la academia de la historia*, 72:327 (July–September 1999), pp. 157–81.

Duarte French, Jaime, *América del Norte al Sur: ¿Corsarios or Libertadores?*, Bogotá: Biblioteca Banco Popular, 1975.

Dueñas Vargas, Guiomar, 'Adulterio, amancebamientos, divorcios y abandono: la fluidez de la vida familiar santafereña, 1750–1810', *Anuario colombiano de historia social y de la cultura*, 23 (1996), pp. 33–49.

Dueñas Vargas, Guiomar, 'Gender, Race and Class: Illegitimacy and Family Life in Santafé, Nuevo Reino de Granada, 1770–1810', University of Texas at Austin, unpub. Ph.D., 1995.

Duffy, Michael, *Soldiers, Sugar and Seapower. The British Expeditions to the West Indies and the War against Revolutionary France*, Oxford: Clarendon Press, 1987.

Duncan, James and Derek Gregory (eds), *Writes of Passage: Reading Travel Writing*, London: Routledge, 1999.

Dunkerley, James, *The Third Man: Francisco Burdett O'Connor and the Emancipation of the Americas*, London: Institute of Latin American Studies, 1999.

Dunkerley, James, *Americana: The Americas in the World around 1850 (or 'Seeing the Elephant' as the Theme for an Imaginary Western)*, London: Verso, 2000.

Dunkerley, James (ed.), *Studies in the Formation of the Nation-State in Latin America*, London: Institute of Latin American Studies, 2001.

Earle, Rebecca, "Padres de la Patria' and the Ancestral Past: Commemorations of Independence in Nineteenth-Century Spanish America', *JLAS*, 34:4 (November 2002), pp. 775–805.

Earle, Rebecca, 'Indian Rebellion and Bourbon Reform in New Granada: Riots in Pasto, 1780–1800', *HAHR*, 73:1 (1993), pp. 99–123.

Earle, Rebecca, 'Creole Patriotism and the Myth of the Loyal Indian', *Past and Present*, 172 (August 2001), pp. 125–45.

Earle, Rebecca, 'A Grave for Europeans? Disease, Death and the Spanish American Revolutions', *War in History*, 3 (1996), pp. 371–93.

Earle, Rebecca, 'Rape and the Anxious Republic: Revolutionary Colombia, 1810–1830', in Elizabeth Dore and Maxine Molyneux (eds), *Hidden Histories of Gender and the State in Latin America*, Chapel Hill, NC: Duke University Press, 2000, pp. 134–42.

Earle, Rebecca, *Spain and the Independence of Colombia 1810–1825*, Exeter: University of Exeter Press, 2000.

Earle, Rebecca, '*Sobre heroes y tumbas*: National Symbols in Nineteenth-Century Spanish America', *HAHR*, 85:3 (2005), pp. 375–416.

Echeverri, Aquiles, *Sangre irlandesa en Antioquia: Biografía del doctor Hugo Blair Brown, miembro de la legión británica, y médico coronel de los ejércitos patriotas*, Medellín: Academia Antioqueña de Historia, 1972.

Elías Ortiz, Sergio, *Franceses en la independencia de la Gran Colombia*, Bogotá: Editorial ABC, 1949.

Elías Ortiz, Sergio, *Agustín Agualongo y su tiempo*, Bogotá: Banco Popular, 1974.

Elsching, Hans Dieter, *Cementerios en Venezuela. Los camposantos de los extranjeros del siglo XIX y los antiguos cementerios en Caracas y el Litoral*, Caracas, 2000.

Eltis, David and Stanley L. Engerman (eds), 'The Importance of Slavery and the Slave Trade to Industrializing Britain', *Journal of Economic History*, 60:1 (March 2000), pp. 123–44.

Emsley, Clive, 'The Impact of War and Military Participation on Britain and France 1792–1815', in Emsley and James Walvin (eds), *Artisans, Peasants and Proletarians 1760–1860: Essays Presented to Gwyn A. Williams*, London: Croom Helm, 1985, pp. 57–80.

Escorcia, José, 'Haciendas y estructura agraria en el valle del Cauca 1810–1850', *Anuario colombiano de historia social y de la cultura*, 10 (1982), pp. 119–38.

Esdaile, Charles J., *Fighting Napoleon: Guerrillas, Bandits and Adventurers in Spain 1808–1814*, New Haven, CT: Yale University Press.

Esdaile, Charles J., *The Duke of Wellington and the Command of the Spanish Army, 1812–1814*, London: Palgrave Macmillan, 1990.

Esdaile, Charles J., *The Peninsular War: A New History*, London: Allen Lane, 2003.

Estrada, Jenny, *Mujeres de Guayaquil: Siglo XVI al Siglo XX*, Guayaquil: Banco Central del Ecuador/Archivo Histórico del Guayas, 1984.

Feijoo, Rosario, 'Indios y esclavos negros en el Valle del Chota', *Sociedad Amigos de la Genealogía* (Quito), 38 (1988), pp. 171–87.

Ferguson, Niall, *Empire: How Britain Made the Modern World*, London: Penguin, 2003.

Fernández-Martínez, Luis, *Torn between Empires: Economy, Society and Patterns of Political Thought in the Hispanic Caribbean, 1840–1878*, Athens, GA: University of Georgia Press, 1994.

Ferry, Robert J., 'Encomienda, African Slavery and Agriculture in Seventeenth-Century Caracas', *HAHR*, 61:4 (1981), pp. 609–35.

Ferry, Robert J., *The Colonial Elite of Early Caracas: Formation and Crisis, 1567–1767*, Berkeley, CA: University of California Press, 1989.

Fey, Ingrid E. and Karen Racine (eds), *Strange Pilgrimages: Exile, Travel and National Identity in Latin America 1800–1990s*, Wilmington, DE: Jaguar Scholarly Resources, 2000.

Filippi, Alberto (ed.), *Bolívar y Europa: En las crónicas, el pensamiento político y la historiografía*, Caracas: Ediciones de la Presidencia de la República, Vol. 1 1986, Vol. 2 1992.

Fisher, John R., 'Soldiers, Society and Politics in Spanish America 1750–1821', *LARR*, 7:1 (1982), pp. 217–22.

Fisher, John R., 'Commerce and Imperial Decline: Spanish Trade with Spanish America 1797–1820', *JLAS*, 30:3 (1998), pp. 459–79.

Fisher, John R., 'The Royalist Regime in the Viceroyalty of Peru 1820–1824', *JLAS*, 32:1 (2000), pp. 55–84.

Fisher, John R. and James Higgins (eds), *Understanding Latin America*, Liverpool: Liverpool University Press, 1989.

Fisher, John R., Allan J. Kuethe and Anthony McFarlane (eds), *Reform and Insurrection in Bourbon New Granada and Peru*, Baton Rouge, LA: Louisiana State University Press, 1990.

Florez Álvarez, L., *Acción de la marina colombiana en la guerra de independencia 1806–1830*, Bogotá: Talleres del Estado Mayor General, 1919.

Foote, Nicola, 'Race, Nation and Society in Ecuador, c. 1900–40', University of London, unpub. Ph.D., 2004.

Fortique, José Rafael, *Cirujanos británicos en el ejército de Bolívar 1817–1821*, Maracaibo, pub. by the author, 1962.

Fortique, José Rafael, *Dos legionarios irlandeses en el ejército de Bolívar*, Maracaraibo: pub. by author, 2001.

Fortique, José Rafael, *Dr John Robertson: Cirujano del ejército de Bolívar*, Caracas: Academia Nacional de Historia, 1972.

Fortique, José Rafael, *Sir Gregor MacGregor: General de división del ejército venezolano*, Maracaibo: pub. by the author, 2001.

Foster, R. F., *Modern Ireland 1600–1972*, London: Penguin, 1988.

Foster, R. F., *The Irish Story: Telling Tales and Making It Up in Ireland*, London: Allen Lane, 2001.

Fowler, Will, 'Joseph Welsh: A British *Santanista* (Mexico, 1832)', *JLAS*, 36 (2004), pp. 29–56.

Frey, Sylvia R., *The British Soldier in America: a Social History of Military Life in the Revolutionary Period*, Austin, TX: University of Texas Press, 1981.

Friede, Juan, 'La expedición de Mac-Gregor a Riohacha, Año 1819', *BCB*, 10:9 (1967), pp. 69–85.

Friede, Juan, *La otra verdad: La independencia americana vista por españoles*, Bogotá: Tercer Mundo Editores, 1972.

Frye, Northrop, *The Anatomy of Criticism: Four Essays*, Princeton, NJ: Princeton University Press, 1957.

Fundación de Bello, *Bello y Londres*, Caracas: Fundación de Bello, 2 Vols, 1980.

Fyfe, Janet, 'Scottish Volunteers with Garibaldi', *Scottish Historical Review*, 57 (1978), pp. 168–96.

Galán, Angel María, *Biografía del coronel de la independencia, Felipe Mauricio Martin, escrita para el 'Papel Periódico de Bogotá'*, Bogotá: Papel Periódico de Bogotá, 1882.

Galán, Angel María, *Las legiones británica e irlandesa*, Bogotá: Imprenta de J. Casis, 1919.

Gallagher, John, *The Decline, Revival and Fall of the British Empire: The Ford Lectures and Other Essays*, ed. Anil Seal, Cambridge: Cambridge University Press, 1992.

Gallagher, John, and Ronald Robinson, 'The Imperialism of Free Trade', *Economic History Review* 6:1 (1953), pp. 1–15.

Gallo, Klaus, *Great Britain and Argentina: From Invasion to Recognition 1808–1826*, New York: Palgrave, 2001.

García Arrieche, Carlos, 'La legión británica en la emancipación de Venezuela y Colombia', *Boletín histórico*, 27 (1971), pp. 346–95.

García Chuecos, Hector, *Estudios de historia colonial venezolana*, Caracas: Tipografía americana, 2 Vols, 1937–38.

García Hernán, Enrique, Miguel Angel de Buenes, Oscar Recio Morales and Bernardo J. García García (eds), *Irlanda y la monarquia hispánica: Kinsale 1601–2000, Guerra, politíca, exilio y religión*, Madrid: Universidad de Alcala, 2002.

García Mejia, Aydee, 'The Transformation of the Indian Communities of the Bogota Sabana during the Nineteenth Century Colombian Republic', unpub. Ph. D., New School for Social Research, 1989.

García Vásquez, Demetrio, *Los hacendados de la otra banda y el cabildo de Cali*, Cali: Imprenta Gutiérrez, 1928.

García Vásquez, Demetrio, *Revaluaciones históricas para la ciudad de Santiago de Cali*, 2 Vols, Cali: Velásquez, 1924.

Garrido, Margarita, *Reclamos y representaciones: Variaciones sobre la política en el Nuevo Reino de Granada 1770–1815*, Bogotá: Banco de la República, 1993.

Geggus, David Patrick, *Slavery, War and Revolution: The British Occupation of Saint Domingue 1793–1798*, Oxford: Oxford University Press, 1982.

Geggus, David Patrick (ed.), *The Impact of the Haitian Revolution in the Atlantic World*, Columbia, SC: University of South Carolina Press, 2001.

Gilmore, Robert L., *Caudillism and Militarism in Venezuela 1810–1910*, Athens: Ohio University Press, 1964.

Gilmore, Robert L., *Federalismo en Colombia 1810–1858*, Bogotá: Sociedad Santanderista de Colombia y Universidad Externado de Colombia, 1995.

Gilroy, Amanda (ed.), *Romantic Geographies: Discourses of Travel 1775–1844*, Manchester: Manchester University Press, 2000.

Giraldo Jaramillo, Gabriel, *Bibliografía colombiana de viajes*, Bogotá: Editorial ABC, 1957.

Girouard, Mark, *The Return to Camelot: Chivalry and the English Gentleman*, London and Hartford, CT: Yale University Press, 1981.

Goebel, Dorothy Burne, 'British Trade to the Spanish Colonies 1796–1823', *American Historical Review*, 43 (1938), pp. 288–320.

Gómez Canedo, Fray Lino, *Los archivos históricos de Venezuela*, Maracaibo: Universidad del Zulia, 1966.

Gómez Hoyos, Rafael, *La independencia de Colombia*, Madrid: MAPFRE, 1992.

González, Margarita, *Ensayos de historia colombiana*, Bogotá: Editorial La Carreta, 1975.

Graham, Richard, *Independence in Latin America: A Comparative Approach*, New York: A. A. Knopf, 1972.

Grant, Alexander and Keith Stringer (eds), *Uniting the Kingdom? The Making of British History*, London: Routledge, 1995.

Grases, Pedro and Arturo Uslar Pietri, *Los libros de Miranda*, Caracas: La Casa de Bello, 1979.

Green, Martin, *Dreams of Adventure, Deeds of Empire*, London: Routledge and Kegan Paul, 1980.

Green, Martin, *The Adventurous Male, Chapters in the History of the White Male Mind*, University Park, PA: Pennsylvania State University Press, 1993.

Greenberg, Kenneth S., *Honor and Slavery: Lies, Duels, Noses, Masks, Dressing as a Woman, Gifts, Strangers, Humanitarianism, Death, Slave Rebellions, The Proslavery Argument, Baseball, Hunting and Gambling in the Old South*, Princeton, NJ: Princeton University Press, 2000.

Greene, Jack, 'Liberty, Slavery and the Transformation of British Identity in the Eighteenth-Century West Indies', *Slavery and Abolition*, 21:1 (April 2000), pp. 1–32.

Gregory, Desmond, *The Brute New World: The Rediscovery of Latin America in the Early Nineteenth Century*, London: British Academic Press, 1992.

Griffin, Charles C., 'Economic and Social Aspects of the Era of Spanish American

Independence', *HAHR*, 29 (1949), pp. 170–87.

Griffith Dawson, Frank, *The First Latin American Debt Crisis: The City of London and the 1822–25 Loan Bubble*, New Haven, CT, and London: Yale University Press, 1990.

Groot, José Manuel, *Historia de la Gran Colombia 1819–1830, Tercer volumen de la historia eclesiástica y civil de Nueva Granada*, Caracas: Academia Nacional de la Historia de Venezuela, 1941.

Guardino, Peter, *Peasants, Politics and the Formation of Mexico's National State: Guerrero, 1800–1857*, Stanford, CA.: University of California Press, 1996.

Guenther, Louise, *British Merchants in Nineteenth-Century Brazil: Business, Culture and Identity in Bahia, 1808–1850*, Oxford: Centre for Brazilian Studies, 2004.

Guerra, François-Xavier, *Modernidad e independencias. Ensayos sobre las revoluciones hispánicas*, Madrid: MAPFRE, 1992.

Guerrero Vinuenza, Gerardo León, *Pasto en la guerra de independencia*, Bogotá: Tecniimpresores, 2 Vols, 1994.

Hagemann, Karen, 'Of 'Manly Valor' and 'German Honor'. Nation, War and Masculinity in the Age of the Prussian Uprising against Napoleon', *Central European History*, 30:2 (1997), pp. 187–220.

Hall, Catherine, *Civilising Subjects: Metropole and Colony in the English Imagination 1830–1867*, London: Polity, 2002.

Halperin Donghi, Tulio, 'Economy and Society', in Leslie Bethell, (ed.), *Spanish America after Independence c. 1820-c. 1870*, Cambridge: Cambridge University Press, 1987, pp. 1–48.

Halperin Donghi, Tulio, *Hispanoamérica después de la independencia. Consecuencias sociales y económicas de la emancipación*, Buenos Aires: Paidos, 1972.

Halperin Donghi, Tulio, *Contemporary History of Latin America*, Durham, NC: Duke University Press, 1993.

Hamerley, Michael T., *Historia social y económica de la antigua provincia de Guayaquil, 1763–1842*, Guayaquil: Archivo Histórico de Guayas, 1975.

Hamnett, Brian R., 'Process and Pattern: A Re-examination of the Ibero-American Independence Movements', *JLAS*, 29:2 (May 1997), pp. 279–328.

Hanham, H. J., 'Religion and Nationality in the Mid-Victorian army', in M. R. D. Foot (ed.), *War and Society: Historical Essays in Honour and Memory of J. R Western 1928–71*, London: Paul Elek, 1973, pp. 159–81.

Harrison, J. P., 'The Colombian Tobacco Industry from Government Monopoly to Free Trade 1778–1876', University of California, unpub. Ph.D., 1951.

Harvey, Robert, *Liberators*, London: John Murray, 2000.

Harwich Valenilla, Nikita, *Inversiones extranjeras en Venezuela, siglo XIX*, 2 Vols, Caracas: Academia Nacional de Historia, 1992.

Hasbrouck, Alfred, *Foreign Legionaries in the Liberation of Spanish South America*, New York: Columbia University Press, 1928.

Hebrard, Veronique, 'Patricio o soldado: ¿Qué uniforme para el ciudadano? El hombre de armas en la construcción de la nación (Venezuela, primera mitad del siglo XIX)', *Revista de Indias*, 225:62 (2002), pp. 429–62.

Helg, Aline, 'Simón Bolívar and the Spectre of Pardocracia: José Padilla in Post-Independence Cartagena', *JLAS*, 35:3 (August 2003), pp. 447–71.

Helg, Aline, *Liberty and Equality in Caribbean Colombia 1770–1835*, Chapel Hill, NC: University of North Carolina Press, 2004.

Helguera, J. Leon, 'The Changing Role of the Military in Colombia', *Journal of Inter-*

American Studies, 3 (1961), pp. 351–58.

Hernández Brito, Wilfredo José, 'Notas sobre el arriendo de nueve misiones del circuito Caroní a los ciudadanos británicos James Hamilton y John Princep', *Boletín histórico del IRCOPAHIDEC* (Ciudad Bolívar), 1 (December 1985), pp. 12–21.

Herrera Angel, Martha, 'Configuración territorial, dominación y resistencia. Provincia de Popayán, siglo XVIII', unpub. paper presented to XII Congreso de Historia, Popayán, Colombia, August 2003.

Herzog, Tamar, *Defining Nations: Immigrants and Citizens in Early Modern Spain and Spanish America*, New Haven, CT: Yale University Press, 2003.

Heuman, Gad (ed.), *Out of the House of Bondage: Runaways, Resistance and Marronage in Africa and the New World*, London: Frank Cass, 1986.

Hilton, Boyd, *Corn, Cash and Commerce: The Economic Policies of the Tory Governments*, Oxford: Oxford University Press, 1977.

Hilton, Boyd, *The Age of Atonement: The Influence of Evangelicalism on Social and Economic Thought 1785–1865*, Oxford: Clarendon Press, 1988.

Hobsbawm, Eric J. and Terence Ranger (eds), *The Invention of Tradition*, Cambridge: Cambridge University Press, 1983.

Hobsbawm, Eric J., *Bandits*, London: Weidenfeld and Nicolson, 3rd edn. 1998.

Hobsbawm, Eric J., *The Age of Revolution, 1789–1848*, New York: Mentor, 1962.

Hoenigsberg, Julio, *Influencia revolucionaria de la masonería en Europa y América. Esbozos históricos*, Bogotá: Editorial ABC, 1944.

Holmes, Richard, *Redcoat: The British Soldier in the Age of Horse and Musket*, London: Harper Collins, 2001.

Hopkins, A. G., 'Informal Empire in Argentina: An Alternative View', *JLAS*, 26:2 (1994), pp. 469–84.

Howard, Michael, *The Lessons of History*, Oxford: Oxford University Press, 1991.

Humphreys, R. A., 'British Merchants and South American Independence', *Proceedings of the British Academy*, (1965), pp. 153–74.

Howard, Michael, *The Invention of Peace and the Reinvention of War*, London: Profile Books, 2000.

Hutchinson, John and Anthony D. Smith (eds), *Nationalism: Critical Concepts in Political Science*, 5 Vols, London: Routledge and Kegan Paul, 2000.

Ibanez Sanchez, Roberto, 'La independencia', in Alvaro Valencia Tovar (ed.), *Historia de las fuerzas militares de Colombia*, Vol. 1, Bogotá: Planeta, 1993, pp. 287–380.

Ignatieff, Michael, *The Warrior's Honor: Ethnic War and the Modern Conscience*, London: Henry Holt, 1998.

Ignatiev, Noel, *How the Irish Became White*, London: Routledge, 1995.

Ivereigh, Austen (ed.), *The Politics of Religion in an Age of Revival*, London: Institute of Latin American Studies, 2000.

Izard, Miguel, *Series estadísticas para la historia de Venezuela*, Mérida: Universidad de los Andes, 1970.

Izard, Miguel, 'El comercio venezolano en una época de transición 1777–1830', *Miscelánea Barcinoseia: Revista de investigación y alta cultura*, 10:30 (1971), pp. 7–44.

Izard, Miguel (ed.), *Política y economía en Venezuela 1810–1976*, Caracas: Fundación John Boulton, 1976.

Izard, Miguel, *El miedo a la revolución: La lucha por la libertad en Venezuela 1777–1830*, Madrid: Editorial Tecnos, 1979.

Jaksic, Ivan (ed.), *The Political Power of the Word: Press and Oratory in Nineteenth-Century Latin America*, London: Institute of Latin American Studies, 2002.

Jaramillo, Juan Diego, *Bolívar y Canning 1822–1827: Desde el congreso de Verona hasta el congreso de Panamá*, Bogotá: Banco de la República, 1983.

Jaramillo Agudelo, Darío (ed.), *Nueva historia de Colombia*, Bogotá: Instituto Colombiano de Cultura, 8 Vols, 1978.

Jaramillo Uribe, Jaime, 'Bentham y los utilitaristas colombianos del siglo XIX', *Ideas y Valores*, 4:13 (January–June 1962), pp. 11–28.

Jaramillo Uribe, Jaime, *El pensamiento colombiano en el siglo XIX*, Bogotá: Editorial Ternis, 1974, first pub. 1964.

Jaramillo Uribe, Jaime, *La personalidad histórica en Colombia y otros ensayos*, Bogotá: Instituto Colombiano de Cultura, 1977.

Jaramillo Uribe, Jaime, *Ensayos de historia social*, Vol. 1, Bogotá: Tercer Mundo Editores, 1989.

Jeffrey, Keith (ed.), *An Irish Empire? Aspects of Ireland and the British Empire*, Cambridge: Cambridge University Press, 1996.

Jiménez López, Hadelis, *La armada de Venezuela en la guerra de la independencia*, Caracas, 2000.

Johnson, Lyman L. and Sonya Lipsett-Rivera (eds), *The Faces of Honor: Sex, Shame and Violence in Colonial Latin America*, Albuquerque, NM: University of New Mexico Press, 1998.

Jones, Charles, '"Business Imperialism" and Argentina, 1875–1900: A Theoretical Note', *JLAS*, 12 (1980), pp. 437–44.

Jones, Gareth A., 'Latin America Geographies', in Philip Swanson (ed.), *The Companion to Latin American Studies*, London: Arnold, 2003, pp. 5–25.

Jordan, Gerald and Nicholas Rogers, 'Admirals as Heroes: Patriotism and Liberty in Hanoverian England', *Journal of British Studies*, 28:3 (July 1989), pp. 201–24.

Joseph, E. L., *Warner Arundell: The Adventures of a Creole*, Kingston: University of the West Indies Press, 2001, ed. Lise Winer, first pub. London, 1838.

Joseph, Gilbert M., 'On the Trail of Latin American Bandits: A Re-examination of Peasant Resistance', *LARR*, 25:3 (1990), pp. 7–53.

Joseph, Gilbert M., Catherine C. LeGrand and Ricardo D. Salvatore (eds), *Close Encounters of Empire: Writing the Cultural History of US – Latin American Relations*, London and Chapel Hill, NC, Duke University Press, 1998.

Kahle, Gunter, *Simón Bolívar y los alemanes*, La Paz: Editorial Los Amigos del Libro, 2000, first pub. in German, Bonn, 1980.

Karras, Alan L., *Sojourners in the Sun. Scottish Migrants in Jamaica and the Chesapeake, 1740–1800*, Ithaca, NY: Cornell University Press, 1992.

Karras, Alan L. and J. R. McNeil (eds), *Atlantic American Societies: From Columbus through Abolition*, London and New York: Routledge, 1992.

Karsten, P., 'Irish Soldiers in the British Army 1792–1922: Suborned or Subordinate?', *Journal of Social History*, 17 (1983–4), pp. 31–64.

Kaufmann, William W., *British Policy and the Independence of Latin America 1804–1828*, New Haven, CT: Yale University Press, 1951.

Kaur, Raminder and John Huytnyk (eds), *Travel Worlds: Journeys in Contemporary Cultural Politics*, London: Zed Books, 1999.

Kearby, Peadar, *Ireland and Latin America: Links and Lessons*, Dublin: Trocaire and Gill and Macmillan, 1992.

Keeble, T. W., *Commercial Relations between British Overseas Territories and South America, 1806–1914: An Introductory Essay*, London: Institute of Latin American Studies, 1970.

Keegan, John, *The Face of Battle*, London: Pimlico, 1991, first pub. 1976.

Kelly, James, *'That Damn'd Thing Called Honour' Duelling in Ireland 1570–1860*, Cork: Cork University Press, 1995.

Kiernan, V. G., *The Duel in European History: Honour and the Reign of Aristocracy*, Oxford: Oxford University Press, 1988.

Kinsbruner, Jay, 'The Political Influence of the British Merchants Resident in Chile during the O'Higgins Administration 1817–1823', *The Americas*, 27 (1970–1), pp. 26–39.

Kinsbruner, Jay, *Independence in Spanish America: Civil Wars, Revolutions and Underdevelopment*, Albuquerque, NM: University of New Mexico Press, 1994, first published 1973.

Knight, Alan, 'Britain and Latin America', in Andrew Porter (ed.), *The Oxford History of the British Empire, Vol. 3 The Nineteenth Century*, Oxford: Oxford University Press, 1999, pp. 122–45.

Knight, Franklin W. (ed.), *UNESCO General History of the Caribbean: Vol. 3: The Slave Societies of the Caribbean*, London: UNESCO Publishing, 1997.

Koebel, W. H., *British Exploits in South America*, New York: The Century Co., 1917.

König, Hans-Joachim, *En el camino hacia la nación: Nacionalismo en el proceso de la formación del estado y de la nación de la Nueva Granada 1750–1856*, translated from the German 1988 edn. by Dagmar Kusche and Juan José de Narvaez, Bogotá: Banco de la República, 1994.

König, Hans-Joachim, 'Nacionalismo y nación en la historia de Iberoamérica', in König, Tristan Platt and Colin Lewis (eds), *Estado-nación, comunidades indígenas, industria: Series cuadernos de historia latinoamericana, viii*, Ridderkerk: AHILA, 2000.

Kuethe, Allan J., *Military Reform and Society in New Granada 1773–1808*, Gainesville, FL: University Presses of Florida, 1978.

Kuethe, Allan J., *Cuba, 1753–1815, Crown, Military and Society*, Knoxville, TN: University of Tennessee Press, 1986.

Lambert, David and Alan Lester (eds), *Colonial Lives: Imperial Careering in the Long Nineteenth Century*, Cambridge: Cambridge University Press, 2006.

Lambert, Eric T. D., 'La muerte y entierro del General English', *Boletín histórico*, 24 (1970), pp. 317–27.

Lambert, Eric T. D., *Carabobo 24 Junio 1821 Algunas relaciones escritas en inglés*, Caracas: Fundación John Boulton, 1974.

Lambert, Eric T. D., 'General Francis Burdett O'Connor', *Irish Sword*, 13:51 (Winter 1977), pp. 128–34.

Lambert, Eric T. D., *Voluntarios británicos e irlandeses en la gesta bolivariana*, Vol. 1, Caracas: Corporación Venezolana de Guayana, 1983, translated from English by Teodosio Leal.

Lambert, Eric T. D., *Voluntarios británicos e irlandeses en la gesta bolivariana*, Vols 2–3, Caracas: Ministerio de Defensa, 1993, translated from English by Teodosio Leal.

Lambert, Eric T. D., 'Irish Soldiers in South America 1818–1830 (Illustrated)', *Irish Sword*, 16:62 (Summer 1984), pp. 22–36.

Lambert, Eric T. D. and F. Glenn Thompson, 'Captain Morgan O'Connell of the Hussar Guards of the Irish Legion', *Irish Sword*, 14:53 (Winter 1979), pp. 280–82.

Lecuna, Vicente, *Crónica razonada de las guerras de Bolívar: Formada sobre documentos, sin utilizar consejas ni versiones impropias. Conclusiones de acuerdo con hechos probados, y la naturaleza de las cosas*, New York: Colonial Press Inc., 1950.

Lester, Alan, *Imperial Networks, Creating Identities in Nineteenth-Century South Africa and Britain*, London: Routledge, 2001.

Lewis, Gordon K., *Main Currents of Caribbean Thought: The Historical Evolution of Caribbean Society in its Ideological Aspects, 1492–1900*, Baltimore, MD: Johns Hopkins University Press, 1983.

Liehr, Reinhard (ed.), *América Latina en la época de Simón Bolívar: La formación de las economías nacionales y los intereses económicos europeos, 1800–1850*, Berlin: Biblioteca Ibero-América: Colloquium Verlag Berlin, 1989.

Linebaugh, Peter and Marcus Rediker, *The Many-Headed Hydra: The Sailors, Slaves, Commoners, and the Hidden History of the Revolutionary Atlantic*, London: Verso, 2000.

Liss, Penny K., *Atlantic Empires: A Network of Trade and Revolution 1713–1826*, Baltimore, MD: Johns Hopkins University Press, 1983.

Lombardi, John V., 'La invención de Venezuela en el marco mundial: El siglo de transición 1750–1850', *Boletín de la academia de la historia*, 83:332 (2000), pp. 8–31.

Lombardi, John V., *The Decline and Abolition of Negro Slavery 1820–1854*, Westport, CT: Greenwood Press, 1971.

Lombardi, John V., *People and Places in Colonial Venezuela*, Bloomington, IN: Indiana University Press, 1976.

Lombardi, John V., 'Los esclavos negros en las guerras venezolanas de la independencia', *Cultura universitaria*, 93 (October–December 1966), pp. 153–66.

Lomnitz, Claudio, 'Nationalism as a Practical System: Benedict Anderson's Theory of Nationalism from the Vantage Point of Spanish America', in Miguel Angel Centeno and Fernando López-Alves (eds), *The Other Mirror: Grand Theory through the Lens of Latin America*, (Princeton, NJ: Princeton University Press, 2001), pp. 329–49.

López, Francisco Miguel, *Contribución al estudio de la ley de haberes militares y sus repercusiones*, Caracas: Centro de investigaciones históricas, Universidad Santa María, 1987.

Loy, Jane, 'Forgotten Comuneros: The 1781 Revolt in the Llanos of Casanare', *HAHR*, 61 (1981), pp. 235–57.

Lucas de Grummond, Jane, *Renato Beluche: Smuggler, Privateer, and Patriot, 1780–1860*, Baton Rouge, LA: Louisiana State University Press, 1982.

Lucena Salmoral, Manuel, *Piratas, bucaneros, filibusteros y corsarios en America: perros, mendigos y otros malditos del mar*, Madrid: MAPFRE, 1992.

Lynch, John, 'British Policy and Spanish America 1783–1808', *JLAS*, 1 (1969), pp. 1–30.

Lynch, John (ed.), *Andrés Bello: The London Years*, Richmond: Richmond Publishing, 1982.

Lynch, John, 'Bolívar and the Caudillos', *HAHR*, 63:1 (1983), pp. 3–37.

Lynch, John, *Caudillos in Spanish America 1800–1850*, Oxford: Clarendon Press, 1992.

Lynch, John (ed.), *Latin American Revolutions 1808–1826, Old and New World Origins*, Norman, OK: University of Oklahoma Press, 1994.

Lynch, John, *Latin America Between Colony and Nation: Selected Essays*, London: Palgrave and Institute of Latin American Studies, 2001.

Macdonagh, Oliver, *The Hereditary Bondsman: Daniel O'Connell 1775–1829*, London: Weidenfeld and Nicolson, 1988.

Mackenzie, John M., 'Empire and National Identities: The Case of Scotland', *TRHS*, 6th Series, Vol. 8 (1998), pp. 215–32.

MacShane, Frank (ed.), *Impressions of Latin America: Five Centuries of Travel and Ad-*

venture by English and North American Writers, New York: Morrow, 1963.

Madden, Robert, *United Irishmen, Their Lives and Times*, London: Catholic Publishing and Bookselling Co., 1860.

Mallon, Florencia E., *Peasant and Nation: The Making of Post-Colonial Mexico and Peru*, Berkeley, CA: University of California Press, 1995.

Marchena Fernández, Juan, *Oficiales y soldados en el ejército de América*, Sevilla: Escuela de Estudios Hispano-americanos de Sevilla, 1983.

Marichal, Carlos, *A Century of Debt Crises in Latin America, from Independence to the Great Depression, 1820–1930*, Princeton, NJ: Princeton University Press, 1989.

Marshall, Oliver, *European Immigration and Ethnicity in Latin America: a Bibliography*, London: Institute of Latin American Studies, 1991.

Marshall, Oliver, *The English Language Press in Latin America*, London: Institute of Latin American Studies, 1996.

Marshall, Oliver (ed.), *English Speaking Communities in Latin America*, London: Institute of Latin American Studies and Palgrave, 2000.

Marshall, Oliver, *English, Irish and Irish–American Pioneer Settlers in Nineteenth-Century Brazil*, Oxford: Centre for Brazilian Studies, 2005.

Marshall, P. J., Presidential Address, 'Britain and the World in the Eighteenth Century: III, Britain and India', *TRHS*, 6th Series, Vol. 10 (2000), pp. 1–16.

Marshall, P. J., Presidential Address. 'Britain and the World in the Eighteenth Century: IV The Turning Outwards of Britain', *TRHS*, 6th Series, Vol. 11 (2001), pp. 1–17.

Marshall, P. J. and Glyndwr Williams, *Great Map of Mankind: Perceptions of New Worlds in the Age of Enlightenment*, London: Dent, 1982.

Marshall, Peter J., *'A Free though Conquering People': Britain and Asia in the Eighteenth Century. An Inaugural Lecture in the Rhodes Chair of Imperial History Delivered at Kings College London on Tuesday 5 March 1981'*, London: Kings College, 1981.

Martínez, Frédéric, 'Apogeo y decadencia del ideal de la inmigración europea en Colombia, siglo XIX', *Boletín cultural y bibliográfico*, 34:44 (1997), pp. 3–45.

Martínez, Frédéric, *El nacionalismo cosmopólita. La referencia europea en la construcción nacional de Colombia, 1845–1900*, Bogotá: Banco de la República/ Instituto Francés de Estudios Andinos, 2001.

Martínez Garnica, Armando, 'El debate legislativo por las calidades ciudadanas en el régimen representativo del Estado de la Nueva Granada (1821–1853)', *Boletín de historia y antigüedades*, 90:821 (April–May–June 2003) pp. 241–63.

Martínez Guarda, María Antonieta, *La región histórica de Coro y su articulación en tres momentos de la Historia de Venezuela: 1528–1824*, Caracas: Consejo Nacional de la Cultura, 2000.

Martínez-Alier, Verena, *Marriage, Class and Colour in Nineteenth-Century Cuba: A Study of Racial Attitudes and Sexual Values in a Slave Society*, London: Cambridge University Press, 1974.

Massey, Doreen, 'Places and their Pasts', *History Workshop Journal*, 39 (Spring 1995), pp. 181–91.

Masur, Gerhard, *Simón Bolívar*, Albuquerque, NM: University of New Mexico Press, 1969, first pub. 1948.

Mathews, Robert Paul, *Violencia rural en Venezuela 1840/1858: Antecedentes socioeconómicos de la guerra federal*, Caracas: Monte Avila, 1977.

Maxwell, Kenneth, 'The Atlantic in the Eighteenth Century: a Southern Perspective on the Need to Return to the "Big Picture"', *TRHS*, 6th Series, Vol. 3 (1993), pp.

209–36.

McBride, Ian, *Scripture Politics: Ulster Presbyterians and Irish Radicalism in the Late Eighteenth Century*, Oxford: Clarendon Press, 1998.

McCalman, Iain, *Radical Underworld: Prophets, Revolutionaries and Pornographers in London, 1795–1840*, Cambridge: Cambridge University Press, 1988.

McCalman, Iain (ed.), *'The Horrors of Slavery' and Other Writings by Robert Wedderburn*, Edinburgh: Edinburgh University Press, 1991.

McFarlane, Anthony, 'Comerciantes y monopolio en la Nueva Granada: El Consulado de Cartagena de Indias', *Anuario colombiano de historia social y de la cultura*, 11 (1983), pp. 43–69.

McFarlane, Anthony, 'Civil Disorders and Popular Protests in late Colonial New Granada', *HAHR*, 64:1 (1984), pp. 17–54.

McFarlane, Anthony, *Colombia before Independence: economy, society, and politics under Bourbon rule*, Cambridge: Cambridge University Press, 1993.

McFarlane, Anthony, *The British in the Americas 1480–1815*, London: Longman, 1994.

McFarlane, Anthony, 'Identity, Enlightenment and Political Dissent in late Colonial Spanish America', *TRHS*, 6th Series, Vol. 8 (1998), pp. 309–36.

McFarlane, Anthony and Eduardo Posada-Carbó (eds), *Independence and Revolution in Spanish America: Perspectives and Problems*, London: Institute of Latin American Studies, 1999.

McGann, Thomas F., 'The Assassination of Sucre and its Significance in Colombian History, 1828–48', *HAHR*, 30:3 (August 1950), pp. 269–89.

McKenzie, John M., 'The Imperial Pioneer and Hunter and the British Masculine Stereotype in Late Victorian and Edwardian Times', in J. A. Mangin and James Walvin (eds), *Manliness and Masculinity: Middle Class Masculinity in Britain and America, 1800–1940*, Manchester: Manchester University Press, 1987, pp. 176–95.

McKillop, Andrew, 'Military Recruiting in the Scottish Highlands, 1739–1815: The Political, Social and Economic Context', unpub. Ph. D., University of Glasgow, 1995.

McKillop, Andrew, *'More Fruitful than the Soil': Army, Empire and the Scottish Highlands 1715–1815*, East Linton: Tuckwell Press, 1999.

McKinley, P. Michael, *Pre-Revolutionary Caracas: Politics, Economy and Society 1777–1811*, Cambridge: Cambridge University Press, 1985.

McLean, David, *War, Diplomacy and Informal Empire: Britain and the Republics of La Plata, 1836–1853*, London and New York: British Academic Press, 1995.

McNerney, Robert F., 'A Famous Paralelo Entre Bolívar y Washington and its Authorship', *Hispania*, 24:4 (1941), pp. 416–22.

Mecham, J. Lloyd, 'The Papacy and Spanish American Independence', *HAHR*, 9 (1929), pp. 154–75.

Mecham, J. Lloyd, *Church and State in Latin America: A History of Politico-Ecclesiastical Relations*, Chapel Hill, NC: University of North Carolina Press, 1934.

Mena García, María Carmen (ed.), *Venezuela en el siglo de las luces*, Seville and Bogotá: Editorial Munos Maya y Montravela, 1995.

Miller, Kerby, Arnold Schrier, Bruce D. Boiling and David N. Doyle (eds), *Irish Immigrants in the Land of Canaan: Letters and Memoirs from Colonial and Revolutionary America, 1675–1815*, Oxford: Oxford University Press, 2003.

Miller, Rory, *Britain and Latin America in the Nineteenth and Twentieth Centuries*, London: Longman, 1993.

Miller, Rory, 'Informal Empire in Latin America', in W. Roger Louis (ed.), *The Oxford*

History of the British Empire, Vol. 5, Historiography, Oxford: Oxford University Press, 2001.

Minguet, Charles, 'El concepto de nación, pueblo, estado, patria en las generaciones de la independencia', in Jean-Rene Aymes (ed.), *Récherches sur le Monde Hispanique au dix-neuvième siècle*, Lille: Université de Lille, 1973, pp. 57–73.

Minh-ha, Trinh T., 'Other than Myself/My Other Self', in George Robertson, Melinda Mash, Lisa Tickner, Jon Bird, Barry Curtis and Tim Putnam (eds), *Travellers' Tales: Narratives of Home and Displacement*, London: Routledge, 1994.

Moliner de Arévalo, Matilde, 'Ingleses en los ejércitos de Bolívar: El coronel Enrique Wilson', *Revista de Indias*, 51 (1953), pp. 89–111.

Monsalve, (General) José Dolores, *Las mujeres de la revolución de la independencia*, Bogotá: Biblioteca de la Revolución de la Independencia, Imprenta Nacional, 1926.

Moreno de Angel, Pilar, *Santander*, Bogotá: Planeta, 1989.

Moreno Fraginals, Manuel and José J. Moreno Masó, *Migración y muerte: El ejército español en Cuba como via migratoria*, Colombres, Asturias: Ediciones Jucar, 1993.

Morgan, Prys, 'Early Victorian Wales and its Crisis of Identity', in Laurence Brockliss and David Eastwood (eds), *A Union of Multiple Identities: The British Isles c. 1750–1850*, Manchester: Manchester University Press, 1997, pp. 93–109.

Mörner, Magnus, 'Economic Factors and Stratification in Colonial Spanish America with Special Regard to Elites', *HAHR*, 63:2 (1983), pp. 335–69.

Mörner, Magnus, *Adventurers and Proletarians: The Story of Migrants in Latin America*, Pittsburgh, PA: University of Pittsburgh Press, UNESCO, 1985.

Mörner, Magnus (ed.), *Estudios y documentos suecos relativos al movimiento emancipador de Hispanoamérica*, Madrid: Ediciones Guadarrama, 1961.

Mulhall, Michael G., *The English in South America*, New York: Arno Press, 1977, first pub. Buenos Aires, 1878.

Múnera, Alfonso, 'El caribe colombiano en la república andina: Identidad y autonomía política en el siglo XIX', *Boletín cultural y bibliográfico*, 33:41 (1996), pp. 29–50.

Múnera, Alfonso, *El fracaso de la nación: Región, clase y raza en el Caribe colombiano (1717–1821)*, Bogotá: Banco de la República, 1998.

Murray, Pamela S, '"Loca" or "Libertadora"?: Manuela Saenz in the Eyes of History and Historians, 1900–c. 1990', *JLAS*, 33:2 (May 2001), pp. 291–310.

Navarro, Luis (ed.), *Las élites urbanas en Hispanoamérica*, Seville: Universidad de Sevilla, 2005.

Naylor, Robert A., *Penny Ante Imperialism: The Mosquito Shore and the Bay of Honduras, 1600–1914: A Case Study in British Informal Empire*, London and Toronto: Associated University Presses, 1989.

Nerlich, Michael, *The Ideology of Adventure: Studies in Modern Consciousness, 1100–1750*, Minneapolis, MN: University of Minnesota Press, 1987, trans. Ruth Cowley.

Nieto Arteta, Luis Eduardo, *Economía y cultura en la historia de Colombia*, Bogotá: Editora Viento del Pueblo, 1975, first pub. 1941.

Nye, Robert A., *Masculinity and Male Codes of Honour in Modern France*, New York: Oxford University Press, 1993.

Ocampo López, Javier, *El proceso ideológico de la emancipación en Colombia*, Bogotá: Editorial Planeta Colombiana, 1999, first pub. Tunja, 1974.

Ocampo López, Javier, 'El proceso político, militar y social de la Independencia', in Darío Jaramillo Agudelo (ed.), *Nueva historia de Colombia*, Vol. 2, Bogotá: Instituto Colombiano de Cultura, 1989, pp. 9–64.

Ortiz Sarmiento, Carlos Miguel and Bernardo Tovar Zambrano (eds), *Predecir el pasado*,

Bogotá: Archivo General de la Nación, 1997.

Ortuño, Manuel, *Xavier Mina: Guerrillero, Liberal, Insurgente*, Pamplona: Universidad Pública de Navarra, 2000.

O'Shaughnessy, Andrew Jackson, *An Empire Divided: The American Revolution and the British Caribbean*, Philadelphia, PA: University of Pennsylvania Press, 2000.

Ospina, Joaquín, *Diccionario biográfico y bibliográfico de Colombia*, 3 Vols, Bogotá: Editorial de Cromos, 1927–39.

Ospina Vásquez, Luis, *Industria y protección en Colombia 1810–1930*, Medellín: E.S.F, 1955.

Otero D'Costa, E., *Asesinato de Córdova: Proceso contra el Primer Comandante Ruperto Hand*, Bogotá: Academia Colombiana de Historia, 1942.

Ots Capdequi, José María, 'The Impact of the Wars of Independence on the Institutional Life of the New Kingdom of Granada', *The Americas*, 17:2 (1960), pp. 111–98.

Pabón Núñez, Lucio, 'Colombia y Gran Bretaña al borde de la guerra', *BCB*, 20:1 (1983), pp. 236–44.

Pagden, Anthony, *Spanish Imperialism and the Political Imagination: Studies in European and Spanish American Social and Political Theory 1513–1830*, London and New York: Yale University Press, 1990.

Pakenham, Thomas, *The Year of Liberty: The Story of the Great Irish Rebellion of 1798*, London: Weidenfeld and Nicholson, 1997, first pub. 1969.

Palacios, Belisario, *Apuntaciones histórico-geográficas de la provincia de Cali*, Ibagué: Imprenta del departamento, 1896.

Palacios, Marco, 'Las consecuencias económicas de la independencia en Colombia: Sobre las orígines del subdesarrollo', *Boletín cultural y bibliográfico*, 29:31 (1992), pp. 3–23.

Parra Pérez, Carracciolo, *Mariño y la independencia de Venezuela*, 5 Vols, Madrid: Ediciones Cultura Hispánica, 1954–56.

Pearce, Adrian J., 'British Trade with the Spanish Colonies, 1788–1795', *BLAR*, 20:2 (April 2001), pp. 233–50.

Pellicer, Luis, *La vivencia del honor en la provincia de Venezuela 1774–1809*, Caracas: Fundación Polar, 1996.

Peloso, Vincent C. and Barbara A. Tenenbaum (eds), *Liberals, Politics and Power: State Formation in Nineteenth-Century Latin America*, Athens, GA: University of Georgia Press, 1996.

Pendle, George, 'British Adventurers in the South American Wars of Independence', *History Today*, 10 (1960), pp. 274–80.

Peñuela, Cayo Leonidas, 'Coronel Jaime Rooke', *Repertorio Boyacense*, 6:64 (February 1923), pp. 777–85.

Pérez Jurado, Carlos, 'Tras las huellas del Coronel George Woodberry', *Boletín de la academia nacional de historia*, 84:335 (July–September 2001), pp. 116–18.

Pérez Mejía, Angela, *A Geography of Hard Times: Narratives about Travel to South America, 1780–1849*, New York: State University of New York Press, 2004.

Pérez Ordóñez, Diego, *El Quiteño Libre: El más espectacular periódico de oposición de la República*, Quito: Abya-Yala, 1999.

Pérez Ortiz, Eduardo, *Guerra irregular en la independencia de la Nueva Granada y Venezuela*, Tunja: Ediciones La Rana y el Aguila, 1982.

Pérez Vila, Manuel (ed.), *Indice de los documentos contenidos en las 'Memorias' del general Daniel Florencio O'Leary*, 2 Vols, Caracas: Sociedad Bolivariana de Venezuela, 1957.

Pérez Vila, Manuel, *Vida de Daniel Florencio O'Leary: Primer edecán del Libertador*, Caracas: Imprenta Nacional, 1957.

Pérez Vila, Manuel, *Ensayo sobre las fuentes para la historia de la diocesis de Guayana durante los períodos de la colonia y la independencia*, Caracas: Archivo General de la Nación, 1969.

Peristiany, J.G. (ed.), *Honour and Shame: The Values of Mediterranean Society*, London: Weidenfeld and Nicolson, 1966.

Perotin-Dumon, Anne, 'Les Corsairs de la liberté', *Histoire*, 43 (1982), pp. 24–29.

Perotin-Dumon, Anne, 'The Pirate and the Emperor: Power and Law on the Seas, 1450–1850', in James D. Tracy (ed.), *The Political Economy of Merchant Empires: State Power and World Trade, 1350–1750*, Cambridge: Cambridge University Press, 1991, pp. 196–228.

Phelan, John Leddy, *The People and The King: The Comunero Revolution in Colombia 1781*, Madison, WI: University of Wisconsin Press, 1978.

Phillips, Richard, *Mapping Men and Empire: A Geography of Adventure*, London: Routledge, 1997.

Pi Sunyer, Carlos, 'Las expediciones de los legionarios británicos vistas desde Inglaterra', *Separata de la revista de la facultad de ciencias sociales*, Caracas: Universidad Central de Venezuela, 1970.

Pi Sunyer, Carlos, *El General Juan Robertson: Un prócer de la independencia*, Caracas: Editorial Arte, 1971.

Pi Sunyer, Carlos, *Patriotas americanos en Londres*, Caracas: Monte Avila, 1978.

Pérez Jurado, Carlos, 'Tras las huellas del Coronel George Woodberry', *BANH*, 84:335 (2001), pp. 116–18.

Piccato, Pablo, 'Politics and the Technology of Honor: Dueling in Turn of the Century Mexico', *Journal of Social History*, 33 (December 1999), pp. 331–54.

Pino Iturrieta, Elías A., 'Antecedentes generales y esbozo del comercio inglés en Angostura', *Latinoamérica: Anuario de estudios latinoamericanos* (1968), pp. 131–43.

Pino Iturrieta, Elías, *Las ideas de los primeros venezolanos*, Caracas: Monte Avila, 1993.

Pino Iturrieta, Elías, and Pedro Enrique Calzadilla, *La mirada del otro: Viajeros extranjeros en la Venezuela del siglo XIX*, Caracas: Fundación Bigott, 1996.

Pino Iturrieta, Elías, *Fueros, civilisación y ciudadanía*, Caracas: Universidad Católica Andrés Bello, 2000.

Pino Iturrieta, Elías, *País Archipiélago: Venezuela 1830–1858*, Caracas: Fundación Bigott, 2002.

Platt, D. C. M., 'Dependency in Nineteenth-Century Latin America: An Historian Objects', *LARR*, 15:1 (1980), pp. 113–30.

Platt, D. C. M., *Latin America and British Trade 1806–1914*, London: Black, 1972.

Platt, Tristan, 'Simón Bolívar, the Sun of Justice and the Amerindian Virgin – Andean Conceptions of the Patria in Nineteenth-Century Potosí', *JLAS*, 25:1 (1993), pp. 159–83.

Plaza, L. M., 'Notas históricas sobre la ayuda inglesa a la independencia venezolana', *Boletín de la academia nacional de la historia*, 33 (1950), pp. 29–44.

Plazas Olarte, Guillermo, 'La legión británica en la independencia de Colombia', *Revista de las fuerzas armadas*, 1:2 (June–July 1960), pp. 287–93.

Pocock, John, *Wilberforce*, London: Constable, 1977.

Polanco Alcántara, Tomás, *Simón Bolívar: ensayo de una interpretación biográfica a través de sus documentos*, Caracas: Ediciones E. G., 1994.

Polanco Alcántara, Tomás, *José Antonio Páez, fundador de la república*, Caracas: Ediciones

E. G., 2000.

Porter, Andrew (ed.), *The Oxford History of the British Empire, Vol. 3, The Nineteenth Century*, Oxford: Oxford University Press, 1999.

Porter, Bernard, *The Absent-Minded Imperialists: Empire, Society and Culture in Britain*, Oxford: Oxford University Press, 2004.

Posada, Eduardo, *Apostillas*, Bogotá: Imprenta Nacional, 1978, first pub. 1926.

Posada-Carbó, Eduardo (ed.), *Wars, Parties and Nationalism: Essays in the Political and Social Order of Nineteenth-Century Latin America*, London: Institute of Latin American Studies, 1995.

Posada-Carbó, Eduardo (ed.), *In Search of a New Order: Essays on the Politics and Society of Nineteenth-Century Latin America*, London: Institute of Latin American Studies, 1998.

Pratt, Mary Louise, *Imperial Eyes: Travel Writing and Transculturation*, London: Routledge, 1992.

Pratt, Mary Louise and Kathleen Newman (eds), *Critical Passions: Selected Essays* [of Jean Franco], Durham, NC: Duke University Press, 1999.

Racine, Karen, 'Imagining Independence: London's Spanish American Community 1790–1829', Tulane University, unpub. Ph.D., 1996.

Radcliffe, Sarah and Sallie Westwood, *Remaking The Nation: Place, Identity and Politics in Latin America*, London: Routledge, 1996.

Ramos Pérez, Demetrio, *Bolívar y su experiencia antillana. Una época decisiva para su línea política*, Caracas: Academia Nacional de la Historia, 1990.

Rausch, Jane M., *Territorial Rule and the Llanos Frontier*, Gainesville, FL: University Press of Florida, 1999.

Rayfield, Jo Ann, 'O'Leary y Córdoba: Un resumen historiográfico y nuevos documentos', *Boletín de historia y antigüedades*, 57:663–65 (January–March 1970), pp. 162–75.

Read, Jan, 'Independence or Death: British Adventurers in South America', *History Today*, 25 (1975), pp. 381–90.

Read, Jan, *The New Conquistadores*, London: Evans Bros, 1980.

Reddy, William, *The Invisible Code: Honor and Sentiment in Postrevolutionary France, 1814–1848*, Berkeley, CA: University of California Press, 1997.

Reid Andrews, George, *The Afro-Argentines of Buenos Aires, 1800–1900*, Madison, WI: University of Wisconsin Press, 1980.

Restrepo Canal, Carlos, 'Mensaje inédito de Nariño sobre el caso del General D'Evereux', *Boletín de historia y antigüedades*, 46:531 (January–March 1959), pp. 77–86.

Rheinheimer, Hans P., *Topo: The Story of a Scottish Colony near Caracas 1825–1827*, Edinburgh: Scottish Academic Press, 1988.

Riano, Camilo, *La campaña libertadora de 1819*, Bogotá: Editorial Andes, 1969.

Rippy, J. Fred, 'Latin America and the British Investment 'boom' of the 1820s', *Journal of Modern History*, 19 (1947), pp. 122–29.

Robinson, David J., 'Liberty, Fragile Fraternity and Inequality in early Republican Spanish America: Assessing the Impact of the French Revolution', *Journal of Historical Geography*, 16:1 (January 1990), pp. 51–76.

Rodgers, Nini, 'Ireland and the Black Atlantic in the Eighteenth Century', *Journal of Irish Historical Studies*, 32:126 (November 2000), pp. 175–92.

Rodriguez O., Jaime E., *The Independence of Spanish America*, Cambridge: Cambridge University Press, 1998.

Rodriguez, José Angel, 'Viajeros alemanes a Venezuela en el siglo XIX', *Jahrbuch für Geschichte Lateinamerikas 37* (2001), pp. 234–41.

Rodriguez, Pablo, 'Noche sangrienta en San Vitorino. Asesinato de un consul norteamericano en Bogotá', *Credencial historia,* 169 (2004), pp. 3–6.

Rodriguez-Bobb, Arturo, *Exclusión e integración del sujeto negro en Cartagena de Indias en perspectiva histórica,* Madrid: Iberoamericana-Vervuert, 2002.

Rogers, Anthony, *Somebody Else's War: Mercenaries from the 1960s to the Present Day,* London: Harper Collins, 1998.

Roldán Vera, Eugenia, *The British Book Trade and Spanish American Independence: Education and Knowledge Transmission in Transcontinental Perspective,* Aldershot: Ashgate, 2003.

Roniger, Luis, and Mario Sznajder (eds), *Constructing Collective Identities and Shaping Public Spheres: Latin American Paths,* Brighton: Sussex Academic Press, 1998.

Roper, Michael, 'Re-remembering the Soldier Hero: the Psychic and Social Construction of Memory in Personal Narratives of the Great War', *History Workshop Journal,* 50 (Autumn 2000), pp. 181–204.

Rydjord, John, 'British Mediation Between Spain and her Colonies', *HAHR,* 21 (1941), pp. 29–50.

Saavedra Galindo, José Manuel, *Colombia libertadora: La obra de la Nueva Granada y especialmente del Valle del Cauca, en la campaña emancipadora del Ecuador y del Perú,* Bogotá: Editorial de Cromos, 1924.

Saether, Steiner A., 'Independence and the Redefinition of Indianness around Santa Marta, 1750–1850', *JLAS,* 37 (2005), pp. 55–80.

Saether, Steiner A., 'Identities and Independence in the Provinces of Santa Marta and Riohacha (Colombia), ca. 1750–ca. 1850', University of Warwick, unpub. Ph.D., 2001.

Safford, Frank, 'Commerce and Enterprise in Central Colombia 1821–1870', Columbia University, unpub. Ph.D., 1965.

Safford, Frank, 'Social Aspects of Politics in Nineteenth-Century Spanish America: New Granada, 1825–1850', *Journal of Social History,* 5 (1971–2), pp. 344–70.

Safford, Frank, 'Foreign and National Enterprise in Nineteenth Century Colombia', *Business History Review,* 39:4 (1965), pp. 503–26.

Safford, Frank, 'Race, Integration and Progress: Elite Attitudes and the Indian in Colombia 1750–1870', *HAHR,* 71:1 (1991), pp. 1–33.

Safford, Frank, *Aspectos del siglo XIX en Colombia,* Medellín: Ediciones Hombre Nuevo, 1977.

Safford, Frank, *The Ideal of the Practical: Colombia's struggle to Form a Technical Elite,* Austin, Texas: University of Texas Press, 1976.

Safford, Frank, 'The Problem of Political Order in Early Republican Spanish America', *JLAS,* 24 (Quincentenary Supplement, 1992), pp. 83–98.

Safford, Frank, and Marco Palacios, *Colombia: Fragmented Land, Divided Society,* Oxford: Oxford University Press, 2002.

Sales de Bohigas, Nuria, *Sobre esclavos, reclutas y mercaderes de quintos,* Barcelona: Ariel, 1974.

Salomon, Frank, and Stuart B. Schwartz (eds), *The Cambridge History of the Native Peoples of the Americas, Vol. 3, South America, Part 2,* Cambridge: Cambridge University Press, 1999.

Salvatore, Ricardo, Carlos Aguirre and Gilbert Joseph (eds), *Crime and Punishment in Latin America: Law and Society since Late Colonial Times,* Durham, NC: Duke University Press, 2001.

Salzman, Paul (ed.), *Oroonoko and Other Writings*, Oxford: Oxford University Press, 1994.

Samper, José María, *Ensayo sobre las revoluciones políticas y la condición social de las repúblicas colombianas*, Paris: E. Thunot, 1861.

Sánchez, Gonzalo, and María Emma Wills Obregón (eds), *Museo, Memoria y Nación*, Bogotá: Museo Nacional, 1999.

Sánchez, M. S., 'O'Leary y su misión a Antioquia: Documentos', *Boletín de historia y antigüedades*, 17:196 (November 1928), pp. 253–63.

Santana, Arturo, *La Campaña de Carabobo (1821) Relación histórica militar*, Caracas: Litografía del Comercio, 1921.

Sanz Tapia, Angel, *Los militares emigrados y los prisioneros franceses en Venezuela durante la guerra contra la revolución: Un aspecto fundamental de la época de la pre-emancipación*, Caracas: Instituto Panamericano de Geografía e Historia, 1977.

Schmidt-Nowara, Christopher, 'Big questions and answers: Three Histories of Slavery, the Slave Trade and the Atlantic World', *Social History*, 27:2 (May 2002), pp. 209–17.

Schwartz, Pedro (ed.), 'The Iberian Correspondence of Jeremy Bentham', manuscript held by The Bentham Project, University College London, 1979.

Schwartz, Stuart B. (ed.), *Implicit Understandings: Observing, Reporting and Reflecting on the Encounters Between Europeans and Other Peoples in the Early Modern Era*, Cambridge: Cambridge University Press, 1994.

Scott, Drusilla, *Mary English: A Friend of Bolivar*, Lewes, The Book Guild, 1991.

Semmel, Stuart, *Napoleon and the British*, New Haven, CT: Yale University Press, 2004.

Shafer, R.J., *The Economic Societies and the Spanish World 1763–1821*, Syracuse, NY: Syracuse University Press, 1958.

Shoemaker, Robert, 'Male Honour and the Decline of Public Violence in Eighteenth-Century London', *Social History*, 26:2 (May 2001), pp. 190–208.

Silva, Renán, *Universidad y sociedad en el Nuevo Reino de Granada: Contribución a un análisis histórico de la formación intelectual de la sociedad colombiana*, Bogotá: Banco de la República, 1992.

Slatta, Richard W., *Bandidos: The Varieties of Latin American Banditry*, Westport, CT: Greenwood, 1987.

Smith, A. W., 'Irish Rebels and English Radicals 1798–1820', *Past and Present*, 7 (1955), pp. 78–85.

Smith, Alan, *The Established Church and Popular Religion, 1750–1850*, London: Longman, 1971.

Smith, Anthony D., 'War and Ethnicity: The Work of Warfare in the Formation, Self-images and Cohesion of Ethnic Communities', *Ethnic and Racial Studies*, 4:4 (1981), pp. 375–93.

Smith, Anthony D., *Nationalism and Modernism: A Critical Survey of Recent Theories of Nations and Nationalism*, London: Routledge, 1998.

Smith, Anthony D., *Nationalism: Theory, Ideology, History*, London: Polity Press, 2001.

Sommer, Doris, *Foundational Fictions: The National Romances of Latin America*, Berkeley, CA: University of California Press, 1991.

Soriano de García Pelayo, Graciela, *Venezuela 1810–1830: Aspectos desatendidos de dos décadas*, Caracas: Cuadernos Legoven, 1988.

Sotomayor Tribin, Hugo Armando, *Guerras, enfermedades y médicos en Colombia*, Bogotá: Escuela de Medicina Juan N. Corpas, 1997.

Sowell, David, *The Early Colombian Labor Movement: Artisans and Politics in Bogotá, 1832–1919*, Philadelphia, PA: Temple University Press, 1992.

Spence, James Mudie, *The Land of Bolivar; Or War, Peace and Adventure in the Republic of Venezuela*, London: S. Low, Marston, Searle and Rivington, 1878.

Spierenburg, Pieter (ed.), *Men and Violence: Gender, Honor and Rituals in Modern Europe and America*, Columbus: Ohio State University Press, 1998.

Steedman, Carolyn Kay, *The Radical Soldier's Tale*, London: Routledge, 1988.

Stern, Steve J. (ed.), *Resistance, Rebellion and Consciousness in the Andean Peasant World, Eighteenth to Twentieth Centuries*, Madison, WI: University of Wisconsin, 1987.

Stern, Steve J., *The Secret History of Gender: Women, Men and Power in Late Colonial Mexico*, Chapel Hill, NC, and London: University of North Carolina Press, 1995.

Stradling, R. A., *The Spanish Monarchy and Irish Mercenaries: The Wild Geese in Spain 1618–68*, Dublin: Irish Academic Press, 1994.

Straka, Tomás, *La voz de los vencidos. Ideas del partido realista de Caracas 1810–1821*, Caracas: Universidad Central de Venezuela, 2000.

Street, John and Manuel Pérez Vila (eds), 'El aporte británico en la independencia venezolana, I (1817–1819): Selección de documentos', Caracas, 1964, held by FJB, Archivo Histórico, C–825.

Subero, Efrain, *Grandes forjadores de la nacionalidad: La independencia y sus próceres de origen extranjero*, Caracas: CORPOVEN, 1979.

Taylor, William B., *Drinking, Homicide and Rebellion in Colonial Mexican Villages*, Stanford, CA: Stanford University Press, 1979.

Tellez, Edgar, Oscar Montes and Jorge Lesmes, *Diario íntimo de un fracaso: Historia no contada del proceso de paz con las FARC*, Bogotá: Planeta, 2002.

Tenenbaum, Barbara A., 'Merchants, Money and Mischief: The British in Mexico, 1821–1862', *The Americas*, 35:5 (1979), pp. 317–39.

Thernstrom, Stephen, and Richard Sennett (eds), *Nineteenth Century Cities: Essays in the New Urban History*, New Haven, CT: Yale University Press, 1969.

Thibaud, Clément, *Repúblicas en armas. Los ejércitos bolivarianos en la Guerra de Independencia (Colombia-Venezuela, 1810–1821)*, Bogotá: Planeta, 2003.

Thomson, Janice E., *Mercenaries, Pirates and Sovereigns: State-Building and Extraterritorial Violence in Early Modern Europe*, Princeton, NJ: Princeton University Press, 1994.

Thurner, Mark, *From Two Republics to One Divided: Contradictions of Post-Colonial Nation-making in Andean Peru*, Durham, NC: Duke University Press, 1996.

Thurner, Mark, and Andrés Guerrero (eds), *After Spanish Rule: Postcolonial predicaments of the Americas*, Durham, NC, Duke University Press, 2003.

Tirado Mejía, Alvaro, *Aspectos sociales de las guerras civiles en Colombia*, Bogotá: Instituto Colombiano de Cultura, 1976.

Tosh, John, *A Man's Place. Masculinity and the Middle-Class Home in Victorian England*, London: Yale University Press, 1999.

Tovar Pinzón, Hermes, 'Guerras de opinión y represión en Colombia durante la independencia 1810–1820', *Anuario colombiano de historia social y de la cultura*, 11 (1983), pp. 187–232.

Tovar Pinzón, Hermes, 'Cartas de amor y de guerra', *Anuario colombiano de historia social y de la cultura*, 12 (1984), pp. 155–69.

Tovar Zambrano, Bernardo, 'Porque los muertos mandan. El imaginario patriótico de la historia colombiana', in Ortiz Sarmiento and Zambrano (eds), *Predecir el pasado*, 1997, pp. 125–69.

Townsend, Camilla, *Tales of Two Cities: Race and Economic Culture in Early Republican North and South America*, Austin, TX: University of Texas Press, 2000.

Triana y Antorveza, Humberto, 'La abolición del comercio de negros de Africa en la política internacional de la Gran Colombia 1821–30', *Boletín de historia y antigüedades*, 82:788 (January–March 1995), pp. 9–73.

Troconis de Veracoechea, Ermila, *El proceso de la inmigración en Venezuela*, Caracas: Academia Nacional de la Historia, 1986.

Turner, Mary, *Slaves and Missionaries: The disintegration of Jamaican Slave Society 1787–1834*, Urbana, IL: University of Illinois Press, 1982.

Tutino, John, *From Insurrection to Revolution in Mexico: Social Bases of Agrarian Violence, 1750–1940*, Princeton, NJ: Princeton University Press, 1986.

Twinam, Ann, *Miners, Merchants and Farmers in colonial Colombia*, Austin, Texas: University of Texas Press, 1982.

Twinam, Ann, *Public Lives, Private Secrets: Gender, Honor, Sexuality and Illegitimacy in Colonial Spanish America*, Stanford, CA: Stanford University Press, 1999.

Uribe Urán, Victor M. (ed.), *State and Society in Spanish America during the Age of Revolution*, Wilmington, DE: Jaguar Scholarly Resources, 2001.

Uribe Urán, Victor M. and Luis Javier Ortiz Mesa (eds), *Naciones, gentes y territorios. Ensayos de historia e historiografía comparada de América Latina y el Caribe*, Medellín: Editorial Universidad de Antioquia, 2000.

Uribe Urán, Victor M., *Honorable Lives: Lawyers, Family and Politics in Colombia, 1780–1850*, Pittsburgh, PA: University of Pittsburgh Press, 2000.

Uslar Pietri, Juan, *Historia de la rebelión popular de 1814, contribución al estudio de la historia de Venezuela*, Caracas: Edime, 1962.

Valarino, Veronica, 'Voluntarios británicos e irlandeses en la independencia de Venezuela', unpublished paper, 2001.

Vale, Brian, *Independence or Death: British Sailors and Brazilian Independence 1822–1825*, London: I. B. Tauris, 1996.

Vale, Brian, *A War Betwixt Englishmen: Brazil Against Argentina on the River Plate 1825–1830*, London and New York: I. B. Tauris, 2000.

Valencia Tovar, Alvaro (ed.), *Historia de las fuerzas militares de Colombia*, 6 Vols, Bogotá: Planeta, 1993.

Van Aken, Mark J., *King of the Night: Juan José Flores and Ecuador, 1824–1864*, Berkeley, CA: University of California Press, 1989.

Van Young, Eric, *The Other Rebellion: Popular Violence and Ideology in Mexico 1810 to 1821*, Stanford, CA: Stanford University Press, 2001.

Vargas, Francisco Alejandro, 'Sesquicentenario luctuoso: Coronel Jayme Rooke', *Boletín de la academia de la historia*, 208 (October-December 1969), pp. 718–23.

Vela Witt, María Susana, *El Departamento del Sur en la Gran Colombia 1822–1830*, Quito: Abya-Yala, 1999.

Velandia, Roberto, *Indice de biografías y notas biográficas de personas colombianas y algunos extranjeros publicados en el 'Boletín de historia y antigüedades' del Vol. 1 (septiembre 1902) al Vol. 86 (diciembre de 1999)*, Bogotá: Academia Colombiana de Historia, 2001.

Venegas Filardo, Pascual, *Viajeros a Venezuela en los siglos XIX*, Caracas: Monte Avila, 1973.

Verna, Paul, *Robert Sutherland: un amigo de Bolívar en Haiti. Contribución al estudio de los destierros del Libertador en Haiti, y de sus Expediciones de Los Cayos y de Jacmel*, Caracas: Fundación John Boulton, 1966.

Verna, Paul, *Petión y Bolívar: Cuarenta Años (1790–1830) de relaciones haitiano-venezolanas y su aporte a la emancipación de Hispanoamérica*, Caracas: Oficina Central de Información, 1969.

Vetencourt Guerra, Lola, *El imperio británico en la economía de Venezuela 1830–1870*, Caracas: Universidad Central de Venezuela, 1981.

Villaveces, Manuel, 'El Proceso D'Evereux', *Boletín de historia y antigüedades*, 19:217 (February 1932), pp. 119–43.

Vittorino, Antonio, *Relaciones colombo-británicas de 1823 a 1825, según los documentos del Foreign Office*, Barranquilla: Ediciones Uninorte, 1990.

Vogel, Hans, 'War, Society and the State in South America, 1800–70', in Patricio Silva (ed.), *The Soldier and the State in South America: Essays in Civil-Military Relations*, London: Palgrave, 2001, pp. 39–51.

Waddell, D. A. G., 'British Neutrality and Spanish American Independence: The Problem of Foreign Enlistment', *JLAS*, 19 (1987), pp. 1–18.

Waddell, D. A. G., 'Anglo-Spanish Relations and the 'Pacification of America' during the Constitutional Triennium 1820–1823', *Anuario de estudios americanos*, 46 (1989), pp. 455–86.

Waddell, D. A. G., *Gran Bretaña y la independencia de Venezuela y Colombia*, Caracas: Ministerio de Educación, 1983.

Waddell, D. A. G., 'International Politics and Independence', in Leslie Bethell (ed.), *CHLA*, Vol. 3, Cambridge: Cambridge University Press, 1987.

Waddell, D. A. G., 'Los británicos y la política británica frente a Bolívar', in Alberto Filippi (ed.), *Bolívar y Europa: En las crónicas, el pensamiento político y la historiografía*, Caracas: Ediciones de la Presidencia de la República, Vol.1, 1986, Vol. 2, 1992.

Wade, Peter, *Blackness and Race Mixture: the Dynamics of Racial Identity in Colombia*, Baltimore, MD: Johns Hopkins University Press, 1993.

Walne, Peter (ed.), *Guide to Manuscript Sources for the History of Latin America and the Caribbean in the British Isles*, Oxford: Oxford University Press, 1973.

Way, Peter, 'The Cutting Edge of Culture: British Soldiers Encounter Native Americans in the French and Indian War', in Martin Daunton and Rick Halpern (eds), *Empire and Others: British Encounters with Indigenous Peoples, 1600–1850*, London: UCL Press, 1998, pp. 124–43.

Weber, David J. and Jane M. Rausch (eds), *Where Cultures Meet: Frontiers in Latin American History*, Wilmington, DE: Jaguar Scholarly Resources, 1994.

Welch, Thomas L. and Myriam Figueras (eds), *Travel Accounts and Descriptions of Latin America and the Caribbean 1800–1920: A Selected Bibliography*, Washington: OAS, 1982.

Wheatley, Christopher J., '"I Hear the Irish are Naturally Brave": Dramatic Portrayals of the Irish Soldier in the Seventeenth and Eighteenth Centuries', *Irish Sword*, 19:77 (Summer 1995), pp. 187–96.

Whitehead, Neil L., *Lords of the Tiger Spirit: A History of the Caribs in Colonial Venezuela and Guayana 1498–1820*, Dordecht, Netherlands: Foris Publications, 1988.

Wielopolska, Maria, 'Polacos de la Independencia de Venezuela', *Revista de la Sociedad Bolivariana de Venezuela*, 331: 103 (1974), pp. 69–74.

Wilson, Kathleen, 'Empire, Trade and Popular Politics in Mid-Hanoverian Britain: The Case of Admiral Vernon', *Past and Present*, 121 (1988), pp. 74–109.

Wilson, Kathleen, *The Sense of the People. Politics, Culture and Imperialism in England, 1715–1815*, Cambridge: Cambridge University Press, 1998.

Winn, Peter, 'British Informal Empire in Uruguay in the Nineteenth Century', *Past and Present*, 73 (1973), pp. 100–26.

Woodward, Margaret L., 'The Spanish Army and the Loss of America 1810–1824', *HAHR*, 48 (1968), pp. 569–96.

Woolf, Stuart, 'The Construction of a European World-View in the Revolutionary–Napoleonic Years', *Past and Present*, 137 (November 1992), pp. 72–101.

Wright, Christine, '"Really Respectable Settlers": Peninsular War Veterans in the Australian colonies, 1820s and 1830s', Australian National University, Canberra, unpub. Ph.D., 2005.

Wright, Winthrop R., *Café con leche: Race, Class and National Image in Venezuela*, Austin, TX: University of Texas Press, 1993.

Zahler, Reuben, 'Honor, Corruption and Legitimacy: Liberal Projects in the Early Venezuelan Republic, 1821–50', unpub. Ph.D., University of Chicago, 2005.

Zuluaga Ramírez, Francisco, *Guerrilla y Sociedad en el Patía: Una relación entre clientelismo político y la insurgencia social*, Cali: Universidad del Valle, 1993.

Electronic Resources

http://genforum.genealogy.com/venezuela/page4.html#13

http://www.venezuelagenealogia.org/basededatos.html

http://www.bisa.btinternet.co.uk

Carson, Roy S., 'How Venezuelan Independence (and South America's) was won by the Irish!' (1996), www.vheadline.com/readnews.asp?id=27560

Eltis, David, Stephen D. Behrendt, David Richardson and Herbert S. Klein, *The Trans-Atlantic Slave Trade: A Database on CD Rom*, Cambridge: Cambridge University Press, 1999.

Fundación Polar, *Diccionario de Historia de Venezuela*, CD Rom, Caracas: Fundación Polar, 2000.

Index

abolitionism 133–136, 139, 143–145
  see also slaves
Achaguas 44, 87
Adlercreutz, Fredrick Thomas de 179, 204
adventure, culture of 7–8, 111–112
Africa 19, 28, 133, 139
agriculture 17, 45, 175–176
Albion battalion 40–41, 51–52, 54–55, 122–125, 164, 178
alcohol 46, 68, 70–72, 97, 99–100, 113–114, 189, 191–192
Alexander, Alexander 23, 138, 145–146, 149, 205
allegiance, oaths of 96–97
Alvarez, Dominga 179–180
amazons, myth of female warriors 16, 45
ambushes 84–85
Angostura ix, 40–44, 63, 70–71, 86, 90–102, 145, 158, 176, 179, 181
Antioquia 51–52
Apure, river 40, 48, 147, 186
Arismendi, Juan Bautista 45, 114, 120, 157–158, 180
arms trade 18–19
Ashdown, Charles William 179, 184, 186, 192, 213 n. 64
Atlantic, context of events 13, 20, 88, 124
auxiliaries, terminology x
Aylmer, William 116, 120

banditry 53, 140–143, 153 n. 69
Barbados 19, 87, 92
Barbacoas 147
Barcelona 40, 45–46, 68, 72, 114–115, 118

Barclay, David 18
Barquisameto 178
Barrancas 181
bayonets, 'Nothing is impossible for British …' 192
Belfast 19, 87, 115, 203
Bello, Andrés 3, 184
Blosset, John 18, 87, 98
Bogotá ix, 50–51, 83, 142, 157–158, 160–162, 164, 167, 174–178, 180–181, 183–185, 188, 191–192, 204
Bolívar, Simón, ix-x, 5–7, 69, 100, 167, 188, 215
  idea of Gran-Colombianness 113, 123–124
Boyacá
  battle of 40, 51, 63
  commemorations 83, 209–210
Brand, Edward 193
Brazil, comparison with 100, 134, 149, 182–183, 210, 216, 218–219
Briceño Méndez, Pedro 120, 165, 186
Brinkworth, Robert 26
Brion, Luis 18, 21, 71, 89, 119, 121
British Army 22–27
British Legion 40, 112–115, 119, 160, 164, 209–210
Brown, John 96–97
Brown, Thomas 179, 194
Brown, William 140
Bucaramanga 100
Buenaventura 140, 147
Buenos Aires 140, 182–183
Byron, Lord 16, 85, 215

Cachaví, mine 147
Cali 52, 73, 140–142

calumnies
  see insults
Calzada, Sebastián de la 140
Canning, George 1, 15, 18, 85
Cannon, George 72–73
capitalism, vanguard of 4, 205
capitalists, gentlemanly 17, 18
Carabobo
  battle of 25, 40–41, 44, 47, 63, 67, 90
  veterans 66, 207, 209–210
Caracas 46–47, 160–161, 165–167, 175–
  177, 179–181, 191, 204
Caribbean, Gran Colombian commercial
  relations 17, 20, 44, 48–49, 65
Cartagena de Indias 49–50, 135, 148,
  177–179, 182
Castlereagh, Lord 16, 18, 85
Castro, Julián, 186
Catholicism
  see Church
Cauca Valley 52–53, 140–143
Chamberlain, Charles 22, 68, 179
Chesterton, George Charles 23, 65, 204
chivalry 68, 82–84, 101
Chocó 51–52
Church, Catholic 29–30, 47–53, 182
Ciénaga, La 41, 64
Cifuentes, Antonio 140–141
citizenship, of Gran Colombia 156, 162–
  168, 195, 215,
Ciudad Bolívar
  see Angostura
civilisation, belief in British 136–138,
  216–217
colonies, British 22–29, 139
colonies, Spanish 69, 134, 136–137, 184
commemoration
  of adventurers 202–210
  of Independence 158–159, 185–189,
  192
commerce 16–18
  see also merchants; networks
Commissions 146, 157–162, 168
Concha, José 140–143
Conde, Juan José 161
Conrad, Joseph 206–207, 209
cooks 84, 135
Córdoba, José María 167, 188
Cork 15, 20, 29, 115

Coro 40–41, 45–46, 71, 180, 193
courage
  see heroism; masculinity
Court proceedings, as site for negotiating
  honour 91, 189
Cowardice
  see masculinity
Cox, George 179
Creoles
  identity, x, 3, 8, 13, 16
  relations with foreigners 89–93, 96–
  97, 99, 138, 164, 216–217
Crofton, Richard 22
Cúcuta
  Congress 134, 158–159
  town 175, 179
Cuenca 178–180, 194
Cumaná 45–46, 87, 160, 179

debts 17–18, 159
  see also loans
Demerara 145
  see also colonies, British
desertion 61–67, 119–120, 141–143, 191
Devereux, John x, 18, 30, 40, 89–90, 101,
  115–116, 119, 135, 215
Dinnon, Peter 20
diplomacy, 1–2, 14–16, 73, 133, 148,
  173–174, 204
disease 43, 45, 49–50, 62–65, 67, 111,
  141–142, 214
  see also health; medicine
Dowd, Daniel 176
drunkenness
  see alcohol
Dublin 29, 115–116
duelling 64, 85–90, 193

Ecuador ix, 54–55, 112, 134, 146–149,
  176–177, 186–190
Elsom, George 40, 114–115
emigration, from Britain and Ireland
  18–22
empire, British, historiography of 3,
  136–138, 206–210
  see also informal empire; colonies,
  British
England ix, x, 27–29
English, James Towers x, 19, 20, 22, 40,

113–114, 117
English, Mary x, 18, 19, 89–90, 114, 175,
    183, 185, 194
enterprise
    see commerce
Escovar, Manuel 162
Esmeraldas 146–149, 178
executions 64–65, 93, 142–143, 188
expeditions
    see recruitment

family 156, 163–168, 186, 192–195
    see also kinship
farming
    see agriculture
fear of unknown 84–88
Ferguson, William 82, 124
Ferrera, Asunción 94–95
Ferrier, Thomas 22, 209
Finlay, George 20–21
Flores, Juan José 54, 181, 187, 189–190
Foreign Enlistment Act 1819 4, 14, 19
Forsyth, Samuel 44, 94–95
Fortoul, Eduardo 183–184
Fortoul, Pedro 180, 183
Fortoul, María Josefa 180
foundational fighting 111–113, 185–189
France 14–16, 27, 112
Fraser, James 61, 162, 175, 179
fraternity 84, 163, 191
free trade, desire for 13, 14, 164
friendship 18, 39, 99, 119, 160–162, 165,
    168, 173, 188–189, 210, 218
Fuge, Francis 26
funerals 68

gambling 98–102, 173–174
García, Basilio 140
García Vásquez, Demetrio 141
Gardiner, John 191
gender
    see kinship; marriage; masculinity;
    women
Genoy, battle of 192
geography
    as obstacle to adventure 7–8, 84–85,
        115, 167, 192, 203–205
    of Gran Colombia 42–55
Germany 27–28, 40, 46, 118, 124

Gillmore, Joseph 23, 61
Goldschmidt, L.A. 18
Gow, William 66
Granados, Francisca 181, 194
Gran Colombia
    state ix, 110, 156,159–160, 164, 167–
        168, 188, 217–218
    national identity 111–113, 119–125,
        156–160, 164–168, 187
    see also kinship; nations
Grant, Peter 23, 95–96, 176
Greenup, Mary
    see English, Mary
Guayana 42–44, 65, 92, 98, 148
    see also Angostura
Guayaquil 54–55, 177–178, 180, 189–190
Guedes, Pascual 189
guerrillas 52, 67, 137, 140–143, 210

haberes militares 146, 156–162, 168
Haiti, influence of 13, 14, 65, 117, 136,
    139
Hall, Francis 8, 22, 25, 148, 165, 167,
    177, 188
Hallowes, Miller 179
Hamilton, James 18, 20, 44, 92, 176
Hamilton, John Potter 73
Hand, Rupert 87, 92–94, 188, 193–194
Hands, John 179
Hanoverians
    see Germany
Hasbrouck, Alfred 1, 4, 25, 47, 64, 90–
    91, 139
Hatoviejo 87
health 26, 63, 67–68, 70–71
Henderson, James 164
Herrera, José 94–95
Herring, Charles 17, 18, 20
heroism, stories of British 6–7, 47, 61,
    82, 90, 192, 208
Hill, John 180, 193
Hippisley, Gustavus Butler (author of
    Siege of Barcelona) 97, 100
Hippisley, Gustavus Mathias (author of
    Narrative of the Expedition) 5, 22,
    40, 65
Hodgkins, Ann 185
honour
    concept 6–8, 67–69, 73

in Britain and Ireland 82–83
in Gran Colombia 81–102, 133–142, 157–159, 183–192, 195
see also duelling; masculinity
horse-racing 100, 173–174
Hubble, John Benjamin 146, 160
Hughes, Hugo 175–176, 178
Humboldt, Alexander von 8, 137
hunting 99
Hyslop, Welwood 163–164

identity
concepts 3, 6, 110–113, 122–124, 137, 202
difficulties in proving 159
multiple 192
Illingworth, John 5, 22, 123, 180, 184, 190, 206
Illingworth, Richard 160–161
illiteracy
see literacy
Imperial eyes
see Pratt, Mary Louise
independence in Hispanic America, historiography 3, 217–219
Independent army x, 18, 43–44, 51, 70–73, 82, 140
see also desertion; military; professionalisation
indigenous peoples 44, 48, 51, 64, 72–73, 82, 85, 120, 136–138
informal empire, historiography 2, 4, 215–217
insults 68, 89–90, 93, 97, 192
international, context of events
see Atlantic
Ireland ix, x, 27–29, 85–86, 117, 143–144, 149
see also Devereux, John; Irish Legion; O'Leary, Daniel; United Irishmen
Irish Legion 40–41, 49–50, 83, 115–116, 119–120, 136, 143, 191, 203, 209
see also Devereux, John; Ireland
Isaacs, Jorge 208–209
Italy 27–28

Jackson, Thomas 21
Jaffray, Richard 18, 20
Jamaica 65, 117, 143–145, 149, 163

see also colonies, British
Johnston, John 121, 162, 164

Kean, Francis 180, 182
Keats, John 16
kinship 167, 183–184, 186, 192–195

La Guaira 45–46
Lambert, Eric T.D. 1, 4, 19, 25, 39, 85, 90–91, 139
land
grants 18–19, 20, 159–162
ownership 146, 162–163, 166, 175, 182, 206
Landaeta, María del Carmen 179, 184
Langan, Jack 203
languages
adventurers' competence in or ignorance of 21–22, 74 n. 1
see also literacy; newspapers, bilingual
Lawless, Mary 185
legionaries, terminology 4
leisure activities 98–100, 173–174
liberty, belief in 4, 13, 16, 114–116, 120–122, 138–139, 147–148, 156, 186, 188–189, 191, 193
see also liberalism; romanticism
liberalism 166, 185–186, 188, 207
see also liberty
literacy 21
llanos 40, 47–48, 71, 160
inhabitants 100, 137–138, 159, 161–162
loans 17, 18, 52
Lons, Private 92–95, 98
López Méndez, Luis 19, 33 n. 50, 40
Loyalists
army x, 24, 51, 66–67, 121
property confiscated from 158–159
loyalty, political 167–168, 189
Lynch, William 87, 176
Lyster, William 22, 94, 116

M'Mahon, Benjamin 143–145, 149
MacDonald, Donald 22, 84–85, 96, 136, 147
MacGregor, Gregor x, 6–7, 24, 28–29, 40–42, 49–50, 65–66, 116–118, 121, 139, 180

MacGregor, Josefa María 206
Maceroni, Francis 40–41
Mackay, John 158, 162
McKean, Felix 26
Mackintosh, James 17
Mackintosh, John 17, 90, 162, 164, 186, 188–189, 192, 209
Maclaughlin, Daniel 74 n. 1, 146, 180
Macmanus, Henry 185, 191–192
MacPherson, John 180
Magdalena, river 50, 177
Manby, Thomas 22, 164, 178, 180, 183–184, 186, 193, 205
Maracaibo 40–41, 45–46, 65–66, 160, 162, 180–182
Margarita 40–46, 63–64, 71, 87, 119, 144, 180–181
Mariño, Santiago 45, 92
markets 17, 70–73
maroons 136
marriage 178–185
see also family; kinship
Martín, Felipe Mauricio 146, 180
Marx, Karl 85
masculinity
accusations of cowardice 89–90, 96, 119, 136, 141, 192, 208
concepts 6–8, 85
physical demonstrations 92–4, 189, 192, 203
see also honour; padre de familia
masons 99
Maturín 87, 98, 135
Mayne, Henry 180, 189, 209
Meates, George 162
Medellín 178–179
medicine 71, 175, 193
doctors 71, 174, 178, 209
mercenaries x, 4, 167, 183, 191, 208
see also insults
merchants 26, 55, 83, 93–96, 98, 100, 135, 149, 158–167, 174, 176, 185, 215
mestizos 50–51, 138
military 29, 43, 110–112, 157–159
see also Independent army
Minchin, Charles 180, 193
mining 17, 18, 175–176, 189
Miranda, Leandro 165, 167

missions 20, 43, 63, 138
Mompox 176, 185
monkeys, allegation that British had tails like 68
Montilla, Mariano 21, 89
Morillo, Pablo 50, 99
Mosquera, Tomás Cipriano de 183, 186
Murray, Thomas 178
musicians 24, 26, 83, 135, 160

Napoleonic Wars 14–16, 22–27, 47, 114, 204
Nariño, Antonio 89–90, 101
nations
in Britain and Ireland 112–117, 164
in colonial and republican Gran Colombia 110–113, 119, 121–125, 157, 183, 207
national history writing 208–209
naturalisation 156, 162–164, 173, 183
naval forces 65–66
Neiva 71–72
Netherlands 27–28
newspapers, bilingual 146, 165
networks 3–4, 17–18, 42, 85, 146, 159, 161–162, 177, 183–184, 189, 217
neutrality, policy 14–6
New Granada ix-x, 47–53, 112, 124, 134, 176–177, 193

O'Connell, Daniel 85, 116, 119–120, 203
O'Connell, Morgan 116, 119–120, 203
O'Connor, Francisco Burdett 100, 181, 206
O'Leary, Daniel 5, 21–22, 84, 87, 100, 124, 148, 162, 167, 181–182, 184, 188, 192–193, 204–205, 209–210
O'Mullan, Cornelius 182
Orinoco, river 20, 42–44

Padilla, José 6, 46, 82
padre de familia 183, 190, 192, 194
see also honour; masculinity
Páez, José Antonio 5, 6, 21, 25, 48, 71, 138, 186, 191, 208
Páez Lobrera, Trinidad 179, 195
Pamplona 51
Panama 50
Pantano de Vargas, battle of 51, 63, 82,

90, 187, 192
paradise, earthly 20
pardos 13, 44, 47–48, 52, 138, 142–143
Pasto 53
Paterson, James Duff 206
Patía 53, 137
patriotism
    during independence period x, 8, 82,
        111–112, 121–125
    post-Independence 156, 166–168,
        185–195
    see also nations
patriots
    see Independent army
payment 72–73
Peterson, Catalina 184
Phillips, Charles 29, 115–116
Piar, Manuel 6, 43, 82
Pichincha, battle of 54
Piggott, Richard 23, 138
pillaging
    see plunder
pirates 20, 48, 121
Pisba, páramo de 44, 51, 63, 84, 137
plantations 140, 143–146, 175
    see also slaves
plunder 4, 46, 72, 118, 124, 140
Poland 146, 180–181
Poole, Capitán 98
Popayán 52, 72–73, 140–143, 178–179,
    182
Portobello 41, 63, 65, 72, 135
Posada Gutierrez, Joaquín 188, 208
Power, William Middleton 23, 87
Powles, J.D. 17
Pratt, Mary Louise 4, 136–137, 204–205,
    217
privateers 65–66
professionalisation of army 61–62, 137–
    138
property
    see land
Protestantism 29–30, 47, 182, 209
    see also religion
Puerto Cabello 45–46, 179

Quito ix, 54, 100, 141, 146–147, 175,
    178, 180–181, 204

race 82, 100, 110, 123, 133–136
radical newspapers in Britain 16, 139
rape 95–96, 107 n. 107
Ramos, Eulalia 68, 179
ranks, military 82–3, 87, 99–100, 189–
    190
Rasch, Frederick 181
rationing 70–73
recruitment, of expeditions 10, 14–22,
    27–30, 40–45, 63, 97, 139
religion 19, 29–30, 67–70, 116–118
Republican army
    see Independent army
respect
    see honour; trust
Restrepo, José Manuel 2, 122–123, 143,
    165, 208
Richards, Thomas 18, 21, 71, 162, 181,
    184
Rifles battalion 53–54
Riohacha 41, 48–49, 63, 72, 118–119,
    121, 124, 136
Robinson Crusoe 8, 203
romanticism 6, 7, 16, 82
Rooke, Ana 92, 181
Rooke, James 5, 23, 51, 63, 82, 92, 181,
    187, 209
Royalist army
    see Loyalist army
Royal Navy 22–24, 62, 66
Rudd, Charles 23, 147–148
Ruiz, María Francisca 179, 194
Runnel, John 42, 52, 138–143
rustling 72–73
Ryan, James 206

sacrifice, language of 68, 141, 158, 186,
    191, 206
Sáenz, Manuela 84
St Bartholomew 18, 87
St Thomas 18
Samper, José María 208
Sandes, Arthur 5, 23, 100, 120, 137–138,
    178
San Juanito, battle of 140–141
San Rafael de Onoto 161
Santa Ana armistice 99
Santa Fe de Bogotá
    see Bogotá

Santa Marta 48–49, 137, 145, 178, 180–181, 202–203
Santander, Francisco de Paula 48, 120, 140, 142–143, 173, 184
Santo Tomás de Angostura
    see Angostura
Santuario, El, battle of 167, 188–189, 208
Sarmiento, Seferino 95–96
savagery, talk of 53, 68, 85, 99, 124, 136–138
Scotland ix, x, 20, 27, 116–118
Scott, Walter 82
shame, at beating of black adventurer 135
    see also honour
Sheridan, Richard 85
Skeene, Coronel 23
Simpson, Thomas 96–97
slave trade 19–20, 133, 135
slaves 44, 52–53, 82, 133–136, 138–150
Socorro 50–51, 73, 175
Soledad 72
Soublette, Carlos 18, 161, 181, 184
Soublette, Soledad 181, 184
Spain 14–16, 27, 68, 139, 156, 167
Spanish army
    see Loyalist army
Stagg, Leonard 22, 181
status 6–8, 82–83, 93–94, 191
Stopford, Edward 18, 23, 146, 160–162, 165–167, 181, 193
Sucre, Antonio José de 54, 100, 182
swords, symbolism of 68, 93–94, 98, 116, 209

Talbot, John 194
Teeson, Jacob 192
thieving 176
    see also plunder
toasting 119
Tocaima 177
trade
    see commerce
travel
    practical difficulties 40, 47–50, 84, 202–205
    writing 3, 7–8
    see also geography
Trinidad 16, 148, 179

    see also colonies, British
trust 5, 17–18, 67, 100, 114, 158, 166, 173, 191
    see also honour
Tunja 50–51
turnover of personnel 61–67
tyranny 16, 113–115, 121–122, 148
    see also liberty

United Irishmen, rebellion of 15, 115
United States of America 19, 27, 148
Upata 98
Urbaneja, Diego Bautista 90
Urdaneta, Rafael 46, 65, 98–99, 120, 162, 188–189
Uslar, Johannes (Juan) 23, 118, 181

Valdés, Manuel 141–143, 147
Valencia 179–181
Vélez 178
Venezuela ix, 42–48, 112, 134, 176–177
veterans 156–168, 173–178, 191–192
Villa del Ortiz, battle of 63
virtue, republican 39, 81, 101, 112, 120, 156, 165–166, 186–188, 195
volunteers, terminology x, 4, 191
Vowell, Richard 136–138, 205

Wales ix, x, 27–28, 118
Wall, George 72
war to the death 124
washing-up, dying while doing the 185
Waterloo, battle of 22–26, 90
Weatherhead, W. Davidson 25, 204
Wedderburn, Robert 139
Weir, Henry 182
Whittle, James 186–187, 197 n. 38
widows 184–185, 194
Wilberforce, William 133
Williams, James 189
Wilson, Henry 5, 23, 96–97
Wilson, Belford Hinton 124, 148, 209
Wilthew, Charles 188
Wilton, John 162
women 6, 19, 84, 92, 95–96, 101, 184–185
    see also honour; widows
Woodberry, George 21, 71
Woodbine, George 148, 182
Wright, Richard 204

Wright, Thomas Charles 5, 182, 184, 189–190, 210

yellow fever
  see disease
Young, Brooke 23, 146–149, 178

Young, Robert 203

Zea, Francisco Antonio 20, 39, 119, 133, 179
Zipaquirá 189
Zulia, campaign of 46